DISCARD

By Oscar Handlin

The Americans

The Americans

A NEW HISTORY OF THE PEOPLE
OF THE UNITED STATES

by OSCAR HANDLIN

with Illustrations by SAMUEL H. BRYANT

An Atlantic Monthly Press Book

LITTLE, BROWN AND COMPANY · BOSTON · TORONTO

LIBRARY OF CONGRESS CATALOG CARD NO. 63-8951

Fifth Printing

The author gratefully acknowledges permission to use the following excerpts from copyrighted material:

Excerpt from a song entitled "Don't Swat Yer Mother, Boys,
Just 'Cause She's Old," words and music by Brian Hooker and
Porter Steele, from *Four Heart Songs of Hearth and Home*,
copyright © 1919 by Brian Hooker and Porter Steele.

Eleven lines from *Winterset*, by Maxwell Anderson, copyright
© 1935 by Anderson House.

The cover design includes a photograph of a
brass eagle by sculptress Lily Swann Saarinen.

ATLANTIC-LITTLE, BROWN BOOKS
ARE PUBLISHED BY
LITTLE, BROWN AND COMPANY
IN ASSOCIATION WITH
THE ATLANTIC MONTHLY PRESS

*Published simultaneously in Canada
by Little, Brown & Company (Canada) Limited*

PRINTED IN THE UNITED STATES OF AMERICA

For the memory of
Samuel S. Flug

Preface

M ORE THAN TEN YEARS AGO, having completed an account of the influence of America upon the immigrant, I determined to describe the influence of migration upon the people of the United States. That task called for a canvas large enough to contain the whole history of the nation, for the continuing process of settling a continent was the central experience of the American people.

The history of that process is the subject of this volume. From small beginnings in an empty corner of the New World there grew a great nation, detached yet never separate from its European sources. The trials it suffered and the triumphs it enjoyed created a new type of man and inspired him in the effort to reshape his environment. Although he succeeded only partially, his achievements were far from negligible and had a profound effect upon the world which emerged from the nineteenth century. His history explains the changes that have shaped American society and that are now at work in other parts of the globe.

I have tried to tell the whole story, making room for the failures as well as the victories and for the heavy human costs even victory entailed. This is not simply a glorious success story; its grandeur is the product of the tragic elements that run through it.

The experience of the people — in all their variety — provides the continuity of the narrative. The characters are the men and women, exceptional and ordinary, whose lives responded to the pressure of the great social forces of their times. But the focus is fixed upon the context and on developments common to the whole people, rather than on the individual. What impelled men to move and how they earned their livelihood, their thoughts of life and death and the ways in which they expressed themselves are among the subjects that reveal some aspect of that common experience.

I have tried to write this book so that anyone who wishes may read and understand it. I have therefore made no effort to find room for every detail, but only for those relevant to the basic themes of the story. Nor have I here assembled the apparatus of proof with which I would confront a purely scientific audience. Those who are familiar with the great body of writing that has enriched American historiography in the past century will understand my indebtedness to the labors of others. But this work is new, in the sense that I have thought through afresh every problem on which it touches, tracing each to its original sources. To document this account adequately would call for another volume fully as large. Most readers will not require that; and I hope in the future, as I have in the past, to make that data available to scholars in other forms.

I am deeply grateful for a grant from the Guggenheim Foundation which gave me a year of essential freedom in 1954; without that leisure for reflection and writing, I could not have carried this work forward. I should acknowledge also my utter dependence upon the incomparable resources of the Harvard College Library. I remain, as ever, indebted to Mary F. Handlin for patient collaboration. Janice Shapiro, Jan M. Matthews, Janet W. Lowenthal and Norma Coté prepared the manuscript with cheerful efficiency.

Oscar Handlin

Cambridge, August 31, 1962

Contents

I

The Old World and the New

1

The Way to America

OUT TO THE limitless distance ran the ocean. From its near edge, the generations of Europeans had watched the turbulent waters recede into the unknown space, within which imagination crowded all the fantastic beings of fable. Here began the end of the world; the mariners hugged the margins of the continent, fearful as in Odysseus's day of losing sight of the familiar universe of rising cliffs and jutting promontories that was their home.

For the mass of men in 1600, the ocean still held the terrors of the past. That a succession of adventurers had reached the outer shores of these uncharted wastes did not in the least allay the fears of the earthbound. Nothing in the chronicles or in the tales that passed by word of mouth gave a friendlier aspect to the waters of the Atlantic.

Yet soon, in their scores, in their hundreds and thousands and later in their millions, the earthbound men and women of Europe passed across the unfriendly sea. In their coming they created a nation.

First there had been the slim craft of the Norsemen. The daring prows had cut through the swirling northern waters and carried the fierce warriors to the farthest ends of Europe. Also westward to Vinland where, about 1000 A.D., Leif's men tasted the ripe fruits of the virgin shore and thought to come back, but never did, and consequently left no trace of their having been there save in the bold lines of the sagas.

Later, the Genoese captain had turned his back upon the coast of Spain and had sailed his ships into the setting sun. His dreamer's eyes had caught the vision of a magic kingdom, hidden at the ocean's outer depths, rich beyond imagining, yet waiting to be conquered and redeemed. From the rambling tales of wanderers to the east, Christopher Columbus had seized upon bits of knowledge that might help him on his way. He had mastered the arts of seamanship and the lore of the geographers to be the better prepared for his mission. And with unfailing conviction he had dedicated his life to this single end; for a mad certainty possessed him that he had been called by destiny to be the discoverer of an unknown realm that would bring the king new subjects, the Church new communicants and himself eternal glory.

On that bright morning of the early Caribbean autumn of 1492 when Columbus made his landfall at Hispaniola he shattered forever the Western Hemisphere's calm. His own longings for some imperial prize proved vain. But his Spanish master gained a glittering empire, and the spreading fame of its worth attracted a host of eager men hopeful of turning it to their own advantage. From everywhere in Spain and Portugal the knights in plated armor, bored with the relative calm of countries now united and peaceful, staked their hopes for quick wealth and their zest for action upon the marvelous lands now laid open to them. The acquisitions of Pizarro and Cortez outdid their greediest speculations and spurred on a host of emulators. On the crowded decks of the outgoing caravels, the high-born hidalgos peered impatiently toward the west while the proud women who occasionally came with them pulled tight the lace shawls against contact with the shuffling retinue who were to hew and draw.

Meanwhile the outsiders looked hungrily on. The two Iberian powers had divided the Americas between them. But that comfortable arrangement, though it enjoyed the Pope's approval, did not avert the envious glances of the other European monarchs. With their more limited means, the French and English stabbed out into the Atlantic on voyages of discovery of their own, only to find the richest territories already preempted. Yet the gold and silver of the laden galleons coming home to Spain sorely tempted the bolder of the captains; when war offered the excuse — and sometimes even when no excuse was available — the British raiders, for glory and for gain, swooped down upon the treasure ships and plundered the somnolent coastal cities. The wealth they brought home was visible evidence of the new continent's opportunities.

For the century onward from the date of Columbus's discovery, the intruding Europeans transformed the New World. The ceaseless coming and going of the little ships laid bare the outlines of the Atlantic coast and of much of the Pacific. Splotches of settlement reached inward toward the interior and the fame of what had been found here continued to excite the imaginations of the men of the old continent. But as yet those who held the new outposts were all Spaniards and Portuguese, and their holdings did not extend north of the Gulf of Mexico, where an empty land still awaited another kind of conqueror.

In the northern countries of Europe as the sixteenth century drew to a close, the New World more and more frequently held a prominent place in the calculations of crafty men. In all the centuries, since international trade with the East had broken the molds of the medieval economy, the Englishmen, Frenchmen, and Hollanders had resented their dependence upon southern Europe. First the merchants of Italy and then those of Spain and Portugal had held the channels of that lucrative trade; their cupidity and power had reduced the less fortunate outsiders to almost colonial dependence.

The northerners labored under a profound disadvantage. While the more advanced East produced a wealth of goods they desired, they themselves created little that could be exported in return. For the silks and spices, the sturdy ironwork and the delicate leathers, payment had to be made in gold, and that kept them poor, disrupted internal trade, and threw the monetary system into disorder.

The difficulty had long since been apparent — and also the solution to it. Those envious of the Italians and Spaniards knew that they too must find direct access to the areas of trade, import their own raw materials, gain their own gold, and come to export the products of their own industries. The means however were lacking. They could not lift themselves by their own bootstraps. So long as they were poor, they were weak, and so long as they lacked power, they could not grasp the resources from which wealth flowed. This had been the dilemma of the maritime nations of the north for a century and more.

Toward the year 1600, however, unsettling elements appeared in the situation. Far-flung expansion had sapped the strength of the Mediterranean powers while Elizabeth's England, the France to which the Bourbons had just come to power, and the newly independent Dutch states were all feeling the renewed vigor of their adolescence. At the same time the northern countries found that their situation on the Atlantic, once a liability was now a real asset. These nations had come through their time of troubles and had emerged with strong, modern, centralized governments capable of acting vigorously. Among their leaders were men of enterprise and initiative, eager to push for new strength.

The great ocean now led not to a mysterious emptiness but to the New World. Here were taking form the novel routes of trade that were to assume major importance in the European economy; and in the struggle for the mastery of these routes, the Atlantic powers were in a decidedly advantageous position.

In their internal life, therefore, overseas trade now assumed a fresh importance. Earlier, the merchant had given over his attention to dealings in his own markets. Organized in the traditional companies and gilds, the drapers and silversmiths, the ironmongers and chandlers had made and sold goods to the folk around them. Commerce with the more distant lands, and finance, had been left to the strangers, to the Jews and Lombards and the Germans of the Hanseatic League. Now the value of the imported stuffs rose steadily in importance and played an ever more prominent part in the life of these economies. At the same time, all local industries were transformed by the hope and the desire to produce for wider markets, to see the products of London or Paris sold in all the distant marts of the world, where they would command in return the precious wares of the Orient and America.

The excitement of these changes and the attractions of the new fortunes that could visibly be made from them, now and then swayed an old trader to take the risk of venturing outside his proper sphere. Occasionally a draper or grocer, excited by the possibility of earning by a speculative coup the fortune that would advance him at a stroke to a level a lifetime of cautious calculation could not hope to achieve, took such a flyer. But more usually the new trade fell into the hands of men of a different sort who had the capital, the skill and the daring to take a hand in hazardous enterprises.

Often the consolidation of power in the new states left the nobility and gentry in relative idleness. Back in the early days a man with a good sword and the ability to command others found employment in plenty, and the possibility of fortune, in the alternations of success between the rival parties struggling for power. But the long Elizabethan reign had ushered in a period of stability in which the restless and ambitious were compelled to look outside their own borders for adventure. It was the same in France now that the Fronde was over and the Bourbons firmly in power; the same even in Holland, at last independent and at peace. The gentry, with time and capital on their hands, restless in spirit, looked westward toward the Atlantic where opportunity awaited them. And it was they who animated the new lines of trade.

Yet these ardent spirits, avid for gain and for action, sometimes complained there was little they could do. They were driven by chance from one fugitive opportunity to another.

In time of war, it was not so bad. The occasional breaks with Spain in the sixteenth century gave them the excuse to fit out marauding expeditions that singed the beard of His Catholic Majesty and incidentally plundered his ships to the goodly advantage of the freebooters who organized these expeditions. Only peace brought the sea dogs idly back, except for the few who continued as pirates the careers they had launched as patriots. At the most, however, all these ventures were sporadic and unsatisfactory to men who wished long to enjoy the glory and the gains of their daring.

What should be stressed is that they were willing to take flyers in trading enterprises promoted in hitherto untouched corners of the earth. For instance, the ships of the English searched out the waters of the Baltic, and made their way to the unfamiliar coasts of Africa, India, and the Levant. Other vessels entered the fishing fleets in distant waters. Here were certainly the prospects of profit along with the hazards of long voyages in distant waters, of hostile action by pirates or by the rulers of the barbarian states. The trials of searching out these new trades and establishing them were well enough, if only those who took the risk could be sure of the gain. Yet too often, it seemed, such a route would hardly be established when interlopers would come in and reap the profits.

For that reason the most energetic looked for another way out. If they could but emulate the Spaniard and, like him, plant trading depots in the unexplored parts of the world! Then they would command the resources of virgin territory, draw as they wished upon the gold and precious metals certain to be found, and have also a monopoly of the business. By this one stroke they could resolve all the dilemmas of their situation.

It was thus that two favorites of the queen dreamed as her reign entered upon a period of peace and stability. Sir Humphrey Gilbert in 1583, having served her well in war, secured a patent to establish a colony in Newfoundland. Unskilled in the business, and handicapped by an unpropitious site, he found the venture disastrous. Two years later, Sir Walter Raleigh sent out another expedition and at great cost established it in Virginia. But this effort, though the site was better, was no more successful and vanished without leaving a trace. These projects lacked the ability to establish themselves permanently; though Raleigh invested thousands of pounds, he still found himself short of the necessary capital. The resources of a single individual were inadequate to the needs of the situation.

As the sixteenth century drew to a close, therefore, the hopeful men of England, and of France and the Netherlands, cast about for some alternative. Neither piracy, nor trade in its traditional forms, nor colonization by individuals had gained them the rewards the season's fresh opportunities promised.

The need was for power that would permit the makers of schemes to capitalize on opportunity, and for power it was necessary to turn to the Crown, in whose hands were concentrated all the instruments of force. As the necessities of the situation became clearer, rival groups of merchants and of others who wished to enter trade turned to the government for aid and favor.

The state was interested. To further such enterprises might well add to the Crown's strength in its rivalry with other monarchs. And no king was now so free of the pressures of cash that he could afford to forego the possibility that he himself might profit were the ventures successful. In return, therefore, for a share of the profits or from the expectation that the royal domains would be extended, the government granted what aid it could. Financial assistance it could rarely afford. But it did have at hand a variety of medieval techniques for encouraging enterprise and upon these it drew freely.

A favored project could receive aid from the Crown in the form of a grant of privileges — relief from taxation, the right to perform acts illegal for others, or the ability to exploit some resources.

The most important privilege was that of creating a monopoly. The common law and practice forbade monopolies. But special grants to enterprises particularly worthy of support were permissible. The advantage was clear. Monopoly closed the markets of the nation to the sale of competing products and left the favored enterpriser free to set what price he wished.

Monopoly was gingerly bestowed. By its very nature, it created one friend and a score of enemies. Disappointed rivals and competitors were likely to complain, so that it was worth giving only to some great enterprise with a claim to public utility. Most often, therefore, it was associated with the grant of the privilege of acting as a corporation, and increasingly monopolies went only to companies.

The corporations were steadily to grow in importance. They too were created by privilege and were already well known in the sixteenth century. Often they were referred to as bodies politic or nations, and although they differed in detail, they had in common one essential feature. They were agencies to which the state delegated some of the power to govern. In them, the Crown created little enclaves of power within which laws could be made, force administered, and taxes levied. These governmental powers were handed over to groups of individuals for specific commercial purposes just as they had earlier been bestowed on municipalities or gilds or universities for other ends.

In the second half of the sixteenth century a number of such regulated companies were created to trade with distant lands. The justification was that the particularly hazardous condition of this trade made necessary the instruments of control and the monopolies with which such companies were endowed. In England, the Muscovy

Company was formed in 1554 to direct all trade with Russia, in 1581 the Levant Company for trade with the Near East, and in 1599 the East India Company for trade with the Orient. This was a technique, however, that was common to all western Europe.

An innovation appeared just after the turn of the century. Until then the regulated companies were purely governing bodies. Each of the merchants who was a member traded on his own account, earning his own profits and losses just as if he were a member of a municipality. In 1602, the Dutch East India Company departed from that pattern by establishing a joint stock to which each of the participants contributed and which the company managed for the common advantage. This created a remarkably strong agency, capable of recruiting capital from many sources, including the noncommercial. In 1612, the English East India Company adopted the same pattern and the joint stock corporation thereafter spread rapidly throughout western Europe.

The corporation acquired in the process a fixed character, the influence of which would be transmitted to the maturing colonies of the New World. Since its powers were essentially those of government, it came into being through an act of the Crown. The charter that created it also defined its powers and established the means for its internal regulation. By the charter the holders of stock or members of the corporation and their successors were constituted a common body; they were directed to meet at stated intervals in an assembly or general court which would pass upon the affairs of the enterprise and make rules for its control; in the intervals between meetings a smaller body or council of directors or assistants, presided over by a president or treasurer, was to manage its affairs.

Special provisions in the charter or by-laws enabled the corporation to conduct its overseas business at a great distance from home. In the land with which it traded — India or Turkey or Russia — the company built its warehouses and residences in a plantation, a fortified place ruled by its own laws and subject to its own discipline. Of necessity, at its head was a military character, the governor.

In the arrangement of particular details, there were often significant differences among the corporation charters. The institution was only in process of development, and unresolved perplexities about its character left room for variations. For instance, although the company received a monopoly of trade, it was not clear whether it was an exclusive body or whether anyone was free to join. The first enter-prisers wished to reserve the privilege to themselves; the Crown was often anxious to widen it. On this issue the well-established merchants divided from newcomers crowding in.

Or again, the existence of the joint stock created difficulties. The freemen of a borough or the members of the gild were all equal, all entitled to one vote and no more. Was the same rule to hold in a corporation the associates of which contributed unequal amounts of capital? In some corporations it did. In others, the members were divided into two groups of large and small stockholders. Only rarely was there the effort to make the voting right proportional to the amount of stock. But these issues were only now being raised and not really settled; they would hang over to plague the colonies that sprang from the corporations.

For the development of these corporations, from which emerged the colonial governments of the future, was not significantly in-fluenced by America or American needs. They had emerged as a result of changes in the economy of the late sixteenth century that had thrust overseas trade into new channels. The alliance of the state's political power with the capital of private venturers took ad-vantage of the opportunities created by the disorders of commerce and by the shift in economic balance away from the Mediterranean. The corporation had grown out of the application of medieval pat-terns to the exigencies of overseas trade in this period. It had been founded by people who still thought in terms of the gild or town or borough.

The chartered companies dedicated to overseas trade appeared in almost all the countries of western Europe in the first half of the seventeenth century. They were set on foot to develop commerce with all the remote corners of the earth — and incidentally with America. In that period their plantations were slowly dotted along the Atlantic coast of what was to be the United States. The Massa-chusetts, the Plymouth, the Dutch West India, the New Sweden, and the Virginia companies all had the same end in view. Not colonization but trade was their objective. In the thinking of all but a few of their sponsors, the discovery of a Northwest passage or the opening of gold mines was more important than the foundation of colonies, which were primarily the means of sustaining and furthering trade. The companies operating in America, at the start, considered themselves on an identical footing with those operating in India or Turkey.

The corporate form had spread because it was far more effective than the individual quasi-feudal forms that Raleigh and his predecessors had used. The new technique enabled overseas enterprise to mobilize and govern the men and to accumulate and manage the capital essential to the successful conduct of overseas trade. The corporation united the adventurers and the planters who were the mainstays of the successful plantation.

The adventurers risked their capital. The large amounts of money absorbed in establishing a going plantation were staggering by seventeenth-century standards; the Virginia Company, for instance, ate up £ 200,000 of its investors' money without ever yielding a return. Yet such sums, particularly in England, were available for investment through the corporation. Some of these funds were still left over from the proceeds of the sequestered church lands earlier distributed among the royal friends. Others came from piracy or trade — legal or illegal — ventures which, while highly risky, were also immensely profitable, so that lucky enterprisers often faced a dilemma when it came to reinvesting the returns. It was futile to go on endlessly speculating in hazardous projects which sooner or later were bound to lead to disaster. Better to plunge in a manner that had at least the hope of stability and security.

The policy of James I in England increased the pressure upon such men. Anxious for peace, the king at last reached an understanding with Spain which brought to a decisive stop the long period when raids upon the Spanish colonies were openly or covertly tolerated. With that means of investment closed off, men of wealth felt even greater pressure for finding some alternative way of placing their funds.

The planters, those who risked their own lives to migrate and settle in the colonies, were driven by other motives. At the start, the fate of the colonies lay largely in the hands of men able to fight and willing to cut themselves off from their homes, to live hard lives among strange peoples and places. The times had also produced the men necessary for expeditions in which the military element played a prominent, indeed, predominant part.

Footloose fighting men were not difficult to find. There was that rascal Tom Verney, for instance. Originally, a rascal, *rascaille* in the French, was a foot soldier, a shade below the mounted knight, but nevertheless a worthy character. It was only now, through such as Verney, that the term acquired its derogatory connotation.

Verney was the offspring of a good county family, but found no niche for himself in the society of his time. He scorned a life in which he would be *fed from hand to mouth, as men do feed young apes to make them pliable to their dispositions.* Yet his troubled parents and brother would no longer indulge him. *Let him suffer for his folly and go his own way.* He wandered in search of the chance that would *make me a fortune for ever* — to Flanders, to France, to Sweden and at last to Barbados. Captain John Smith was a man of similar cut and would play a more important role in the history of the colonies.

These men on the edge of gentility sought most of all the means they could no longer find in their own society of establishing themselves in proper terms. If they were younger sons, or scions of families fallen on hard times, they could not afford to lead the lives they considered appropriate to their station. Neither were they willing to accept the degradation of endless toil at home without hope of quick improvement. Their craft was the sword; they preferred the risks and hardships of life in the battlefields or the wilderness where there was at least hope that a stroke of fortune would redeem their lot and open up the position of security for which they were eager. These were first in the ranks of the planters and constituted the corps of fighting men the hazards of trade demanded.

They found themselves in company with comrades of quite another sort. The economic disturbances of the times set adrift a number of sober artisans, men who had been trained to a handicraft, who knew how to reckon and after a fashion how to write. For them, too, opportunities were scarce, and often it seemed to them more desirable to follow chance elsewhere than to scrounge around in dependence. Such crafty men were occasionally willing to go as the clerks and carpenters these enterprises demanded. They were not numerous, but they were an important contingent in the population of the plantations.

Finally, the special conditions of English life set apart still another group — some gentry, some worthy artisans — willing to take a part in these adventures. The Elizabethan adjustment had by no means stilled all religious disturbances and the accession of the Stuarts raised up once more all the uneasy questions that the compromises of the great queen had pushed to the background. In many regions, earnest men brooded over the state of the Church as it was, and out of their dissatisfactions found cause for leaving their homelands.

There were, for instance, a body of separatists who wished to have no further communion with the Established Church. Some of them had formed a congregation in Leyden in Holland, but had achieved no lasting settlement there. They were willing to fall in with Thomas Weston's scheme for a company that would exploit the furs and fisheries of the New World and for his profit and their security find a more satisfactory place of refuge there. Plymouth would become their home.

So, too, the scattered settlements around Massachusetts Bay attracted the attention of an unusual group of migrants, moved to leave England for reasons of their own. These dissident spirits had not left the Church of England, but they considered the Church corrupted and were eager for its purification. Among them was John Winthrop, a gentleman, but having a difficult time of it. Perhaps his affairs suffered from preoccupation with religious matters. He was struck with the illumination that the best way to reform the Church, for which all at home seemed dark, was to depart to some empty part of the earth where there would be room for an experiment that would demonstrate what the true polity should be. The eager spirits around him embarked on a long series of negotiations with the Council for New England which for some years had sponsored desultory fishing and trading establishments and the result was the Massachusetts Bay Company which in 1630 dispatched its first group of settlers to take up land around Boston harbor.

None of these groups — the religious dissidents, the rascally gentry, or the artisans — was numerous. But they supplied the manpower which the corporation joined to its capital to get these undertakings under way. And large numbers of settlers were not at the start considered essential. For the basis of all these operations, to begin with, was the trading company, and few thought in advance that more men would be needed in the plantations of America than in those of India or Muscovy. These settlements had been projected as a means of giving Europeans, theretofore excluded from it, a place in overseas trade. They did not, in their earliest years, outgrow that design.

2

The Permanence of Plantations

THE COLONIES did not develop as their projectors thought they would. Unexpectedly, the trading corporation did not function in America north of Mexico as it had elsewhere. Again and again, expeditions were sent forth with the old plans and instructions. Again and again, they failed or were transformed.

The source of the difference was the character of the land to which the Europeans came. Along the coast north from Florida, the commercial plantations were repeatedly frustrated. Here they found neither the natives nor the resources they were elsewhere able to exploit. Here, unlike the more fortunate places in Mexico or India, there were no settled populations with which trade could be conducted or which could be set to work. Instead, the country was inhabited by scattered Indian tribes who vanished swiftly into the wilderness. Attempts to establish commerce with these nomads were not fruitful, for the simple indigenous economy boasted few articles of value to the newcomers. And efforts to put the Indians to work were no more successful; the red men fled into the forests at the first efforts to make use of them.

Yet here the labor of the natives was, if anything, more necessary than in other parts of the world. In this corner of America few surface resources were available simply for the taking. Ultimately the oncoming Europeans would find this land rich enough. But its riches were not lying open to the conquerors as they had been in Mexico and Peru; it took labor to bring them forth.

The unexpected situation drove men to the quest for alternatives. Where so much in capital, in energy, in hope had already been invested, they were reluctant to give up; and the magic of America kept drawing newcomers to it. Some soon surrendered and went home. But many remained, struggling on to work out a way of making their enterprises feasible in defiance of adverse conditions.

If there were no population with which to deal, then trade could be nurtured by the discovery of those valuable commodities that found ready sale in all European markets. In the seventeenth century and onwards, the planters' first thoughts were toward the possibility of uncovering stores of raw materials that would supply the staple exports of commerce. Along the whole coast, the hopeful went tapping for gold; or they wove ambitious dreams for the cultivation of silk or sassafras or other exotic crops. These came to nothing.

On the other hand, a number of places made promising starts in the production of other exports. In Virginia a few men had begun to raise tobacco in 1614; and that trade grew steadily in value thereafter. In Plymouth and New Amsterdam, fur provided the staple of commerce. The Massachusetts people found their best medium the catches of fish; and elsewhere men were turning to the timber and naval stores of the forests. With one or another of these products it was possible to earn the means of keeping the colony going, particularly if that income could be eked out by privateering or by illegal trade with the Spaniards or Dutch.

The lack of local labor limited all these expedients. The demand for tobacco or fur or fish was ample. But there were simply not the hands to produce them; neither the Indians nor the gentry, nor the artisans, were fit for these tasks. Cultivation of the tobacco plant called for tillers of the soil; fish and furs had not only to be caught but cured. Above all, the colonies themselves had to be provisioned. So long as they depended on the food and drink that small ships of limited capacity could bring out, the possibilities of growth were restricted.

By 1640, after some four decades of effort, the English colonies could boast only seventy thousand residents, more than half of them in the West Indies. Virginia had eight thousand, Massachusetts fourteen thousand, and four thousand were scattered in the other English continental colonies. The French and Dutch settlements were tinier still.

If the settlements were ever to outgrow these limits, and thus assure their own permanency, they would need a labor force of another sort, one capable of raising their food and the staples of their exports. To recruit such a labor force, they were compelled to take steps that ultimately converted the trading companies into settled communities.

Land alone would draw to the colonies men who could work with their hands. Sooner or later the companies perceived that and acted accordingly. At first, they attempted to give away large tracts to great proprietors who would bear the expense of bringing over the laborers in the usual European pattern inherited from the medieval past. Virginia created particular plantations of this sort and encouraged the feudal schemes of Lord Baltimore in neighboring Maryland; and the Dutch West India Company set aside large areas for the estates of patroons.

To make such grants was one thing; to stock them with people was another matter. Those who received concessions soon discovered that a thousand acres on the Hudson or the James were not worth even a hundred on the Rhine or the Thames. Servile labor was no more attractive on one side of the Atlantic than on the other. Few Europeans wished to leave home if their only reward was the same dependent status as before. To draw newcomers across the ocean, a device was needed that would give peasants what they most desired — the prospect of independent landed proprietorship. In 1618 Virginia hit upon such a device when it initiated the headright system. It gave fifty acres free of charge to every settler and fifty more for each person he brought in. Other colonies began to display similar liberality; and the number of yeomen who arrived in response rose steadily.

But the flow was not adequate. Western European states sought to increase rather than to diminish their populations and imposed legal obstacles to emigration of this sort. After 1640 some of the sources of religious tension abated and dissenters earned grudging tolerance. Above all, people who enjoyed any margin of choice hesitated to risk their lives in ventures that were still tentative and uncertain. The propaganda that described the gentle climate, the abundant food and healthful air of the New World was largely wasted. At mid-century, all the colonies were still unclear about the prospects of future settlement.

Yet simultaneously, in many parts of Europe and especially in England, there had been developing a fund of labor of an altogether different sort. These people would be desperate enough, helpless enough, to be willing to migrate; and free land would be the means of bringing them across.

Again and again, the English records of the seventeenth century referred to an excess of people. The population of the country was then climbing up toward the five million mark, but that total itself did not justify the repeated complaints. The difficulty arose from the increase in the wrong kind of folk in the wrong places, and particularly in London.

The number of inhabitants in the great city rose from about ninety thousand in 1560 to some five hundred thousand a century later, and did so despite plagues, fires, and laws forbidding the city to grow. People lived there *heaped up together, and in a sort smothered, with many families of children and servants in one house or small tenament*; and yet, still others continued to arrive.

The additions were not themselves products of the city, but drawn to it from outside. A fundamental change in the structure of English agriculture was turning hundreds of tiny tracts cultivated by scores of peasants into a few great estates where a handful of shepherds tended their charges.

> *The towns go down, the land decays,*
> *Great men make nowadays*
> *A sheepcot in the church.*
> *Poor folks for bread do cry and weep,*
> *Towns pulled down to pasture sheep —*
> *This is the new guise.*

The placeless, set adrift in the process, took to the road in quest of bread and labor. Hordes of sturdy vagabonds moved from parish to parish, working, begging, threatening, their numbers swelled by the economic hardships of the 1620's. The current flowed always toward London, which in its size offered the refuge of anonymity. Nowhere else in England was there room for the unattached.

All men were presumed to labor as part of a household, the yeomen on their lands, the artisans in their shops, and the unfree in the families of their masters. In a few places, manorial estates still survived, within which villeins transmitted from father to son a permanent servile relationship to the lord to whom they were bound. In the towns journeymen, apprentices, and servants were subject for fixed terms to the control and discipline of their master of whose family they were a part. Everyone was thus intended to have a stable place, personal as well as occupational.

The steady rise in population altered the situation. There were now more men than the masters or landowners wished to take on. It was more advantageous to hire servants who would remain servants forever than to contract with apprentices who expected some day themselves to master a craft. The excess of men destroyed their bargaining power and limited their freedom. Those who had places clung to them and aspired to pass them on to their children. There was little hope of improvement; changes were likely to be for the worse. The evidence was plain in the village marketplace, where each year the placeless desperately waited for someone who might use their service. If there were no takers, the local authorities could auction them off to the highest bidder. Otherwise it was the workhouse for them.

Such were the folk who flocked to London and among them were some for whom America would be an escape from a hopeless future.

Indentured servitude enabled them to come. In return for their passage they contracted to labor in the New World, sometimes directly with the prospective employer, sometimes with the ship captain who would sell them on arrival. Often, but not always, the agreement specified the number of years and the conditions of their bondage. But these details were of minor importance to men eager to break out of the endless round of servitude at home.

For the planters and shipowners too the migration was a boon. For a moderate price the former got four to seven years of labor and, in addition, fifty acres as a headright for each soul they imported. The latter profited from a valuable cargo. The trade boomed, drawing off thousands from London and from the rural countryside of England and southern Scotland.

Expansion of the trade increased the demand; soon the entrepreneurs were no longer content to limit their activities to such servants as signed up of their own accord. By the middle of the seventeenth century they were also drawing upon involuntary laborers from three sources — the wild Irishmen, the African Negroes, and criminals.

In the eyes of the English the Irishmen constituted a simple, if an ancient, problem. For three hundred years the fierce tribesmen had resisted efforts to subjugate them; in the 1640's under Cromwell, the conflict was more intense than ever. A century before, Henry VIII's advisers had wished to undertake the total extirpation and destruction of all the Irishmen in the land and had only put aside the project because it was too expensive. But to seize them as prisoners of war to be sold overseas would be profitable rather than costly and settle the problem as well. Males of an age to labor and women who were *not past breeding* had value in the New World; and the traffic persisted for years. "*We have repeatedly seen husbands torn from their wives, children from their parents, servants from their masters and all forcibly carried off to the West Indies there to be sold as slaves,*" wrote an observer.

The same fate awaited thousands of black men. The earliest interest of Europeans in West Africa was not in its population but in its gold and ivory. The Portuguese had longest been established in the area, but in the seventeenth century the Dutch and English were competing successfully. Whenever the interlopers failed to get the precious wares they wanted, they took on cargoes of lesser value, "Negers" whom they could sell in the Spanish colonies of America, and thus earn entree into a trade from which the King of Spain excluded foreigners.

Sometimes, of course, a royal viceroy was inconveniently present or local conditions prevented the completion of these illegal transactions. Then the blacks could be sold in Curaçao, the Barbados, St. Christopher or later Jamaica; and in time, these islands developed a thriving sugar economy with its own increasing demand for bound labor. Now and then a stray ship dropped some of this human cargo in Virginia and the other mainland colonies, but the numbers were not large until after 1660.

By mid-century also, English and Scottish authorities had begun to transport debtors, paupers and criminals to the New World, a humane solution which relieved these unfortunates of the cruel punishments to which they were otherwise subject and also relieved the parish of the substantial cost of supporting them. All these involuntary migrants were sold on arrival like other servants and for a time mingled with the rest and lost their separate identity. Though the coming was not a product of their own will, they could serve their terms and enter then upon the promise of the New World's freedom.

In one crucial respect, the servants — voluntary and involuntary alike — differed from the gentry, the yeomen, and the artisans, the people of skill and position, who until then had been the sole source of colonial population. The old planters had come to America with their eyes still fixed across the ocean intending to make their fortunes and go back home. For them settlement was a temporary episode, as it was for others who went to India, Turkey or Russia. But for the unfree, the voyage to America was a total commitment. The Old World had been the scene of their wretchedness, where they had been permanently degraded. Even a fortune would not permit such to return and surmount the stigmata of their servile status. They dreamed instead of becoming in the New World what they could never be in Europe, independent landholders. To these people America was not to be a transient episode but a totally permanent experience.

After mid-century, the permanence of the colonies seemed assured. The settlements had struck roots that could hold them up against any likely blows in the future. The risk of migration persisted but in a substantially reduced form. An effective social order held forth the promise of a life free from the gross insecurities of the earliest decades. The Indians were a danger; but after 1664, all the provinces shared a common English rule and were prepared to defend themselves against external attack. America became increasingly attractive to several groups of potential settlers.

The possibility of accumulating great landed estates lured a few gentlemen of good families, even some of the courtiers who returned to power with the restoration of Charles II in 1660. They were in a position to secure favorable grants and eager to rebuild or expand their fortunes. Some of them came to Virginia; others put their hopes further south, in the new Carolina project. The expanding trade of the colonies also drew occasional merchants who settled down in the growing cities to deal on their own account or as correspondents of English houses.

Far more numerous were new arrivals of a humbler sort. The changing English economy continued to deprive some of the population of places. Disturbances in the wool trade, the consolidation of agricultural holdings, and the weakening of traditional handicrafts unsettled numerous yeomen and artisans. Those already established on their holdings, or in their trades, no doubt held on, even if at a disadvantage. But there was not likely to be room for their younger sons. In East Anglia and the West Country, growing numbers of the young and ambitious, with dim prospects at home, responded to the temptations of the New World's opportunities. They went off to Bristol or London where, by now, the well-established system of indentured servitude was ready to carry them across the ocean. They joined the servants and convicts whose number was also increasing, paying for their ultimate freedom the price of a temporary period of unfreedom.

Such migrants, intent upon settling down and establishing permanent homes, were the most valuable instruments of colonization. They came not for immediate advantages, but to stay; and they would help build a permanent society.

All the great powers with overseas interests sought such supplies of unfree labor. But none had the success of England in actually recruiting and replanting such a population. France managed to get several thousand such *engagées* to Martinique by the 1650's; but neither in the West Indies nor in Canada could it accumulate a group sufficient to meet the needs of the colony. It failed to do so because the agricultural population of the homeland was still bound to the soil; and the changes which uprooted masses of men were not to begin for a century more. On the continent of Europe, displacements similar to those in England had occurred only in Germany, which lacked overseas outlets of its own; when emigration there took form, after 1680, it too would flow in the direction of the opportunities of the British settlements.

The French and Dutch colonies in the New World remained underpopulated and dependent on large numbers of Negroes, at a time when the English colonies were already peopled by folk determined to create a new way of life in the wilderness. Those others remained colonial offshoots of commercial empires; while the mainland settlements which began with the same impulses were transformed into stable societies.

II

Europeans at the Edge of the Wilderness
1600–1680

3

Civil Society in a Remote Place

THE NEW WORLD began at the water's edge in Europe.

Tiny vessels, sixty to two hundred tons in the main, bore the voyagers westward. Riding at anchor in the sheltered bays of the homeland, the ships seemed substantial enough. Their sturdy timber and looming masts, their cabins that rose like a castle several stories high in the stern, were impressive in comparison with the harbor craft that flitted about them. At sea, it would be another matter. All became precarious as the isolated specks, buffeted by the elements, beat their way into the unknown immensity before them; and the men below huddled fearfully in the cramped space that set their condition of life.

The Pilgrims who came to Plymouth in 1620 were an unusual group, mostly freemen who paid their own way, with only a few servants among them. Their journey was as comfortable as any could be in the seventeenth century. Two ships carried the company, the *Speedwell* of sixty tons and the *Mayflower* of a hundred and eighty. Into the *Mayflower*, ninety feet long and twenty-four feet wide at its widest point on deck, were crowded twenty-five seamen and a hundred and two passengers together with swine, poultry, goats, and the other supplies adequate for three months at sea, and also the equipment needed to build the plantation. These were their narrow quarters for sixty-seven days while fierce storms and contrary winds sadly shook them and persistent leaks in the upper works exposed the frailty of their protection from the elements.

The Pilgrims were comparatively fortunate. Indentured servants, transported convicts, captive Irish and Negroes fared much worse. Jammed together to economize on space and fed no more than was necessary to keep them alive, such people could find no relief even in the sight of land; forebodings of the difficulties of an uncertain future heightened their anxiety as they pushed out of mind the homes they had forever left behind. For them, more than for other men, the crossing was an impassable barrier in the way of ever going back. Henceforward they would make their lives between the ocean and the wilderness.

At the start, all the colonizing enterprises were tentative. The little troops landed at the edge of the dark forest, the ships withdrew beyond the eastern horizon. Now was the time for survival. All that existed at home as a heritage from previous generations had to be built afresh here, and swiftly, to avert disaster. The people of Charlestown, on Massachusetts Bay, in 1630 took shelter in empty casks before the first rude huts went up. In Jamestown the palisade and magazine for stores took precedence over individual convenience. Only when their toes were firmly dug in could the settlers begin to create the basis for a permanent society, to establish dependable means of earning a livelihood and clear an orderly way of life in the wilderness.

They had in mind the homeland scheme of society, where trade occupied the towns and agriculture the countryside and each man had his place in one or the other. Every newcomer could summon up the picture of a community he knew, where ancient institutions regulated his relationships to work, to other men, and to God. Embedded in the village or the gild were tested habits and the capacity for communal decision adequate to cope with all the problems of daily life. Those who departed hoped to re-create in the New World the whole communities they had known in the Old, only purified of their imperfections. They did not succeed; the wilderness proved uncongenial to such concepts of order. In time, the colonies thrived. But their trade was not that of the established gilds and companies. Their agriculture departed from the patterns familiar to European peasants for centuries. Their people did not sort themselves out into the accepted classes set off from one another by wealth, skill and privilege. Even the towns and villages never acquired the appearance of those of home. The changes intruded into the most intimate human relations and distorted the character of the church and the family. Society here could not establish the same order as at home; it had to contrive new ways of enabling men to live and work with their neighbors.

The planters were not content merely to sustain themselves in isolation; they wished to preserve a connection with Europe and the origin of the settlements in commercial companies made trade their pre-eminent concern. The newcomers were no sooner established than they devoted all their energies to commerce; and the centers through which overseas trade passed became the first cities of American civilization.

The export of commodities which had value in the marketplaces of Europe was long the basis of commerce. Puritan vessels, coasting down to Newfoundland, brought the cod ashore to be cured and packed and then sent abroad. Furs gathered in the interior passed through the warehouses of Plymouth and New Amsterdam. In the Chesapeake colonies, tobacco was the staple and from the Connecticut and the Hudson valleys went the flour and biscuits that made up the bread trade. The ships that bore these commodities headed mostly for Europe, where the colonists had business and family connections. But the settlers learned also to look to the West Indies for a trade; their closeness to the sugar islands swelled the volume of their commerce and sustained the life of their towns.

Unsettled international conditions encouraged these early starts at overseas trade. In the first half of the century, the intruding English and Dutch merchants were still primarily attracted by the prospect of breaking into the closed business of the Spanish and Portuguese colonies. They then acquired the habit and facility for disregarding inconvenient laws. By mid-century, however, conflicting interests arrayed England and the Netherlands as the chief rivals for commercial supremacy. Open war between the two powers in 1652 gave the merchants of New England and New Netherland an opportunity to expand their trade while the mother countries fought one another. By 1680, Boston and New York (by then in English possession) were substantial commercial cities.

These communities were not altogether like the urban places of Europe. In 1673 Boston, the largest of them, boasted a population of five or six thousand. As returning mariners moved up the bay they glimpsed the masts of the ships clustered in the harbor, the steeples of the three churches, and a few windmills. By the time the anchor dropped this side of the seawall or Old Wharf they made out the gothic houses huddled together toward the North End. But when they looked up King Street beyond the Town House they also saw the ample fields rising toward Beacon Hill and the Common, where cattle still peaceably grazed.

The cities were not as yet wholly detached from the countryside. Laid out at first as fortified garrison posts, they subtly mingled in their development the urban features of the medieval town and the rural aspects of the village. Still dependent on their own resources to feed and sustain themselves they nevertheless continued to trade overseas.

The merchants whose hands held the lines of commerce were the most important residents. But the raw setting did not allow them simply to do business as in Amsterdam or London. They succeeded only when they accommodated themselves to the wilderness.

David Pietersen de Vries was forty-six years old and already rich in experience and in capital when he arrived in New Netherland in 1639. As owner-skipper he had taken his ships whaling off Greenland and fishing off Newfoundland. He had bought furs in Canada and spices in the East Indies and alternately bartered with and fought the corsairs of the Mediterranean. Now he dreamed of a grand plantation on Staten Island whence he could tap the trade that moved through the great harbor. But the dream faded. The men he contracted for in Holland did not come; he had trouble with the English on a venture to the Connecticut River; and in his absence the

Raritan Indians swooped down to destroy what he had built. He retired to the calm of rustic life on his Manhattan farm.

Other merchants came to terms with the wilderness. William Pynchon of Springfield had settled in the Bay Colony in 1630 at the age of forty, bringing with him the substantial capital left by the proceeds of his estate in Essex. He had quickly perceived the advantages of a site on the Connecticut River, and built his storehouse opposite the Indian village of Agawam. From the surrounding countryside, the red men and, later, white farmers brought him furs, beef, pork and corn to be shipped down the river, the provisions by way of Hartford to the West Indies, the pelts by way of Boston to London. Back from his correspondents abroad came sugar, molasses, rum, textiles and manufactured goods. This was entirely trade on the book; no money changed hands as Pynchon kept account of the barter transactions. Naturally the squire was the dominant figure in the community, a magistrate and a dignitary of the church. His neatly clothed figure, from which shrewd, calculating eyes surveyed his world, commanded respect and disposed of power.

His counterpart to the south was William Claiborne, the younger son of a well-connected English family. Claiborne had recently left college when he came to Virginia in 1621. A strong man who affected the long flowing hair, the pointed mustache and beard of the courtiers of his time, he built himself a little trading empire on Kent Island in the Chesapeake. Allied with Cloberry & Company of London, he played off Virginians against Marylanders, the parliamentary against the Crown parties, settlers against Indians to keep the flow of goods moving. Such men early rebelled against traditional restrictions on enterprise, whether they came from the company, the church, or the colonial government. European connections remained important for the access to market and the capital they provided. But the successful merchant knew that his prosperity depended upon the ability to adapt quickly and freely to the conditions about him.

The tiny groups of officials, ministers, doctors and lawyers who found their way across the ocean were also unsettled by the new environment. With few exceptions, the men who came to take these posts were those who had no places at home — the failures, the dissidents, the lowborn. Mostly eager to make their fortunes, they were inclined to ally themselves with the dominant merchants.

In this situation, professional men could not simply adhere to European standards. No recognized authority effectively regulated their behavior or practice and they were constantly called on to improvise the means of exercising their skills in the absence of the familiar institutions and tools of home. They had to make do without bishops or libraries, without Inns of Court or surgical instruments, without any of the symbols or artifacts that attested to their competence in the Old World.

In that respect, their problem was analogous to that of a humbler stratum of urban society. Artisans played an essential role in mercantile towns. Coopers and ropemakers and sailmakers fitted out the ships and prepared their cargo; carpenters, tailors and bakers supplied shelter, clothing and food. These men too had to transfer specialized techniques of making and doing to a new environment. Their number grew steadily, sober, skilled heads of households whose craft was at a premium in a new society and who therefore earned substantial rewards. No gild rules and few legal restraints hampered them here in the quest for their own advantage in their own ways.

Below these solid folk was a shifting mass of servants working out their terms, and sailors between ships. Hands were scarce and control was difficult in communities from which escape was easy; and it was no simple matter to keep in their places people tempted by avenues of easy escape.

Commerce also unsettled American agriculture, and shaped it into forms that diverged from Old World antecedents. The desire to develop money crops that could be exported as staples influenced the whole character of settlement. Already from the ship's deck the newcomers could perceive the abundant stands of timber. The forests of western Europe had long since been destroyed. Yet wood, drawn at considerable expense from the Baltic, remained essential to the European economy. Tall masts and stout planks, tar and turpentine, built ships for war and commerce. Trees supplied the fuel for domestic heating and for the iron, copper, and glass industries. Potash and dyes for the wool manufactures, shingles and barrel staves were among the other valuable products to be drawn from the forest. In the New World all were abundant. Many a husbandman who went out to plow and reap was tempted instead to hack away at the pine and oak already raised for him and to move on as the line of timber receded rather than attend to the exacting business of farming. The rural population spread thin in the process.

Tobacco had much the same effect. It too was in high demand. But it quickly exhausted the soil, particularly since the only implements, the spade and the hoe, permitted the farmers merely to scratch away at the surface. The tobacco growers therefore preferred not to use scarce labor on plots that had been worked over for four or five years, but to shift to the abundant virgin land. British policy after 1660 encouraged the trend. The Navigation Acts protected the market for American tobacco, but also taxed it heavily and put a premium on the best grades, which could more readily be raised on fresh soil.

Other efforts to grow exotic staples failed. Schemes to plant vineyards or lay out fields of flax or graze great flocks of sheep all came to nothing because they required intensive cultivation and hard labor, for which hands were not available in the New World. But as the merchants developed the West India trade, they did create markets for grain and cattle, products to which the farmers of the Hudson and Connecticut valleys could devote their efforts. The enterprising learned also that the herring of the rivers and the clams of the seashore could profitably be packed for export.

Only a few treated agriculture simply as a means of subsistence. As they became familiar with the forest, the settlers supplemented their diet by fishing and hunting. But they did not lose sight of the goals of commercial agriculture; they devoted their energies primarily to production for overseas markets that would yield returns for expansion and some of them were drawn directly into trade to add to their incomes.

The efforts to create staples for export, the premium on production for the market and the dispersal of population fashioned a distinctive system of landholding in the colonies. In most parts of Europe, the peasants still lived together in villages and walked out each day to labor in the fields. Often their plots were scattered, an acre here, an acre there, in complex fragments that were the products of generations of subdivision, inheritance and marriage. And most holdings, whether for a fixed or indefinite term, were conditional, that is, subject to continuing obligations to the Crown or to intermediary landlords. By the 1670's, the colonies had developed quite different patterns. In the New World, the characteristic farm was a single unified piece of land on which the farmer lived apart from his neighbors and which he owned outright as a freehold, subject only to general taxes.

The first projectors of the colonies had not expected this development and had long sought to establish older feudal forms. The Virginian, Plymouth, and New Netherland companies, and the proprietors of Maryland and Carolina attempted in vain to retain a grasp on the land. Ultimately each yielded in the face of evidence that settlers would come only in response to the lure of the freehold.

In some places, there remained an obligation to pay a nominal annual fee to the proprietor or the Crown. Later, in the eighteenth century, the Americans would regard that quitrent as an intolerable burden, having forgotten that it was a relic of their liberation from all the charges that still encumbered land held in Europe, but which could not be transferred to a new society.

This was the striking difference between the development of the mainland colonies and of the West Indies. The latter were islands, the amounts of land limited. What there was of it was quickly allocated among a few large landholders. Incapable of attracting voluntary settlers by the offer of small freeholds, the island planters depended increasingly on involuntary servants who worked on larger and larger plantations. They never developed the substantial group of independent farmers that occupied the coast between Maine and Carolina.

The individual freehold penetrated the New England colonies more slowly than elsewhere on the continent. In the towns of that region, older forms survived through the seventeenth century, sustained by coherent, disciplined communities. Serving at once economic, political and religious functions, the town could resist for a while the disruptive impact of the American environment.

The town was long an economic entity. It received the grant of land from the legislature and retained part of it in common fields. It also held corporate privileges, like that of taking fish from the rivers. Of the plots it gave away, some were in the center where the residents built their homes. But the arable land was usually dispersed in strips as in the Old World, so that agriculture was to some extent a communal enterprise. There were efforts also to subject trade to traditional restraints, although with less success.

The town was also a political and religious unit. It selected representatives to the General Court and governed the lives of its residents. Its power and resources supported the church and compelled all to attend services and accept its discipline. All these interlocking concerns sustained one another. The individual who wished to follow his own course in business or farming faced the religious and political disapproval of his neighbors; and those who persisted in error were excluded, banished or punished.

New England was unique not in the conception of the town but in the ability to keep it alive so long. The particular plantations and patroonships to the south were also corporate bodies within the larger company, but they quickly disappeared while the New England town persisted and spread wherever the Yankees settled — in Long Island and New Jersey as well as east of the Hudson.

No single element accounted for the persistence of the New England town. The intense religious drive that brought many settlers to Plymouth, Massachusetts Bay, and Connecticut generated a concern with preserving an instrument to keep men walking in a godly way. The danger of attack from the north by the Indians and by the French emphasized the desirability of clustering together for defense. The New England colonies were also freer of royal interference than the others. The founders of Massachusetts had taken the precaution of bringing their charter with them; and its neighbors also evaded control from London. They could therefore proceed to create new towns as the occasion arose without fear of restraint by the Crown.

Above all, the character of its population made New England more conservative. The town repeated in a modified form the central features of village communal agriculture, of gild trade; its political activities were modeled on the practices of manor courts and local borough government; and its religious discipline was familiar in all of western Europe. The Puritan element in the migration to New England was able for a time to transfer these institutions despite the hostility of New World conditions. Their leaders were a small but influential group, settled men rather than adventurous wanderers or displaced peasants and artisans, who migrated as a result of a considered resolution to build in America a purified counterpart of the society they had left at home. For three decades their objectives shaped the destiny of New England.

After the middle of the century their influence waned and their conservatism was a less effective brake on changes that thereafter steadily accelerated. The communal land system broke down as holdings were consolidated and the common fields distributed. Merchants and artisans were ever less responsive to the claims of conscience in setting prices. As the population scattered, control by the church loosened and the fragmentation of the old community, already more advanced to the south, proceeded apace here too. Even the iron devotion of the Puritans could not permanently hold off the corrosive effects of the New World wilderness.

The settlers therefore discovered that they could not simply carry to their new homes the orderly structure of society they had known in Europe. It was all very well to respect differences in rank, to distinguish among the gentry, the great merchants, the yeomen, the traders, the artisans, and the servants. The law could dictate what clothing each class should wear and determine who should be addressed as "sir," "mister," "goodman," and who without title. But such distinctions early lost their importance, despite all efforts to preserve them. Shifts in status came quickly and easily and mobility emptied the formal rankings of significance.

The law, for instance, could fix the regulations of servitude — length of term, conditions of labor, and rewards in cash, land or clothing. But masters had to be increasingly liberal in these matters if they wished to attract the laborers who alone could add value to empty lands. The aggrieved hands could run off into the forest or to another settlement; and harsh treatment lowered the reputation of a colony and made difficult the recruitment of newcomers (except in the case of the Negroes who had no choice about their coming and remained depressed while others rose). Relatively favorable terms of employment enabled many bondsmen to improve their lot quickly; like Michiel Jansen, who began as a farm servant in Rensselaerswyck, they made their fortunes in a few years. Such alternations in status were common in a society where position was less often inherited than acquired.

Mobility of this sort raised a question it had not been necessary to answer in Europe, where differences in rank were in large part hereditary and were marked by visible distinctions in speech, clothing and style of life. The people of the Old World had long since learned that every man had a place or station to which he was assigned by God and which had its own peculiar rights and obligations. The servant and master were what they were not through any particular merit or blame of their own but as a result of forces and decisions they could not control. Each could strive only to play his own role to the best of his ability.

American experience required a subtler explanation. The settlers had to account both for the stratifications in their society and for the ability to move from one level to another. Men were not born, but rose or descended, to their ranks. That one met with fortune and another with disaster could not have been fortuitous; merit and deficiency had to be part of a larger design. He whose holdings grew larger and purse longer manifestly enjoyed God's favor as his neighbor visited by misfortune did not. It was tempting under these conditions to fit rise and fall into a Calvinist scheme, to divide human society into the saved and the damned, the saints and the sinners, the prosperous and the poor.

In the Puritan areas where Calvinism was strongest, there was a tendency to identify divine election with rank and to regard the acquisition of wealth as a sign of divine justification. Acceptance of that logic strengthened existing leadership, fortified social discipline, and helped protect the community against untoward change.

Elsewhere differences in rank were not so readily explained and the disparity in conditions created uncomfortable tensions. The people of Virginia and Maryland learned quickly to question the authority of the would-be gentry. Men who had sustained themselves by their own efforts, who made their own estates, and lived by themselves were not likely to be passive or acquiescent. Now and again they burst into turbulent disorder and, in 1676, rose up under Nathaniel Bacon to defy the governor in his mansion. Such a rebellion was as yet unthinkable in New England. The colonists had begun to create a social order but it would not be simply copied from that of the Old World.

As soon as the settlers understood that they would not continue under the provisional forms of company life, they tried to put into operation the kinds of institutions they had known in Europe. They had to hold together and act together, be a civil society; this the Puritans knew from the start and the others learned in the struggle to survive. They needed no abstract theory to tell them that only by covenanting with one another toward common goals could they provide for God's worship, regulate family life, and establish the means of governing themselves. Experience taught them that unless they did so they would sink to the level of the beasts of the wilderness.

The seventeenth-century settlers shared a common religious background, but marked divergences appeared among them as they established their churches in the wilderness. The people of New England followed a course unlike that of their neighbors to the south.

The initial difference stemmed from the presence in Massachusetts and Connecticut of a small but influential body of religious leaders who had no counterpart elsewhere. The learned clergy and devout laymen who participated in the Puritan migration were a unique, leavening element, drawn from a higher level of society than the rest of the population, and animated with zeal. Although a minority, they commanded not only power but also esteem and respect, and they were long able to impose their conceptions of order and discipline upon the churches they founded.

The first Puritans had no intention of cutting themselves off from the Church of England; they were no separatists such as were to be found in Plymouth. But they carried with them the belief that the Church was the product of a covenant among its members and that quickly brought them to Congregationalism. In practice, the members were a small, self-selected group, convinced of each other's piety, who chose the minister, regulated worship and governed the whole congregation. The tendency to identify spiritual election to the body of saints with material evidences of divine favor put such membership within easy reach of people of wealth and rank, yet often excluded the common mass who had to attend services and listen to the sermon but who lacked any voice in decisions. The same influential personages therefore exercised religious as well as political and economic power, a fact which elicited the obedience of the rest of the community. Moreover, the town was a setting that encouraged a tight religious order. So long as all lived and worked together there was no room for secret transgression, dissent or open rebellion.

The planters of Virginia were no less religious than those of Massachusetts. But their settlements lacked the organizational strength of the New England town and, without the religious commitment to Calvinism, they could not develop such local roots as the Congregationalists did. Their churches were therefore weak and unstable, despite the fact that they were established by law and had the support of government.

In theory, Virginia was under the charge of the Bishop of London, as all the English colonies were held to be down to the American Revolution. But that cleric before 1670 was not overly concerned with the fate of the remote outposts of his immense diocese; and without rigorous episcopal oversight, the church fell into disorder. It proved difficult to recruit a reputable clergy. Given the opportunities for comfortable livings in the Established Church at home, it was not likely that any but the failures and the disgraced would choose to come to the colonies. Undistinguished by either piety or learning, such men acquired the lax manners of those among whom they resided in the dispersed settlements. The result was a breakdown of the habit of worship and widespread apathy toward the obligations of faith. Religion could not serve as an instrument of social discipline as it did in New England. Personal misbehavior could only be dealt with by the government. A certain David Spiller, who, in 1653, was repeatedly brought to court for excessive drinking, name-calling, slander and immorality, in Massachusetts would certainly have been curbed by the religious authorities. In Virginia, he could only be controlled by force; usually, such types were not controlled at all.

The Virginia situation tended to become the norm everywhere south of the Hudson. The few Roman Catholic priests in Maryland and the few Calvinist ministers in New Netherland could not hold together patterns of religious life shaken by migration. The failure to do so outside New England profoundly influenced all social relationships. What in the wilderness would induce men to obey without fear of divine retribution?

Neither habit nor the inner discipline of the family could be counted on here to hold men to conventional ways. However appearances remained unchanged, beneath the surface the alchemy of the wilderness transformed traditional modes of behavior.

The seventeenth-century colonist often imagined himself a Biblical patriarch; again and again, in sermons, the family life described in the Scriptures was held up as a model for emulation. He was hardly aware that the institution evolving in America was different not only from that of ancient Palestine, but also from that of contemporary England. And the alterations weakened its capacity for controlling men's conduct.

In Europe, the family had been a functioning economic unit, in which were joined husband, wife, children, and also relatives and servants who participated in the work of the household. On the land or in the workshop, each person had duties defined by age and status and each was subject to the authority of the master who was responsible for the welfare of all. The community of which it was a part assumed general oversight of the family; its sanctions assured respect for the mutual rights and obligations of the members. The disapproval of neighbors, the reproof of the church, and the punishment of the state hung above those who failed to comply with the accepted code.

Only in the very largest cities, like London, did relative anonymity permit deviations. There the mass of drifting laborers were not parts of households but individuals who struggled in isolation for a livelihood. There the conventions of family behavior did not apply; nor were priests or judges there powerful enough to hold parents and children, husbands and wives, masters and servants to a strict adherence to communally defined duties. Each man and woman, without control, could move in his own direction. The situation was abnormal but significant, for a large part of the population destined for America experienced it.

After the long disorganized interval between departure and settlement every family sought to regain its stability by re-establishing the old forms of behavior; but wilderness conditions often frustrated its efforts to do so.

In Virginia and Maryland the dispersal of settlement destroyed the possibility of close supervision of personal life. Each family was isolated on its own farm, remote from any neighbor and dependent upon its own resources. Yet it was a strain to see only the same faces, day after day in the strange environment. In the lingering tensions, quarrels erupted; children and servants were disobedient, and husband and wife abused one another. As a result, gaps appeared in the network of intimate relationships that organized household life. The sermons of troubled ministers revealed the concern with the consequences. But rarely was there an authority to step in to establish an order of what was right and what was wrong.

Such an order was more necessary here than in settled societies. Concentration upon the staple eliminated the diversification of the old household economy. Between the tobacco field and the wilderness there was nothing — rarely a yard or garden to occupy the women and children at traditional tasks. The only alternative to idleness was man's work; and the wife or son who labored by the side of a husband or father ceased to accept authority as a matter of course. Boys no sooner emerged from adolescence than they insisted on being off to fend for themselves; and the abundance of land permitted them to break away easily.

Often then the husband and wife were left alone and the family ceased to be what it had seemed to be in Europe — a durable institution, reaching back across many generations and extending widely through many relationships in the society. Instead, it was an arrangement that held together the conjugal pair and, temporarily, their dependent children.

Marriage lost its religious significance. In the South, where the clergy were few and far between, the traditional rites became a burdensome formality readily dispensed with. In New England, the Calvinist rejection of the sacrament of marriage had the same result. But common to the general secularization was an altered view of what the ceremony meant. Marriage was not the solemnization, in a manner ordained by God, of a relationship that would perpetuate the family as a pillar of society. It was an arrangement, effected through a civil contract before a magistrate or simply by a voluntary agreement, in which two individuals undertook to work together for the satisfaction of their own needs.

That transformation, slower in New England than elsewhere, but everywhere apparent by the 1670's, was symptomatic of a much broader change in the whole society. The colonists were not able to bring intact with them the corporate order of family and church within the community that had governed their lives in Europe. If men were to live by rules, and not as brutes in the wilderness, other means of control would have to be made effective.

4

The Body Politic

ORDER WAS the immediate and continuing need of the colonists at the edge of the wilderness. Remote from traditional sources of control, the anxious men and women who struggled for survival quickly learned that they would fend off the dangers from the enemies of the forest and from among themselves only if they could labor together in some organized way. Yet the soil of the New World proved inhospitable to the inherited European community that they wished to bring with them across the ocean. Neither church nor family, nor any other institution, survived the crossing intact. If the venturers in these hazardous enterprises were to co-operate it would have to be according to fresh rules compatible with the strange conditions; and, all too often, force was required to make the rules binding.

But the Europeans who became Americans were, by habit and training, hostile to the naked use of violence. The experience of a thousand years had taught them to distinguish between the compulsion cloaked in legitimacy and that which was simply the oppressive exercise of power by one man over another. And precisely because all else in the new universe they explored was uncertain and unfamiliar they wished to preserve the clarity of the line between brute force and the restraint of law. Otherwise they would find themselves, one man set against another, all helpless and without order.

Seventeenth-century Europeans understood that violence was tolerable and even desirable when those subject to it accepted it, of their own will, as a means of attaining a goal they could not individually pursue. Men banded together because they could not live alone. In doing so, they agreed to accept the government of the ruler placed over them in order to further their common interests. They thereby formed a body politic within which were lodged the legitimate instruments of coercion. It was so that the passengers of the *Mayflower* had acted when they covenanted to combine themselves into a civil body politic that could frame just and equal laws to which they could promise all due submission.

The chartered company was one such body politic and those who voluntarily joined it accepted its governance. But it derived its authority from the sovereign only for a specific purpose, set forth in the document that brought it into being. It controlled so much of the lives of its members as was relevant to that purpose and no more. In the wilderness, however, these commercial enterprises became civil societies and were expected to maintain order in all men's relations with one another. The new role transformed transplanted institutions. The governor discovered that despite his commission, he was not all-powerful but had to secure the collaboration of those who could give effect to his orders. Rules promulgated in Europe proved less binding than those adopted locally. Diverse groups tried to use the polity in their own interest; and the participants became aware that all were concerned with establishing the regularity of law and the security of privileges. By 1680, the metamorphosis was almost complete; the companies had turned into the political instruments of functioning civil societies.

The process modified the traditional European conception of political power. In the Old World, the monarch stood at the pinnacle of the body politic. His anointment in a religious ceremony lent a sacred quality to the mutual obligations of sovereign and subject. To him all owed obedience. From him all authority emanated;

standing at the head of the hierarchy of power, he issued all commissions and gave validity to every action at law.

No one, among the immigrants to America, questioned the supreme position of the king at the head of the state. The problem was to give it meaning in a remote place under conditions radically different from those of Europe. The character of the people who became colonists and their distance from the source of authority decisively conditioned the way in which the institutions of government passed across the ocean.

The settlers were not a complete cross-section of the population of the lands from which they came. Among them were almost no men who had had any experience with the upper levels of political administration. The mass had had no contact with power except as subjects; in a vague way they were conscious of the links between neighborhood officials and Westminster, but they had no way of knowing how the mechanism actually functioned. Some of the gentry among the migrants had held local office and knew something about the practice of borough or manor courts. But none was familiar with the operations of Parliament or of the king's councils; and none was learned in the law.

As a result the colonists were often compelled to improvise, not out of any love of novelty but out of misunderstanding or ignorance. Lacking a secure grasp of proper procedures, they were driven to act in accord with their own approximations of what seemed right under their own circumstances. That opened the way to significant, though often unperceived, deviations from what had been usual at home.

The sheer distance of the colonies in America from the capitals in Europe had somewhat the same result in impeding the simple transfer of political institutions across the ocean. The slowness of communications left an imposing gap between every order and its fulfillment. A command issued in London in March was not likely to reach Virginia until June; and news of whether it had been accepted would not come back until September. If there was any uncertainty or disinclination to obey in the colony, correspondence on the matter could prolong itself a year or more. Under these conditions, large measures of local discretion were unavoidable and the intentions of the rulers only incompletely became the realities of the New World.

The governors sent out by the Crown were men of power. They commanded respect not only because they were often gentlemen of quality, not only because they stood at the head of colonial society, but also because they represented the king's majesty. In the rude clearings, where all others sank to the level of the savage surroundings, the governors still embodied what was royal and sacred in the Old World. Helmeted and armored, they were force in its traditional guise.

In 1642 and 1643, three such men came to the New World. Sir William Berkeley was then thirty-six years old, scion of an influential family, a graduate of Oxford who had already made his mark as a courtier and a playwright. From his impressive brick mansion in Jamestown he was to rule Virginia in its most critical decades. Johan Printz was almost fifty, a veteran of the Thirty Years War; a nobleman by birth, he had been a student at the University of Rostock when he drifted into a fighting career and had served one German princeling after another until he arrived to command the settlement at New Sweden on the Delaware River. Later he was to die of a fall from a horse. But he was now a monumental figure: awed by his four hundred pounds, the Indians called him "Big Guts" and the colonists feared his wile and his soldierly anger. The career and character of Petrus Stuyvesant were somewhat similar. Of the same age as Printz, he too had lived by the sword and was a faithful servant of the Dutch West India Company. He came to America as governor of Curaçao and there lost his right leg in battle. But the stump proved no impediment when he was assigned to New Netherland in 1646. There he established himself in his great bowery and ruled like a czar — vain, choleric, impatient of advice. All three were competent administrators, men accustomed to large enterprise, conscious of their rank and insistent upon unquestioning obedience.

Yet despite the staunch front they maintained, despite their habit of command, all the governors found themselves making subtle changes in the structure of government not because of open challenges to their authority, but because only thus could they get themselves obeyed. The process was well under way by the time Berkeley and Stuyvesant arrived.

Virginia for almost two decades was the property of a chartered corporation. The seat of its government was London; there the stockholders, meeting in General Court, enacted the rules for its management. Thence instructions went to the governor and his council, in Jamestown, who actually administered the colony. Under garrison conditions, the officials on the spot exercised total jurisdiction; within the broad mandate from the company they made rules, enforced obedience, and tried and punished the refractory.

The system never worked. Unforeseen conditions in the New World and distance from the Old impeded the execution of the company's wishes and forced the governor to arrive at his own decisions. Yet the spread of settlement outside Jamestown made it difficult for him to make his will felt throughout the colony. As the individual families drifted away from the sheltering but confining palisades they removed themselves from the governor's power.

In 1618, the company recognized the problem and resolved to deal with it. It marked out a number of territorial jurisdictions in each of which it asked that a court or meeting consider various matters of local business. No existing term was exactly appropriate to describe these areas, which for the time being were sometimes called shires, sometimes towns, and sometimes counties. Eventually, the last designation became permanent; and as the sessions became formalized, convening regularly four times a year, they were known as the County or Quarter Courts. Their concerns were not simply judicial. They controlled the militia, made rules of their own, and in effect administered local government.

Meanwhile, in 1619, these bodies were directed to choose representatives to meet together to consider matters that concerned the whole colony. That assembly would become known as the House of Burgesses — again an inappropriate designation because no English word fitted it exactly. It had, in its early years, no precise functions or defined procedures. Nor did it meet at regular intervals. It was simply a convention of the prominent men in the colony who came together to act upon matters of common concern, often sitting with the Council. After a decade or so, the meetings became more regular and more systematic and the House of Burgesses gradually took on the character of a legislature, not through any deliberate plan but because the situation required that general rules be made by people drawn from all parts of the settlement, who alone could see to their enforcement.

The first session in 1619 occupied a good part of its time with petty details, the complaints of servants, the control of drunkenness, the punishment of misdemeanors and the like. But as the political system developed, it became clear that the effective power to get anything done resided not in the grand assembly that met in Jamestown but in the county courts which could muster the military power to support the general laws. Although the courts met only quarterly, they quickly worked out means of exercising their control throughout the year.

By the 1620's, they were accustomed to designating those members who lived in a particular district or parish to act as a vestry, or local governing body. Here the men of influence came together to administer the affairs of their area in accordance with the broad directives of the County Court, on which they also sat in its quarterly meetings. As settlement became stable, power was fixed in the hands of the families of wealth and position; and the vestries were chosen by co-option. Later, the practice of public election became common, but that consisted only of the approval by the people of the list the vestry presented them. The election was not a means of selecting officers but rather a way of giving general recognition to those already designated.

The system was comprehensible in terms of the conditions of the time. The great landowners were not only the wealthiest individuals in a region; because they controlled large numbers of servants, they also disposed of the most power. They alone could exact obedience and therefore they alone could sit on the vestry effectively. For the same reason they appeared on the bench of the County Court, which could rule only with the sanctions they supplied. And only by securing their attendance could the House of Burgesses expect its wishes to be carried out. The governor in theory had the power to commission justices of the peace. But he too realized that the sealed paper had value only in the hands of men with power to use it, that is, of exactly the same persons who appeared in the vestry, the County Court and the House of Burgesses. The system worked because it rested on local power.

Here was a significant inversion of the relationship to authority. In England and France, the king's legitimate right to rule was delegated by successive steps down to the justice or the bailiff who acted on his behalf in each village. The American colonists of the seventeenth century never questioned the propriety of that scheme. But it did not work in the New World. Instead, authority accumulated on the local level and passed upward by the representation of those who held it.

Only when those who held local control themselves divided into antagonistic groups were these nascent political institutions further altered. In Virginia, that occurred in the 1670's when families that possessed exceptionally large landed estates began to set themselves off from the rest of the county gentry. The Blands, the Byrds, the Carters, the Ludwells and the Masons were often men with capital who had arrived since the first pioneering days; and their holdings were far greater than those of their neighbors. Generally, the instrument of their participation in politics was the Council.

In the earliest days, that had been the only body with which the governor had shared power. But it had sunk in importance in the half-century between 1620 and 1670, when it seemed often simply to merge with the Burgesses. Then, as the difference between the great and the greatest men in the colony became more distinct, the Council took to meeting by itself as the agency of the uppermost group in society. At that point the characteristic features of the provincial polity were clearly defined; the governor appointed from London, an assembly of the local gentry, and a smaller council of would-be aristocrats shared power.

The developments in Virginia were representative of those in the other mainland colonies. Nearby Maryland was the possession of a lord proprietor rather than of a chartered company. But it had been settled by much the same kind of people as Virginia and followed a very similar course.

The Dutch and Swedish colonies differed in their failure to develop an assembly, in part at least because the companies retained greater control and preserved the military character of the early government. A smaller population, confined to a restricted area, was also more readily cowed. Yet even in New Netherland, authority tended to drift toward the holders of local power. And after mid-century, calls for some representative governing body showed that the dominance of the governor and council would not long remain unchallenged.

In New England, too, power shifted to a local base, although the compact communal nature of settlement complicated the evolution there.

The Pilgrims came to Plymouth with a clouded title and with powers derived not directly from the Crown but from the larger Virginia Company. Properly speaking, there was no legitimate authority; whatever right to govern existed, emanated entirely from the agreement among those who held power. While the settlers clung together in the place of their first landing, they ruled themselves in meetings under the leadership of a governor and assistant. Their town embraced features of the organization of English boroughs grafted onto company forms. But when in the next two decades the Plymouth folk spread out into a half-dozen different centers, a more elaborate structure appeared. Each cluster of families became a town and from 1639 onward, each sent deputies to an assembly which, with the governor and assistants, exercised political power in the colony.

The town was also the nucleus of power in Massachusetts. Salem was already functioning after this fashion before the Bay Company formally took possession; and thereafter each penetration of new settlers into the interior proceeded through the creation of new communities. In each place, the freemen met regularly, made the important decisions of common interest, and designated the selectmen who governed in the interim. Of course they chose the prominent men, the godly and wealthy most properly entrusted with authority. But the character of the office-holders did not change from year to year and those once elected tended to retain power indefinitely. When vacancies occurred, moreover, they were in the best position for co-opting new men to share their responsibilities. In practice therefore the role of the meeting was that of approving their choices and of resolving conflicts within the ruling group. Like the vestrymen of Virginia, the selectmen of New England ruled because they held local power. It was obvious, John Winthrop pointed out, that *some must be rich, some poore, some highe and eminent in power and dignitie; others meane and in subieccion.*

As settlement spread, the leaders in each town, eminent in wealth, power and dignity, reached out for a share of control in the colony. Within a decade they had transformed the company organization transferred from England. Who were the stockholders or freemen, entitled to vote in the General Court? Not a narrow group of the original promoters, but all those property-holders admitted to the privilege by the towns. Shortly they became too numerous to gather as a body. Instead the town meeting designated representatives to act for it in the General Court which became a legislative assembly. Here too government was effective because it rested upon the local organization of power.

In Connecticut and Rhode Island the dependence upon local authority was clearer still. There the individual towns actually antedated the organization of any central government. The settlers made their clearings, built their meeting houses and chose their rulers independently, until the needs of defense and common action persuaded them voluntarily to unite in each of the two colonies. There, as elsewhere on the mainland, the Assembly remained the medium through which the holders of local power joined to establish general order.

Each colony developed along parallel but separate lines. In each, the immigrants who were making homes in the wilderness contrived a political system as best they could to give them an equivalent of the stable relations they thought they had known at home. Bringing with them a common heritage and confronting similar conditions, they converted the company form into workable governments that represented the actualities of power.

In the process, the connections with the Crown were relatively unimportant. Through this whole period Englishmen had closer and more pressing subjects of political concern. The disturbances that began under the Stuarts continued through the Cromwellian decades and were by no means resolved by the Restoration. Few gave much thought to the remote and unproductive colonies in these years of turmoil and experimentation. As a result, decisions made in London had little effect upon the developing American institutions.

In 1624, for instance, the Crown vacated the charter of the Virginia Company and turned the colony into a royal province. That change, however, had no visible influence upon internal political evolution. Thereafter the king rather than the company appointed the governor. But that official still had to secure the assent of those he ruled; and he had to accept the development of the assembly, of the counties and of the parishes to do so.

Divergences in overseas control were less important than the similarities in wilderness conditions. Maryland remained a proprietary possession, but its political system did not for that reason differ from that of Virginia. The changes from Swedish to Dutch suzerainty in Delaware and from Dutch to English in New Netherland had little influence upon the course of internal development. Such issues as arose in the relationship to authority in Europe were significant insofar as they set precedents for the future rather than for their immediate effect.

That was also true of occasional efforts to draw the separate colonies into some more intimate association with one another. Under the pressure of the fear the Indians stirred up by the Pequot War of 1636, Massachusetts, Connecticut, New Hampshire and Plymouth formed the Confederation of New England. In the next half-century, that loose alliance co-ordinated the activities of the separate colonies, mainly in defense against Dutch, Indian and French threats. But the Confederation had no power. It could act only through the independent member governments. Lacking any means of communicating with the towns directly, it had no way of making decisions that could be locally enforced.

The settlers rarely thought about the remote questions of authority. Government in their eyes was a means of maintaining local order. Justices of the peace and selectmen, courts and assemblies were useful because they could protect men against enemies, punish the disorderly, resolve conflicts among individuals and undertake such projects, useful to all, as the support of schools and churches, the construction of roads and the provision of ferries. All these efforts required the use of force, to ensure obedience and to collect taxes. It was a matter of course that the officials were men who disposed of such force.

Seventeenth-century Americans, like Europeans, were accustomed to thinking of office as a kind of property, the holder of which was expected to profit from the fees and privileges associated with it. The small exactions for every service were preferred to higher taxes on all property. Fees, however, mounted up in the purses of those who received them and were accounted among the legitimate rewards of politics.

Those who held and those who sought power therefore soon turned their attention to distribution of the spoils. Accustomed to thinking in terms of the limited space of the Old World, they considered land the greatest prize at first; and the maps of each province were crisscrossed with enormous grants of thousands of acres. (To make something of these wilderness tracts would be another matter, of course.) Monopolies of various kinds were also deemed precious — of trade with the Indians, of bolting flour, of operating mills and ferries. It was over the allocation of prizes that the local gentry sometimes fell out. Political conflicts generally originated in disputes about the award of these concessions.

In Virginia, the most dynamic and expansive of the provinces, such conflicts culminated in Bacon's Rebellion of 1676. Nathaniel Bacon, a gentleman of good family and liberal education, but very ambitious and arrogant, was a recent arrival who found himself at odds with the clique around Governor Berkeley. Bacon had land, but wanted more; his scheme for a monopoly of the fur trade failed, and he wished an aggressive Indian policy. He drew around him malcontents aggrieved because the country's wealth had been committed into the hands of the men in authority and favor. The challenge to the ruling group also excited some ordinary settlers unhappy about the privileges of the local magnates and about the heavy fees exacted by sheriffs and clerks. The uprising at first had a measure of success. But it dissolved, as did similar insurrections in other colonies, when it became clear that the destruction of privilege might also destroy the order of which privilege was a part. The county gentry who at first followed Bacon wanted a share of the spoils, not their total elimination.

The Puritan colonies established the connection between privilege and order more easily. There, religious sanctions firmly sustained all the institutions of discipline and control. In the first decades of settlement, power and church membership were closely linked. Church membership determined who would participate in government; and respectability, wealth, and position helped to determine church membership. But as the years passed, an increasing number of children of the best families failed to achieve the experience of conversion, were denied membership and therefore excluded from an active role in the polity. If the process continued to shrink the number of members they would not be able to hold power and the original order would dissolve. The concept of the halfway covenant which admitted such people to membership averted the danger. In effect, that compromise allowed a position in the church to pass from generation to generation within the family — pragmatically, within the respectable families — in each community. With that position, too, passed the privileges of sharing political control.

The vastness of what was available, throughout the colonies, relieved the tension of the conflicts over the prizes of politics. There was no end to the land yet untaken; and even the unsuccessful competitor for a grant could not feel totally disappointed when he considered how much remained to be exploited. There was room for all. And as the colonies expanded, old privileges tended to shrivel in value by comparison with the new opportunities constantly being opened. That took the bitterness out of defeat and sustained the evolving order.

Experience demonstrated that, in the long run, men profited most if the society could but assure them an orderly basis for conducting their own operations. The wilderness, once men learned to exploit it, offered them all the goods their hearts desired; it most lacked regularity, predictability, security. The fertile virgin soil would amply reward those who tilled it and there were endless opportunities for trade and for the exercise of craft skills, if only those who applied themselves to their tasks could be sure that none would trespass or break an agreement or take by force or deceit that which did not belong to him. To be sure that they would reap what they had sowed, sell what they had bought and be paid for what they had made, the colonists needed the safeguards of law.

The law administered by the governor of a military plantation was inadequate in a civil society precisely because it was unpredictable and hung upon the whim of a single individual. Yet the inherited system of law was not readily transported across the ocean. At home lawyers and judges in courts argued the meaning of texts; prescribed courses of study prepared them for judgment; and they could consult books and records for confirmation of their views. None of this apparatus was available in the wilderness; neither the trained jurists nor the books. The deficiency was particularly grave in the case of Englishmen, for their common law rested largely on an accumulation of precedents with which few colonists were familiar. Some had had experience with the local courts of the Old World in which custom and tradition counted heavily. But their recollections were necessarily imperfect and in any case there were significant variations among the practices of the different districts from which the settlers came.

The law therefore could not simply be transplanted from European to American soil; and those who attempted to do so encountered a hostile reception. The Burgesses of Virginia in 1658 considered the question *Whether a regulation or total ejection of lawyers?* They answered: *By the first vote. An ejection.* The law was not to be received but improvised in response to immediate practical conditions.

The men who made the judgments that became law were swayed by personal interest and by the prejudices of their time and position. But they were also guided by some notion of what was just; religious faith and habit persuaded them that there was a standard by which to recognize and punish wrongs, by which to resolve disputes, and by which to preserve the peace. To rule in accord with that standard it was necessary to consult experience, the Bible and other sacred or learned texts, and the teaching of the ministers.

But memory was a fallible instrument; the recollection of past decisions faded with the passage of years and with the death of those who had made them. Records were not well kept and were difficult to consult. Often the members of an assembly or the officers of a court could not be sure of what precisely their predecessors had actually done. In the Puritan colonies, concern with maintaining a standard of justice and with letting the people know what it was led to the promulgation, from time to time, of restatements of the law or codes. But in most parts of the continent judges and representatives had to determine the merits of each issue as it arose with no more guidance than their own sense of justice gave them.

In this fluid situation, men could not rely for protection on status, custom or tradition; there was always the danger of some infringement by the ignorant or heedless others and it was essential that each be vigilant in the protection of his own rights. Even in New

England the community could not be counted upon to help those who did not call upon it; and elsewhere he who did not guard his own privileges would surely find them trampled on. Hence the sensitivity of the colonists to their liberties, a term then still synonymous with privileges or rights.

The colonial charters had assured the people who went to the New World that they would continue to enjoy the liberties and immunities of free and natural-born subjects. Those phrases in England had a meaning defined through the centuries by the common law; they were intended to guard the individual in a remote place against arbitrary action by the company or its officers. They assured those who enlisted in hazardous enterprises of their own will that they would not, in doing so, lose the privileges to which their respective stations at home entitled them.

But the relevance of these guarantees to wilderness conditions was by no means clear. As the colonists developed their own polities, they had to begin slowly and imperfectly to work out their own definitions of their liberties. Claims were made in petitions and affirmed in codes or ordinances. No man's life was to be taken or his good name stained or his person arrested, or his wife, children or goods seized, or his labor pressed to public service unless by the terms of some law applicable to all. Each had the right to a trial by jury, to move away if he wished, and to fish and fowl in the great ponds and bays. There were to be no monopolies, nor any bond slavery, villeinage or captivity, except according to law.

Affirmations such as these were broad and general not out of any conscious denial of the importance of differences in rank nor out of any desire to maintain that all people were equal. It was not at all incongruous that they should go on, for example, to provide one punishment for gentlemen and another for common folk. Rights often were associated with all men, rather than with particular classes, because the distinctions were less readily perceived in the wilderness than in the Old World. Men alone could turn the forests into homes, the more men the better and faster. The settlements eager to expand therefore welcomed immigration. The landowner, teased by a shortage of the labor which alone could make his holding profitable, and the merchant, whose trade would thrive with an increase in the number of producers and consumers, were alike eager to do all they could to attract newcomers. The assurance that all men in the New World were secure in the enjoyment of extensive rights was one of the means of doing so.

The effects were visible in the steady improvement of the status of servants. Their complaints were heeded, not only out of fear that they might otherwise run away, but also out of concern for the reputation of the colony. Stories of ill treatment would surely affect the future number of arrivals. Terms were shortened, discipline relaxed, and the interpretation of unclear contracts was heavily weighted in their favor. By 1680, although they were bound for the years of their service, they had substantial rights, for they were on their way to being freemen.

By contrast, the Negroes, who served for life, remained sunk in the degradation that was the lot of all servants at the beginning. Totally strange, they did not even know how to complain. They had in any case been brought against their will; their fate once they arrived had no effect whatever upon the volume of the traffic. Therefore all doubts were resolved against them and the discipline by which they were bound became steadily more severe. They were totally devoid of rights.

The distinction which now became clear between the freeman and the slave hinged upon the relationship to rights. The European society the settlers left had known no such sharp distinction; it had rather recognized a gradation of ranks at each level of which men enjoyed particular privileges or freedoms, wider at the top, narrower on the bottom. The New World, by 1680, however, had come to distinguish between the totally free and the totally enslaved, those with rights and those without.

The Americans as yet were far from carrying the logic of that position to its extreme. On through the next century there would remain elements in the population that were free and yet disadvantaged in respect to some of their rights — women, the poor and the aliens, for example. For there was not, in this period, any complete or comprehensive statement of rights, everywhere binding. Rather, sporadically as the occasion demanded, individuals arose to assert boldly, and sometimes successfully, that a privilege was theirs and was not to be violated. Not everyone was in a position to raise his voice. Nor did the succession of such claims, as yet, erect a reliable barrier against those who held power and were determined to use it. But a body of precedents was accumulating that would have genuine importance in the future.

The emphasis upon rights reflected the vagueness of the law and the looseness of society. The colonists were concerned about their freedoms precisely because these freedoms were not securely grounded in a stable community and had to be defended.

They had hoped to maintain orderly relations among themselves through a government of laws and had created a polity out of the materials they had brought with them in the company form. The governments that emerged were instruments of local power, generally used for the advantage of those who controlled them. But in the process of creating these agencies, the colonists had in practice discovered that the authority to rule depended upon consent and that free men had rights to defend. The next century would attach profound meanings to these vague propositions.

5

New World Ideas

ALL THE LABORS of colonization bore unexpected fruits. The trading companies turned into a settled society; the planters and adventurers became farmers, merchants and artisans; and a political order appeared quite unlike any familiar to its creators. The men and women engaged in these efforts moved, in the process, from one world to another entirely distinct from it. Whatever illusions of return some of them may have cherished died quickly. They knew soon enough that the move was a permanent, not a temporary one.

They were therefore compelled to ask themselves questions that never occurred to those of their former neighbors who stayed at home. The villagers and townsmen of Europe looked back to a past unbroken in its continuity. They believed that they were where they were because their ancestors, to a time out of mind, had been there; and they could see everywhere about them the monuments of their heritage. They did not have to wonder, as Americans did, what had been the meaning of lives interrupted in mid-course.

For the immigrants, of this and later generations, that question recurred again and again in the countless moments when vital decisions depended upon uncertain interpretations of novel experiences. Is it now the time to sow or sell? The unfamiliar roots and berries, birds and beasts, fish and clams — are they edible? What remedies will heal the sick and who will bury the dead? All life consisted of such specific queries; and each led back to the one question that was the source of all others: why had they left the land of their fathers, to wander in a wilderness where none could tell what would become of them?

There were no formal philosophers among the Americans of this generation; and the answers they devised appeared in no systematic treatise. But they did frequently consider how they could account for themselves; and the unconscious assumptions and habits of thought their every action expressed revealed the answers they gave.

The character of the participants in the migrations and the nature of their adjustment shaped the views they would hold of themselves and of their place in the universe.

Few among the permanent settlers were men learned in an orderly way. A handful of ministers who came with their flocks, an occasional company or royal official and a scattering of gentlemen who had passed through a university, were educated up to a respectable European level. But the mass of settlers had the knowledge appropriate to men of humbler stations. Many of them, particularly among the Puritans, could read and write after a fashion, but the learning they brought with them was practical rather than speculative. Their knowledge came not from books but from folklore and tradition passed on orally; their skills were acquired by imitation on the farm or in the workshop rather than by abstract analysis. And they were not accustomed to questioning the basic premises with which people of their time explained the universe in which they lived. When they wondered why their universe had changed in the course of the Atlantic crossing they looked not to general theories for an explanation, but to the practical circumstances of their positions.

Most of these people lived through their years in personal and social disorder. Already at home, the lives of religious dissenters, of placeless servants, of vagabondsmen, and of the gentry without prospects had departed from any normal expected pattern. Unlike other men, they had moved about, from parish to parish, from the country to London, across to Holland and back. The migration to America was but the most dramatic manifestation of their unsettlement. Then the ocean voyage, the shifting fortunes of settlement, and even the strange forms in which the new communities were ordered showed that they were not among the usual run of men and prodded them also to wonder why.

Harsh conditions of existence prolonged the disorder the colonists brought with them. Everywhere those who survived looked back upon a starving time, a period when the margin between life and death narrowed perilously, when the very existence of the feeble societies hung by a thread. The Virginia Burgesses, thinking back to those early days, recalled that the handfuls of meal and peas allotted them were so moldy, rotten, full of cobwebs and maggots that some settlers were driven to steal or to flee for relief to the savage enemy. Many, through these extremities, being weary of life, dug holes in the earth and hid themselves till they famished. So lamentable was the scarcity that they were constrained to eat dogs, cats, rats, snakes and toadstools. Some even set upon the corpses of dead men and one, out of the misery he endured, killed his wife and powdered her up to eat, for which he was burned. Later prosperity never dimmed the memory of these early difficulties; and there remained always areas where the trying experience of survival was being repeated. At the edge of the spreading settlements, there was frequently a brutal and disorderly struggle for existence.

A high death rate remained constant. In the first winter at Plymouth, one-half the Pilgrims died. Between 1606 and 1623 about five thousand immigrants came to Virginia, had children and raised families. Yet at the end of that period there were only one thousand left. This cruel mortality was characteristic of seventeenth-century life in the New World. The chances that any infant would survive were distressingly low, even after the early, most rigorous, years. It was rare in these decades that a husband and wife should live until old age together. The frequency of remarriages by widowers and widows showed how familiar a factor in life was death.

Those who lived on suffered from nagging difficulties that prevented them from managing properly their homes or farms or shops. Old habits did not apply to the new circumstances. The men-at-arms forced by hunger to labor in the fields were hardly worse off than the husbandmen accustomed to the neat plots of the Old World who had to struggle with the dense underbrush and the great trees of the virgin forest before they could spread their seed to the ground. What splendid visions of themselves as conquering lords or masters of many acres some colonists brought with them faded in the light of the expedients by which they struggled to survive.

The colonists were always making harsh judgments of one another because they were unable to fulfill the personal, family, religious or communal roles they were expected to play. The head of the household, the worshiper, the dutiful subject could not behave in the wilderness by the standards they and others accepted, for nowhere there could they count on stability or order. Often, therefore, they were tempted to reminisce with nostalgia of the old homes where everything had its time and place and every man knew what was expected of him.

All that was missing. The visible world itself was different. The countryman's landscape, the familiar silhouettes of villages and towns, all had disappeared. In their place were patches of clearings in the ragged forest. The climate was not the same nor the cycle of the seasons; and the fixed holidays appeared in unfamiliar contexts. Above all, each man, in some way, sensed the pain of severance from the monuments of his past; he had left forever behind him the graveyard of his forebears, the church of his baptism and marriage, the familiar lanes and structures that had framed the world of home.

Nor were these generations to discover any equivalent permanence in the New World. Individuals and families moved frequently about in that quest for an ideal location that was to keep Americans restless for generations. And if they stayed, then the place itself changed as others came, and what had already been built was torn down and built over again. Everything was new and transient and remained so.

Each stage of migration seemed to remove people farther from the old home which was the source of all orderly values. In a literal sense, the settlers were still dependent upon Europe for every object of their culture; glass and Bibles, cloth and medicine, law and literature, all the products of civilization were imported. Each step from the seacoast was a step away, a further desertion, and raised troubling questions. Must they depend on the feeble connections to hold off the debilitating effects of the wilderness? If not, could they improvise for themselves? Or could they do without? Thus was born that ambiguous sense of dependence and antagonism that would long mark the relations of the Old World with the New.

Permanence and order were not to be obtained even in the most intimate personal relationships. In building, the colonists followed the old-country models. But the edifices they erected were not the homes they had known before they migrated, where every person and object had a place. However much they attempted to imitate the physical appearance, they could not restore the order. The early makeshift huts gave way to more substantial houses, but they never offered adequate protection against the rigorous alternations of winter cold and summer heat. Above all, there was no space; men, women, children and servants of all sorts crowded together in an enforced intimacy that made normal family life impossible. Children, always underfoot, were or seemed disobedient. Courtship under these conditions became casual; even in New England, church records were dotted with confessions of fornication before marriage and elsewhere marital arrangements were conveniently consummated without benefit of clergy. Instances of adultery and bestiality were not uncommon. Close contact with servants of diverse backgrounds and with Negroes, whose ways were utterly alien, increased the likelihood of delinquency inside and outside the home. This was a far cry indeed from that sheltering hearth around which a harmonious household moved and which was the symbol of continuity across the generations. Even the settlers who had never themselves enjoyed that warmth or had lost it before the crossing valued it in the loneliness of the new place. Therefore all eagerly longed for people of their own kind who would help them restore the conditions of home.

But that was not the only source of difficulty. All the elements were hostile to man's desire for order. The Europeans had been accustomed to open spaces; in the folk literature the woods had been occupied by inhuman creatures; in the shadows, out of sight of heaven, was the place of elves and fairies, spirits good and bad, witches and demons, werewolves and the strangely formed shapes that lost souls took. Here children wandered off mysteriously, never to return. Yet in the New World the forest had become home for men. They could not be sure if they would survive without being transformed, without losing their humanity.

The virgin forest reached to the water's edge. When the settlers moved inland, they were engulfed by the endless wilderness. Though they hacked out their tiny clearings, the tall trees still shut out the sun and made the day dark. Men cut off from all neighbors feared the loneliness of the pathless wilds. Strange beasts and crawling things threatened them; mosquitoes and flies assailed them; and a certain bug, called by the Spanish the cockroach, creeping into tents and boxes, defiled all it met with. As the settlers expected, there was neither safety nor decency in the wilderness.

Among the creatures of the forest were the Indians whom the colonists dreaded and despised. At the arrival of the Europeans, the scattered tribes east of the Appalachians probably numbered fewer than thirty thousand souls; and they were soon to be weakened by a smallpox epidemic. The sparse population lived in scattered villages, supported by the hunting of the men and the farming of the women. Toward the newcomers the red men were unaggressive and even friendly. Powhatan, indeed, hoped to make allies of the Englishmen in his own effort to build an empire; and Squanto and Pocahontas were generous and helpful. The settlers at first contact were also cordial, deluded as they were by the hope that the native kings would some day reveal such stores of gold as the Aztec and Inca had possessed. Furthermore, these were worthy objects of the task of conversion that was one of the ostensible purposes of colonization and exploration.

Efforts to persuade the Indians to adopt Christianity continued through the seventeenth century. The results, apart from John Eliot's village at Natick, were negligible. The Indians were at first willing enough to pray to the Christian God if it pleased their friends or promised to be helpful. But more was demanded of them; they were expected also to put aside their own gods and to emulate the life of the newcomers. The apostle Eliot was firm: men were not to be idle more than a fortnight, nor lie with unmarried girls, nor beat their wives, nor wear long locks, nor kill their lice between their teeth; nor were women to cut their hair or go with naked breasts. It made no sense to the Indians. They persisted in remaining children of the forest. In time their resentment mounted at the pushy, crowding strangers who seemed never satisfied with what they had and were incomprehensible in their limitless claims for land. The running tension between the two groups then burst into open hostility and each matched the other in savagery.

These encounters embittered the settlers not only by the losses they suffered but also by the damages wilderness fighting compelled them to inflict. That resentment meshed in with the disappointment and frustration of the dawning awareness that these, after all, were not such Indians as were to be found in the East or in Mexico, loaded with wealth and susceptible to exploitation. The tribesmen's stubborn opposition both to conversion and labor brought back memories of those wild Irish who had also resisted civilization.

The colonist who met brutality knew that the fault was not his but theirs; indecent habits and heathenish practices set them apart from other men. Manifestly they would not come to terms because the evil forces of the forest in which they lurked encouraged their wild and dissolute behavior. They were imps of Satan, literally, and therefore to be exterminated as such. Apart from the genuine danger they presented, they revealed the dreadful dehumanizing power of the wilderness that threatened all who came into contact with it.

The forest shielded other enemies as well. In the north and the south, the French and Spanish Papists represented the Romish Whore of Babylon and were potential allies of the red men. When the Indians attacked and swept through the frontier in the 1670's, the whole colonial enterprise seemed 'in danger. The furious cruelty of the fighting was evidence of what the satanic wilderness could do.

What then was man?

Pulled away from the places of his birth, overwhelmed by disorder, his very existence precarious from the moment he boarded ship, he was tossed about by uncontrollable, and often hostile, forces. What was man that he should be subjected to this trying experience?

There were answers to these questions. The seventeenth-century colonists firmly believed that these trials could be explained, for every event had a deep meaning. The ministers were rationalists who had faith in the power of logic to resolve the most difficult theological problems; and the people had to think matters through for themselves when they could not depend on habit. Neither the learned, nor the plain folk could regard their trials simply as incomprehensible chance occurrences.

Indeed nothing that occurred in the world was simply a random event. Everything was the product of the intent of some mover. A tree did not fall; it was felled. When a monstrous child was born or a school of porpoises seen, that was a sign of something designed. Life was full of signs and portents which indicated the direction of events and the intentions of the forces at work in the universe. Curses, spells and imprecations were severely punished because they could very well take effect; *Be Damned* or *Go to the Devil* might ruin a soul for eternity. All things were part of a causal system which involved God Himself, but also angels, devils, witches, and other spirits. In the pilgrimage of life, man cautiously made his way, examining every incident for clues to his destiny. Certainly therefore it was necessary to search out the significance of that painful process that had taken these men from the Old World to the New. The learned did so in writing histories and sermons; the less articulate, in listening, in believing and in forming the new habits expressed in their actions.

The colonists explained every happening in terms of a familiar dichotomy. On the one hand, they could perceive in their own experience that some actions were the products of evil impulses emanating from dark desires within themselves or from the influence of the Devil, who was by no means a figure of speech or an abstract conception but a real being consciously at work in the universe. On the other hand, they understood that other incidents were the manifestations of good impulses derived from God and evidence of His divine benevolence.

The same confrontation of good and evil existed in the social world that surrounded the individual. There in the external wilderness, in the savagery of life without reliable guides, were the sources of corruption. Were not the Indians imps of Satan, and the Papists creatures of the Devil, and was not therefore the whole American experience one which endangered man's salvation? By contrast, Europe, from the perspective of the beleaguered settlements, was the source of law, of order, of morality, and of Christianity. But in that event how was the colonist to explain his migration, away from order to disorder, away from law to savagery, away from Christianity to the spiritual perils of the New World?

These questions had to be answered. No man was willing to believe that he had endured the sufferings of migration merely to be delivered to eternal damnation. Furthermore, ministers, theologically sophisticated, could not concede that good and evil, God and the Devil, operated on a parity; that was Manichaeanism, a heresy against which they frequently inveighed and to refute which they drew upon a traditional Christian explanation. Even the existence of evil, they had learned, was an expression of God's inscrutable Providence. For reasons of His own He permitted Satan to do his work and tolerated the evil that followed upon man's original sin.

God's Providence therefore was the key to understanding the personal experiences of the colonists and the history of their settlements; and the explanation of the one offered by analogy an explanation of the other.

In the 1660's, a grieving grandmother in Massachusetts wrote a poem to explain to herself the death of three grandchildren within four short years. All were under the age of four. She had of course suffered other losses in those years, but that of the children was particularly poignant. Surely these tender innocents had been stricken down through no fault of their own, through no evil deed such as might condemn the mature sinner!

There was, however, a reason. Anne Bradstreet pointed out:

> *By nature trees do rot when they are grown.*
> *And plums and apples thoroughly ripe do fall,*
> *And corn and grass are in their season mown,*
> *And time brings down what is both strong and tall.*

> *But plants new set to be eradicate,*
> *And buds new blown, to have so short a date,*
> *Is by his hand alone that guides nature and fate.*

Ordinary events that followed an ordinary course were not particularly meaningful. But the unexpected and unnatural — even when a misfortune — was evidence of a particular divine concern. While the fallible human understanding could not clearly grasp God's intentions, the event itself was surely endowed with some special supernatural purpose. It was an assurance of heavenly interest and foresight. Just so, too, the Indians, who swooped down on the frontier towns, were themselves devilish beings and therefore to be destroyed.

But in a larger sense they were also the agents of God's wrath, no doubt bearing a salutary warning to His people that they repent and mend their ways.

A society's way of life totally out of the usual course was also evidence of some particular design. The whole character of the planting of the settlements, by its very abnormality, indicated that there had been some special purpose to the coming to America. The fact that this whole area had been withheld from previous civilized habitation indicated that there was some deliberate, unique intention for its use. The fact that the institutions that flourished there did not follow any usual pattern was itself a sign that the colonies had an unusual destiny.

Examining their own experiences, the immigrants could make out evidence that a larger will than their own had shaped their careers. Their migration was largely the product of their helplessness, of social forces they could not control — persecution by the Established Church, changes in agriculture and the unavailability of land, the disruption of the wool trade and the growth in the number of men without employment. So much was clear. But then the migration was also the product of a choice on the part of those who participated in it. Not all who were persecuted or displaced or unemployed had come; only some. Why these and not others?

In retrospect it seemed that the movement had stemmed both from the compulsion that forced the emigrants to leave and also from the positive act of will by which they decided to go. They might thus be compared to legates dispatched on a mission by a potentate; the errand was given them, but they accepted it voluntarily. The fact, too, that not all who went arrived also showed the operation of a process of selection that set some apart from the rest.

In no other way could these people account for their experience but by the conclusion that somehow and for some special purpose they had been chosen to depart from the ways of ordinary men to become in their own lives extraordinary.

Some colonists were able to describe their errand to the wilderness with considerable sophistication. The New England Puritans knew that Divine Providence had led them to a new Canaan where, like the ancient Israelites, they were to create a new Jerusalem. The wilderness was evil and did conceal ruinous temptations. But that was precisely why the chosen people had been exposed to it, to do battle with Satan under terms that would demonstrate the glory of God, whose envoys they were. There they would build a virtuous society that would be a model for the whole world. All men would ultimately emulate the city upon a hill erected in America.

This poor pilgrim people was thus doing the wonderful work of Christ, carrying forward the cosmic scheme of redemption that had begun with the Creation and that would end in the Second Coming. God had tried other instruments of His purpose, most recently in the Reformation; they had failed Him. But these forerunners of His army in New England had been tried and found not wanting. The marvelous providences they had experienced were *the very finger of the Lord* who had sent this people to preach in this wilderness and to proclaim to all nations the near approach of the most wonderful works that ever the sons of men saw.

Elsewhere the explanation was less sophisticated, less explicit, and less literate. But there nevertheless emerged again and again the expression of conviction in a sense of mission—to convert the Indians or to civilize the wilderness. The newness of a New World reserved for some ultimate purpose and waiting for those who would bring it under cultivation or who would use it as the setting for their own experiments in salvation confirmed the successive groups of immigrants, in the seventeenth century and later, in the belief that there was a profound importance to their coming. Even an involuntary servant, captured in Ireland or shipped out of an English gaol, could stir with the wonder of events that chose him from among the others, that carried him this long distance, and that raised him from the lowliest of estates.

Alone among the newcomers, the Negroes had no share in the vision. Muted by their total strangeness, they gave no expression to their interpretation of the brutal seizure and harsh confinement that brought them to the New World. Perhaps in the earliest decades while opportunity was open to them, they too may have caught a glimpse of meaning in their coming to the New World. But the definition of their status as slaves, after 1660, removed all sense of purpose from their migration. Their arrival could only be evidence of a blind, incomprehensible fate devoid of the meaning other men gave to America.

As the years passed, the number of native-born among the colonists increased steadily. A second generation appeared and then a third. By 1680 among the men prominent in the affairs of these societies were such as had themselves never made the crossing. Their interpretations of themselves and of the world about them were not altogether the same as those of the immigrants.

The native-born were at home in the wilderness as their parents had never been. The forest had been their playground; its sights and sounds were the familiar environment of their growing up. They had no fear of the wilderness, but rather confidence in their ability to master it. Never having known Europe, they were not pressed by the necessity for making comparisons with that which had been left across the ocean. Their experience was not one of loss or deprivation, but of steady gains, as the frontier moved back, as population grew, as the cities expanded. They were rootless, mobile and unstable; but they had never lived under any other condition and they were therefore not subject to the strains of the decisions that had burdened their parents or grandparents. They were likely to accept as a way of life to which they could adjust the disorder and precariousness that troubled the immigrants.

Indeed, in the eyes of those who had preceded them, the second generation seemed a ruder, less cultivated, less decent, and wilder people. Even in New England they were no longer moved by religious zeal, never having known the fear of persecution. Frequently the elders complained that the society was threatened with declension and that the sense of mission of the founders was fading.

But the second generation had not so much lost the sense of mission as transformed it. The very fact that they were a wilderness people, thoroughly at home in the New World, gave them a feeling of power. They could deal with the forest and the savage as their fathers could not; and the frontier was not to them a threat but an opportunity. The young man impatient with the oversight of his parents, the servant irked by the restraints of his master, found the wilderness a mode of escape.

For such people Europe was a source not of security but of inherited bonds, often irrelevant to the needs of the time and place. Beyond the influence of the values and standards of the Old World, they developed their own. Not having known London, they could count Boston a great city; not having seen the Guildhall or Abbey, they could take pride in the meetinghouse. They did not fear a loss of contact with a Europe they never knew. Their experience, limited when it came to what lay beyond the ocean but not when it came to what was near at hand, generated confidence in their own capacity for achievement.

Therefore, they too, although in a different form, were moved by a conviction of the grandeur of their destiny which they linked to the potentialities of a land not alien to them as it had been to their parents. They believed in the future greatness of their societies because they were proud of their own power. They saw themselves as a people certain to conquer not by virtue of their suffering but of their strength. The faith by which the immigrants had justified the hardships of their departure from Europe became, for their children, the simple confidence in the future.

By 1680, the native-born were the dominant element in colonial society. Far removed from the humble beginnings of the old company plantations, they took their peculiarities for granted and turned their energies to building upon the foundations already laid for them.

III

Provincial Society, 1680–1750

6

An Imperial Economy

THE SEVENTY YEARS after 1680 were decades of rapid development. The colonies adjusted to the terms of their environment and grew steadily in population, wealth, and power. By 1750 they had developed a culture and an identity of their own, one dependent on England, yet distinctive — in that sense, provincial. A thriving economy, flourishing cities, settlements spread far to the west, and a bountiful agriculture were evidence of the permanence and durability of settlement.

The colonists built substantially upon the foundations laid by their predecessors, extending many tendencies that had already taken form. But the success of their efforts depended also on two additional elements. A steady, more diverse, stream of later comers strengthened the population; and the international situation gave the provincials elbow room for development.

After 1680, the flow of immigration continued, interrupted only by outbreaks of war and fighting at sea that sometimes increased the hazards of the journey. By now, the recruitment and transportation of the newcomers had become a systematic business. Agents searched out the potential emigrants on behalf of ship captains and made the necessary arrangements so that redemptioners who were unable to pay their own way could work out their time across the ocean. Servants, younger sons of yeomen and artisans still left England although, after 1720, the law put obstacles in the way of the departure of men with skills. Some merchants and a few gentlemen went abroad upon adventures to rise by enterprise and make themselves famous. But the sources of emigration were more numerous than before. Although Ireland was now relatively peaceful, the drain on its population continued; the movement was particularly vigorous out of Ulster in the north where Presbyterians only a few generations displaced from Scotland responded in considerable numbers to the attractions of America. The fever for migration spread also to Wales and Scotland, and even to the continent where it affected Germans, Swiss and Frenchmen.

Religious refugees from England, Germany and France supplied substantial fresh contingents to the flow of transatlantic passengers. Monarchs grew ever less zealous about matters of faith as the seventeenth century drew to a close and were more likely to regard dissenters as political nuisances than as heretics. From this point of view it was as useful, and more convenient, to allow those who disturbed the establishment to depart, rather than to attempt to convert or exterminate them.

A goodly share of the exiles thus created were drawn to America, and particularly to the new colony of Pennsylvania. This territory had once been a possession of the Duke of York, who had used it to pay an old debt to William Penn, son of a well-known admiral. As a student at Oxford, Penn had become a convert to Quaker doctrine; and in the 1670's he had participated in a scheme to create a religious refuge in New Jersey. The venture had not gone well and Penn feared a revival of persecution; in 1681 he persuaded Charles II to grant him as a proprietary province the land to the west which he already owned. Accounts of its freedom and opportunities, spread by pamphlets in English, French, Dutch, and German, at once made this the goal of thousands of newcomers. In time, furthermore, the examples of Pennsylvania and Rhode Island forced the other colonies also to tolerate religious dissent in order to attract the flow of population essential to growth.

Another motley company of men driven by conscience therefore descended upon American shores. English, Welsh and German Quakers, soberly garbed, frugal in their habits and careful in their speech, became successful merchants and farmers. In the cities, they encountered French Huguenots who left home with the revocation of the Edict of Nantes in 1685 and also Spanish, Portuguese and English Jews, all of them engaged in overseas trade. Meanwhile there was room in the interior for the coherent, homogeneous settlements of various German pietistic sects, each of which found here the space for its own New Jerusalem. The religious refugees were a minority of the immigrants, but they brought with them exceptional skills and commercial and intellectual contacts of considerable importance.

The volume of immigrant traffic became an object of grandiose schemes; usually a combination of charity and greed swayed the promoters. Many kind hearts in the London of 1709 were thus touched by the plight of the thirteen thousand poor Palatines who subsisted on the ninepence a day of Queen Anne's charity. The region of southwest Germany from which they had fled had been repeatedly fought over during the wars of Louis XIV; and these fragments of the Protestant minority, after a winter when the very birds had perished on the wing, had escaped with empty hands and bare backs. There were no more worthy objects of assistance; so thought Governor Robert Hunter who set forth with three thousand of them to create a center for the production of naval stores on the banks of the Hudson. The venture failed. Fully four hundred and seventy were buried at sea; two hundred and fifty more died before they reached the settlement; and four hundred single women and children were left to shift for themselves in New York City. The remainder struggled on miserably and unsuccessfully for a year before they wandered off to the Schoharie region where they could keep the fruits of their own labor.

Pity also moved the heart of James Oglethorpe when he contemplated the lot of the paupers and prisoners of England. Impoverished through no fault of their own, many were confined because of inability to pay their debts or for petty thefts into which starvation tempted them. The good-hearted observer envisioned a settlement where he could redeem the victims of misfortune; and in 1733 he led the first contingent to Georgia with the blessing of the Crown, which hoped there to establish a buffer against the Spaniards. The scheme failed, but the colony survived and, after 1750, would thrive in a fashion its founder never imagined. These experiences showed that while the immigrants would come, they wished to come voluntarily to realize their own and not other men's dreams.

In that respect, by now, the white immigrants stood completely apart from the Africans who after 1680 were slaves, acting only in response to the will of others.

Although the number of Negroes had grown through the seventeenth century, there was still little demand for their services in the mainland colonies. Though they served for life, the cost was far higher than that of servants for a term and the risk greater. No man could tell whether they would live long enough to justify the substantial investment. In any event, the planters of Virginia and Maryland who still lived in close contact with their laborers preferred those of their own kind who would be less disruptive elements in the household. When they asked for more hands, it was always for white servants rather than for slaves. Indeed occasional laws in the colonies attempted to prohibit or discourage the importation of Africans.

The increase in the number of slaves was, to begin with, a product not of demand but of supply. In 1672, Charles II chartered the Royal African Company and gave it a monopoly of trade with the Dark Continent. The courtiers and merchants who held shares in the enterprise were interested primarily in gold and ivory but they were not above taking on a cargo of the Negroes, highly valued in the Spanish colonies. Slaves who could not be sold to the Spaniards could be disposed of to the French, Dutch and English. The resources of the Company were sufficient to expand all the branches of its business; and when its monopoly terminated in 1697, a host of independent merchants flocked into the trade and further raised the volume of the traffic.

The availability of black labor, bound to perpetual slavery, encouraged the development of a new form of agricultural organization among the sugar growers of the West Indies. To produce sugar called for a large-scale enterprise, with heavy investments in land and machinery and also a disciplined army of laborers. The terrified Negroes, formed into gangs and housed in barracks, were led into fields by overseers and taught with the whip to toil. The slave-traders, eager to find buyers, were liberal with credit; and Europe's markets took all the sugar that could be raised. This was the modern form of the plantation, a far cry from the earlier company settlements.

The plantation spread from the sugar islands to the new mainland colonies, like South Carolina, where rice, cotton and indigo cultivation also profited from large-scale units of production. In time too, for other reasons, it transformed tobacco growing in Virginia and Maryland. Everywhere the development of the plantation enhanced the value of slaves. The market for these helpless survivors of the harsh crossing expanded steadily until the 1730's.

The settlers of these decades had little in common. They differed in color, faith and language. They left various birthplaces, some in pursuit of dreams — of gold, or land, or freedom — and some blindly in a nightmare of terror. They shared only a common destiny, to mix with the waiting soil their labor which would make a new country grow.

These colonies, now English from Maine to Georgia, were part of a world of European empires perennially locked in conflicts which influenced all their constituent parts. France was Britain's great antagonist, both in the Old World and the New. In the eighteenth century, the Dutch and Portuguese played a minor role in America; their primary interests were in Africa and the Far East. Spain's possessions in the Western Hemisphere were still largely intact, but it was content to follow the lead of Paris, particularly after a dynastic alliance brought a Bourbon to its throne. It was with France that England would fight the contest for mastery; and France was the great power of the European continent, in wealth, population and military strength. It gave shelter to the Stuart pretenders who were potential threats to the security of the Hanoverians on the throne of England. French forces challenged Britain around the world, in India as in America, in the commercial rivalry of peacetime as in the open hostilities of war. The issues that divided the two countries would endure on into the nineteenth century.

Each contrived alliances to beat its rival down. This was the diplomats' war waged in the courts of monarchs eager to advance their own and their dynastic interests. The Hapsburgs, the Hohenzollerns, the Romanovs and scores of lesser houses were persuaded to take sides, change partners, and give what aid they could in the pulling and pushing for advantage. From time to time brief encounters of the armies punctuated the continual regrouping of forces and gave new bargaining points to the negotiators. There were extended periods of peace by treaty between 1683 and 1688 and again between 1713 and 1739; but the diplomatic game went on from year to year.

The nature of the struggle was quite different in the American colonies that were among the stakes. Both France and England now perceived the value of possession of the lands north of Mexico; and the subjects on the spot had an even clearer apprehension of the prizes to be gained. These territories were producing such important staples as sugar, tobacco and timber; here was access, through Indian intermediaries, to the fur trade; here the fisheries could best be exploited; and here was a strategic base from which to break in on the precious trade of the Spanish colonies which Madrid could no longer control.

The Mississippi Valley was the key to French strategy. Louis de Buade, Count Frontenac, had come as governor to New France in 1672 at the age of fifty-two. A nobleman, with long military experience, he was determined that achievements in the New World should compensate for both a frustrated career and abandonment by his wife. He outlined the plan France would continue to follow even after his death in 1698.

A chain of fortified posts would stretch along the Saint Lawrence, through the lakes and on down the great river to the Gulf of Mexico. Firmly entrenched in this semicircle, the French would profit immediately from control of the fur trade and establish a solid alliance with the Indians. Then they could put pressure from the north and the west upon the extended English frontier that reached from Maine to Virginia while the friendly Spaniards attacked from Florida in the south.

Plausible as the plan was, it did not work. The French were unable to push back, halt or seriously retard the spread of English settlement. The steady growth of colonial population proved a more potent weapon than superior strategy. On the other hand, the English enjoyed little success in counterattacks against the center of French power in Canada. In the 1690's a direct assault upon Montreal launched from New York and Connecticut by way of the Hudson River and Lake Champlain, failed and made plain the obstacles of that long inland route. In the approach by sea, by way of the Saint Lawrence, the English possessed superiority of naval power, but Quebec nevertheless proved impregnable; and Port Royal had to be twice taken before the diplomats transferred it permanently. More than a half-century of conflict thus proved indecisive. In 1750, the French were still entrenched in Canada; the annoying base at Louis-bourg on Cape Breton Island, seized by a Massachusetts expedition earlier, had been returned; and they were busily engaged in building Fort Duquesne at the forks of the Ohio.

For some time, British administrators imagined that improved organization would strengthen the colonies. The French system seemed neater and more efficient. All power was centralized and a single chain of command led from each outpost to the Crown. By contrast, their own system was a conglomeration of provinces, divided and decentralized, each with its own political forms, related to one another only through a tenuous connection with London. Some governors were appointed by the king, others by proprietors and still others were elected; and there was no ready device for co-ordinating their activities, much less those of the assemblies. It was not possible even to manage the militia, which constituted a substantial fighting force but which was locally controlled and fought when it wished to. The colonists also followed their own fancy when it came to raising funds for the support of royal government.

The first — and last — step toward rationalizing the administration came with the arrival of Sir Edmund Andros in Boston in 1688. He was to be governor of all the New England states, now united into a single dominion, as well as of New York and New Jersey. Through him the Crown expected to replace the anarchy of the early charters with the order of centralized control. The scheme proved unmanageable and Andros had already encountered local resistance when the news arrived early in 1689 of the Glorious Revolution in England that dethroned James II and ended the experiment in the colonies.

The sorry history of the dominion remained a standing warning to royal authorities who preferred thereafter to let each province manage itself with only the very loosest supervision. Officials occupied with problems in every part of the world were tempted to let the colony which could take care of itself go its own way. As long as the French and Spanish threat persisted, they could not afford the risk of internal dissension. An expanding population and a thriving economy were more valuable assets in the struggle than neat administration.

The Crown had already learned to be permissive when it came to enforcement of the Acts of Trade. Britain, like every other colonial power, operated under the assumption that it was beneficial to create a closed circle of imperial commerce; and in addition, the measures that aimed to do so were tactics of commercial warfare, designed to strengthen the empire by excluding outsiders from the advantages of colonial production and navigation. The colonies were to ship their goods only in English craft and to send their staples only to the mother country. Such restrictions were not particularly burdensome. The vessels of merchants in Boston or New York qualified as English and were protected from foreign competition. Planters who could not sell their tobacco directly to France or Germany were consoled by the monopoly they enjoyed of the British market.

Other provisions were more annoying. Admiralty courts appointed from London were not subject to local control and operated with unfamiliar procedures. The colonists disliked also attempts to force them to purchase molasses from the British rather than from the French West Indies or to forbid them to manufacture woolens or hats. But these inconveniences were readily surmounted by smuggling or evasion; and colonial commerce thrived as the merchants accepted the protection of the Navigation Acts when it suited them and disregarded such restrictions as were to their disadvantage.

The officials who winked at violations of the law were not simply corrupt and inefficient, although some of them were that; they realized that, in a larger sense, it was in the interest of the Crown to encourage the development of the colonies. Whatever immediate losses the acquiescent policy might entail, it stimulated the growth of population and the spread of settlement; and the prosperity of the provinces was more important in the struggle with the French than a flawless government organization.

For the same reason, the Crown offered outright subsidies to American producers of such commodities as naval stores and indigo and also tolerated enterprises of dubious legality that might weaken the

French. Down to the middle of the eighteenth century there were few impediments to colonial piracy. Ships fitted out in New York cruised to the southeast coast of Africa, where they preyed on Far Eastern traffic; or else, they drifted off to the Spanish Main where they found victims in the merchantmen trading with the islanders. These ventures were not much different from the lawful privateering of wartime; and they were organized as businesses with respectable merchants and officials among the investors. By the same token, it was sometimes expedient to tolerate direct trade with the enemy; the costs to the colonies in repressing it would have been greater than the gains to the French in permitting it.

The international conflicts among the great European empires thus offered the colonists a strategic opportunity. The conflict in North America made their prosperity vital to Britain and earned them exemption from the restrictions of the Acts of Trade. They were then able to use their expanding population to develop an independent commercial system.

Under these amiable circumstances colonial trade thrived. The most important cargoes moved directly across the Atlantic to and from the mother country. Furs, timber, fish and tobacco on the eastward passage crossed cloth and iron, books and glass and every manner of manufactured goods moving westward. The workshops of England and the fields of America thus drew together in a mutually profitable exchange.

But the commerce of the colonies was not limited to such orderly dealings with the mother country. The disturbed conditions of the times created interstices in the imperial commercial system, through which ingenious merchants elaborated intricate patterns of indirect trade. Ships laden with biscuits, barrel staves, horses, or fish left Boston, Newport or Philadelphia for the West Indies where they took on cargoes of molasses or sugar which they could bring back home or carry to London. The molasses brought to Newport was turned into rum, that to London, traded for cloth, iron or silver. All those commodities could be taken to the coast of Africa and bartered for slaves which in turn were salable in Jamaica or Martinique. The possibilities of combination were endless; and enterprising captains could trim their sails to every gust of opportunity. There was room here for every type of new enterprise and new enterpriser.

There were risks, of course, not only from storms at sea and loss to hostile corsairs, but also from unexpected gluts in remote markets and the errors men could make in strange places negotiating in unfamiliar languages. There were chances for failure as well as for success. Therefore it was helpful to have access to reliable correspondents, preferably to such as were linked by kinship. The bonds of loyalty and of family feeling alone could persuade them to send useful advice, to honor drafts, to extend credit and to furnish other assistance as the numerous hazards of trade might require. In this respect, such tight communities with overseas connections as the Quakers, Jews, and Huguenots had an advantage; their scattered members could depend upon one another. But English, Scottish and Irish commercial clans also worked out networks spread wide throughout the Atlantic world.

Other lines of connection hastened the flow of goods to the consumers. Well into the eighteenth century, even the wealthiest merchants were not above dealing directly at retail. Some continued to do so; newspapers in the 1740's still carried advertisements in which overseas traders offered for direct sale commodities from recently arrived ships. By then, however, the most enterprising had developed more elaborate means of distribution. A separate group of retail shopkeepers who measured out cloth by the yard and counted out pennyworths of nails relieved the merchant of the chore of doing so. In addition, a motley crew of hawkers and peddlers moved from door to door in the towns and in the country and carried wares from foreign parts into the household itself.

A steadily growing internal trade also linked the cities and added to the prosperity of the merchants. Intercolonial mercantile connections facilitated the traffic of ships that plied the coast, darting into the smaller harbors, cruising up the rivers in the endless buying, selling, and swapping that consistently raised the level of American exports and imports. This profitable round of commerce drew together all the provincial centers permitted to expand by the exigencies of imperial policy.

Colonial cities therefore increased rapidly in number and size after 1680. On the seacoast, Philadelphia, Newport and Charleston came to rival Boston and New York, both by then well established. All grew rapidly in population; in the half-century after 1690, Boston climbed from seven thousand to seventeen thousand and New York from four thousand to eleven thousand while Philadelphia, more recently founded, already boasted thirteen thousand residents. These were respectable totals even by comparison with the ancient provincial cities of Europe. Inland, thriving entrepôts appeared at places like Hartford, Albany and Lancaster. In scores of smaller ports from Falmouth in Maine to Savannah in Georgia local traders distributed goods to their neighborhoods and, aspiring to emulate their big-city models, undertook such ventures overseas as their resources permitted.

The merchants who dominated the cities were a various lot. No simple formula explained their success. Some were newcomers; others were offspring of families long in the land. Some began with substantial assets; others worked themselves up by their own efforts. They were of every religious and ethnic background. The sole attribute they shared was the ability to make connections that enabled them to exploit opportunity when it appeared.

Some inherited their places.

Thomas Hutchinson, for instance, was the fourth generation of his family to trade in Boston. Born in 1711, he was indulged in a Harvard education but trained for a mercantile career. While still in college he carried on a little trade by sundry ventures in his father's vessels, kept careful accounts and at the age of twenty-one had £ 500 in capital of his own and was part owner of a ship. He married a Newport Sanford and was allied by blood and business with the Olivers. By the time he entered politics in 1737 he had amassed a considerable fortune.

Israel Pemberton was also native born, one of ten children who were to constitute a redoubtable Philadelphia clan. His father was a wealthy Quaker merchant who drew him into trade in association with such prominent local partners as James Logan and John Reynell. The younger Pemberton thrived; political activity and good works still left him time for enterprise. His great town house and three country estates were the visible evidence of his shrewdness.

Even the career of such an immigrant as Caleb Heathcote showed the value of connections. Heathcote had been no poor boy in England, but the son of a mayor; and when he came to the New World in 1692 out of disappointment in love, it was not as a servant but with resources enough to permit him to enter trade. He was twenty-seven years old when he settled in New York. The profits of an expanding commerce quickly enabled him to branch out. He became a contractor and a farmer of taxes for Westchester County; he speculated in land and built grist, leather, fulling, oil and saw mills, all of which added to his returns. As was expected of a man of his position, he entered politics and became a colonel in the militia, a judge, the receiver general of customs, and the mayor of New York; these posts added both to his status and to his access to wealth. His daughter Anne became the wife of James DeLancey, the son of a Huguenot refugee who had married into the old Van Cortlandt family.

But connections could be made as well as inherited. Thomas Hancock, whose fortune was to rival Hutchinson's, had been the son of a poor minister in Lexington. Apprenticed at the age of thirteen to a bookseller in Boston, he worked hard, opened his own shop, and thrived. A fortunate marriage gave him additional capital and he expanded his activities. In 1746 when he undertook to supply the British forces in Nova Scotia he was on the verge of achieving great wealth. He continued to act as a contractor for the government but was not thereby inhibited from smuggling tea and paper from Holland by way of St. Eustatius or from loading French molasses in English hogsheads. When he died in 1764, he left an estate of well over £ 70,000.

Pierre Manigault also made a lowly start when he came to Charleston in 1695. He was of a good Huguenot family but he could at first do no better for himself than set up as a victualler. His next step was to build a distillery. But it was years before he embarked in trade as a merchant. Then fortune smiled. His son Gabriel invested happily in plantations, made a good marriage and became the wealthiest man in the province.

The merchants created an urban world through which to move their goods. They built wharves at which to unload the ships and markets and exchanges for convenience in buying and selling. A multitude of artisans and laborers assisted in the transactions. This population itself became a center of consumption to be policed, supplied and serviced by officials, ministers, physicians, bakers and tailors.

The tasks of construction and contrivance called for skills that were still rare and at a premium; and those who could make the needed objects or provide the wanted services were respected and well to do. Printers, goldsmiths, distillers and scores of other craftsmen formed a substantial and prosperous element in urban society. Benjamin Franklin was the pre-eminent example. He came as a poor boy to Philadelphia, served his apprenticeship and became his own master. His ability and enterprise earned him success and he took a prominent part in the political and cultural life of his town.

Nevertheless, the artisans were not able to copy the orderly corporate life of the gilds of the Old World. Apprenticeship persisted, but in an ever less stringent form; and it proved impossible either to exclude outsiders or to set up uniform standards. Even physicians and attorneys were unable to monopolize the practice of medicine and law. Carpenters and cordwainers were hardly in a position to do better.

In any case, many artisans were anxious not so much to improve the status of their craft as themselves to move out of it. Hancock and Manigault, from lowly starts, had become great merchants; other bookbinders and distillers could do the same or dream of it. There were fortunes to be made; the evidence was plain about them. Diligent labor and careful calculation set aside the surpluses for speculative investments that craftsmen hoped would open a way into trade for them. The merchant's fine coat and great house were then within reach. Some succeeded; more did not. But the failures left only a faint impression on their times, while those who won paraded the gains of their risk-taking in open sight.

For many artisans and shopkeepers, as for the merchants whom they emulated, speculation was an essential aspect of business. These people could not be creatures of habit or routine; the newness and instability of their situation prevented it. No accepted standards limited their visions; there was no proper income or place for the son of a carpenter or minister. Each could aim as high as he wished.

Furthermore, chances were worth taking because there was in any case no security. With the cargo safely in and profitably sold, the fortunate trader always faced the question of what to do next: hold the paper and risk depreciation; accumulate idle coins that earned no interest and risk theft; double the stakes of the next voyage and risk the loss of all. The prudent merchant had to speculate and the venturesome artisan followed his lead.

Therefore every possessor of surplus capital was on the lookout for schemes in which to invest. They took flyers in manufacturing and shipbuilding; they sought mill rights, contracts to supply the armies, monopolies and other privileges; and they made each other loans at interest. Above all they were intrigued by the possibility of speculation in land, of which the continent still afforded plenty and which remained the destination of the greatest number of immigrants.

By the middle of the eighteenth century, the merchants and their imitators had built an urban world between Europe and the wilderness. The autonomy of their enterprises was quite out of accord with contemporary conceptions of what a colony should be. But the anomalous commercial development, which England could not repress, shaped the forms in which a growing population would press on in the tasks of settlement.

7

The Varieties of Agricultural Experience

A THRIVING TRADE and an expanding frontier sustained the agriculture that occupied most colonists. The growing new cities consumed many of the products of the farm; and what they did not themselves use, they sent off to more distant markets. The rising demand assured those who lived on the soil that there would always be a reliable demand for the fruits of their labor. At the same time the surplus capital available for speculative enterprises hastened the spread of settlement and increased the supply of goods. These elements shaped the varieties of American agriculture in the eighteenth century.

Again and again, the men who itched with anxiety to invest their extra funds turned their attention to the frontier. The empty spaces beyond the edge of settlement extended toward remote and unknown horizons. There were no limits to the hopes and expectations displaced there. Everyone who could afford it was greedy for a share of the future that each advance into the wilderness revealed. Even those who would never themselves struggle with the forest, could approach its potential wealth by the twin avenues of the fur trade and land speculation. Success in both depended upon grants of government privilege; and the battle for those prizes promised to be more rewarding than the contest with the virgin soil.

Fur remained a precious staple. Beaver supplied most of Europe's hats and the pelts of deer and otter were not far behind in value. But the spread of settlement was hostile to the trade; as farmers cut down the trees, the animals retreated and the trappers were forced to follow farther and farther into the interior. That was why Massachusetts, in the eighteenth century, no longer played a large part in the business.

Three routes then opened into the important trapping areas. From the region of the Great Lakes furs moved down to Albany or to New York. From western Pennsylvania and the Ohio River they came either to Lancaster and Philadelphia or to Virginia. And from the South Carolina frontier they reached a market in Augusta and Charleston. In all these districts the activities of the traders involved relationships with the Indians, and with foreign powers, of vital concern to the colonial governments. Everywhere, success depended on the services of red men who collected the skins and who sometimes also acted as middlemen. Yet the colonists knew that their bitter rivals, the French in the north and the Spaniards in the south, could also bid for the favor of the tribesmen.

It was reasonable to control by licensing a trade so closely entwined with diplomacy. Otherwise unscrupulous adventurers might stir up hostility and endanger the frontier by selling guns and liquor to the Indians. But any attempt at licensing, by favoring some and excluding others, touched off a struggle for privilege. And the question of who should gain complicated that of who should administer. Western boundaries were by no means clear and each province claimed the right to make its own regulations, to say nothing of the fact that the superintendents of Indian affairs appointed by the Crown also exercised some authority in the matter. Here certainly was an important subject of political controversy.

The outcome was hardly decisive. Difficult as it was to resolve the contending claims by law, it was more difficult still to secure compliance. Reckless interlopers felt free to move through the disputed areas, trading on their own without licenses, and generally without scruples, fraternizing and fighting with the Indians, reaching deeper and deeper toward the heart of the continent. Altogether apart from the immediate value of the furs, which brought wealth to some merchants and was the cause of acrimonious political controversy, the trade played an important function in the colonies. It was the preliminary to settlement. Its agents blazed the trails along which the farmers would follow.

The wilderness also occupied the thoughts of those who could see, in the future, its forests cleared away and its acres tilled by contented husbandmen who paid rents or substantial purchase prices to the possessors of the title. The rapidly rising population virtually assured profits from speculation. Political influence smoothed the way to desirable grants. The Indians, who had never thought in terms of ownership, were readily persuaded to sign away immense tracts of uncertain limits and the provincial authorities generally interposed no objections.

There were nuisances. The boundaries of many colonies were unprecise; there were already conflicts over the line between New York and Connecticut and Massachusetts. Sometimes the governors and assemblies fell out over distribution of the spoils; and it was not quite clear under what circumstances the approval of London was needed. But the saving element was plenty; there was land enough for prizes for all. Merchants and country gentlemen whose influence was greatest were the most likely beneficiaries. But it was not unusual to find a grant to a group of which the leading figures were a pewterer, a shopkeeper, a stonecutter and an innkeeper. Generally the grantees undertook to establish a stated number of families on their holdings; but no one expected to enforce such requirements. The millions of acres thus given away were counted on, of themselves, to draw the settlers on.

They did. Largely this was a north-south rather than a westward movement, for it followed the river valleys and the coast, which offered the most convenient means of transportation. New England settlement ran up the Maine shore to Waldoboro, and up the Merrimack, Blackstone, Connecticut and Housatonic rivers through central Massachusetts to a point north of Concord, New Hampshire. New York's population spread up the Hudson and Mohawk valleys and Pennsylvania's pressed on toward the mountains. In the latter province, by the 1740's energetic German and Scotch-Irish were drifting down the valleys to western Maryland and Virginia.

For a time, Massachusetts and Connecticut tried to keep the process orderly, laying out new towns as the old ones were settled and encouraging the movement of groups large enough to support churches and organize governments. But in the 1720's those restraints began to break down. The concern with the continuity of settlement faded and grants went to proprietors who expected not to move themselves but rather to sell to any comer for a speculative profit. Elsewhere such scruples had never existed; it was always each family restlessly probing for a place for itself. The Virginians and the Scotch-Irish were particularly likely to wander off alone, confident of their ability to survive in solitude. Such men, everywhere along the frontier, by the second quarter of the eighteenth century, squatted without title, reckoning that the labor of clearing any empty space gave them a better claim than a paper stamped in a distant capital. The frontier attracted impatient people of every variety; respectable men eager for a quick way to wealth, servants unwilling to serve out their terms, mulattoes, and rebels against church or society formed the vanguard. Behind them came a tide of families that never ceased to spread the area of settlement.

The land thus uncovered became available to agriculture. The use to which it was put varied with its situation, its relationship to the marketplace and the character of those who exploited it.

The Pennsylvania Germans were almost unique in the ability to transfer to America the essential features of Old World agriculture. Their farms quickly took on a neat settled look, were carefully tilled, never were burdened with debt, and year after year yielded an abundance of diversified crops. That the soil was fertile and close to markets contributed to their success but did not altogether explain it.

The Germans brought with them the inherited assumption that land was scarce and precious, while human labor was abundant and expendable without stint. These ideas, more appropriate to the limited spaces of the Rhineland than to Pennsylvania, called for immense outlays of energy and constant vigilance against the temptations of the environment. The carefully tended cattle and orderly fields were exceedingly costly in labor; and only rigid discipline could keep at their tasks the men, women and children who worked together. The Germans toiled as they did, not only to gain a livelihood but also to protect and develop the land, because they expected to stay where they were forever. The religious sanctions of the Mennonites and other sects held them in tight communities that regulated clothing, speech, and habits as well as labor, and prevented them from flying off in the pursuit of their own inclinations. They would long remain apart from the main currents of American life.

Most colonists of the eighteenth century, however, regarded land in a different light; it was not the setting for a communal experience but an individual investment and treated as such. Frontier farming came to terms with the wilderness, by recognizing that labor was scanty, precious and to be economized, while the land was abundant and could be wasted. The first tasks of clearing and building were performed as expeditiously as possible. The trees were chopped down and burned, the stumps left standing, and a shelter quickly thrown up. The first crop was planted in the spaces between the stumps and what livestock there was fended for itself. Meanwhile hunting and fishing kept the larder stocked. Often such families never struck roots at all. It was not worth the effort to pull out the stumps or to harness themselves to a routine of careful husbandry. They preferred to trap, to trade a little with the Indians and to wait for a purchaser with capital to buy out their claim. If the game ran out before that time came, they were ready to move on to a likelier situation. They simply mined a living from the soil. When such people stopped moving, it was either because they had amassed the capital to launch themselves in more substantial enterprises directed toward the market or because they had lost hope and would thereafter be content with a mere subsistence.

Either course was possible. Each man was an individual entrepreneur, left to sink or swim on his own — even in New England, once the town lost its communal character. The failures sank into the ranks of the small marginal farmers who existed in every rural community. The successes became the masters of extensive estates.

The failures scratched miserably about to keep alive. In every region there were subsistence farmers who sought from agriculture no more than the means of feeding themselves. They were the sons who got the poorer share of the inheritance; or they were unlucky or off the main roads and lacked access to market; or their fields were pitched on hillsides or were stony beyond redemption; or they were themselves unenterprising and failed to recognize opportunity. They could make ends meet when all went well, but no more; they lacked any leeway when misfortune struck, and a single poor harvest, an illness, or the death of the cow drove them at once to the wall. They were therefore prone to borrowing small sums to tide them over; and debt, once contracted, pulled them steadily down, for even if they laid their hands on the cash to repay the interest and principal they were still as vulnerable as ever to the next blow. In time some lost their land, became other men's tenants or laborers, or wandered away to the frontier. Those who hung on did so sullenly, nurturing unspoken grievances against the more fortunate and resenting any taxes, no matter how slight.

The successful farmer was one able to produce beyond his own needs to supply the rapidly expanding markets the city opened to him. The labor and the capital such a man brought to the land returned substantial rewards indeed.

The consolidated freehold was now the characteristic farm; even in New England, the strips and common fields had all but disappeared. The old communal ways faded, to be replaced by more efficient methods responsive to the needs of the market. In eastern Massachusetts and in the valleys of the Connecticut, the Hudson, the Delaware and the Susquehanna rivers, a style of agriculture attuned to commerce took hold. Here farmers were not content to feed themselves, but focused their energies on production of goods they could sell. Their calculated enterprises were closely dependent upon the merchants who supplied them with outlets both in nearby cities and overseas.

The connection with trade encouraged specialization in the staples most likely to yield a good price. There was a steady demand for meat and grains. Drovers regularly led herds of cattle and hogs to the city slaughterhouses where the fresh beef and pork was sold locally and the pickled meat packed for export. Corn raised in New England and wheat from the middle colonies were turned into bread and biscuits and shipped down to the West Indies. In many places timber was still near at hand and found ready buyers. Then there were such local specialties as that of Wethersfield, Connecticut, which supplied a good part of the continent with its onions.

The market farmers often supplemented their income from the river fisheries. The annual run of herring, scooped up in nets, could be salted and packed for export; and what was not eaten or sold was spread upon the fields as fertilizer. The coastal shores also yielded good harvests of clams which were dried in the sun and sent off to the West Indies or traded to the interior Indians. Then too, in the slack season on the farm, some men left their families to take a hand in the offshore fisheries. In Nantucket and eastern Massachusetts the cod and the whale supplied useful additions to agricultural earnings.

The knowledge that buyers waited for their products also tempted the farmers into manufacturing. Wood was abundant and could be turned into shingles or barrel staves when inclement weather kept men from the fields. The sheep's wool became thread on the spinning wheel and the hides, stretched and tanned, were fashioned into boots, all to be traded at the store. Farmers with political influence enough to acquire the sites used their saved-up earnings to build saw, fulling, grist and iron mills; and the fees they received from their neighbors were available for other investments. The more prosperous made loans at good interest to the less fortunate, speculated in land, and sometimes themselves opened a store to carry on local trade on the side. They thus became capitalists of a sort, living in time not only on the returns from their own labor but also on the profits of an ingenuity stimulated by the widespread markets colonial trade opened to them.

Some such men developed considerable estates, and began to aspire to aristocratic pretensions. But not many could act the part; a restricted labor force set limits to their ambitions. In the Hudson and Connecticut valleys there were some hands willing to serve for hire or as tenants, but not many even there; it was too easy even for the poor who were free to remain their own masters. The opportunities of imperial trade enabled market farmers to expand as far as the work of their own households would carry them. Larger estates called for a slave labor force; and that could be managed only under the special plantation conditions not readily created on a diversified farm.

The plantation appeared in its modern form, in this period, mainly in the Southern colonies where it left an indelible impression upon society. It was a well-organized, rationalized system of production that involved distinctive relationships among land, capital and labor. All the units were much larger in scale than anywhere else in colonial life. At his death in 1732, Robert "King" Carter of Corotoman in Virginia left an estate of three hundred thousand acres, one thousand slaves and £ 10,000. His holdings were certainly unusual; but they were indicative of the trend.

The new plantation encompassed thousands of acres; it utilized scores of slaves and entailed a substantial investment of capital, in land, equipment and labor. An operation of this size could not function by the rules of the household. It had to be organized, disciplined and governed by plan. Its master was frequently an absentee, who lived in Charleston or held more than one plantation. He therefore required the services of salaried managers who acted as intermediaries between him and the laborers. In the interest of maximum efficiency, the planters imposed rationalized techniques on production, concentrated upon a staple crop, and arranged the tasks of the labor force to get the utmost exertion from it.

The plantation in this form appeared on the mainland toward the end of the seventeenth century, brought over from the West Indies, where it had already emerged in the cultivation of sugar. The speed of its spread depended upon the appearance of crops to which it could be advantageously applied, the accumulation of capital to finance it, and the development of an adequate supply of slaves. Those conditions were ripe after 1700.

There had been no advantages of scale in the cultivation of tobacco; each of the three or four hands on twenty-five acres was as efficient as each of the two hundred on two thousand acres. That was not the case with the tropical crops that took hold in South Carolina and later in Georgia. Rice, indigo and cotton required heavy fixed overhead in irrigation ditches and processing equipment; and they were profitably raised only in large units. The introduction of these staples, in response to opportunities created by imperial trade, gave a marked impetus to the development of the plantation.

In the same years, substantial sums became available for investment in this form. In some cases these were proceeds from the sale of tracts of land granted earlier and now become valuable with the growth of population. Families which held title to thousands of acres could readily sell some off for the cash with which to improve the rest, particularly if a privileged position in the government enabled them to secure more for speculation. Some immigrants brought considerable capital with them from the West Indies where they had been cramped by lack of empty land. Trade endowed many other planters with the funds to set up plantations. Robert Carter, William Byrd and William Fitzhugh were among those who profited from traffic with the Indians or who bought and sold furs and sent their own ships to England. The Manigaults, like other Charleston merchants, used the returns from commerce to invest in plantations.

Once started from any of these sources, the new form of agricultural organization yielded phenomenal returns that could be plowed back into expansion. In a good year a rice planter earned as much as forty per cent on his investment; and a few such years made available a satisfying surplus for extending his holdings. What was more, the slave was capital that reproduced itself by breeding. The Manigaults, starting with eighty-six Negroes, bought only twelve more in the next thirty-eight years, yet at the end of the period owned two hundred and seventy. At the same time, the steadily increasing demand raised the value of each hand. The plantation owner therefore drew a triple profit from his slaves. The crops produced by their labor in the fields, their children, and the rise in price they themselves brought all contributed capital to the expansion of the system.

The worth of the Negro as an investment accounted for the spread of the new form of organization to Virginia and Maryland. Those provinces raised no rice or cotton; and there were no advantages to the large-scale cultivation of tobacco. But they did raise slaves and as long as the surplus could be sold farther south it did not matter if the return from the sales of tobacco were meager. Essentially, planters there were speculators; agriculture was a means of keeping their Negroes and lands occupied, at a slight profit, while waiting for the larger gain that came from rising values. In anticipation, many were willing to go into debt; and all knew that their future welfare depended upon further expansion which would continue to lift values.

The evolving system depended upon the Negro and required his total subjugation to controls that confirmed his utter helplessness. That was why the planters of Georgia ultimately got a repeal of the regulations that had orginally excluded slavery from the province. Only thus could the new plantation function. The masses of black men had to be totally disciplined. Otherwise, treated like brutes, they might indeed become brutes and turn upon their masters; or, with nothing to lose, they might run away to the forests or join hands with the Indians. Forbidden to hold weapons, to signal one another, to assemble in groups or to strike a white man, they were kept incommunicado. The law defined them as chattels, held them incapable of giving evidence, punished them savagely for misdemeanors, and deprived them of their humanity. Even the names they received — Juno or Sambo — set them off from other men. Above all, they could have no families; encouraged to breed though they might be, the plantation treated them as units of production available for purchase or sale. The completion of the slave codes fixed the character of the plantation. An unfree labor force could then be mobilized efficiently to turn out the staples the colonies poured into trade.

North of Maryland the plantation appeared only in the Narragansett region of Rhode Island. There the Hazard, Updike and Champlin families gave over their great estates to raising cattle and horses for sale to the West Indies. Negroes there could be organized and controlled as in the South.

Elsewhere in the North, slavery was concentrated in the cities where it could be controlled. The plantation system could not serve the unspecialized market farms which required labor endowed with diversified skills and individual judgment incompatible with slavery. The scattering of Negroes in the rural districts of New England and the middle colonies were members of the household, were treated like servants but also like human beings, and often earned their freedom.

The plantation system confirmed the divergence in experience between the provinces to the north and those to the south of the Mason-

Dixon Line. The owners of the great estates remained a minority of the white population everywhere; in Virginia and Maryland most freemen still tilled their own plots or were served by a handful of Negroes. But slavery dominated the life of the regions in which the plantation took hold. Great capital resources enabled masters to buy up the best lands, while the yeomen, unable to compete, drifted westward to the uplands or northward to Pennsylvania. With land went political power, social primacy, and a distinctive style of life.

The great planters took as their model the English country gentry. Some had actually been educated in the mother country, many more had traveled there. Impressed by the new Georgian architecture, they brought back builders' manuals and set themselves to constructing appropriate homes. Drayton Hall, Westover, Shirley and Rosewell were small by comparison with their Old World counterparts but they were spacious beyond any other structures yet raised in the colonies. Specially imported bricks and columns of Portland marble, fine panels and lavish furnishing embellished them, while carefully planned grounds set them off both from the streams on which they were generally situated and from the quarters where the slaves lived and labored.

The lofty central hall gave out on a verandah and led to wings in which the master and his lady learned to behave according to their station. Their clothes came from England at considerable expense; and they had, or acquired, the graces to go with them. A little learning was a gentlemanly thing; a standard fare of books and journals found its way into homes where the ability to read a page of Greek was a valued sign of position. The men were also sturdy drinkers and took readily to sports. By the 1740's they were riding to hounds, racing blooded horses and, occasionally, getting up elevens for a cricket match. The women had a more difficult time of it, what with the worry of frequent childbearing and the supervision of incompetent households.

But however they played the gentlefolk, the setting remained different. Here no loyal family retainers discreetly served or respectfully tipped their caps. The uncouth black slaves who swarmed through the house made a mockery of pretensions to elegance; though the porcelain were ever so fine, it was always presented in a black hand. Not quite enough county families were close enough to permit the round of sociability of the English countryside; occasional visitors, whatever their quality, were eagerly welcomed to break the monotonous isolation. Williamsburg was far from the capital London was; the planters' visits took them not to fine town houses, but to inns, promiscuously crowded with strangers. At the county court house or in the muster of the militia, there was no challenge to their superiority of status. But they dealt with rude farmers who, though respectful, were vocal in their grievances, were persistent in the pursuit of their own interests and lacked the mannerly habits of deference.

It was difficult to be an aristocrat in a society without an orderly array of classes. But the difficulty was especially severe in a period when rural life everywhere in the colonies grew increasingly disorderly.

Two structures were symbols of the dominant tone — the farmhouse, set off by itself in the clearing, and the tavern. Even in New England now the village community had declined in importance; the process was already far advanced elsewhere. As the population dispersed, all social connections weakened; the occasions for common action declined; and men grew accustomed to going their own way alone. The family lived apart from its neighbors on its own land. It neither interfered with others, nor wished to be interfered with. Its only external contacts came weekly in church, if there was one in the vicinity.

In some regions, the church became superfluous. Half-remembered ancestral traditions were not binding, the habit of worship had decayed and competent ministers were in any case hard to find. The structure seemed scarcely worth the effort or expense of construction and maintenance. Gradually the inn supplanted it as a common meeting place. At the crossroads, it might be only a store, with a space for refreshments and a room for occasional lodgers. In the town, which was itself but an expanded crossroads, the tavern very likely occupied a building of its own with a sign to mark its dignity. Here the men of the district met, to do business, to discuss common problems, to find an excuse for conviviality. The inn was neutral ground, a private rather than a communal enterprise. Each individual came when he wished and without commitment; each paid for his entertainment and went his own way. In every respect it differed significantly from the meetinghouse of the seventeenth century.

In some places, on the frontier, there was not even an inn. There the rural families were completely detached from one another and might not catch sight of a stranger in months.

Travelers through the back country in these years frequently commented on the marked deterioration of the country population. The wild and rustic children stared like sheep when a stranger entered their home. Their shyness reflected the growing rudeness of manners of the parents, the loss of some of the European habits and skills the immigrants had brought with them, and the widening distance that cut neighbors off from one another. Since visitors rarely came it was not necessary to be over-careful about dress; the mirror hung in the corner, unconsulted for days on end. There was a decline in literacy and orthography; and speech became brusque, almost monosyllabic, and infused with strange words locally coined or borrowed from other languages. The homes of well-to-do farmers often presented a grim contrast between material prosperity and cultural poverty. Such quantities of meat appeared upon their boards as only lords enjoyed in Europe, yet a dour silence hung over the hasty meals, in dark rooms bare of any adornment. In some households there were practically no utensils; everyone around the table reached into the common pot with his fingers. Others boasted a few pewter spoons with which to scrape away at the wooden bowls.

For all, the days passed in a grim round, scarcely marked by feast or ceremony. Many places had not even the Sunday visit to church to tell off the weeks. Sociability for people who lived there focused rather on the court days when pent-up conviviality flowed over in drunkenness and violence. Under such circumstances, each family, though it got what it wished from the soil, was no longer sure what it wished for. Perhaps that accounted for the perpetual restlessness that drove them on, ever discontent, to seek more land, better places.

Isolation and rusticity encouraged a looseness in behavior and manners, most marked outside of New England and in the new settlements. The curse, no longer taken literally, entered common speech; and blasts of profanity were casually interjected in the most commonplace sentences. The consumption of spirituous liquors was enormous; intemperance became the frequent recourse of lonely men who lived without routine and who were tempted to fight off boredom, fear, and physical discomfort by drinking themselves into insensibility.

Rural family life, having lost many of the communal features that had enveloped it in Europe, increasingly depended upon the personal convenience of the participants. It was troublesome and expensive to arrange marriages according to the letter of a distant law; by 1750, most were formed by a simple agreement among the partners. Courtship was relaxed and informal; it became customary for couples to spend evenings together in bed, presumably to economize on light and heat. However innocent the intentions of the bundlers, the tolerance of their parents reflected the erosion of traditional restraints. Whatever controls remained emanated from within the individuals concerned.

From this experience emerged men and women who learned to live without restraints imposed from without or inherited from the past. Separation from established communities compelled them to get on by themselves and to live by such rules as their own consciences devised. Costly as the process was, it nurtured in those who survived a sense of self-reliance and of power and a will for achievement.

Therein, most colonists differed from the German sectarians who transplanted their communities intact and insulated themselves, by the discipline of faith, against the American environment. Except for those few little enclaves, the provincial farmers accepted the challenge of their New World. Spurred on by horizonless opportunities, they strained to spread themselves out. Their personalities, developed without the constraints of accepted limits and rules, needed a sense of the boundless expansion of acres and possessions. Some went under in the effort; they lost out to debt and to ceaseless moves and were never able to do more than earn a hand-to-mouth subsistence. The market farmers and planters won a measure of contentment. But few were able fully to satisfy the urges that pressed them on in search of more. This was the common experience of agricultural life in provinces stimulated by an empire's growth.

8

Politics and Society

THE COLONIES never lost contact with the European world. Immigration, trade and the flow of ideas kept the connection alive. But the colonists gradually ceased to be Europeans; the new way of life shaped people for whom there were no precise counterparts in the Old World; and, in time, all the transplanted institutions of their culture mirrored the change.

The landed gentry and merchants, the farmers and artisans did not reflect upon their situation in general or theoretical terms. They became aware of it gradually and sporadically as they tried in specific matters to make their wishes real. To get land and to keep it, to trade and to profit from it, often called for the use of power; and that involved them in contests for political control. By 1680, their governments had acquired fairly stable forms derived from, but not identical with, the European antecedents described in the charters. The decades that followed brought no radical changes in form. Innovations in the way it operated subtly adapted the political system to the kind of people the colonists had become.

For a while, in the 1680's, threats to the earlier governmental adjustment persisted. The uncertainties about the intentions of James II, suspicion that a small group of aristocrats might engross all privileges, and disputes about the established churches evoked widespread discontent. In New York, Jacob Leisler led a group of rebels who seized power and controlled the government briefly. In Massachusetts, the heirs of the Puritans prepared to defend their position, and in Pennsylvania and Maryland there were grumblings against the proprietors. But by the end of the century, all these malcontents knew what the followers of Bacon had earlier learned, that they had more to lose by destroying the existing order than by accommodating themselves to it.

In the eighteenth century, the forms of government remained stable. The Revolution of 1688 had quieted the fear that dynastic changes might alter relations with the mother country; and the conflict with France left the colonies relatively free of interference from London. There were therefore no significant alterations in the organization of the polity. A governor — elected by the freemen in Connecticut and Rhode Island, appointed by the Crown or the proprietor elsewhere — an assembly representing the freemen, and a council of the greatest merchants and landowners shared the responsibilities of administration.

While there was no dispute about the framework, there was frequent debate about how the mechanism within it should function. The actions of the government pleased some men and antagonized others; differences of opinion led to divisions as each group sought to have its own way; and the contests for power profoundly influenced the operations of politics.

On the surface, the significant conflicts aligned the governor as representative of the king or proprietor against the assembly. Each governor wished no check upon his power to designate members of the Council which helped him make all appointments and all grants of privilege. Each urged the legislature to make general appropriations and to leave the details of expenditure to him. Each demanded a fixed and permanent salary in order to be independent of the whims of the assembly. On the other hand, the governor sought to control the legislature by asserting the right to convene and adjourn it and by vetoing laws of which he disapproved. The assemblies fought back, withholding salaries and appropriations and balking at taxes when the governors proved intransigent. Such contests enlivened provincial politics for decades.

No doubt the governors were conscious of their roles as agents of the Crown and were determined to preserve the royal prerogative. But that solicitude was not the only element that animated these struggles. The elected chief executives of Connecticut and Rhode Island did not altogether escape political conflict. The office was troublesome because those who held it were animated by incentives of their own in wielding the power attached to it.

Joseph Dudley, for instance, was Massachusetts-born and linked with a cluster of prominent families in the province. His father had been governor under the old company charter, his sister married a Bradstreet and his own wife was a Tyng. He had chosen the wrong side when Andros appeared in New England and had to leave America when the dominion regime collapsed. But Dudley was determined to edge his way to wealth and preferment through royal service. He discarded the Puritanism of his ancestors for the Church of England, held a succession of royal positions, and was finally sent back to Boston as governor in 1702. He held the position for thirteen hard-fought years, zealously making the most of his opportunities.

Alexander Spotswood was an Englishman who arrived as lieutenant governor in Virginia in 1710. He had been wounded in battle with the French, and the post was the reward for his valor. The titular governor never actually appeared and Spotswood exercised his powers for twelve years. His efforts to regulate the fur trade, to inspect tobacco, to control the Indians, and to make appointments to the church and the courts involved him in acrimonious controversy, with the Byrds and Ludwells prominent among his enemies. Nevertheless, when relieved, he decided to remain in Virginia, where he had somehow acquired an estate of eighty-five thousand acres.

Dudley and Spotswood were representative of the royal governors of these years. Certainly they were sincere in the desire to serve their king. But the good servant was to be well rewarded, and office was a kind of property, from which the holder expected to profit. The salary attached to the post was useful, but the privileges within its reach were even more attractive. As a matter of course, every governor set about creating a following among the local gentry, with a share of the spoils as the cement that held the alliance together. The difficulty was that those left out could strike back through the assembly. Since they could not act effectively without the collaboration of the colonists, the governors were thus part of a larger political system and were guided by its rules.

The business of government called for skills and patience that governors and legislators often lacked. Someone had to read the maps to keep land grants from overlapping, check the amounts of the bonds printed and redeemed, account for finances, negotiate with the Indians and keep track of correspondence. The helpful mediators who assumed these responsibilities in many provinces acquired a limited power of their own.

Late in life, James Logan complained that he had been a public drudge for twenty-five years. He had been glad enough, as a youth of twenty-five, to come to Pennsylvania as William Penn's secretary; and he had been flattered to be designated clerk of the Council and secretary of the province two years later. But the business of state that passed through his hands involved him in repeated conflicts. On the other hand, it had brought him the pleasant estate at Stenton where he passed his declining gentlemanly years.

Cadwallader Colden had practiced medicine in Philadelphia for eight years when the governor of New York asked him to come to that province. The Scottish physician was then thirty, well educated and eager to serve. He became surveyor general, then a member of the Council and, for a time, lieutenant governor, an earnest efficient bureaucrat who kept a keen eye on his own interest.

Or there was Speaker John Robinson, scion of a good Virginia family and a graduate of William and Mary. His inherited estate gave him a seat in the House of Burgesses at the age of thirty-two and two years later made him treasurer and speaker. For decades he handled the finances of the province; and the executors of his will would one day learn with a shock how much had stuck to his fingers.

The governors and the bureaucrats, the members of the assemblies and of the councils were always concerned with the privileges that provincial politics put within reach. The advance of settlement promised soon to raise the value of great tracts of empty land which could now be liberally parceled out to the fortunate favorites. No man by himself was powerful enough to extort a grant. But in union there was strength; a group of strategically located individuals could further the advantage of all. Some got grants of land, others monopolies or bounties or offices or the enactment of special laws that rewarded them for collaboration with the faction.

A faction formed naturally about a family connection. In New York, for instance, William Smith, James DeLancey, Stephen Van Cortlandt and Caleb Heathcote were all close relatives by blood or marriage; when they co-operated, they and their hangers-on could exert potent pressure on the assembly, the governor and the Council. But kinsmen sometimes also fell out or saw greater chances for gain in co-operation with outsiders. Since no discipline held them together, the groupings were not always durable; the lines among them frequently shifted as their members jockeyed for advantage. The constant formation and dissolution of factions accounted for a good deal of provincial politics.

From time to time, the colonial governments also faced more complex issues than were involved in the distribution of privileges. On these matters, opinion divided and forces aligned themselves in a different manner.

Again and again, the problem of the currency plagued governors and assemblies; it was not to be resolved until long after independence. The rapid expansion of the economy called for increasing quantities of some dependable circulating medium; yet the English government in 1684 forbade the provinces to operate their own mints. A miscellany of coins passed from hand to hand — Spanish dollars and pieces of eight, Portuguese half-johannes and moidores, as well as some English gold and silver. All had values fixed by a proclamation in 1704. But there were frequent erratic fluctuations for the amount available was small and inflexible. The country did not itself produce these metals, and international trade did not usually add to the store, indeed sometimes seriously depleted it. Most overseas trade was conducted by barter or by the exchange of drafts by merchants on their correspondents. Local internal transactions also depended heavily on similar arrangements and on makeshift expedients such as Indian wampum or tobacco. As a result values were uncertain and unstable and occasionally no money at all was to be had except at a premium. The lack of a dependable currency hampered business enterprise and sometimes caused hardship for farmers; those who needed even the small sums to pay taxes or fees had to sacrifice their produce to get the cash.

Those damaged by shortages were likely to raise a cry for paper money to compensate for the deficiency of specie. Few imagined that the government itself could be trusted at the printing press. But it seemed reasonable that a bank could safely perform the function, for it would be responsible for redemption of the notes it issued and would therefore emit only as many as the economy required. Those who wished an expansion of the currency consequently kept reverting to the hope that banks would be authorized to take the matter in hand.

A good deal, of course, depended upon the character of the bank. One required to redeem its notes in silver on demand would have only a moderate effect, for it would always operate within the limits set by the existing supplies of specie. No such restraints would hamper a land bank, for land was abundant as silver was not. At such an institution, the farmer in need could pledge his holding and receive a purseful of banknotes to pay his taxes and debts. The notes would then pass from buyers to sellers, circulating at par, for they would command confidence, backed as they would be by acres whose value would surely rise. In time the farmer would sell his produce, getting back notes which he could return to the bank to clear his debt. So the paper would pass round and all would profit as commerce shook off the restraints of the currency shortage.

When internal dissension and the hostility of the Crown prevented the colonies from pursuing such ingenious schemes, promoters were ready with alternative paper money devices. The recurrent wars burdened the provinces with heavy expenditures and made the royal government tolerant of the means employed to raise the necessary resources. Taxes were unpopular and difficult to collect; it was much more convenient to borrow, particularly since the debt could expand the currency. Bonds in small denominations were used to pay the militia and purchase supplies. The soldiers and purveyors passed them on to meet their own expenses and the paper continued to circulate indefinitely. In Rhode Island, the bills once issued never were redeemed and formed a permanent, expanding currency. Massachusetts was more scrupulous; it periodically redeemed each issue only to replace it with another. Other provinces varied in their policies, responding to the push of various groups that had a stake in the matter.

For decades on end, the currency question agitated the assemblies. Those who favored an inflating or expanding currency, whether through a land bank or through the free use of paper, were men with debts or with ambitious designs who needed easy access to credit. Those who favored a stable, less flexible currency, whether through a silver bank or through strict reliance upon specie, were creditors and merchants in established lines of trade who feared any fluctuation in values. Both groupings were heterogeneous. Among the debtors were shiftless or unlucky subsistence farmers, but also enterprising merchants and artisans who wished to enlarge their stocks, speculators of every sort, and great Virginia planters. Among the creditors were merchants who needed specie for international transactions and who feared a flood of paper; and also well-to-do market farmers who wanted the loans to their neighbors repaid in silver rather than in notes of uncertain value. The two groups were set off only by their common position on the currency issue. In that sense each was an interest.

Other issues precipitated other interests. When it came to fixing the prices of commodities or services, for instance, the interest of the artisan divided from that of the merchant. Farmers wanted a low tax on land and the right to vend their goods in the city when they wished; merchants and artisans feared taxes on trade and wanted goods brought in on fixed market days. To that extent a mercantile interest was arrayed against an agrarian interest. The Tidewater was generally satisfied with the distribution of seats in the assembly; the spreading back-country kept asking for redistricting that would give it the weight justified by its growing population. To that extent there was an eastern and a western interest. Communicants of the Established Church sought to protect its position; Baptists and Quakers sought to divest it of its privileges. To that extent there was a church and a dissenting interest.

Some interests were aligned in fairly regular patterns which, in provinces like New York, held consistent over fairly long periods. A great merchant was likely to be a creditor, to live in a coastal city and to belong to the Church of England. But even he would collaborate on some matters with men who differed markedly with him on others. For the interest was not a fixed group with a stable configuration of members; individuals who worked together on one set of measures could as well be antagonists on another. And the simultaneous interplay of factions always complicated the outcome.

The participants in provincial politics thus played a complicated game. Each was a local power in his own right, bound by no external discipline. Furthermore each maneuvered with considerable freedom because his position was personal rather than representative. Rarely did a legislator feel the pressure of an electorate. These affairs, after all, generally occupied the attention of but a minority of the population. The servants and the tenant farmers had neither voice nor concern in them. Nor did the frontiersmen in the remote settlements. Yeomen, artisans, planters, and merchants voted but mostly they had only a limited role in elections. They appeared in town meeting or at the county courthouse to confront a single candidate or slate to which they consented. There was a choice only when the local dignitaries fell out. Once elected, an office-holder generally held his position indefinitely and often passed it on to his son.

On this foundation, provincial politics developed the mechanisms of faction and interest through which the holders of local power struggled for accommodation. The assemblies differed from the English parliament in this respect, mainly insofar as remoteness from the Crown and the paucity of patronage prevented the growth of more formal party organizations.

Most men were content to leave government in the hands of the powerful; that was the price of the order that enabled them to live peacefully together. Judges, sheriffs, and selectmen brought lawbreakers to trial, protected the helpless and adjudicated quarrels. That was as it should be. The decent subject obeyed.

Now and again someone who knew no better asked unmannerly questions. On June 11, 1744, Governor Thomas of Pennsylvania addressed the assembled populace from the Courthouse stairs in Philadelphia. About two hundred gentlemen attended him and thirty flags, borrowed from the ships in the harbor, marked the dignity of the occasion. A rabble of some four thousand listened. The Governor informed them that war had been declared against the French and directed the militiamen to arm themselves. One bold fellow stepped forth and spoke out: he and many other poor men had neither the money nor credit to procure a musket or the third part of a musket. What about it? The Governor made no reply but smiled and went off to drive homeward in his chariot.

This was not a revolution nor a gesture of defiance, nor even, properly speaking, a demand for political reform. But the incident revealed among the colonists a weakening of the habit of deference to the great ones of the land, a disposition to talk back and ask why, rather than spontaneously and unreflectively to accept orders.

The tendency had been growing steadily. Some years earlier, John Peter Zenger, the printer of the *New York Weekly Journal*, published a scurrilous attack upon the governor of the province and was indicted for seditious libel. By the common law, the offense was clear and the case should have been cut and dried. The only issue was one of fact — whether Zenger had indeed printed the criminal lines, which were, on the face of it, libelous. But two novel doctrines introduced by the attorneys for the defense got the printer off scot free. Andrew Hamilton, an ornament of the Philadelphia bar, had come up to New York, expressly to join James Alexander in making the argument. They maintained that their client had a right to publish the statement since it was true and that the jury had the duty of deciding the issue of law as well as that of fact.

The two propositions were linked, for the law of England would sustain neither and the first could not stand without the support of the second. In England, the truth of a libel compounded the offense; Zenger could escape punishment only by claiming that in New York some vague and undefined right to publish the truth mitigated the damage caused by his seditious statement. But the judges would hardly recognize a right not described in any charter, statute or previous judicial decision. Therefore it was necessary to maintain that the ultimate verdict lay in the hands of a jury of colonists, which found that the concept made sense. And the governor could only smile and ride off in his chariot.

The Zenger Case by no means established complete freedom of the press in the colonies. Nor did it put an end to prosecutions for seditious libel. But it showed that, on occasion, considerable numbers of people, not ordinarily involved, took an interest in politics and treated law as a safeguard not of particular privileges but of general rights.

Earlier still, John Wise, minister in Ipswich, had wandered toward similar assertions. In 1717 he had attempted to vindicate the government of the churches of New England against those who sought to change the old congregational system. His argument led him to the conclusion that it followed reasonably from the native liberty of man's nature that every subject ought to share, through his representatives, in making the law and, through the jury, in administering it. His little treatise met with approval, although none could guess then what inferences would be drawn from its ideas a half century later.

These views were symptomatic. Experience slowly taught the colonists that the statute book was not sacrosanct. It could not turn natural and useful actions into crimes. It could not legitimize unreasonable, unjust or unequal privileges. And if the lawyers and the common law tried to do so, then they were to be disregarded. In 1750 a placid sermon explained that a civil ruler who injured the subjects instead of defending their rights and doing them good dissolved the obligation to obey. The resistance of the subjects, under such circumstances, was not rebellion but a righteous stand in defense of the natural and legal rights of the people against the unnatural and illegal encroachments of arbitrary power.

Such opinions were still embellished with professions of the utmost loyalty to the Crown. But they nonetheless revealed that there was more to provincial politics than the normal contest of factions and interests. The polity was also a means by which subjects defended their rights and pursued their welfare. These ideas were part of no abstract theory; nor were their implications fully perceived. They were the simple observations of men cut off from tradition, who applied the standards of reason to governments created through their own consent.

In the last analysis, controls were not strong enough to rule men who did not wish to be governed. The assembly made a law, the governor approved, and the court passed judgment in accordance with it. It still remained to be enforced. Off went the sheriff. Now and again, he came back with his writ still unserved. On the back was the eloquent endorsement: *not executed by reason there is no road to the place where he lives.* Or, more eloquent still, in a frontier county: *not executed by reason of a gun.* Or, *not executed by reason of an axe.* Or, simply, *defendant swore that he would shoot me if I touched any of his estates.* Everywhere, juries had to be persuaded; nowhere could those who held power be sure that a mob would not take matters into its own hands and pull apart the insecure fabric of a society loosely woven together. Order was only beginning to appear; it could not be taken for granted.

The governors could only smile. They commanded neither the power nor the respect to silence the questioners. Even the support of the gentry, when they enjoyed it, gave them only limited control. In these exposed communities they could never assemble the display of force or go forth in the ceremonial panoply of their office that might elicit instinctive awe. They had to borrow the flags to add pomp to the parade, and for music they could often muster only a pitiful, scraping Negro fiddle. Provincial society was not stable or stratified enough to connect the whole population with the ruler in a dependable chain of obedience.

It grew ever less possible to preserve the significance of distinctions of rank. New families were constantly elbowing their way in to dispute the primacy of the old, even in Virginia and Maryland where the continuity was greatest. Few therefore could claim any tradition of command. Furthermore, the symbols of social status, even when recognized by the law, were rarely meaningful in the colonial context. The old sumptuary regulations were forgotten; people wore what clothes they could afford and lived in what style they pleased. Formal titles fell into disuse; the promiscuous "mister" began to replace the carefully graduated "sir" and "goodman" and men entitled to be known as "cacique" or "baron" did not bother to make a claim to their dignities. Nor did the great landowners often trouble to tie up their estates by primogeniture and entail; a whole continent was, after all, available.

By the middle of the eighteenth century, their lavish houses did mark the landed gentry off from other folk. The master of Westover in Virginia or of Wentworth Hall in New Hampshire lived and behaved like an aristocrat. The buildings themselves, standing out upon the rural landscape, were evidence of wealth and of the command of labor and they were the setting of a distinctive round of activities. Here the justice held his court and here sometimes the great men of the county met on public business. The Byrds of Westover and the Wentworths of Wentworth Hall were aristocrats in the sense that their homes were significant symbols of a status established by family, land and political function. Fairfax, Randolph, and Dulaney in the South, and Van Rensselaer, Schuyler, DeLancey and Waldo in the North were names that bore a similar connotation.

No other group in colonial society was able similarly to entrench itself. The Hutchinson, Bowdoin, and Morris families had wealth and political power. But riches derived from trade were not visible and lacked the relationship of land to the life of the community. Merchants' homes were solid two-story structures, sometimes built of brick, but they were not large, for urban labor was costly and scarce. Nor were they the setting of significant political activity; public affairs were transacted on the neutral ground of public buildings. Moreover, the provincial city frustrated every effort to develop a gentlemanly style. Select clubs could only meet in the tavern, where every outsider curiously looked on. In the Exchange, all sorts of men jostled the respectable merchant; and only price counted in the business of buying and selling.

Professional people had no more success in establishing a distinctive status. Such men as Cadwallader Colden, David Lloyd and Benjamin Franklin played prominent roles in the life of New York and Philadelphia. But the doctors, lawyers and journalists of those towns could not make their callings exclusive or distinctive. Neither the law nor private associations established an effective licensing system. Any man of more than common education — and some of none — could set himself to devising cures, or filling out writs or composing essays. A doctor from Scotland was shocked to find a colleague in a worsted cap who had once been a shoemaker but who had discovered he could use his great black fists more profitably in the practice of physic than in cobbling. Even the ministry had to make room for those moved to preach by some spontaneous call rather than by any formal ordination. The professional men were no better off than the yeomen or artisans whose stations depended entirely upon their own capacity for achievement.

Only the landed aristocracy occupied a status that was fixed and orderly. Their estates set them apart and gained recognition of their families, wealth, political power and social primacy. That was why all others — merchants, lawyers and farmers — aspired also to establish landed estates and did so as soon as a surplus permitted it. By the 1740's, many a merchant was taking capital out of trade to build himself an appropriate country house on the outskirts of town. These aspirations were the result of a curiously disjointed social structure. The landed aristocracy alone formed a coherent class. The rest of the population was fluid and disorganized, with each individual occupied by himself in the quest for profit and place.

That situation had a direct influence upon provincial politics. In the abstract the colonists recognized that there ought to be an order in society, with each man in his station attentive to his own duties. But in practice constant movement, from place to place and from rank to rank, prevented the society from settling down in any fixed set of molds; and the whole remained disorderly. Even the landed aristocracy, though it acquired stability, was on uncertain ground when it dealt with other, less fixed sectors of the population.

Therefore no long-term group objectives shaped the operations of government. Power remained mostly in the hands of the gentry who used it in the factional struggle for privilege. Now and again some issue of policy momentarily arrayed larger interests against one another. But by and large, the men involved thought of politics in terms of personal advantage.

Yet, at the same time, precisely because the free colonists reacted as individuals and not as members of coherent groups, they came to value what they all had, certain rights as men. They would have been hard put, in 1750, to define those rights or to explain how they came to possess them. But the conviction that such rights existed was nonetheless genuine. And by then, this provincial society had created a culture that compelled the colonists to reflect on the nature of the world in which they lived in terms that established a new setting for political ideas and action.

9

Sources of a Modern Culture

THE CHILDREN of Mr. Parris, the minister of Salem Village, knew perfectly well that witches were among the most perilous beings in the invisible world about them. In 1692, when they became aware of a malevolent influence in their home, they were quick to communicate their suspicions to their elders. The town authorities, of course, took action. The normal judicial proceedings followed their investigation; one hundred and fifty persons were arrested and twenty were convicted and executed, among them the Reverend George Burroughs.

There was nothing out of the ordinary in this incident. Only a few years earlier a witch had been detected and hanged in Boston; and the learned divine Cotton Mather had then taken the occasion to publish a sermon which revealed the significance of these demons and the modes for recognizing them. Nor was the concern with hostile spirits peculiar to the colonies. All western Europe was on the hunt for witches in the seventeenth century; and literally hundreds of thousands were ferreted out and killed.

Salem Village was not unusual in tracking down and persecuting those who had intercourse with familiar spirits; such an outburst could then have appeared anywhere. This particular incident was significant, rather, for the afterthoughts it evoked. Before long there were grave doubts about the whole affair. In 1700 a number of tracts attacked the courts; and Samuel Sewall, who had served as a judge, himself in time confessed to serious doubts about the propriety of the action. Before long, the witchcraft episode was regarded as a tragic delusion, not to be repeated.

Even those who recanted or who questioned the action of the judges did not deny that witches actually existed or that they might appear to do their evil work on earth. Those ideas remained unchallenged; and the reversal of attitudes was not due to a change in theoretical beliefs. The witchcraft prosecutions halted when they did because men decided that however correct the theory, it made no sense in practice. Accusations pointed against some poor demented creature had been plausible enough; but then the charges had spread and had condemned substantial, respectable townfolk who *lived Christian like in their families, and were ever ready to help such as stood in need.* Even though the evidence was sound by accepted standards and though some of the defendants had actually confessed, it simply was not credible that they should have been guilty.

Therein lay the true meaning of the outbreak. In rejecting the results of the trials, the colonists applied to the supernatural not the tests of authority or tradition, but those of experience. The learned books and ancestral wisdom proved that there were witches and set forth the signs by which to recognize them; but the people who knew the victims as good neighbors were not persuaded. Whatever the dogmas of scholars and ministers, whatever the practices of the past, most colonists by now preferred to rely upon their own observations interpreted by their own common sense.

Increasingly in the next half-century the colonists gave evidence that they used a new way of thinking. They less often applied to events about them the explanations handed down from the past by father to son; they more often looked afresh and wondered why. In doing so they frequently rejected the interpretations that had been conventional in the seventeenth century. The comet that flashed through the heavens, the earthquake that tore through the ground were no longer signs of God's displeasure. They were by no means accidental, but neither were they manifestations of any supernatural will. Rather, they were the results of causes that operated with some regularity in the universe and that were comprehensible to men who had the wit to understand them.

Few colonists, by 1750, had actually read the works of Sir Isaac Newton or of John Locke. But the ideas connected with those great names had slowly filtered across the Atlantic; and they had seized hold of many imaginations because they seemed to conform to experience. Man was not a creature endowed at birth with all his attributes and located by Providence in a situation in which he would remain fixed and helpless in the face of forces he could not control. Certainly that had not been his fate in America. Man at birth was all potentials, his mind a clean slate; he acquired habits, skills and ideas by training and by contact with the environment. Nor was the world subject to the fitful intervention of good and evil powers. Properly understood, the same rules that accounted for the ripening of apples on the mature tree also accounted for the blight that eradicated new-set plants. The universe and all that was in it functioned according to laws inherent in its own nature. The movement of the heavenly bodies, the shape of the earth and the cycle of birth and decay reflected the workings of mechanisms which, while divine in orgin, operated by rule rather than by caprice.

There were, therefore, vast areas to be explored but no secrets or mysteries. What was as yet not known could be known through the exercise of right reason, that faculty of man which enabled him to sort out the results of his own experience and observations and to combine them into meaningful patterns. Those who studied nature carefully could plainly read and understand its laws.

The colonists, in practice, had long since become accustomed to this way of thinking. Their situation had compelled them to cast loose from tradition and habit and to depend upon reason and trial and error or experiment. In the absence of doctors, schools of medicine and folk remedies, they depended upon simple natural remedies; in the absence of lawyers and lawbooks, they relied upon fair standards of justice. In every sphere of life, the lack of a binding tradition, of established institutions and of a technically skilled leadership, and the obduracy of novel conditions had driven these people to act upon observation and reason. They were all converts to Newton and Locke before they had ever heard the names.

The new ways of thought lashed men on in the pursuit of knowledge, for learning was the key to the command of nature. Thomas Godfrey, for instance, had been an infant when his father died. His mother, the widow of a poor farmer, had no alternative but to remarry; and the boy grew up in Philadelphia without prospects or formal education. Apprenticed to a glazier, he himself took up that trade, and spent the rest of his life cutting glass and fitting panes to windows. But something drove him to expect universal precision in everything and from counting and measuring he advanced to a study of mathematics.

Godfrey knew of Newton's *Principia Mathematica* and somehow learned that James Logan, secretary of the Province, had a copy. Presenting himself at the door of the secretary, he secured access to Logan's personal library and, incidentally, got the job of putting windows into Stenton. He turned his knowledge to a useful end in the invention of a new quadrant, but he reckoned that less important than his continuing study. Logan himself was an eager student and encouraged others, among them John Bartram. That self-taught botanist and farmer traveled along the river banks for years, picking and sorting the plants he dispatched to Europe to assist in the great work of classification. Benjamin Franklin, who for a time shared a house with Godfrey, pursued a succession of explorations that earned him fame. He was also the moving spirit in the Junto, a group of young men who pooled their books and resources in a library company and met regularly for heated discussion.

Everywhere along the coast curious students repeated the experience of the Philadelphians. Great planters, merchants, printers and artisans, government officials and farmers, ministers and physicians, set themselves eagerly to scanning the heavens and scouring the earth, hoping to see the work of God through a telescope and to learn the laws of nature from the fresh world about them.

Some among these inquirers boasted degrees from Edinburgh or Harvard. But most were self taught and all were amateurs, who pursued their studies independently of any formal institutions. They placed only slight reliance upon inherited cultural agencies; insofar as they needed media for communication, they preferred to create new ones. That was why churches, schools and colleges languished while the press thrived.

Down to the 1730's the churches and their ministers steadily lost influence. Even in New England the ties to the community loosened and support from the government grew weaker; elsewhere the process had long been under way and now accelerated. The increasing religious diversity of the population wore away the basis of establishment particularly since the dissenters were among the most respectable men in the colonies. Quakers once driven out of Massachusetts were merchants of wealth in Newport and Philadelphia. Some owners of great estates in Pennsylvania and Maryland were Roman Catholics; and little groups of Jews played a prominent role in trade in most large cities. All this was apart from the Presbyterians, Baptists, Huguenots and Moravians who followed their own sectarian practices. Moreover, some persons in each of these faiths shared political power and influence; and together they formed a far from negligible force.

Such conditions cast doubt upon the claim of any particular group to election or to special privilege. It was easy to slip into tolerance, to deal with people as individuals rather than as members of religious bodies, and to accept the parity of all forms of worship. But, as a result, the minister ceased to be the spokesman of the whole community and lost the authority and sanctions once attached to his position. Except in some small, stable New England towns, he became but one among many expounders of ideas, attempting to persuade rather than simply to reveal the truth to others.

Furthermore, the old pattern of persuasion was not as effective as it had once been. Eighteenth-century audiences did not listen patiently to long sermons delivered in a plain style and setting forth accepted propositions based on recognized authorities. They judged these expositions by the standards of their own experience and observations and by what they knew through other sources of the new learning; and by those tests the traditional disquisitions did not make sense. Increasingly, therefore, some ministers felt the pressure to adjust to the new conditions and absorb the new ideas. Those who held to the old ways lost their followings — to other sects or to apathy.

The altered role of the church in the community profoundly affected colonial education. Seventeenth-century schools had been primarily religious in orientation, whether their direction was actually in the hands of ministers or not. The Bible was the primary text, for the end of learning was the ability to make out the holy writ and to understand its authoritative expositors.

Those functions steadily declined in importance as men placed greater reliance upon their own experience and less upon ancient texts. Insofar as the schools remained bound to the older tasks, they lost relevance and ceased to attract support. Ordinarily, parental instruction or the teaching by a dame in the neighborhood was enough to impart the elementary ability to read and to reckon. More than that was inessential.

South of Pennsylvania there was scarcely a sign of formal development in this period. Education was a private arrangement, worked out by each family in accord with its own aspirations. Apprenticeship was available in the cities and planters commonly took on tutors for their sons. That generally left no provision whatever for the rest of the population which, however, seemed not to suffer from the lack.

The contrast with New England was striking — on paper. Massachusetts had enjoined each town to provide for a school back in the 1640's and the other provinces had early followed its example. But the reality was less impressive. In the cities, the sons of merchants and of ambitious artisans, who did not wish to be apprenticed, could attend regular schools under settled masters. But the farming communities frequently saw little utility in book-learning and found the expense unnecessary. It was cheaper to pay the moderate fine exacted for failure to comply with the law; or to make a pretense of obedience by hiring some available youth for a four- or six-week term each year. In practice, New England children grew up no more literate than their peers in Virginia.

Nor were the results significantly different in the middle provinces. There the schools remained in the hands of the church — English, Dutch, Presbyterian or Quaker — and the cast of education was primarily religious. The cities sustained a few strong institutions. The country districts were deliberately negligent.

A burst of enthusiasm in 1693 and 1701 increased the number of colonial universities to three by adding William and Mary and Yale to Harvard, then already a venerable institution. But these colleges had little to do with learning. They were, in the first instance, seminaries for training ministers and also, in imitation of Oxford and Cambridge, places of refuge where well-to-do parents sent their adolescent sons to learn to carry themselves handsomely and come into a room genteelly. Each entering class was rarely above twenty in number; and the handful of harried pedagogues divided their time between instructing the serious minority and disciplining the majority given to indecent language and the liberal use of spirituous liquors. If an occasional tutor found time for intellectual pursuits of his own, it was generally despite the environment rather than because of it.

Genuine education was otherwise conceived by those more earnestly involved in it. Schools and books were useful insofar as they taught men skills that enabled them to deal with the practical problems of their lives. The classics were worth consulting insofar as their wisdom still had meaning in answering immediate moral, political and scientific questions. But study was certainly not to be limited to the classics. There were those in every town capable of conveying the skills of Italian double-entry bookkeeping, surveying, mathematics, geography, astronomy, navigation and the languages the trader needed — French, Spanish and Portuguese.

Furthermore, learning was not a function of status; a glazier was as likely a subject as a minister or gentleman. Nor was it confined to youth or channeled through schools. Study was a continuing process that occupied the scholar's whole life. Sustained by the libraries that appeared in the larger cities, it brought him into contact with others similarly engaged through discussion groups such as the Junto and through the web of correspondence that tied all the colonies and England together.

These students therefore were not isolated and they were in a position to address the whole population, which listened to them through new media of communications. Newspapers, for instance, were rapidly becoming the most important purveyors of information and molders of opinion in the colonies. The *Weekly News-Letter* that first appeared in Boston in 1704 waited fifteen years for an imitator; but after 1719 the number of gazettes mounted rapidly. In 1750, only New Jersey, Delaware and Georgia lacked their own journals, and those places were served from nearby cities in other provinces.

The demand that encouraged these enterprises was not for local news which passed by word of mouth in towns still small enough so that a curious pedestrian could walk from end to end without difficulty. The weekly sheets served other functions. About half their space went to advertisements and shipping notices that made known the flow of goods. They also recorded governmental actions and proclamations and found room for long accounts of events in Europe and in other colonies. The newspaper thus devoted itself primarily to the needs of people in trade, for whom such information was immediately useful.

But without design or plan, it also became a means of communicating instruction. The printers filled what columns still remained empty with essays copied from the English press and with original disquisitions on political, religious, moral and scientific subjects. They assembled this miscellaneous reading matter haphazardly, often taking whatever came most readily to hand. But the successful ones, like Franklin, learned to be selective, making judgments about what would most likely interest, edify and amuse their readers. Those who published annual almanacs also filled up the little spaces in the calendar with useful literature. Thus snatches of poetry, accounts of the virtues of Seneca Snake-Root Oil as a cure for pleurisy, merry jokes and wise sayings, advice on law, politics, and marriage all were conveyed to wide audiences in a concise and effective form. Imperceptibly the newspaperman became the rival of the minister and the essay competed successfully with the sermon.

This was an unequal contest. The advantage of the newspaper emanated from its greater relevance to the situation of the colonists. The culture it communicated was not a fixed body of immutable ideas and practices handed down by tradition but rather an aggregation of techniques upon which men drew when they had need. The essays, aphorisms and poems were nuggets of practical truth that helped a variety of different people deal with the problems of health, family life, business and politics.

This culture embodied the experience and common sense of its participants without demanding of them a commitment to any total belief. It was therefore also individual rather than communal in character. The Bostonian or Philadelphian of 1750 made a choice of which of several journals he took; he carried each issue into his own home and read what parts of it he wished; and he agreed with some opinions and not with others. He had come a long way from the men of his grandfather's time who had met together in a worshiping communion and had shared a corpus of ideas which explained to them all there was to be known.

Toward the end of the 1730's there was a change. That perceptive observer Benjamin Franklin noted it with interest.

Franklin had seldom attended any public worship; the preachers' arid discourses seemed to him chiefly either polemic arguments or explications of the peculiar doctrines of one sect, with not a single moral principle inculcated. He devised instead a little liturgy for his own private use and guided himself by scientific charts and tables that he expected would lead him to moral perfection.

But in 1739 and 1740, the discourses of George Whitefield did move him. Knowing that a collection would be made, the canny printer went resolved not to give a penny. The words of the preacher dissolved that resolution; as he spoke, Franklin thought first to give whatever coppers he had on hand, then mentally added the silver, but when the climax came emptied his pockets altogether. Evidently Whitefield's sermon was of altogether another order from the labored discourses of the usual minister.

Whitefield was riding the crest of a great awakening which had burst into prominence with the spread of accounts, a few years earlier, of the surprising work of God in Northampton and Enfield in Massachusetts. There the eloquent exhortations of the local minister, Jonathan Edwards, had induced a feverish revival of religion. The men who welcomed Whitefield to Philadelphia and other cities in his long tour of the coast did so in excited anticipation that he might effect similar great things among them. Everywhere in the colonies the materials were ready. For some time now, Theodorus J. Frelinghuysen had been urging his Dutch Reformed congregation in New Jersey to strive for personal holiness; William Tennant moved on a similar mission among the Scotch-Irish of Pennsylvania; and the newly arrived German Schwenkfelders and Moravians bore with them their own gospel of repentance and redemption. Fed from these various sources, the flames of revivalism burned fiercely on into the 1740's.

The Great Awakening was part of a movement which also encompassed much of Western Europe. Whitefield's friend John Wesley in England, the pietistic sects in Germany, and even the Hasidic Jews of Hungary had in common the mystical certainty that the true believer could find communion with God through an experience which was essentially emotional. Disdaining the formality of the churches, they preached anywhere directly to the masses of men and led them in the singing that would open their hearts to the saving impulses of God's grace. That much the revivals of the New World shared with those of the Old.

But the converted sinners of Enfield and Philadelphia were not the same as those of Halle or Bristol. The difference in situation led also to a difference in response in America.

The tense men and women winced as they listened. They were half beasts and half devils, hypocrites steeped in sin. Their hideous behavior, their readiness in yielding to evil made them loathsome in the sight of God who held them over the pit of hell, much as one held a spider over the fire. For the moment they could go heedlessly their own way. But they hung, though they did not know it, by a slender thread over the furnace where the flames of divine wrath flashed about.

Was it not all true? The laxity of behavior and the failure of respect, the bold nightwalker in town, the tippler in the tavern, the disobedient child, the faithless spouse, the surly servant and the disloyal subject, all showed the effects of a falling away from virtue. All had cut themselves off from the rules that could guide them to goodness and, blinded by selfishness, all were in danger of losing their souls. They were all guilty and all sinners. Weaknesses in their own nature and the temptations of the world had made them so and eternal perdition awaited them.

But there was still time. Through regeneration they could achieve a new birth that would restore them to God's favor.

Sin, regeneration and new birth were familiar Christian terms; but as they passed from the preacher to his audience they acquired a distinctive connotation. That new birth of which he spoke was not to occur after death in a hereafter in which they believed but which was unimaginably remote. It was to occur at once, on earth and in the present life, and was to manifest itself in a change in behavior, in manners free of sin, in actions laden with goodness.

Regeneration was to be effected not through an incomprehensible gift of God's grace for which the supplicant could only humbly wait. The exhortations of the preacher assured his listeners that they would be saved if they would only will it. Regeneration was a reward bestowed on those who through their works showed that they earnestly desired it.

And sin was no longer the product of the positive force of evil working upon man's original corrupt nature. It was a product of man's inadequate will to be good. He was not driven to sin by the devils or any other external powers; he lapsed from virtue by reason of his own insufficient desire to do good.

The preacher thus moved his listeners to a consciousness of guilt for having fallen away from the faith of their fathers; but it was not to the old faith that he brought them back. As the words passed through the crowded fields, they effected a significant inversion in the older drama of salvation. By Adam's fall we sinned all to be saved for life eternal by God's mysterious grace — the old lines acquired a new meaning. I failed to do good through lack of will but if I wish to, and try, I can make my life virtuous.

By 1750, the fever had abated. But the Great Awakening left a permanent imprint upon colonial culture, and not quite that which its promoters had anticipated. The revivals had not restored the religious practice of the seventeenth century but had recast it to accommodate novel views of God, man and the universe.

The call to personal piety, reiterated again and again, fixed the emphasis of those who responded on the exercise of the will to do good. It was right action that was demanded of them, not right belief; and that confirmed what experience had already taught, that sectarian differences were of but slight consequence. When the people of Philadelphia put up a building for Whitefield's use, they designed a structure that could serve any preacher of any denomination so that even were the Mufti of Constantinople to send a missionary to teach Mahometanism, he would find a pulpit available.

Such people thrilled to descriptions of divine wrath, yet it was not really an angry God they recognized. A stern judge, yes, who rewarded the good and punished the bad, but one who had, as it were, benevolently arranged all the mechanisms of the trial to assure a favorable outcome for those who sought it. Increasingly, He bore a striking resemblance to the Celestial Mechanic described by the English deists — the Heavenly Watchmaker, whose creation was so perfectly regulated by natural law that man had only to adjust himself to it to be carried along in a pattern of correct behavior.

This God was not punctilious in the matter of creeds; it was therefore unnecessary for the preachers to devote themselves to studying and expounding nice points of theology. They could more usefully spend their energy in the discussion of ethical principles. But even that was secondary. Their listeners required most of all stimulus to the will; those who wished to be good, would be. And it was not by means of tedious argument that the will was aroused, but by a dramatic appeal to the emotions. Hence the wild gyrations and gesticulations, the lurid descriptions of hell and the accusations pointed at the unconverted. The listeners did not actually believe that they would fall to Satan, for they knew that once they believed at all, they were saved; and as they joined in the mass singing of the rousing psalms that opened their hearts in gladness, they knew that they would be saved.

The emotional experience that was the essence of religious conversion was accessible to all. God had not designated a few as saints and left the rest to sin. Every man, rich or poor, learned or ignorant, could respond to the appeal to the heart and could assert the will to be good. Thereafter, the dictates of conscience and reason would enable the regenerate to display true piety in their personal lives.

The new ideas had a profound effect upon colonial life. They did not substantially increase religiosity; membership and attendance in the established churches did not rise. The settled ministers, who were often shocked by the outbreaks, pointed out somewhat smugly that once the excitement subsided, people reverted to their old ways. The result in some colonies was a reaction, expressed in the 1740's in laws against itinerant preaching.

The long-term consequences of the Great Awakening pointed in another direction. The movement weakened traditional denominational loyalties by its stress upon the emotional experience of the individual rather than upon the creedal communion united as a group. Not the attendance at one church rather than another, but ethical behavior unrelated to theological affiliations, brought salvation.

The ground was thus prepared for the spread of deism — the total denial of any need for institutional religion — and for the proliferation of separate churches, formed through no authority but the will of their members. The colonists thereafter resisted any centralizing or episcopal pattern and moved toward an extreme of congregationalism in which each local group governed itself. Even the Anglicans rejected proposals that they be given a bishop; and every body of worshipers assumed the right to adopt what practices and forms it desired.

Each congregation could also call upon the services of whatever minister it wished. Since the necessary qualifications were those not of learning in a particular doctrine or authoritative ordination but of the ability to appeal to the emotions and to exhort to moral behavior, every listener could seek out the preacher he pleased. Indeed, the summons to right action need not come from the pulpit at all; it could as well be heard from the columns of a newspaper or the pages of a book. For in the last analysis each individual, in his own fashion, responded to whatever impulses toward goodness suited him. Conscience and reason were the only useful guides.

The conception that salvation was accessible to all and not a gift limited by the Donor to a few also had deep implications. If none were thoroughly predestined to be damned and all shared the hope of salvation, then there was some common element of worth in every man, whatever his place, rank or station.

The explosive corollaries of this idea were not, at the moment, apparent. For the time being, it was mostly important in stimulating practical efforts to do good. Even earlier in the century, such men as Cotton Mather and Benjamin Franklin had explained that spontaneous acts of virtue were steps toward moral perfection. Now there was a greater reason for furthering projects of self-help and help to others. The colonists began to draw together to provide for the poor, the sick and the aged, to establish new academies and colleges, to moderate the use of spirituous liquors, to ameliorate the conditions of the slaves and to improve their cities. Significantly almost all these enterprises were initiated not by the established institutions of the community, the government and the church, but by individuals associating freely together and mostly on a nonsectarian basis. Good works were exercises of man's moral faculty which demonstrated his own worth and developed the worth of others.

The analogous movements in Europe moved in the same direction but arrived at a different destination. English Methodism and German Pietism were similar to the American revivals in method and also stressed the importance of philanthropy as an expression of personal virtue. But the Old World limited the sphere within which the regenerate could act. John Wesley and Count Zinzendorf recognized that the society about them was evil, and had no hope of recasting it. They counseled withdrawal. Piety was a fence that excluded the hostile forces they could not defeat but could only escape. English Methodists and German Moravians tried to draw as many souls as possible to safety within the fence; they did not aspire to reorder the world outside it.

The situation in the New World was entirely different. Here evil was not entrenched in tradition; nor sustained by rigid corporate communities; nor protected by an unchangeable political system. Here all was in flux and redeemable. In a new and expanding society, men could control all the terms of their relationships, among themselves, with others, and with their past. They could use will and reason to shape their lives in accordance with those natural orderly regulations that governed the benevolent operations of the universe.

The Great Awakening left the colonists imbued with confidence in their capacity for achievement. They had the will and the power to reorder a world not yet encrusted with restrictive institutions, but fresh and still malleable, ready to take whatever form they would give it. They were now ready to reinterpret in their own terms that faith in a special American mission which their seventeenth-century ancestors had bequeathed them.

IV

A Nation in Being, 1750–1810

10

The Imperial Crisis

I *shall soon be no more*, wrote the boy, *and all the reward I shall get will be — "Poor Will is dead!"*

He could be forgiven the indulgence in self-pity. When the men mounted guard, they passed first among their fellows, assembling what bits of patched and darned clothing had not yet fallen apart. Some could do no better than wrap themselves in blankets against the Pennsylvania winter. Bloodstains in the snow reminded the general that some troops had come barefoot to the parade; he reckoned that half were without breeches, shoes and stockings. There was shelter of a sort in cabins no gayer than a dungeon. But there had been times before Christmas when there was no food at all; and in happier seasons it was hard biscuits and water, meal after meal and day after day.

Poor Will had no fear of death in battle. He was more likely to waste away on a bed of straw and be carried off by pneumonia or consumption, typhus or smallpox. In the improvised hospital, one third of the patients failed to survive.

This was Valley Forge. When at last the spring dawned in 1778, one third of the army which had pitched camp in the war-torn village in December had melted away; and others had stayed only out of numb inertia or because they were so naked they were ashamed to be seen on the way home.

Like poor Will, the commander was given to broody introspection. His teeth troubled him; now and again he tinkered with the plates in a vain effort to ease the discomfort. He was forty-five now and felt his middle age. Yet outwardly he still presented an appearance of serene dignity. He was exceptionally tall, so that he stood always a little above others; and the calm of his countenance, the steadiness of his gaze, elicited instinctive respect.

In the small farmhouse he shared with his staff he tried to hold the war effort together; but the burden of decision was heavy, for he had to keep track in his mind of the politics of Congress, of the intrigues of his subordinates, and of the misery of his men, as well as of the intentions of the British comfortably ensconced in Philadelphia, eighteen miles away. Often he thought with nostalgia of the simpler round of duties and pleasures that might even then be occupying him on his great estate at Mount Vernon. But then when he reviewed the events of his own lifetime and the reasons that took him so far from home, he was certain that the cause justified every sacrifice.

And the men too endured this trial; contrary to expectations, they did not mutiny. Later, one of them recalled, that it was at Valley Forge that he had been confirmed in the habit of considering America as his country and Congress as his government.

It had begun a quarter of a century earlier with the liquidation of the French foothold on the mainland. In 1748, his Fairfax connections got George Washington a place as surveyor in a western expedition; the sixteen-year-old boy, spying out the riches of an unclaimed land, had looked with wonder at the limitless forest as his party followed the courses of fresh streams that flowed from the unknown heart of the continent. Five years later, when the news came that the French were entrenching themselves at the forks of the Ohio River, Governor Dinwiddie of Virginia sent him on a futile mission to warn the intruders away. The published journal of that trip earned its author renown and spread word of the attractions of the region.

Then the two empires were locked in combat. Washington came back three times, once with his own militia, once with Braddock's professional British troops, and again with Forbes's. Each force was beaten back; the French and their Indian allies were too strong. Washington spent the remaining years of the war in command of the Virginia frontier, patiently occupied with the wearisome task of protecting against attack the steady advance of settlement that was to win the area as armies could not.

The conflict reached around the world before the Treaty of Paris ended it in 1763. All the great powers took part; and years of intermittent fighting shaped the final outcome — at Louisbourg, Ticonderoga and Quebec, at Rossbach and Leuthen in Europe, along the Senegalese coast, before ancient Asian cities, and on every traveled sea lane. But in the New World, the issue was never in doubt. When Washington traveled overland in 1755 to consult the British commander in Boston, he passed through societies so deeply planted no foreign conqueror could hope to root them out.

In 1763, France lost Canada and Spain lost Florida. Britain acquired total hegemony over the mainland; it also acquired a set of problems that would soon lose it more than it had gained. It had then to develop an efficient pattern of administration to govern its far-flung possessions; and it had to take steps to reduce a debt enlarged by war to £140,000,000 — no mean burden for a country with a population of eight million. The two concerns were related in their implications for America. In the effort to deal with them the royal administrators touched off heated conflicts over trade, land, taxes, and government; and they made bitter enemies of the colonists who had only recently rejoiced in the triumph of British arms.

Consistently the king's ministers attempted to normalize the situation, to bring these provinces to conform to a general pattern that governed all the other dominions. Consistently the colonists resisted any effort to modify the political and social order they had themselves developed in the earlier permissive decades. Impasse!

Colonel Washington, a dutiful subject and respectable landowner, certainly disapproved of the lawless men who destroyed the property of others when they poured the East India Company's tea into Boston harbor in 1773. Yet he could understand the course that brought his countrymen to that pass.

In the perspective of London, it had seemed only proper that England should profit from an empire gained at considerable expense. The Acts of Trade were among the means of doing so. The basic measures had long been on the statute books. It remained only to enforce them. The Sugar Act of 1764 and the Townshend Acts of 1767 compelled the colonies to direct their commerce through British ports, strengthened the vice-admiralty courts, the justices of which were agents of the Crown, and permitted customs officers, when they wished, to use writs of assistance in the search for contraband. The Currency Act forbade the provinces to print their own legal tender; the Stamp Act subjected them to a moderate tax; and the Quartering Act shifted some of the cost of supporting the army to those it was expected to defend. None of these laws put greater burdens on the colonists than Englishmen at home accepted as a matter of course.

The colonists did not see it that way. British policy threatened their foreign trade and limited the possibilities for internal expansion. It taxed them without their consent and imposed upon them a tyrannical standing army. It gave unlimited license to any royal prowler to enter their homes and warehouses in the search for illicit goods and deprived them of the protection of their own local courts. They protested and, when protests proved unavailing, embarked upon a boycott that damaged English commerce.

Washington perceived even more clearly the results of the failure to settle the fate of the western lands vacated by the French, for he himself and many of his associates were heavily involved. In 1763, the royal ministers had concluded they needed time to work out an adjustment. Canada and Florida were therefore to remain as they were. British troops were to continue to man the interior posts to prevent such Indian uprisings as Pontiac had just led, and further settlement in the trans-Allegheny West was forbidden pending a final decision about its future.

London could distinguish two long-term alternatives. The region might remain a permanent wilderness as the fur-trading interests wished. Or it might be opened to settlement for the profit of investors in land companies and of the manufacturers whose goods would move to ever-expanding markets. The only question was which path was more advantageous to Britain.

To the colonists, the question of whether to people the West or not was meaningless; the steadily advancing settlers were taking care of the answer. The important decisions were, rather: under whose auspices and to whose advantage? Was the Crown to dispose of the vast new tracts or were the provinces to do so? Were the areas now to be populated to remain parts of old colonies or form new ones? How were the overlapping claims of various governmental jurisdictions and speculative companies to be reconciled? Those questions the royal ministers could not answer.

The Tea Party was merely an incident in the developing crisis. When the other Townshend duties had been repealed, that on tea survived and the East India Company received a monopoly of the sale to the colonies. The people of Massachusetts were already indignant; just a year earlier the Crown had decided to pay the salaries of the judges and the governor directly to relieve them of local control. The Bostonians responded to this latest provocation by direct action.

Opinions hardened. Parliament closed the port, abolished the existing government, and strengthened the Quartering Act. At about the same time, it at last made a decision about the West, that was least likely to please the colonists. In 1774 it gave the whole trans-Allegheny region to Quebec, thereby favoring the fur-trading interest and frustrating settlers and speculators alike. The heart of the continent was to be French, in customs, government and language, and the Roman Catholic Church was to be permanently established by law. For a while yet, moderate men argued that commercial pressure through a refusal to buy English goods would turn the mother country toward a conciliatory policy. But however they cried peace, peace — there was no peace. Washington, like most other colonists, saw no retreat from the intolerable acts but *submission and slavery*. The war had already begun.

So opened a division that was never to be bridged. The Americans and the English, though they spoke the same language, could no longer understand one another.

Imperial policy had been formed by the king in Parliament. George III had come to the throne determined to rule effectively. He was neither avaricious nor stupid. But he knew nothing of America; in 1762 he was not even sure whether it was the Ganges or the Mississippi that flowed through that continent. And of government he knew only that he could have his way by strengthening his own party in the House of Commons, thus compounding the corruption he found there.

Nor was greater understanding likely to come from a Parliament controlled by selfish peers and the puppets of their rotten boroughs. Pitt and Shelburne were exceptional in their perception of a larger duty. More typical was the Marquis of Rockingham, who boasted that he was none the worse for having kept himself *in fact, continually drunk or elevated for eleven hours* on end. The spoiled child of the House of Commons was, after all, Charles Townshend, a gay young man about London, when gaiety was identified with dissolution. No broad conceptions of empire were likely to emerge in his witty comments to the House. The fate of Wilkes — deprived of his seat for speaking out — showed what happened to members of a more liberal disposition.

And Parliament reflected the ruling element in English society, overspread with the luxury gained by its conquests. Clerks and factors from the East Indies loaded with the spoils of plundered provinces, contractors fattened by the wars, usurers and jobbers of every kind suddenly translated into a state of opulence, hastened to London where they gorged like shovel-mouthed sharks upon the blubber of privilege. The colonists knew that they had the sympathy of many honest Whigs in England, but they despaired of any effective assistance against the powers entrenched in government.

Certainly George III assured *the unhappy and deluded multitude* which had risen against him that he was ready to receive *the misled with tenderness and mercy* once they had become *sensible of their error.* He did not realize that the provinces were no longer dependencies humbly waiting upon his grace; when they sent agents to treat with him, it was almost as if they were themselves sovereign and as if the connection with the Crown were an alliance from which they expected to gain as much as they gave. Nor could he comprehend the *fierce spirit of liberty* that Edmund Burke warned him *was stronger in the English colonies than in any other people of the earth.* Deceived by ritual protestations of loyalty and by superficial resemblances to the mother country, the king and his ministers failed to perceive that across the Atlantic there had appeared a new society capable of taking autonomous political action, of raising an army, and of fighting for its rights.

After 1774, it ceased to be a matter of bargaining over the redress of grievances. When the Earl of Carlisle came bearing concessions, early in 1778, Washington and the Congress, desperate though their situation was, were in no mood for compromise. The men at Valley Forge were no longer fighting for exemption from the Navigation Acts or for western lands. Those immediate issues had opened their eyes to the wider objectives of the struggle.

The years of debate had compelled them to consider and to justify. Parliament was wrong to levy the stamp tax. Why? Because that amounted to taxation without representation. And the Acts of Trade? Because they lacked the consent of the governed. But were the Americans not virtually represented in Parliament? No, because they did not participate directly in selecting members of their own choice who would speak for them. Well then, on the basis of what grant or charter did they claim that privilege? None; the rights they claimed were not such as were conceded in any document but were assured them by the spirit of the constitution on the basis of which their own polity had developed.

Since 1750, the colonists had grown ever more confident in making such assertions. The constant exercise in politics had familiarized them with the terms of the debate and eloquent spokesmen were ready to formulate their ideas. A generation of young men trained in the law had searched classical and modern political theory for the ideas that would fit the peculiar experience of this society; and with growing frequency, since the Great Awakening, ministers had speculated about the just forms of government that would enable men to live a good life. From the pulpit, through the press, and in a flood of pamphlets, the colonists pointed their discussions by way of the immediate issues — the grievances — at the ultimate issue of rights.

Not every sector of their audience was equally attentive; those who least felt the grievances were least likely to worry about the rights. The Anglican clergy were bound to the king as head of their church and were comfortably established. The great merchants allied with English houses mostly did business directly with the mother country and were but slightly inconvenienced by the Acts of Trade; some indeed had been willing to act as agents of the East India Company. The holders of royal office and privileges and some landowners were also satisfied with things as they were; they had been willing enough to distribute the hated stamps. On the other hand, merchants whose trade ran out of the usual channels faced ruin by strict adherence to the law and were annoyed by customs racketeers willing to wink at evasions for a consideration. Plantation owners in debt to English factors were squeezed by the shortage of currency, worried by the possibility that an end to expansion would limit the market for surplus slaves, and frustrated by the collapse of all schemes for the exploitation of western lands. In fact, every speculative type — merchant, farmer and artisan — saw in the measures that pricked their hopes of expansion the end of their dreams of growth.

As the debate unfolded, positions hardened, not in an exact correspondence of calculations of advantage with attitudes toward rights, but in a tendency of those who suffered from grievances to be readier in defiance of the Crown than others. The rebellion also attracted support from elements of the population which had not theretofore been active in politics. Already in the 1750's, farmers, artisans, religious dissenters and other folk of the lower sort were emboldened not only to vote but to offer their own candidates for office. After 1763, their anger too turned against the British. The Boston caucus, led by Sam Adams, and the New York Sons of Liberty, led by Isaac Sears, helped elect patriots and joined the mobs that attacked the lieutenant governor's house, or threatened the stamp collector, or burned a customs vessel, or played at Indians in Boston Harbor. They too spoke of rights and liberty, generally in sweeping terms unsoftened by qualification. Their growing prominence as the resistance became revolutionary gave further pause to the respectable minority fearful of change.

In 1776, the Loyalists perceived that they would have to part company from their countrymen. There was no hope of conciliation; and in time many would go into exile. The colonial army, for more than a year, had stood in open rebellion; and there had been pitched battles at Lexington and Concord and at Bunker Hill. In January, 1776, the shrill voice of Tom Paine the pamphleteer had urged the Americans to recognize the actuality of separation. *Common Sense* pointed out that faith in kings was dead; it was time to proclaim the republic that already existed.

The Continental Congress held off until July. Prudence dictated that governments long established should not be changed for light and transient causes. Yet by now it was time to display the seriousness of separation, particularly since the embattled colonists sought the aid of foreign powers. In taking this momentous step, however, it was desirable to put the case for independence in such a form as would convince the hesitant at home and earn the decent respect of the opinions of mankind. The task of framing the Declaration was assigned to a committee of which John Adams and Thomas Jefferson were the most active members. The text was largely Jefferson's.

The Americans, it explained, had become independent by resisting a design to subject them to an absolute tyranny. It had been their duty to end a long train of abuses for which the English people, Parliament and the king were jointly responsible. The colonists had appealed to the native justice and magnanimity of their British brethren, who had however been deaf to the request that they disavow these usurpations. Parliament had improperly assumed the power of pretended legislation, quartering a hostile army upon the colonies, cutting off their trade, imposing taxes, and subverting their free system of government. The king had connived at these transgressions and, in addition, had dealt improperly with the assemblies, had sent over swarms of officers to harass the people and eat out their substance, had prevented the growth of population and had dispatched foreign mercenaries to complete the works of death, desolation and tyranny.

The people had to throw off an authority which had become destructive of its proper ends. All governments derived their just powers from the consent of the governed, who instituted them to secure the unalienable rights of life, liberty and the pursuit of happiness with which the Creator had equally endowed men. It was a self-evident truth that a political system which attacked the rights it was designed to defend, deserved itself to be attacked.

Enlightened men everywhere recognized Jefferson's vocabulary. That an orderly universe operated by natural law, that men formed governments to protect their natural rights, were assumptions common to all readers of Locke, to all contemporaries of Rousseau and Montesquieu. But the phrases of the Declaration had a meaning at Valley Forge even for the man innocent of bookish political theory. They described his experience of the past and his hope for the future. He had created governments by consent; his rights had not been granted but assumed as inherent in the nature of things; and he aspired to live in an orderly society that would give him access to the goods of life. Therefore he stayed to fight.

The war dragged wearily on in the eighteenth-century manner. There were months of preparation, then days of maneuver for strategic position, then a brief encounter, a retreat, the consolidation of positions and preparation once more for the next move. For almost three years the enemy had thus dogged Washington's steps as he withdrew from Boston to New York and then to Pennsylvania. Yet in the spring of 1778, the American prospects were brighter than ever before. The army had been kept intact; victories at Bennington and Saratoga had ended English expectations that the rebellion could quickly be crushed; and those successes had drawn the French into an alliance against their traditional enemy.

These developments virtually assured the United States its independence. But there was as yet no basis for expecting that the terms would be favorable. Even were George III to recognize that he could never again make colonists of these men, the British forces still were powerful enough to nurture his vain hopes of regaining the lost provinces or of restricting them in a way that would doom them to failure.

Three more years of war barely altered the situation. French troops, money and supplies poured steadily across the Atlantic; and the Spaniards and Dutch were of considerable assistance. Yet peace was no closer than formerly. The British still enjoyed military superiority and were entrenched in the seaports from New York to the southward. In May, 1781, the Comte de Vergennes, Louis XVI's minister of state, calculated that the indecisive struggle had stretched on long enough. To put an end to further unprofitable expenditures he was ready to accept a settlement on the basis of the status quo. That would have left the new nation hemmed in along a narrow coastal belt with Boston its only major city. Of course, John Adams, the American envoy to Versailles, vigorously objected.

His objections acquired weight from a sudden reversal of the military position. Washington was able to join forces with the French and, in an imaginative march from the Hudson to the York River, trapped the smaller of two British forces, that under Cornwallis at Yorktown. That maneuver was laden with risk. It depended upon effecting a junction with the French troops coming from Newport, upon the lethargy of Sir Henry Clinton's much larger army in New York City, upon the ability of the French ships to bring artillery and supplies through the British naval blockade, and upon the tricks of weather that prevented Cornwallis from escaping the net drawn about him. Fortune was, in each case, with the Americans. On October 17, 1781, Cornwallis surrendered.

The victory decisively altered the diplomatic balance and shifted the control of British politics out of the hands of George III and into those of ministers more friendly to the American cause. A new cabinet took office, resolved to make peace; and Vergennes could only acquiesce in the informal negotiations that stretched through the months that followed. In November, 1782, the terms of settlement, ultimately written into the treaty of peace, were fixed. Independence was recognized, the new nation's boundaries reached west to the Mississippi, and the English agreed to evacuate the ports and posts they still held. The Americans also retained the fishing privileges they had held as British subjects; and the United States was not bound to compensate the Tories for their confiscated property. The other powers fared less well. France got nothing for all its efforts; Spain received Florida in return for the surrender of its hopes for Gibraltar; and Britain was confirmed in its possession of Canada.

Poor Will and the others who had suffered at Valley Forge had earned their reward. The assistance of the European powers had been substantial; the inefficiency and halfheartedness of the English commanders and government had been monumental; and, in the end, all the vagaries of chance had aided the American cause. Yet, in the last analysis, the determination of a people fighting for its freedom had shaped the outcome of the war, although not the details of the settlement. By the end of 1781, the British had learned that they could win battles but not the war. At enormous expense, they could limit the gains of the Americans; but the colonies were lost beyond redemption. The Continental forces again and again scattered, again and again re-formed to take the field once more. In 1782, the peacemakers only recognized what in actuality already existed, a new nation.

Independence confronted the Americans with novel problems. They had not fought to become a small country, detached and isolated. The grandiloquent rhetoric in which they phrased their aspirations revealed a much wider conception of the significance of their experiment. They expected their achievements to have meaning for the whole world. Yet they could not extend their influence, as the great powers did, by the conquests that made an empire. The very terms that had justified the rebellion prevented the United States from subjugating other peoples. Independence required that it work out new ways of trade, that it assure itself room for expansion, and that it adopt a sympathetic view of the struggle of other men for liberty.

After 1783, the world was no less divided into its exclusive trading spheres than formerly. The English, French, Dutch and Portuguese empires still operated on the old basis; and the Americans now lacked the sheltered position in the British system they had formerly enjoyed. They sought to normalize the practices by which they had formerly thrived, to achieve recognition of their right to do business wherever ingenuity and enterprise carried them. Others were not disposed to make concessions to outsiders who had few bargaining advantages; and some thought that the loss of its international trade would soon drive the upstart country to its knees. But the Americans were sure that the proffer of the opportunity to share the trade of a continent that the British alone had formerly monopolized would open ports everywhere to their vessels.

The United States therefore set about negotiating treaties of friendship, commerce and navigation, beginning with the countries like Prussia which lacked overseas colonies of their own. The tortuous bargaining process was complicated by the limited powers of the general government and was interrupted in 1792 by the renewed outbreak of war between Britain and France. Caught between the two rival powers, the United States attempted, by neutrality, to assure the freedom of the seas to its commerce and its goods. But the belligerents insisted that the control of trade was an instrument of war and refused to exempt the Americans from the decrees that forbade intercourse with the enemy. In 1798, the new country was engaged in an undeclared naval war with France; after the turn of the century it repeatedly clashed with Britain. An embargo on all overseas trade failed to bring the Europeans to terms, and in 1810, the United States was no closer than it ever had been to achieving recognition of its commercial independence.

The struggle for space involved contacts with France, Spain, and England. The Spaniards in Florida were awkward neighbors and in New Orleans held the outlet through which the rapid settlement of the Mississippi Valley poured an ever greater volume of American trade. But Spain was weak and concessions were relatively easy to extort. Pinckney's Treaty of 1795 gave the Westerners what they demanded, the right of deposit that enabled them to transship their goods at New Orleans.

It was a more serious matter when that city passed into the hands of the French. Napoleon for a time nurtured dreams of a revived French empire in America. He hoped to join the tropical islands of the West Indies with Louisiana in a dominion that would reach around the Gulf of Mexico and would be a counterweight to British sea power. At his insistence the Spaniards agreed to cede Louisiana to the French in 1800 and he prepared a great expedition to get his project under way. But the scheme withered as soon as it had begun to flower. General Victor's armada never left the European harbor in which ice held it through the winter of 1802; and meanwhile a rebellion and yellow fever in Santo Domingo decimated the French army already there. In March, 1803, Napoleon determined to liquidate the enterprise; and the American envoys waiting to renegotiate the right of deposit learned that they could have the whole of Louisiana for some $15,000,000. The vast expanse between the Mississippi and the mountains was thus joined to the new republic.

More troublesome were relations with Britain. The former mother country still held the northwest posts on American soil, and from its base in Canada, encouraged the Indians who threatened the American farmers steadily moving into the region. Tecumseh and his brother the Prophet were planning a confederation of all the interior tribes that might pose a permanent barrier to the future advance of settlement. And miscellaneous groups of adventurers wandered about, some of them giving serious consideration to the possibility of breaking away in states of their own. Yet the English evaded every request that they evacuate the posts. Angry Americans demanded direct action and some were so bold as to call for the expulsion of the enemy from Canada to assure the safety of the western spaces.

The defense of unrestrained commerce and of the preserves of western space did not seem parochial concerns to the Americans. They were, rather, vital to the preservation of the revolution which was the cause of all mankind. In that dim past of which eighteenth-century thinkers were becoming conscious, men had been everywhere free; now they were everywhere slaves, even in England, that once fortunate isle. They had been debased by corrupt rulers who selfishly pursued their own ends through war and diplomacy. The New World, protected by its distant situation, alone remained a bulwark of liberty and a refuge for those who hated tyranny. Its desire for space beyond any immediate requirement and for the natural connections of trade therefore served the interest of all who some day wished to be free. That was why so many young men from every part of Europe had come to take a part in the struggle against Britain. That was why so many continued to sympathize.

The course of a republic in a world still dominated by monarchies was difficult. The whole etiquette of diplomacy rested upon dynastic considerations and upon the relationship of one sovereign to another. The United States, therefore, could take no part in the devious dealings by which European rulers sought their own advantage. It guided itself rather by the rule of reason and applied to its collective actions the same code of morality that individuals did. From the start, it had rejected any political alliances with incompatible systems, *because the true interest of these United States required that they should be as little as possible entangled in the politics and controversies of the European nations. The business of America with Europe*, John Adams had discerned in 1776, *was commerce, not politics or war.* Necessity had driven Congress to accept an alliance with France in 1778, but that precedent was not to be repeated and was to be limited as quickly as possible.

Yet most Americans considered themselves citizens of the world as well as of their own country. The rights for which they had fought rested upon universal laws of nature and were universal in import; all men ought some day to share them. No doubt a time would come when the people of England, France, and even Russia would rise against their tyrants; and the United States would then feel a brotherly responsibility for assisting them. But that time was not

ıear and the first republic, for the moment, could best serve man-
ʑind by creating a model and a refuge.

The test came after 1789, when revolution destroyed the Old
Regime in France. The course of events in Europe soon raised
doubts whether the forces at work there were the same as those
which had fought tyranny in the New World. In France, the fall
of the monarchy led not to representative government, but to
Napoleon's empire. The collapse of the established church did not
diffuse a natural virtuous religion through the land but opened the
way to licentiousness, infidelity and corruption. The attempt by
Citizen Genêt to implicate the United States in the war against
England stirred up internal dissension; and the XYZ affair — the
effort in Paris to blackmail the American emissaries — was a final
demonstration of the cynicism of the Gallic revolution. Evidently
Europe was a long way from redemption.

For the time being, at least, Washington pointed out in his
Farewell Address, America would take its own course. The Old
World had a set of primary interests remote from the New World's
and it would be unwise to become involved by artificial ties in the
entanglements of foreign ambition, rivalship, interest, humor or
caprice. *The great rule of conduct was, in extending our commercial
relations to have as little political connection as possible.* In that wise,
America would give to mankind *the magnanimous and too novel
example of a people always guided by an exalted justice and benevolence.*

The full meaning of independence was thus only beginning to
emerge two decades after Valley Forge. The new nation had achieved
its separation from Britain. But in doing so it entered upon an
unusual relationship with the rest of the world; it desired such
natural connections as came with the movement of goods and
people, yet it rejected as artificial any involvement with the old
political system. The Americans, as a people, thereby assumed a
special set of obligations.

11

The American—A New Man

INDEPENDENCE MARKED the political separation of the United States from Europe. But another kind of separation had already been effected by the time that the new state took form. The Americans had become a distinct people. The widening gulf that prevented the colonists and the English ministers from understanding one another was the result of a fundamental divergence of experience. The men on the western shore of the Atlantic had ceased to be the same as those on its older, eastern, shore. In the hearts and minds of those who fought it, therefore, the Revolution was already consummated before the first shot was fired. Even had political developments taken some other turn that permitted the colonies to remain within the empire, the Americans would still have been a nation apart.

The signs of distinctiveness appeared in the middle of the eighteenth century. Earlier, writers who referred to the Americans had in mind the Indian native of the soil. Now the term came consistently to apply to the provincials, as if they were no longer Englishmen living abroad but a separate species. The British officers and men who served in the New World in the wars against France habitually differentiated themselves from the colonists. The Americans did the same. The encounters of travelers — whether the provincials were abroad or the Europeans in the colonies — elicited the same sense of distinctiveness. On the eve of the Revolution, it was clear that a new nationality held together the people of the New World.

Neither then nor later could Americans explain the bonds that held them together as the products of inheritance. The Frenchman or German or Englishman was what he was by virtue of his patrimony; his ancestors had passed down to him a territory, a language, customs and religion which cemented individuals into a unity. Not so the American. His language, laws and customs were mostly English; but that heritage did not establish an identity with the people of the mother country. That was already evident on the eve of the Revolution and the events of the years after 1774 strengthened the convictions that this nation was not simply the derivative offshoot of any other. Heatedly Americans insisted that their English inheritance was only one, if the largest, of several. They were a mixture of many varieties of Europeans who by the alchemy of the New World were fused into a new kind of man.

What then was this new man — the American? Several questions lay hidden in the inquiry. Why did Americans think they were different from other people? Were they actually different? And what made them identify themselves as one nation — rather than as several, as their separate provincial experiences might have forecast. The answers were embedded in the institutions the colonies had developed, in their character as people, and in their aspirations for the future.

Shortly before his death in 1753, William Douglass, a Boston physician, commented on the problem in his *Summary View* of the history and present condition of the British colonies in North America. Douglass had observed that a difference in their experience had set the Americans apart from other Englishmen. Life in the wilderness, the effects of constant mobility, and the necessity of adjusting to strange conditions had nurtured among them novel customs and manners and had created new social forms. He initiated thus a long line of speculation that attributed the nationality of the Americans to their distinctive institutions.

Certainly these factors were important. By the middle of the eighteenth century a variety of circumstances made the culture of the

colonies American, in the sense that it was both intercolonial and
different from that of England. The provinces were all contiguous, so
that men and goods moved freely among them. Ties of trade drew
them together; stagecoaches, inns, and a regular post facilitated com
munications, as did the numerous vessels that plied the coastal sea
Newspapers passed from town to town and made the dispersed popu
lation familiar with a common fund of information and ideas. Despite
local variations, all the governments were unmarked by significan
feudal elements, and notable similarities in style of life knit the
several colonies together.

In addition, a common enemy pressed the Americans toward
unity. At first it was the French, who for a century were a continuing
danger to the frontier. After 1763, when that peril abated, the threa
came from the mother country; and the necessity of joining force
in the struggle developed a consciousness of common interest. A
the crisis unfolded and as men thought of their differences with
England, they became increasingly aware of the similarities among
themselves. In 1765 at the Stamp Act Congress, Christopher Gadsden
had already proclaimed that *there ought to be no New England man
no New Yorker, known on the Continent; but all Americans.* And
ten years later, Patrick Henry had boldly affirmed, *I am not
Virginian but an American.*

The War for Independence was itself a unifying experience and
after the peace the recollection of shared sufferings held the victor
together. The new governments had many features in common and
their emphasis upon free institutions added strength to the sent
ment of nationalism. History had thus created a network of common
institutions that endowed Americans with nationality.

But here was a paradox! One could speak of American institution:
but for a long time there was no America, except insofar as the
term vaguely applied to the whole hemisphere. That designatio
could be attached to no political entity in existence before 1774
Each colony was separate and related not to its neighbors but to th
Crown. Boston's governmental, cultural and business contacts wer
at least as close with London as with Charleston, South Carolina
Efforts to devise schemes for intercolonial co-operation among th
governments were futile; and when the provinces met together it wa
in congresses, as if they were separate states.

Furthermore, not all the English possessions were American in the sense that they joined the rebellion and became states in the Union. Nova Scotia, Quebec and the West Indian islands remained apart, yet they shared some experiences and institutions with those that became independent. South Carolina, in climate, history and economy, was closer to Barbados than to Massachusetts.

Indeed, diversities were as striking as uniformities in the cluster of mainland colonies that formed the nation. Differences in antecedents, history, habits, religious affiliations, and style of life set the New Englander off from the Virginian, the New Yorker from the Pennsylvanian. Nor did those people learn to discount the differences simply by common exposure to the wilderness. In many respects the diversities remained significant; and, in any case, the towns distant from the frontier were as American as the back-country.

Remoteness from the Old World was no criterion at all of the degree of national identification. The Americans were by no means those who were un-European; indeed ties across the Atlantic had never been closer than in the quarter-century before Independence. No colonist seemed more representative of his countrymen than Benjamin Franklin and none was more familiar than he in the cosmopolitan salons of Paris.

And who most eloquently expressed the aspirations of the nation as it approached the test of revolution? The Americans commonly agreed that two works, *Letters from an American Farmer* and *Common Sense*, most carefully described them as a people, most accurately enunciated their ideas and attitudes. Yet Michel de Crèvecoeur, the author of the one, was a Frenchman who had only migrated from Canada after 1763; and Thomas Paine had come off the ship from England little more than a year before he wrote the other. Neither could have been shaped by the influence of distinctive institutions or experience in the brief period after his arrival.

There was no America before 1774. But there were Americans. The people of Maine and Georgia did feel a sense of identification with the nation and did regard their institutions and experience as common unifying forces. The circumstances of their lives in the New World alone were not enough to create a national sentiment; but the people, under those circumstances, developed traits of character that drew them together in pursuit of common goals.

That was Crèvecoeur's conclusion when he attempted to account for the identity of his adopted countrymen. He too had puzzled over the question of who the Americans were. He could see clearly enough that they were a mixture of English, Scotch, Irish, French, Dutch, Germans, and Swedes. From this promiscuous breed that race, now called Americans, had arisen. *He was an American, who, leaving behind him all his ancient prejudices and manners, received new ones, from the new mode of life he embraced, the new government he obeyed, the new rank he held.* But, by what invisible power had this surprising metamorphosis been performed? In part, by that of the laws and of a new social system. But whence proceeded these laws? From the government. Whence the government?

There was the difficulty. The colonies were, after all, English; and although the original genius and the strong desire of the settlers influenced the laws, in the last analysis it was the Crown that ratified and confirmed them. Furthermore, these institutions were neither uniform through the many provinces of British America nor entirely distinctive of them. Crèvecoeur pointed to the significant differences between men who lived in the North and those who lived in the South, between those who earned their livelihood by the sea and those who tilled the soil, between the residents of the frontier and the German Moravians.

It was therefore necessary to look not merely at the laws, but at the mode of living in a new society which shaped the character of the people. To do so Crèvecoeur narrowed the focus of his vision from the continent as a whole to a tiny corner of it — the island of Nantucket. Here a society of five thousand individuals exemplified the traits distinctive of the Americans.

Crèvecoeur reviewed at length the topography of the place, the manners of the inhabitants, the way in which they earned their bread, the upbringing of their children and the form of their government. He then passed to a description of the whale fishery, which had begun as the simple pursuit of offshore strays but which now carried the Nantucketers far from home, northward by the coast of Labrador to Cape Desolation and southward by Brazil to the Falkland Islands and even to the South Seas.

In one of these characteristic ventures, a little company forms and sets out in a brig of about 150 tons burden. They have no wages; each draws a certain established share in partnership so that all are equally vigorous and determined. They sail for weeks in readiness for the moment of their great encounter. When they sight the whale, two boats are launched, each with a crew of six, four at the oars, one on his feet in the bow holding a harpoon, and the other at the helm. At a reasonable distance, one boat stands off as a witness, the other approaches.

The harpooner is still; *on him principally depends the success of the enterprise. In his hands he holds the dreadful weapon — made of the best steel, to the shaft of which the end of a cord is firmly tied. The other end is fastened to the bottom of the boat. They row in profound silence, leaving the whole conduct of the contest to the harpooner and to the steersman. At a distance of about fifteen feet, the harpooner bids them stop.*

He balances high his harpoon, trying at this important moment to collect all the energy of which he is capable. He launches it forth — the whale is struck! Sometimes, in the immediate impulse of rage, she will attack the boat and demolish it with one stroke of her tail. At other times she will dive and disappear from sight or swim away and draw the cord with such swiftness that it will set the edge of the boat on fire by the friction. The boat follows her course until, tired at last with convulsing the elements, she dies and floats on the surface.

The handful of men, venturing freely forth to impose their will upon the natural power of sea and whale, are American in character. Why?

The Nantucketers are not alone in the pursuit of the great whale; in the eighteenth century, vessels from England and Scandinavia also expose themselves to the danger. But the motive that leads Nantucketers to the sea marks them off from other seafaring men. Neither failure at home nor despair sends them to that element; it is a simple plan of life, a well-founded hope of earning a livelihood. The sea becomes to them a kind of patrimony; they go to whaling with as much pleasure and tranquil indifference, with as strong an expectation of success, as the landsman undertakes to clear a piece of swamp.

And they go to come back home. Not for them the wild bouts of carousing in port, by which other seamen punctuate their repeated encounters with danger. There are no material irregularities when the fleet returns to Nantucket. All is peace and a general decency prevails. The long abstemiousness to which these men are exposed, the frequent repetitions of danger, the boldness in surmounting them, do not lead, when on shore, to a desire for inebriation and a more eager pursuit of those pleasures of which they have been so long deprived and which they must soon again forego. They come home to their wives and children; and the pleasures of returning to their families absorb every other desire. In their absence, their wives have managed their farms and transacted their business. The men at their return, weary with the fatigue of the sea, full of confidence and love, carefully give their consent to every transaction that has happened during their absence, and all is joy and peace. "Wife, thee hast done well," is the general approbation for application and industry.

The Nantucketers were distinctive not in their willingness to take risks or in the fact that they had homes to which to return, but in the unique juncture of the two qualities. They were stable men who cherished ties to family and friends, who left home not because there was no place, but voluntarily and with the intention of returning. The hazards they accepted were not a desperate alternative to, but an accepted part of, an orderly life.

By the 1770's that situation had become characteristically American. The men who moved along the northern and southern frontiers were not simply isolated drifters, placeless individuals, cut loose from any ties. They were often the sons of respectable families who left decent homes, not driven away but drawn on by impatience with the limits of the present. As a matter of course they subjected themselves to hardship and danger, strengthened as they were by the certainty of a limitless future. Habituated to a landscape without horizons, they had no fear of venturing into the unknown distances.

That situation the Nantucket whalemen shared with the Virginia planter. So the young Washington, well connected by good family, hardly hesitated to take himself off to the wilderness, abandoning comfort for the life of the shelterless forest and exchanging the company of the cultivated local gentry at Mount Vernon for that of rude trappers and Indians. It was a matter of course that such men should put in the balance the security of what they already had as against the hazards of a boundless potential.

At every level of society the speculative temperament asserted itself. The son of the prosperous merchant was more likely to go to sea than to college; he carried his wares in little craft subject to all the hazards of the elements, from port to port, appeasing hostile officials, negotiating with strangers, his mind ever occupied in calculation, his will ever hardened to gain. What fortune he accumulated was never secure, but always passed through his hands back to new enterprises. The farmer and artisan could fall in with no rhythm of production, they could not adjust to a regular round of sowing and reaping, of building and making. They too were occupied in the effort to extend themselves. They borrowed and lent, worked to save and saved to invest, driven on by the hope of great winnings, yet recognizing the possibility of great losings.

None of them liked the necessity. All their dreams revealed occasional glimpses of a distant resting place which offered surcease from their constant striving; there the husbandman divided the fruits of his fields with his family, the patriarchal master graciously guided the operations of his great plantation, the merchant neatly balanced his books and all was contentment, harmony and peace. Such was the stability and order these people valued. But there was no confusing dreams with the reality of constant striving and ever-present danger. A situation that compelled men who cherished security constantly to seek out and to take risks formed the character of the Americans.

The willingness to accept risks had originated in the very nature of the first settlement and had been perpetuated by a society that allowed few individuals stability enough to relax in the security of exemption from further hazards. All was and remained precarious; whatever was achieved was not enough to sustain itself without further effort. Nothing stood of itself. Ceaseless striving and mobility were necessary to hold on, for only expansion could preserve what had already been created. The venture to the South Seas or to the Ohio wilderness was necessary to keep the Nantucket home or Mount Vernon from crumbling.

The risk and the constant strain of taking it were tolerable because there was a reasonable chance of reward. Space and opportunity —

and therefore hope — were abundant. Every man, whatever his past, could have a future. Europeans became Americans because they no sooner arrived than they immediately felt the effects of plenty. Their toils were no less heavy than before but of a very different nature. They had put behind them involuntary idleness, servile dependence, penury and useless labor. An ample subsistence was within reach. They became landowners and for the first time in their lives, counted for something. *They ceased to be ciphers and felt themselves men because they were treated as such.* They were then Americans.

The sense of nationality was essentially the awareness of the common situation they shared. They recognized one another not by the identity of their antecedents, nor by similarities in appearance, habits, manners, or institutions, but by those traits of character that came from the effort to maintain a balance between the longing for stability and the exposure to risks. This was their environment and the environment alone molded the nature of men and established the differences among species.

Therefore it was possible for the foreign-born to come off the boat and be transformed immediately into Americans, as Paine was and as countless later immigrants would be. Indeed some could identify themselves with the nation and already be American before even leaving the Old World, if the circumstances of their own lives projected them into the same precarious situation. That identification brought scores of Europeans to fight in the revolutionary armies; and it would continue to pull others across the Atlantic on into the nineteenth century.

Independence gave political form to American nationality and deepened the characteristic traits associated with it. Pride in the achievement of having humbled the great empire, confidence in the ability to do without the trappings of traditional monarchy, and faith in man's capacity for fresh creation stimulated every imagination. It was only necessary to be daring enough! Any risk was worthwhile; and there were no limits to what the independent citizens of a republic could do.

The travelers set themselves ever more distant goals. One of Jefferson's neighbors in Virginia took to dreaming in 1792 of an overland route to the Pacific. He was only eighteen then, of a good family, bright and attractive, with every prospect before him. But he would not settle down to planting. It was ten years before Meriwether Lewis had his chance to make that long tedious journey westward to the mouth of the Columbia River. President Jefferson, who had dispatched him, no doubt remembered another genius who had also yearned to lay eyes on the Pacific. John Ledyard had sailed with Cook to the South Seas, but refused to serve the British against his countrymen. A romantic escape; wanderings through Europe; a meeting with Jefferson and John Paul Jones in Paris; then Ledyard had his idea. He would walk eastward across Russia and Siberia. He left England in 1786, passed through Norway, Sweden, and Lapland to St. Petersburg, reached Yakutsk in 1787 and Irkutsk in 1788, then, seized by order of the suspicious empress, was sent back to Poland. Frustrated, he took it into his head to locate the sources of the Niger and never returned to his native Connecticut. For such men the wish to add to knowledge was but a way of describing their restless curiosity.

Everywhere the pace of movement quickened. Settlers in the thousands hastened to the West; merchants sent their ships along hitherto untraveled lands to remote harbors; and every type of fresh enterprise attracted speculative investors. They could hardly wait, any of them, to expose themselves to risk. They were now conscious of their newness as a people; new principles animated them; and they had to assert themselves in new ideas and new achievements.

The awareness of their peculiar situation which shaped their character as a people gave a national meaning to the culture and institutions of the Americans. The looseness of their society and their desire for order, the local sources of political power and the concern with individual rights, the disregard for tradition and the eagerness for new knowledge, the tolerance of difference and the concern with ethical behavior were the accommodations of men who lived precariously in an environment that did not limit their future.

The few who stood apart alienated themselves from the rest. At the Revolution they mostly became Tories and many left the country; after Independence those who stayed were citizens but did not share the spirit of the Republic. In that sense they were not Americans; though born in the New World, they were not part of it. Particular quirks of their personal situations accounted for the difference in their response. Some great merchants whose business connections were fixed and secure, some great landowners who valued stability on their estates, men of all sorts who clung to political or religious tradition or who refused to surrender the social standards of the Old World formed the minority that emigrated or that remained querulously in opposition at home.

Tiny enclaves, like those of the Pennsylvania Amish, which retained a character of their own and resisted national tendencies also stood apart but were no problem. There was space for them, they did not interfere with others, and the distance they maintained was the result of their own desire. But other, larger groups — in the population yet not fully identified as Americans — posed an intellectual and social challenge of the first magnitude.

The Indians, after all, were the original inhabitants of the New World and had longest been subject to its beneficent environment. Yet despite the effort to persuade them to settle down and enter into the new mixture that was brewing, they preferred their tribal identities. Indeed, there was disconcerting evidence that contact with the white man only introduced them to vice and disease. By the end of the eighteenth century the prospect seemed slight that they would amalgamate with other Americans. Clearly they were separate and independent nations.

That was inconvenient. The lands they occupied were within the territorial jurisdiction of the United States and were covetously regarded by settlers and speculators. The polite fiction had it that the tribes, uncivilized as they were, needed the tutelage of the Great Chiefs in the East who best knew how to safeguard the Indian interests. Solemnly signed treaties spelled out the kindly arrangement. However, they left unsolved the question of how to remove the obstacles to the advance of settlement.

President Jefferson supplied the practical answer in his advice to Governor Harrison of the Indiana Territory: It was the duty of the Indians to *withdraw themselves to the culture of a small piece of land.* Soon they would *perceive how useless to them were extensive forests* and would be willing *to pare them off from time to time in exchange for necessities for their farms and families.* That inclination could be promoted by setting up trading houses where *the good and influential among them would run* up *debts beyond what they could pay* and then would be willing *to lop them off by a cession of lands.* The formula only omitted the whiskey. That was the usual course, before the Revolution and after. Broken promises, bloody wars and deceptive treaties marked the whole history of Indian removal. But these tactics, which might well be expected of European despots, were not appropriate to the representatives of the free people of a republic.

The intellectual question remained. Wistfully, Americans told themselves that the Indians really did not like it where they were. Beyond the Mississippi there was more than enough space where they could better lead the life they preferred. It was in their own self-interest that they should go, until some future time when they would be able to associate, as they should, on equal terms with other Americans. There was no better answer.

The situation of the Negroes was more anomalous still, for they lived not in tribes of their own but thoroughly intermingled with the rest of the population. Earlier in the century, slavery had explained their differences from the whites; lacking freedom or the capacity to make choices, they were cut off from the influences that formed other Americans. But after 1750, and increasingly as the Revolution approached, slavery was condemned as an evil. Those who claimed the natural rights of life, liberty and the pursuit of happiness for themselves could hardly deny them to others. In all the Northern states, slavery disappeared with Independence.

Thereafter, it was expected, the blacks would merge with their neighbors. Few in number, they readily made a place for themselves in the expanding cities. Their peculiarities were explicable in terms of environmental forces; even their color — the result of long exposure to the tropic sun or, as Dr. Benjamin Rush explained, of a disease that had once raged through Africa — ultimately would fade to the whiteness befitting Americans. The polite stanzas of Phillis Wheatley's little book of poems, published in Boston, showed the levels of cultivation to which a former slave could aspire.

In the plantation South, the question had altogether different dimensions. The men of Jefferson's generation were no less ready than their countrymen in the North to admit that slavery was an evil. Abolition was a moral imperative and would shortly have to be effected. The difficulty arose from adjustments to the political and social implications. Gradual emancipation created more problems than it solved; freedom extended to some Negroes made control of the rest less secure, and unscrupulous slaveholders were sometimes tempted to use manumission to rid themselves of those too old to work. Liberty, when it came, would have to come to all.

Yet the consequences of such a radical change were unthinkable. In a republic, citizenship went with freedom; when the Negroes ceased to be slaves they would become potential voters and in some places would surely acquire political power. Was it reasonable to suppose that men who had suffered the cruelest wrongs for generations would then fail to seek revenge? Their own sense of guilt for the crimes of their ancestors gave Southerners the answer even before Toussaint in Santo Domingo confirmed it. Emancipation would lead to violence, bloodshed and the collapse of all order. Everyone would suffer in the aftermath.

Prudential considerations added to the hesitation. Would the freedmen be able to support themselves without capital and land? Those who drove the reluctant bondsman to the fields could not see in him the makings of an enterprising yeoman. Was the Negro really constitutionally equal? Those who did not treat him so found it hard to believe. Would it be safe to mix, on terms of equality, two races so different in manners and antecedents? The masters who had always had their will of the slaves feared the loss of advantages power gave them. The doubts were not strong enough to persuade many to argue that slavery ought to be preserved; but they were strong enough to postpone the day of decision.

Better wait. Soon, perhaps, the problem would solve itself. With the author of the widely read legal commentary on Blackstone, St. George Tucker, many a planter indulged in the dream. If only the Negro would go away! There was land enough in the West, or better still, in Mexico. There the freedmen, removed from the scenes of their past indignities, separated from the masters who had once wronged them, could build their own life in their own way. No doubt the future would reveal the means of consummating this happy outcome. The Negro, like the Indian, was assigned a promissory portion of the New World. For the time being, these people were awkward exceptions to the American's conception of his own identity as a new man, liberated from his past and free to live as an individual by the rule of risks of his own choosing.

For the Americans there was always the future to redeem the shortcomings of the present; their experience and ideas encouraged a faith in improvement and infused fresh vitality into the old conception of mission.

The image of the city on the hill had persisted since the days of the first settlers; and the events of the revolutionary period only confirmed the certitude that a great destiny awaited the Republic. The environment shaped the character of men; and there was nowhere a more bounteous setting for achievement than the continent the Americans were in process of occupying. Painstakingly Jefferson, in the *Notes on Virginia*, marshaled the evidence: nature here was on a grander scale; man would be so too. He thereby reaffirmed Franklin's earlier estimate of the future grandeur of the country.

Their own character was also evidence that the Americans were a new race whose labors and posterity would one day cause great changes in the world. In them were incorporated the sum of all past achievements; and the situation which had made them a nation would soon give their experience universal significance. They were, Crèvecoeur proclaimed, *the western pilgrims, carrying along with them that great mass of arts, sciences, vigor and industry which began long since in the east*. They were the heirs of all the ages, the vanguard of human destiny.

The Revolution proved it was all true, not only by its success, but by its implications for the rest of the world. Enthusiasm, in 1794, swept that cautious divine the Reverend Timothy Dwight into poetry. He hailed the Republic, *by heaven design'd, th' example bright, to renovate mankind*. Its sons would soon claim their home on far Pacific shores, and *their rule, religion, manners, arts, convey and spread their freedom to the Asian sea*. And actions spoke louder than words. In 1806, a small group of students in Williams College, in rural Massachusetts, recalled their duty to the millions living in *the moral darkness of Asia*. Their resolution to do something led to the formation of the American Board of Commissioners for Foreign Missions in 1810. Soon farm wives in every countryside would be saving pennies for the redemption and Americanization of the waiting millions.

Behind such efforts was the utter conviction that the American brought to his mission the irresistible weapons of an entirely new political and social system. Unhampered by a feudal past, he had created forms of government grounded on natural law and universally applicable. His situation made him a trader; nature, which did nothing in vain, had so arranged his geography that all nations, *by a free intercourse with this vast and fertile continent would again become brothers* and forget war. And above all, he had space — to advance agriculture to its summit of perfection and to welcome, in limitless numbers, immigrants from every end of the earth who, becoming free, would all become American.

Laboriously Joel Barlow measured the syllables in the endless lines of his epic. As a youth he had fought for Independence, then had tried his hand at diplomacy and had done what he could for the revolution in France. After years away he came back home in 1805 and converted an earlier innocent poem into a gigantic glorification of his country. *The Columbiad* surveyed the whole span of human history, past and prospective. At the end, man — liberated from fraud, folly, and error, holding sovereign sway over earth's total powers which yield their fruit at his mere call — has banished contention and bound all regions in one confederate league of peace. This was the work the first American, Columbus, had initiated when

> *his pinions led the trackless way*
> *and taught mankind such useful deeds to dare,*
> *To trace new seas and happy nations rear;*
> *Till by fraternal hands their sails unfurl'd*
> *Have waved at last in union o'er the world.*

This was the work it was the destiny of other Americans to pursue.

12

Reorganizing the Polity

HAVING EFFECTED *the greatest and completest revolution the world ever knew,* the Americans were sure they could contribute to humanity the finest system of government ever devised by men. Already in the middle of the eighteenth century their polity had operated effectively; it maintained order and yet assured individual rights. Its only difficulties arose from the interference of outsiders, and Independence ended those. Meanwhile, years of debate had habituated the colonists to the examination of first principles and to experimentation with existing forms. Unembarrassed by the vestiges of a despotic past, they fully expected to be able to fashion the means of ruling themselves in accordance with reason and the laws of nature.

It was not necessary to begin altogether afresh in 1776. Americans believed that their ancestors, coming from England, had not brought with them laws adapted to a *people grown old in the habits of vice,* but had very early established a constitution of government by their own authority, with virtue for its principle and the public good as its object. It remained only to adjust that system to new conditions.

There was, therefore, remarkable continuity in the local arrangements that most affected the mass of men. The New England town meetings continued to choose selectmen and to regulate life in much the same way in 1810 as in 1750. The vestry, the mayors and aldermen, the county courts and the sheriffs functioned after Independence as they had before. The Revolution prevented Loyalist judges from sitting and replaced Tories with patriots; but the nature of the posts and the duties attached to them did not change. The fact that officials, formerly appointed, were now to be elected made little difference; voters usually chose the men with local power just as the governor had.

The Revolution was far more disruptive at the provincial level of government. The severance of the ties to the Crown removed the authority under which the whole apparatus of power had been organized. There was no longer a royal governor to exercise executive power, to summon the assembly, to make appointments, and to issue writs. That vacuum had to be filled. Furthermore, in many colonies the uppermost aristocratic group vanished; many had been close to England and became Tories, others were implicated in unpopular measures that preceded the break. The disappearance of imperial power forced the remaining agencies of government to make decisions about issues relatively new to them. Many colonists had resented the royal prerogative of conducting war and diplomacy, of issuing a currency, and of regulating trade. Now they had to devise means of managing these affairs by themselves.

In the decade of controversy before the Revolution, extra-legal groups had learned to function as shadow governments, sometimes with the connivance of established officials, sometimes in defiance of them. After the Stamp Act Congress of 1765, local committees of correspondence maintained contact with one another. They worked for compliance with the boycott that responded to the Townshend Acts and carried forward the successive stages of protest and rebellion against the Crown. As the crisis approached, they sent delegates to county conventions and, in time, representatives to provincial congresses which assumed the power to rule by either supplanting or infiltrating the assemblies.

Until 1776, of course, these arrangements were of dubious legality. But they nevertheless enabled the provinces to raise military forces, to make ordinances for the orderly conduct of their own affairs, to collect money by taxation and loans, and to wage war. The colonies had in effect become sovereign states.

Yet the issue of legitimacy was troubling. Engaged as they were in resistance to their monarch, the colonists had to assure themselves and others that their steps were legal. They wished to justify not only their own disobedience but also their own claim to future obedience. They had no desire to open the way to the perpetual disorder that would follow if any future group of malcontents were to feel free to assert the right to revolt when it wished.

The rebels were therefore also the founders of states. It was, they argued, proper to resist the king because he had, by arbitrary and usurpative actions, in effect abdicated. By doing so he had left his former subjects in a state of nature; and it was appropriate that they should themselves provide for their future government by new compacts. In the early months of 1776 New Hampshire, South Carolina and New Jersey adopted constitutions; and in May the Continental Congress urged the other provinces to make such arrangements as would *best conduce to the happiness and safety of their constituents in particular and America in general.*

By 1780, all the states had devised constitutions which embodied the consent of the people, except Connecticut and Rhode Island, which assumed that their old charters were the equivalent. The forms were remarkably similar. A Bill of Rights set forth the purpose of government and enumerated the inherent rights of which the citizens, entering into a state of society, could not deprive their posterity; namely, the enjoyment of life and liberty, with the means of acquiring and possessing property, and pursuing and obtaining happiness and safety. There was some caprice in the specific enumeration of rights, although trial by jury and freedom of speech were generally mentioned; the compilers were not making an exhaustive catalogue but illustrating the types of abuses to be prevented. The constitutions went on to provide for an elected chief executive, for a legislature which succeeded to the duties of the assembly and council, and for an independent judicial system. These arrangements were patterned on the experience of the colonies, except that power now emanated from the governed rather than from the Crown.

The statemakers were anxious to avoid the great defect of

provincial politics, the ability of the governor to use office as a means of developing his own faction. They therefore insisted that most positions were to be elective and that all were to be held for a limited term. For the same reason, the legislative, executive and judicial branches were also to be separate from one another. These provisions would forestall the emergence of a body of placemen who might interfere with the free decisions of the people. In this respect, too, colonial experience was a guide.

The character of the struggle against Great Britain also made necessary some general agency to carry on first the protest, and then the war, in the name of all the rebels. But here, experience was no guide at all. Each province had developed separately and each now became sovereign. Neither their own earlier practices nor contemporary political theory offered a clue to the means of uniting a congeries of separate states into an efficient larger entity.

The committees of correspondence had already established links in a chain that stretched from Maine to Georgia. But in the crisis of 1774 the Americans relied not on a national government but on a Continental Congress composed of delegates from each province. So long as future relations with the mother country were unclear, anything more than a provisional arrangement seemed unwise. Yet that subterfuge forced the Congress to conduct diplomacy and carry on the war, handicapped by cumbrous machinery. It was not a legislature but a gathering of the ambassadors of separate though allied states. It did its work through committees and depended for support on the individual states to which it could address requests but not orders. For years there was not even a formal ratification of the Articles of Confederation, for those states like Maryland, which had no western lands, refused to accede until those which did, like Virginia, surrendered their holdings to the United States.

In 1781, Virginia yielded, Maryland ratified and the Articles established a perpetual union. By then, however, the theory of a league of independent states was increasingly becoming a fiction. The United States existed as an entity in its own right; it controlled extensive territories which it ruled through ordinances; and it exercised some, although fragmentary, powers of government. It could declare war and make peace, coin money, charter a bank, establish weights and measures, operate the post office, and admit new states to the union; it thus inherited the general powers formerly exercised by the Crown. But the states would not trust it to interfere with local affairs, or to levy taxes or to regulate commerce, powers they had earlier denied the king in Parliament.

The deficiencies of an arrangement based on pre-Revolutionary standards became particularly apparent after 1783 when the country attempted to negotiate treaties of commerce with foreign powers yet was unable to level obstacles to trade among the states. The debt incurred during the war was unredeemed, current revenues were uncertain, and there was no hope of undertaking significant interstate projects of any sort. These weaknesses impressed the commissioners from Virginia, Pennsylvania, New York, New Jersey and Delaware, summoned in 1786 to a conference at Annapolis to discuss improvements in internal navigation. They concluded that some thorough revision of the general government was necessary; at their suggestion the Continental Congress summoned a convention to meet in Philadelphia in 1787.

The sense of urgency had mounted by the time the fifty-five members of the Constitutional Convention assembled. Shays's Rebellion in Massachusetts had been repressed; but the effort by debt-ridden farmers to prevent courts from sitting had revealed the existence of disorderly elements that threatened to negate the positive achievements of the Revolution. Many of the participants in the task of revision were lawyers, and the others were respectable merchants and planters. Men of property they were, of course, conscious of their own interests and of those of the states which had sent them. But they were also aware of a national interest.

Among them were nearly all the promoters of Independence. Young, almost all of them veterans of the war, they were concerned with the necessity for radical action to bring the revolutionary ideals to fulfillment. They were, Madison thought, about to decide the fate of republican government in the whole world. The general air of earnest endeavor created a mood for compromise; even those who disagreed with the final document did not vote against it, but considering the plan the best that could be obtained, acquiesced in it. The results were impressive.

On the points on which the Convention could follow experience there was little difficulty. The federal government acquired, in addition to the powers of the Confederacy, those of levying a tariff and certain internal taxes, of regulating trade, and of establishing uniform rules of naturalization and bankruptcy. Its three branches were generally modeled after those of the states.

But in many matters the framers of the Constitution lacked precedent. They forbade the states to print paper money or to abrogate the obligations of contracts without giving thought to how those prohibitions, useful to the development of commerce, would be enforced. On the other hand, some ingenious devices were wasted on difficulties that never materialized. It seemed implausible, for instance, to suppose that the people of a vast country could choose a President and Vice President directly; electors in each state therefore were to select their favorite candidates, a joint session of Congress was to compose a slate of the five persons with the largest number of votes, and from that slate the House of Representatives would choose first a President and then a Vice President. The scheme was never to function that way. In other cases, compromises resolved divergent points of view. For the purpose of reckoning representation, a slave was counted as three-fifths of a person in the expectation that the quick disappearance of such bondage would resolve that anomaly. The rights of the large states were recognized by allocating seats in the House on the basis of population, while the small ones were appeased with a uniform number of places in the Senate.

Submitted to the Continental Congress, the Constitution was sent, by a unanimous vote, to each of the states for ratification. A long debate followed, while the special conventions to consider the document were elected and convened. The canvass elicited one important objection. The framers had not included a Bill of Rights; and the First Congress was ultimately to remedy that deficiency. No other changes were necessary for approval. In general, the new Constitution met initial hostility from those suspicious of any large concentration of power removed from local sources. Elements content with their own position in state politics and fearful that a new order might affect them adversely also opposed it. On the other hand, the document drew support from those anxious to stabilize the results of the Revolution by creating a forceful national government and from groups which sought the same end in order to further commercial interests.

More important than any such alignments was the persuasive effect of the extended discussions in the press and in the ratifying conventions which made clear the limited powers of the new government. One by one the states adopted it, with the critical votes coming in Pennsylvania, Massachusetts, New York and Virginia. Rhode Island, unwilling to forego its freedom to print paper money and to trade as it liked, remained apart until 1790; but the new government could take form with the election of 1788.

In little more than a decade the Americans had recast their political institutions, replacing the forms inherited from their period of English tutelage with new ones of their own design. The achievement was substantial and proved remarkably durable. In part, it was the product of the ability of its architects — George Washington, Benjamin Franklin, John Adams, Thomas Jefferson, James Madison and Alexander Hamilton were only the best known of men who brought to the task of framing the federal and state constitutions unusual skills acquired from experience and reading. But not genius alone accounted for the solidity of the edifice they reared; it rested on a solid foundation of institutions developed in the colonial past and it was buttressed by widespread agreement about the nature and purpose of government. A consensus on general propositions was the stabilizing force that induced compromise in every clash of immediate interests.

There was never a question, for instance, but that a single nation would emerge from the war. Conceivably the alliance could have dissolved in 1783 and each of the sovereign states gone its own way. There was no legal impediment; indeed, Vermont flirted with the idea of union with Canada and the New England Federalists of 1803 also toyed with secession. However tolerable in theory, in practice any such developments were unthinkable. The idea of a common national identity that required expression in a political form was too strong. Many factors had contributed to that sentiment — the presence of hostile neighbors, the western lands held by the Union, and the internal migrations which tied the people of the various states together. Above all, the awareness of a shared situation forestalled any serious discussion of an alternative to national union in some form. The Revolution in which all had participated could only be justified by its outcome, a single people under a single government. The debatable questions were of means rather than of end.

Nor was there any dispute but that the American government was to be republican, although the unanimous opinion of the political theorists the colonists respected held that only a king could govern a great country. A republic was appropriate to small areas like the ancient and medieval free cities; experience everywhere had demonstrated that the increase in size also increased the tendency toward monarchy. The classical precedents of Greece and Rome were sobering evidence.

Nineteenth-century European revolutionaries accepted the logic of that argument and provided a steady market for German princelings. The Americans denied it. Except for Hamilton — and he not publicly — no American expressed the desire for a monarchy. No alternative to a republic was conceivable, because the concept meant much more in the new nation than the absence of a crowned head. The elective principle implied also that no person, of whatever rank or status, had any vested right to office. The power to rule was not bestowed by heredity, purchase or favor but by the consent of the governed. Officers drawn from among the people by *frequent, certain and regular elections* and *at fixed periods reduced to a private station* would be *restrained from oppression* by sharing the burdens common to all. Washington was the modern Cincinnatus who, holding great power, willingly yielded it to return to the plow. It followed that there were to be no recognized signs of rank nor any titles of nobility. The Americans were willing to give their President the executive powers of the king but not his regal qualities. The First Congress after a long debate concluded that the proper style of address was Mr. President and it refused Vice-President John Adams a canopied chair from which to preside over the Senate because of its resemblance to a throne. That was one of the meanings Americans gave to republican equality.

Officeholders were merely the temporary custodians of power because the state belonged to no man or no group. It was a Republic or — in its English equivalent — a Commonwealth. Government was instituted *not for the profit, honor, or private interest of any one man, family, or class of men* but *for the common good of the people, nation or community.* It was to promote that general welfare that each citizen covenanted with the whole people, exchanging the agreement to obey for the assurance that the laws would be for the common benefit, protection and security of all.

The magistrates of a republic derived their powers from the people, *were their trustees and servants and at all times amenable to them.* The Constitution spelled out the detailed terms of the relationship. Contemporary political theory, the origins of the colonies in company charters, the federal theology of the Puritans, the practices of the towns, and the experience of the frontier all emphasized the importance of a written compact. Both the rulers and the ruled required a precise definition of which actions were proper, the former, so that they would not transgress, the latter so that they could be vigilant in defense of their rights.

It was not feasible that all the citizens who consented to be governed should participate directly in the process; *they could not march five hundred miles, nor spare the time, nor find a space to meet.* Perforce they acted through a representative system which permitted a balance among the various groups in society and therefore was more efficient both in advancing the interests of all and protecting the liberty of each. It was only prudent to arrange the mode of selecting officers so that the wisest would be chosen. Property qualifications were means to that end, for they restricted voting and officeholding to such men as had given sufficient evidence of permanent common interest with, and attachment to, the community. In a society which offered to all an access to property, the ability to acquire it was a test, as it were, of competence.

In any case, men of every degree retained their natural rights which governments could only advance, never restrict. Thus the states which wished to do so could support established churches; but they could not restrict the exercise of religion as conscience dictated, for reason and free inquiry were the only effectual agents against error. The constitutions set outside the competence of government all matters in which the individual could act for himself without injury to his neighbors.

Having framed constitutions that rested squarely upon these agreed-on assumptions, the political leaders of the 1780's might well have indulged in optimistic self-congratulations. Instead, they set about sounding warnings of impending disaster. Even under a republic, they suspected, reason and concern for the general welfare might not always be the guides of the rulers. The source of these fears was frequently and clearly described. Human nature was subject to the corrupting effects of pride, passion and avarice, which unfortunately influenced men's political behavior. Conflicts of faction and interest had subverted colonial legislatures; they might do the same to the republic!

They did, although not with the dire consequences the constitution-makers anticipated. The play of faction and interest in provincial politics had been as prominent a characteristic after 1750 as before; and the Revolution, far from eliminating these factors, increased the scope of their operations. The states at war had contracts, subsidies, and bounties of which to dispose; and they printed paper money and regulated prices. On these issues groups divided much as before. With the return of peace each sovereign commonwealth was able to establish land and trade policies, to create banks and charter corporations, to take a stand on religious and other freedoms, and to enact new legislation touching on every aspect of life. On these matters, too, men divided into factions and interests.

The Continental Congress, having little autonomous power, was not as frequently the seat of such clashes until it acquired control of the western lands; then it had to decide among contending views of how to dispose of these possessions. Under the new Constitution, Congress had wide-reaching prerogatives; and now politics quickly resumed some of the familiar features of the past. The first Secretary of the Treasury, Alexander Hamilton, framed the critical questions; his three reports on economic policy envisioned a prominent role for the national government in the development of the productive system. To re-establish credit, he asked the country to assume all the state debts contracted during the Revolution and to redeem them, as well as the bonds of the Continental Congress, in full. He proposed the charter of a Bank of the United States to maintain a sound yet flexible currency throughout the country. And he asked for a protective tariff to encourage domestic manufactures. He got all except the last, but in the process stirred up speculators against taxpayers, merchants against agriculturists, and those who feared further extensions of national power against those who favored it.

So much was familiar. But as the eighteenth century drew to a close, political debate also resounded with new tones.

On January 30, 1798, the House of Representatives being in session in Philadelphia, Mr. Griswold of Connecticut made some allusion to a story that Mr. Lyon of Vermont had been obliged during the war to wear a wooden sword for cowardice in the field. Upon this, Mr. Lyon spit in Mr. Griswold's face. Some days later, Mr. Griswold went to McAlister's store on Chestnut Street and bought the biggest hickory stick available. He proceeded to the House where, in the presence of the whole Congress and with Mr. Speaker urging him on, he beat Mr. Lyon about the head and shoulders. An effort to censure both actors in the drama failed by one vote.

The incident had long been brewing. The Vermonter, *a strange, offensive brute, too wild to tame, too base to shoot,* had made enemies from the moment of his arrival. Born in Ireland, he had come to the New World an indentured servant, married a niece of Ethan Allen and, settling on the Lake Champlain frontier, had prospered and entered politics. A resolute foe of aristocratic tendencies, he had antagonized the friends of the new President, John Adams, one of whose followers had appealed to men with the *better blood and accent of Americans* to keep in check *plebeians with an Irish brogue flung on these shores from Europe.* Lyon had boldly spoken back. He had never before *heard of gentlemen boasting of their blood. He could not say, it was true, that he was descended from the bastards of Oliver Cromwell, or from the Puritans who punished their horses for breaking the Sabbath, or from those who persecuted the Quakers or hanged the witches. He could, however, say that this was his country, because he had no other, and he owned a share of it which he had bought by means of honest industry. Being independent, he called no man's blood in question.*

For a long time now such bold fellows had shown a growing inclination to challenge the right of their betters to govern. Already in the 1750's the lower social orders were disruptive. In some provinces, the division into "new lights" and "old lights" effected by the Great Awakening had given form to these contests; elsewhere back-country people with little claim to dignity had asserted their rights as freemen and challenged the Eastern gentry; and urban artisans had disputed the primacy of the merchants. The Revolution had encouraged these rude fellows. Called on to protest, to fight in the armies and to show concern for the rights of man, they became active participants in government, citizens rather than subjects; and they showed no disposition to sink back to an inferior position when the crisis was over. Moreover, they could remember when those who now presumed to lead were themselves men of small estates. The social turmoil of the war period had cut away the old aristocracy and made meaner people persons of power, riches and influence. But the conflict had, after all, not been waged to give them the pomp and privilege for which they hankered.

The role of the populace was still limited and qualified. In the older states it looked for leadership to the gentry, the great merchants, and the lawyers; and it took a place in the following of one or another of the factions that struggled for power. But in new states, like Vermont and Kentucky, the leaders bubbled up from below. And everywhere masses of men, imbued with egalitarian sentiment, sought to express themselves through the governments they had created, whatever the law said of a property qualification.

In many states they had become an active force in politics. The leaders of some factions, like John Hancock of Massachusetts, George Clinton of New York and Patrick Henry of Virginia, themselves wealthy lawyers, planters or merchants, nevertheless learned to draw upon the new source of support; and the intrusion of that element compelled other office-seekers to curry its favor in elections. The press became an agency for diffusing opinion to the populace and debate acquired heat and passion.

The division polarized briefly after 1795. The labored efforts to maintain peace in the war between France and Britain had set the American partisans of the two countries to arguing with one another; and Jay's Treaty that year precipitated the issue. The friends of France saw it as a craven surrender to a former enemy and a base betrayal of a former friend. Furthermore it seemed a step toward subversion of republican principles engineered by those who themselves wished the return of a monarchical aristocracy. In response, the friends of the English connection accused their rivals of a desire to imitate

Gallic anarchy and infidelity; and made out the outlines of a vast international conspiracy of illuminati designed to overthrow all existing order. The political contest thus acquired an ideological overtone that set Francophiles and Anglophiles off in two distinct parties, one Democratic-Republican and the other Federalist. The former tended to oppose, the latter to support, the Hamiltonian economic policies.

The elections of 1796 and 1800 hardened these lines. Washington had come to the Presidency by acclamation, but no one commanded such universal support after his withdrawal. The contestants, anxious to generate a national following, could only do so by interstate alliances which fell generally within the party configuration. The campaigns therefore further spread the impression of a clear-cut division.

The reality was somewhat less distinct than the orators made it. Adams's great conflict in office was with Hamilton, the Federalist; and Jefferson in power was most intense in his struggle with Aaron Burr, the Democratic-Republican. The Federalists were no more anxious to destroy the republic than the Republicans were to imitate the anarchy of the French Revolution, which had, in any case, already settled down in a conservative pattern. The truth was, as Jefferson's first inaugural address put it, Americans were all Republicans, all Federalists.

The party lines did not hold long after his first election. The extreme Federalists, particularly in New England, turned pessimists; *the vices of the government were incurable.* Their advocacy of war in 1798, their support of the measures to limit free speech in the Alien and Sedition Acts, and their loose talk about secession alienated most of their support. They ceased to be a consequential political force. In some places the old labels persisted, but they applied to the local and state groupings of factions and interests which were still the organizing elements in the operations of government. There was, however, this difference: the mass of people drawn into participation remained to be reckoned with; they could be appeased not with privilege but only with such actions as furthered the common welfare. Increasingly those who hoped to rule with their consent would have to take cognizance of their wishes.

The responsible actors in American politics after 1800 realized the need for sensitivity to the wishes of the people, for government was not an institution that sustained itself but one that existed only through the support of those it served. Its structure and forms therefore were not immutable, but subject to change. The constitution-makers had not been infallible and conditions they had not anticipated had already called for substantial alterations before Jefferson took office. The electoral college, for instance, never worked; Washington's popularity made it unnecessary in the first two elections, and party contests made it obsolete in the next two. The Twelfth Amendment took the first step in converting the election of the President into a canvass of opinion in the whole country.

Other changes appeared without debate, in response to practical experience. Thus, the federal bureaucracy proved so large it could not function directly under the President and it was therefore shaped into four departments, each with a secretary at its head. By 1800 the secretaries were meeting regularly as a cabinet to advise the Chief Executive. The cabinet took the place the Council had held in the colonies, a place the Senate had been designed to fill, but which it had refused.

Yet there were limits; change was tolerable only through orderly procedures. The will of a momentary majority expressed in the acts of Congress or a legislature could not deprive men of their rights nor alter the forms established by their constitutions. When the Supreme Court had refused to rule upon the Alien and Sedition Acts, the Virginia and Kentucky resolutions had suggested alternative ways of testing them. But John Marshall, who became Chief Justice in the same year that Jefferson became President, was convinced that questions of constitutionality were primarily the responsibility of the courts, a doctrine he asserted in the case of *Marbury* v. *Madison*.

Jefferson, who suspected that the judges sought to frustrate the popular will, tried to get rid of offenders like Samuel Chase by the process of impeachment. He failed. Though he commanded a majority in Congress, even his own followers were reluctant to destroy the independence of the judiciary.

In the last analysis, the means of effecting change were still available. The people, not the judges, were the ultimate interpreters of the Constitution, through the amending process. The Eleventh Amendment, which protected the states against suits by individuals, had thus overturned the unpopular decision in the case of *Chisholm* v. *Georgia*. All the fundamental charters contained provisions for revision or for periodic review; and several states had already rewritten their constitutions. No one expected that the work of one generation would forever bind its successors. So long as government recognized the obligation of eliciting consent, it would be responsive to changing needs; and if it were not, a free people would rise up once more to assert their rights. Government would thus be constantly refined and improved and approach ever closer to conformity with the basic laws of nature that regulated man's relations with his fellows.

This comfortable assumption both explained the achievements and made tolerable the deficiencies of the present. It was admirably in accord with the temper of a society still engaged in disorderly growth. Americans could envision the most daring leaps into the future because firm continuities with the past sustained them. They confidently expected that their polity, product of their own experience, would continue to adapt itself to their development as a people. That was a reassuring basis for consensus in a period when many other aspects of their existence were in constant flux.

13

The Prospects of a New Society

"*The American war is over,*" wrote Benjamin Rush in 1783, "*but this is far from being the case with the American Revolution.*" New men in a new world, with a new government at their disposal, would certainly create a totally new society, unlike the old in its reasonable and orderly adherence to the laws of nature. Americans thereafter were constantly being enjoined to unshackle their minds and act like independent beings. They had an interest of their own to augment and defend, an empire to raise and support and a national character to establish and extend by their wisdom and virtue. Effort and determination would create a culture that would justify their history.

It was not as easy as the phrases of the orators put it. The Revolution influenced the existing productive system, social order, and modes of expression only to a limited degree; and it created new problems as often as it solved old ones. Where a basis was already laid before 1774, independence released latent energies for great achievements. But where the materials had before been lacking, the mere separation from Europe was not enough to compensate and ambitions outran ability.

The war upset still further the unstable economy of the colonies.

Their prosperity had rested upon a trade that ran mostly outside the normal imperial channels but that found carrying profits for the merchants and markets for the farmers and planters. The recurrent boycotts and the efforts to enforce the Acts of Trade shook severely the flimsy expedients by which the merchants got by. The years of fighting after 1775 were further disruptive. Shortages of manpower and of supplies plagued the districts through which the armies maneuvered and the currency plummeted in disorder as the states and the Congress turned to the printing press to finance the struggle.

Peace was slow to bring relief. Not until the organization of the government under the Constitution did the more pressing fiscal problems abate; and even thereafter currency and credit were still subject to violent fluctuations that seriously affected the internal commerce of the country. More important was the dilemma of the overseas traders, now excluded from the imperial systems of the great powers. The slowly negotiated treaties of commerce with the neutrals did not compensate for their losses. Lord Sheffield had grounds for his gleeful anticipation, in an influential pamphlet published in 1783, that the whole American experiment would soon collapse in failure.

American merchants, however, were habituated to operating in difficult situations. They had earlier learned the tactics of evasion and made crisis their opportunity. Fortunately, plenty of capital was at hand for their ventures. While the speculative atmosphere of the times brought some to the disaster of the debtor's cell, it raised others to affluence. Contracts to supply the army, grants of various privileges, and investments in depreciated bonds or in land built up sizable surpluses that could be hazarded in new enterprises. The fluid situation also nurtured the disposition to take risks that saved American trade after 1783.

The old firms, after the peace, took up the interrupted patterns of direct exchange with England. Other merchants found their chance in service as neutral carriers for both sides in the renewed outbreak of war in Europe in 1792. More important, energetic, enterprising men were able to penetrate markets from which they had theretofore been excluded.

Before the Revolution the fabled East of India and China had been the preserve of the East India Company and almost entirely closed to colonial vessels. Now adventurous skippers began to bring their craft into these strange harbors. While the English, French, Dutch, Spanish and Portuguese were occupied in war, the Americans were able to bring pepper from Sumatra, cottons from India, tea and porcelain from China, not only to the New World but also to the markets of the Old. New York and Philadelphia merchants combined to send the *Empress of China* to Canton in 1784. Two years later the *Grand Turk* brought a cargo to Salem from Mauritius and the *Chesapeake* reached a port in India from Baltimore.

Eastward or westward, it did not matter; profits lay in both directions. The trade had no regular routes, for it depended upon the hazards of fortune and the wit of the enterprisers. The Boston ship *Columbia*, 212 tons, left home in 1788, rounded Cape Horn and set its course north to the mouth of the river that was to bear its name. It remained there for months loading a cargo of furs supplied by the Indians. Sailing westward, it went on to Canton, exchanged pelts for tea, and finally reached home in 1790. Imitators quickly followed, sometimes enlivening their trips with stops at Hawaii or other Pacific islands.

Some ship captains preferred to face the rising rather than the setting sun. The *Belisarius* of the Crowninshield family left Salem in November, 1795, bound for India by way of the Cape of Good Hope with a mixed cargo of rum, iron and specie. In March, 1796, having rounded the Cape, it stopped at the Ile de France where it found an advantageous opportunity to take on a load of coffee destined for Bordeaux. Turning back, the ship reached that port in November. It then returned to the Ile de France carrying miscellaneous French goods and continued on to Danish Tranquebar and French Pondicherry in south India. It shuttled back to the island once more before continuing on to Calcutta, which it reached in December, 1797. There at last it took on the India cargo which it brought back to the United States. In all, the venture lasted more than three years, but it brought a handsome return.

Any extravagant notion might pay off. Traders took it into their heads to cut up the New England ponds and send ice to the Indies. They succeeded. Other merchants sent fish, grain and tobacco to the Baltic and the Mediterranean and wove those areas into the patterns of their commerce. There was no great port into which American vessels did not venture. Nothing was permanent; all was unstable and laden with risk in such business. But it was enormously profitable while it lasted. When William Gray moved to Boston in 1809 he owned thirty-six vessels and was worth three million dollars. He had started in Salem with nothing.

A booming traffic linked the merchants with the interior of the country. The eastern routes were more heavily traveled than before; and west of the mountains a growing fleet of flatboats carried goods along the rivers of the Mississippi basin. New towns bustled with activity at each node of trade as ambitious men appraised the means of linking the undeveloped potential of the West with the trade of the world.

At the forks of the Ohio, where Washington and the French had only recently laid out their forts in the forest, Pittsburgh planned to be a metropolis. Buffalo on the Great Lakes and Richmond in the South had also become substantial cities by 1810. The raw, unfinished look of these places showed that their future was more important than their past. Their people as yet lacked the time to think of appearances. But the coastal ports now reflected the well-being of their merchants. Boston, Philadelphia, and New York, growing rapidly, burst out of their colonial confines. Hills were leveled, marshes and ponds were filled in to make room for the straight new streets along which the solid homes stretched in orderly rows.

Yet even in the older cities the impression of permanence and stability was deceptive. Merchants like Gray were in no position to relax and live easily on the fruits of their earnings. Their business fell into no routine pattern and their capital, growing as it was, required constant attention and constant reinvestment. Everyone engaged in trade was, by his situation, a perpetual speculator.

It was the same with many agriculturists. Maritime prosperity stimulated agricultural expansion. The high prices and inflation of the war years generally favored the market farmers; and the growth of cities and of trade expanded the outlets for their products. But their mode of production barely changed between 1750 and 1810; wheat and corn were planted as before and drovers still led the herds of cattle to nearby markets. The coastal fisheries which had suffered from British depredations during the war had reverted to their earlier state by the end of the century. But though these agriculturists profited by their labors, they could not expand the scale of their enterprises because the shortage of labor was more restrictive than ever. They too, therefore, accumulated surpluses available for speculation.

The position of the plantation South was more precarious still. Here the initial effect of independence was adverse. Deprived of English bounties and marketing facilities, the crops of the region languished. Some planters, particularly in South Carolina and Georgia, turned to the cultivation of cotton, which could be cheaply processed after Eli Whitney's invention of the gin. But most expected to convert their holdings to the diversified production of livestock, wheat and other cereals. The Chesapeake colonies had already begun to do so even before they felt the disruptive effects of the war. In any case, slavery was not likely long to endure; and the planters were not eager themselves to follow the plow, except in oratorical figures of speech. Their minds too turned frequently to the possible stroke of fortune that would bring them stability.

Speculation was every man's escape from inadequate reality. Merchants, farmers and planters all gambled on the future growth of the country. Timothy Dexter, in his great Newburyport house, showed that it could be done. Son of a poor farmer, apprenticed to a leather dresser, he had scraped along on his earnings and on the little property marriage to a widow brought him, until he decided to buy up depreciated continentals after the Revolution. Redemption put him on his feet. Then he flew off into profitable trading eccentricities, sending Bibles and warming pans to the West Indies, cornering the market in whalebone, and investing in bridges and real estate.

More sober men continued to ship timber from the Cape Fear, Mohawk and Piscataqua river valleys; they sought out bog iron to be worked up in scores of furnaces; and they built ingenious mills to turn wheat into flour and timber into boards. When boycott and war cut off the flow of textiles from Britain, thousands of households turned to spinning and weaving. At Lynn, Massachusetts, they made shoes, at Berlin, Connecticut, tinware of every shape, at Germantown, Pennsylvania, stockings, not for local use but to be shipped to distant ports. Local entrepreneurs were often the moving spirits. Mathew Lyon was typical. He had not only farmed in Vermont, but also speculated in land, worked up iron, made paper from basswood, fashioned ship timbers and traded with Montreal. More generally, in these ventures the merchant of the city and a local farmer or squire pooled capital and services.

Land remained the most attractive investment. The complexities of British politics had frustrated the companies that had schemed in the 1750's and 1760's to lay hold of tracts in the Ohio Valley. With Independence, control over the destiny of that region passed to an American Congress tempted by financial stringency to sell off large sections to speculators rather than wait for the slow arrival of actual settlers. The Land Ordinance of 1785 set up the machinery for sale and the Northwest Ordinance two years later created a pattern of government for the territories north of the Ohio River that reassured prospective purchasers. The Ohio and the Scioto companies, promoted by former revolutionary officers, each undertook to purchase more than a million acres; and scores of lesser speculators entered the field with projects of their own. Others took up state-owned lands from Maine to Georgia or bought and developed real estate in the cities.

Independence also enabled the new governments to grant corporate charters. They hoped thereby to create agencies that would perform some useful public function the state could not itself undertake. The shares quickly became media for speculation. Their purchasers gratified their desires for excitement, for gain, and for the satisfaction of acts of civic virtue. The grant of privilege in the charter also promised a hedge against the hazards of investment. Everyone who could lay hands on the cash hastened to get in on the good thing. Here was a more prudent form of the lottery, through which Americans had long tempered their generosity toward worthy causes with the teasing hope of fortune.

After 1790, the corporations multiplied at an astonishing rate. Each was a clear case. Commerce needed adequate currency and credit; a bank would supply it. Insurance would mitigate calculable risks of every sort. Turnpikes, bridges and canals would facilitate the movement of people and wares. Manufactories would set up mills and organize scattered households into an efficient system for producing the goods to move into the channels of trade. That no one knew just how to manage these enterprises seemed no obstacle at all; they would learn by doing. Not until after the company was organized did it look about for an engineer to build the canal or a cashier to run the bank.

The first promoters no doubt aspired to monopolies. They expected that the Massachusetts Bank or the Bank of New York would occupy the position in each state held by the Bank of England in the former mother country or the Bank of Amsterdam in Holland. There was not a chance of it. The Revolution left Americans with a lingering emotional hostility to monopoly; the very mention of the word set the inner Indian in every citizen to dumping tea in the harbor. Moreover, control of the state governments was too local and too unstable to permit any faction to exclude others entirely. Privileges granted *in consideration of services rendered to the public* ought to be available to anyone willing to serve. If a bank would help the trade of Boston, why should not Salem be similarly assisted; and if Salem, why not Newburyport? And if one bank was useful, would not two be more useful, or three? If there was land for one company, there ought to be as much for another. The schemes piled up, one atop the other.

Everyone wished to take a part; but not everyone could do so and those who could not resented both their own exclusion and the superior fortune of those who could. Usually, the subsistence farmers and artisans lacked the temperament and the capital for plunging. Timothy Dexter was exceptional; most leather dressers remained what they were either out of pride in their craft or because they lacked margin with which to speculate. Yet the tailor or carpenter who stayed at his trade, the husbandman who remained in the home of his birth, lost his share of the American future. Worse! Though the journeyman earned good wages and the master good fees and every farmer could feed himself, they were plagued by fluctuating prices and were often short of the cash to pay the taxes that more speculative men accepted as a matter of course.

The very improvements that benefited others damaged the artisans and the subsistence farmers. The former began to resent their dependence upon the merchants who managed the market and the latter felt no neighborliness toward the miller who took their tolls. All men without a surplus slid easily into debt and, once enmeshed, could rarely extricate themselves. Bitterness at their plight made some rise up with Shays in Massachusetts or with the whiskey rebels in Pennsylvania; others vented their anger at the *aristocrats* in politics. More frequently, they sank where they were in apathy, or moved away.

A second chance — or a third — was the ultimate promise of the American future, even for the failures. Bankrupts who appeased their creditors started over again. If the fields were barren and stony here, they were lush and verdant there. If the carpenter or blacksmith was discontent in New York or Boston, Cincinnati and Louisville were eager for his services. There were still no limits to the West's capacity for satisfying the unfulfilled expectations of the East. The long procession that moved in Conestoga wagons across the mountain passes or that floated in flatboats down the rivers contained men and women of every degree and every occupation, some with capital and some with just hope. But all pursued a success the old places had not given them.

As earlier, Europeans filled out their ranks, with Scotland, Ireland, England and Germany supplying the greatest number. In the quarter-century after 1750, the volume of transatlantic traffic mounted steadily. Interrupted by the war, it resumed in 1783 and continued, although at a diminished level, into the nineteenth century. With these additions the population of the country swelled from just about one million in 1750 to well over seven million in 1810. The narrow band of provincial settlements along the coast had spread westward to form a great jagged triangle with its apex at the junction of the Ohio and the Mississippi, and with exposed outposts at New Orleans and St. Louis. And beyond lay still more space for the taking.

The haste for moving west was not reasonable; there was still plenty of empty land in the East. Nor did these migrations follow any plan; it was mostly each family for itself. But then the fantastic mercantile ventures displayed the same characteristic disorder.

An economy that was largely speculative made this growth possible. The looseness of all political and social institutions precluded the development of any orderly plan such as Hamilton had devised, for trade, industry, agriculture, or settlement. The result was frequent overextension followed by panic and failure and then a regrouping of energies for further effort.

The process was costly but also rewarding; it assured promoters of every sort the flexibility to take advantage of every opportunity. The tradition-bound were always the losers. Under such conditions, tinkerers like Oliver Evans or Robert Fulton or Eli Whitney could gain the ear of a backer — nothing ventured, nothing gained — and men were not afraid to make schemes that the future would underwrite. By 1810, the American productive system could assure few security in their fortunes, but it also left few without the scope for dreams of success.

The economy the Americans had fashioned was neither reasonable, nor orderly nor natural by their own standards. Its commerce was not *the simple art of the reciprocal supply of wants* but an adventurous pursuit of contrived opportunities. The farmers were not happy yeomen contentedly tilling ancestral acres, but speculators on the turn of the market. The Revolution had permitted tendencies already present in the New World of the seventeenth century at last to flower.

The members of a new society, unwilling to accept the limits of the past, would form their own fresh ideas and express themselves in novel artistic terms. *It was dishonorable to waste life in mimicking the follies of other nations and in basking in the sunshine of foreign glory.* Architecture, painting and literature must all reflect the new American spirit of republican vigor.

To effect those ends a broad system of education was necessary, preferably one unencumbered by European influences. In New Haven, Noah Webster gave up a lawyer's career and set himself to compiling a grammar and dictionary that would reveal to Americans how their language differed from English. Washington solicitously left funds in his will to establish a national university so that his countrymen would not have to go to foreign countries to acquire *the higher branches of erudition* and there be corrupted by *maxims not congenial with republicanism.* Georgia had already taken the precaution of barring any person educated abroad from public office for as long a period as he had spent away. As a matter of course, therefore, seven of the original state constitutions enjoined upon their governments the obligation of supporting learning.

Performance presented an ironic contrast to professions. Nine years after it adopted the high-sounding phrases of its Frame of Government, Massachusetts recognized reality and exempted towns with fewer than two hundred families from the old requirement that they maintain a grammar school. Nowhere in the country before 1810 was there the least improvement or change in the pattern of elementary education.

By contrast, the earlier multiplication of institutions of higher education continued; in 1800, the United States boasted twenty-two degree-granting colleges — more than France and England combined — in addition to a still larger number of academies of undefined scope which lacked that privilege. The new seminaries, however, were impressive neither for the learning they conveyed nor for the patriotism they nurtured. Local pride and sectarian zeal moved their founders, although rarely to the extent of eliciting substantial financial contributions. Driblets of state support were occasionally helpful, though small. But these remained modest enterprises; in 1804, the total budget of Union College came to four thousand dollars, and the University of North Carolina accommodated about twenty students in the shared facilities of a grammar school. A few possessed libraries and endowed professorships; and a few offered lectures in medicine to aspirants preparing for that profession. But their curriculum was entirely derivative; and most remained what the older colleges had been in the first half of the eighteenth century, vaguely religious agencies to which ambitious parents sent their adolescent boys to be polished by contact with letters. In 1810, Washington's bequest for a university for free Americans was still unused. It never would be.

The arts ornamental of civilization fared somewhat better. History showed, as Jefferson pointed out, that the arts had always traveled westward; there was no doubt of their flourishing hereafter on the new side of the Atlantic. Unrestrained by the dead hand of the past, Americans could express their national genius in architecture, painting and literature. They could erect public buildings, sketch edifying scenes, and write fresh prose and poetry to reflect the sentiments of a free people.

The tasks of construction and composition were pushed forward. Every state wished an appropriate seat of government; and the federal city, as yet a swamp along the Potomac, had to house the President, Congress and the Supreme Court. Cities new and old needed dignified churches and banks that commanded confidence. If there were not architects enough to draw the designs, carpenters and amateurs could improvise. Painters were less plentiful and sculptors fewer still; Benjamin West and John S. Copley, though born in America, found

London more congenial. Nevertheless Gilbert Stuart, John Trumbull and C. W. Peale were certainly skilled in putting oil to canvas. Above all, there was no lack of aspirants for literary honors, eager to indite the poems and novels, the essays and dramas, that would use the new nation's idiom. *"Exult each patriot heart!"* proclaimed Royal Tyler's *The Contrast* — the play that introduced Brother Jonathan to literature —

> *this night is shown*
> *A piece, which we may fairly call our own!*
> *Where the proud titles of "My Lord! Your Grace!"*
> *To humble Mr. and plain Sir give place.*

The results were curiously deficient in precisely those qualities of uniqueness and distinctiveness the Americans sought. For all its self-conscious searching for difference, the literature was thoroughly derivative. Tyler could not shake off the debt to Sheridan and Goldsmith and the heroic couplets of Barlow's grandiloquent *Columbiad* left no doubt about his filiation to Pope.

The building of the Capitol revealed the dilemma. The plan of the future federal city that Major Pierre L'Enfant had drawn for President Washington left a prominent place at the head of a great walk for the House of Congress. It was clear that no structure would be more important and none could better display the relation of design to the function of a republic. After a competition in 1792 had elicited suggestions from every American architect of note, that submitted by William Thornton of Philadelphia was selected.

Thornton was an amateur of many talents, a Quaker who also dabbled at painting, at writing novels and at breeding race horses. His sketch showed most prominently a dome and a portico, the stylishness of which no doubt gained him the award. They were to house a rotunda, the purpose of which was scarcely clear, while the Senate and House were to make space for themselves in little wings. There was the additional practical shortcoming that nothing could be built from the plans as presented; *there were no details whatever.* Yet construction started without any working drawings. As a result there followed a long process of amendment through which the only constants in design were the useless but ornamental dome and portico, which, however, were not erected. By the time the government moved to the city one wing was complete and by 1810 the other — with the eloquent gap between them bridged by a passageway of rough boards.

The troublesome design of the Capitol had little relation to the function of the building and was hardly American. Thornton had simply appropriated it from *Vitruvius Britannicus,* a collection of engravings of English structures. But then every entry in the competition was similarly indebted to a transatlantic model.

In striving for originality, the Americans had outreached themselves. It was unworthy to follow the Georgian pattern that had shaped public buildings between 1750 and the Revolution; those were *colonial.* But new shapes were not to be dreamed up for the wishing. Jefferson, struggling to conceive a new capitol for Virginia, traced the outlines of a Roman temple in Nimes; and Benjamin Latrobe reached back to Greece to borrow the façade for a Philadelphia bank from the Erechtheum.

Americans were even less capable of pulling themselves away from the architectural than from the literary past. It was gratifying to hear Paine declaim that he had *no notion of yielding the palm of the United States to any Grecians or Romans that were born;* and it was easy to substitute corncobs for acanthus leaves on the columns. But sustained innovation called for a command of techniques few possessed in the United States. Even the engineers, James Hoban, Latrobe and L'Enfant, who proved the most competent architects, had been born and trained abroad.

The minds of the Americans concerned with art were stocked with images of foreign derivation. The prints they saw represented European structures. For edification they went to exhibitions of vast painted panoramas of London or Rome or examined the classical copies and plaster casts in the New York and Philadelphia academies of fine arts. They simply could not break away. Timothy Dexter, who pushed everything to an extreme, commissioned Joseph Wilson to represent in forty life-size painted statues all the great men in history, from Adam to Timothy Dexter. His neighbors laughed. But when it came to grandeur, they wanted their domes and porticoes too.

The Revolution produced no monumental outburst of artistic creativity, but rather a decent elaboration of trends already at work. For all the declamation of the writers, the continent could sustain no magazine for any length of time until after 1800, when the *Port-*

Folio and the *Monthly Anthology* gave it stodgy imitations of the British reviews undelivered because of the commercial warfare of the times. On the other hand the press thrived, for *public newspapers* conveyed *the principal knowledge necessary for a free man to have.* Philadelphians received their first daily in 1783 and other cities were soon similarly served.

The merchants and planters, best able to make choices, were sober in their judgments; they ordered silver and chests not for the glory of republicanism, but to pour tea and store clothes. In response Paul Revere and Duncan Phyfe made them objects graceful in line, restrained in embellishment and beautiful in their utility. Every man of note wished the personal recognition of a portrait; he went to the studio of a painter of repute like Stuart or hired a wandering limner and received a forceful delineation of character to hang on his wall. If he wanted a new house or the town needed a new church, he could leaf through the pages of Asher Benjamin's *Country Builders Assistant* and ask the carpenter to adapt a pleasing plan to local circumstances. It was thus Samuel McIntire came to line Chestnut Street in Salem with sturdy merchants' homes whose graceful dimensions and delicately carved mantels and doorways revealed both his knowledge of London practice and his love for the material with which he worked.

The houses, churches, capitols and other artifacts this society produced were not evidence of its newness but of its confidence that it could expand the realm of order in the continent it was settling. With the Revolution, some of the Tory patrons of learning departed and along with them Benjamin Thompson, the most promising colonial scientist. But faith in reason and the patient anticipation of a steady advance in knowledge survived those losses. The philosophical societies in Philadelphia and Boston diligently continued their work, assured that their great achievements were still to come. Meanwhile it was possible to encourage reforms in the criminal code or schemes to supply the towns with pure water.

The constant reiteration during the Revolutionary debates of appeals to reason and to the laws of nature strengthened tendencies implicit in American thought since the Great Awakening. Disestablishment in some states and tolerance in the others minimized sectarian differences and emphasized the common standards of virtue that united all men. Deistic influences grew steadily stronger; the God of nature had endowed the universe with benevolent and orderly laws and reason enabled men to act in harmony with His divine scheme without the crutches of creed or ritual. *Reason was the only oracle of man,* announced the pamphlet to which Ethan Allen put his name. Masonic orders which adhered to those ideas were already in existence before 1776; they gained rapidly in membership during the war.

The same assumptions filtered through the organized religious bodies. The Unitarians and Universalists broke clearly with orthodoxy in their rejection of the doctrine of the Trinity and in their assurance of salvation to all men. But even those who held to the older forms subtly modified them. Americans who had earlier shuddered at the very notion of an episcopate now regarded with equanimity the installation of Anglican, Methodist and even Roman Catholic bishops. There was no danger, for their denominations, like the Congregationalists and Presbyterians, had quietly acquiesced in the underlying assumption that neighbors could live together in order, attend each his own worship or none, and all be judged by their behavior.

Disconcerting exceptions, particularly along the frontier, revealed disturbing signs of strain. Thousands of farmers in the interior suddenly rejected the dominant standards of their times and followed Mother Ann Lee. She had come from England in 1774, a wild enthusiast with only eight disciples, and settled near Albany. By 1810, Shaker colonies dotted the states. There, men and women gave up the struggle for individuality and achievement; they abjured private property, tilled the soil and labored in the workshops together; and they made the ultimate surrender of self in celibacy. In return they achieved the ecstasy of that quivering rhythmic dancing that gave them their name.

They were not alone. In 1801, thousands of people flocked to the Cain Ridge meeting in Bourbon County, Kentucky. They camped upon the plain by families, in tents or under the wagons. At night hundreds of torches lit the contorted faces lifted in hymns that swept through the multitude. By day they listened to the preachers who called them to redemption. Periodic shrieks punctuated the sermons and touched off mass hysteria; in wave upon explosive wave, spasmodic sobs ran through the ranks, then uncontained laughter — the shrill voices of the women rising above those of the men. Some were taken with the jerks as they shook off the devils who laid hold of them. Others broke into clumsy dances, making wild animal sounds before they fainted. They lay motionless for hours, disheveled, abandoned, tossed in unconscious alternations of despair and exaltation.

Such revivals had swept regularly through the frontier in the 1790's; they continued to do so after 1801. They fed on the pent-up tensions of people constantly forced by their struggles to doubt their own adequacy. Yes, they were mastering a continent, but the conquerors, in the rude homes thrown up in the course of their wanderings, took no joy in it. They died young, especially the women, worn out with childbearing and endless chores; they sickened readily, were shaken with agues and pinched with miseries; and through it all, they were nagged with the responsibility for decisions — even their staying or leaving was a choice frequently to be made. There were limits to what they could take. Strong though they were, hardened to risk and self-reliant, they could not forever put off the questions that crowded upon them in the loneliness and isolation. Had they been right to break away, to abandon the certainties of the past, to stake all on themselves in the great separation? They cried, *Sin, Sin, Sin!* as emotion broke down reserves. Was it the sin of pride to have believed too much in themselves?

The feverish attacks of doubt were not confined to the frontier, although most extreme there. Disaster also struck the great cities — yellow fever or fire — and showed the limits of man's competence to control the universe. Not every ship came back to port; and William Duer, the greatest speculator of them all, from having fifteen wines at dinner like a nobleman, was reduced to a debtor's prison. The orderly façades of a style of life somewhat older than that of the frontier kept emotion under cover. But the strain was there too.

Hence the importance of the future. In the separation from Europe, of which the Revolution was the visible expression, the Americans had also cut themselves off from the Old World. Yet in their aspirations for a new start, they discovered that they could not altogether maintain their distance either from the rest of the world or from their earlier experiences. To offset the drags and the dependence they did have a continent, left malleable by its emptiness. It remained their grave responsibility, as individuals and as communities, to shape it into a new society befitting new men.

V

Migration and Expansion, 1810–1860

14

The Frontiers of Migration

AT LAST IN 1815 peace came to the world. The fighting men everywhere put aside their arms and returned to the labor of the fields and the workshops. With Napoleon safely exiled, the statesmen took up the effort to design an order that would repair the ravages of a quarter-century of conflict and prevent the recurrence of similar calamities in the future.

Appropriately, the congress met in Vienna — seat of the Hapsburg empire, which had most to lose from the forces the French revolution had unleashed. Good Kaiser Franz ruled a polyglot conglomeration of German, Italian, Czech, Hungarian and Slavic peoples; his aristocrats jealously guarded their feudal privileges. His minister, Count Metternich, the master architect of the plan of settlement, was utterly determined to prevent changes that might disturb the status quo. In that aim he received the full concurrence of the Russian Romanov, the Prussian Hohenzollern and the French Bourbon, each of whom bore fresh memories of assaults upon the old dynastic order. But Metternich also realized that the shallow pated diplomacy of the eighteenth century could not achieve his objectives. The divisive rivalries of an earlier era were now to yield precedence to the overriding necessity of turning the clock back to before 1789.

More significant than the treaty which resolved the issues of the past were the arrangements to impose order and stability upon the future. A Holy Alliance of the great monarchs was to preserve the peace, protect existing privileges and maintain the status quo. It would form the basis of a durable European system that would keep legitimate rulers on their thrones, define correct boundaries, settle local quarrels and permit a concert of the powers to resist revolutionary impulses anywhere on the continent.

England had participated, as one of the victors, in the congress and had helped establish the terms of the peace with France. But its statesmen were dubious about the grandiose intentions of the Holy Alliance. Their traditional desire to preserve a balance of power on the Continent made them suspicious of any scheme for Continental unity; and they were beginning to doubt that the effort to impose an old legitimacy upon Europe would be any more successful than their own attempt to maintain an old imperial system in the New World.

In the same year that the congress had gathered in Vienna, the English had met with the Americans in Ghent to conclude another treaty of peace. The two countries had just fought a short, inglorious little war within the greater war. Goaded to desperation by the persistent disregard of neutral rights, the United States had laid down an ultimatum in 1810: it would trade only with the belligerent which first repealed the offensive decrees. Tricked into believing that the French had actually yielded, the Americans had declared war on Britain two years later.

The decision was the product of emotion rather than of calculation. Humiliated by repeated seizures of their ships and by impressment of their seamen, many citizens genuinely feared for the safety of the Republic. The disorders in trade depressed prices and threatened agricultural as well as commercial interests. The War Hawks — aggressive young congressmen — resented the encouragement to the Indians from the English posts in the Northwest and expressed the exuberant, reckless faith that a slight effort could clear the British out of Canada and the Spaniards out of Florida.

The conflict had been quite another matter; it dragged on inconclusively by land and by sea, with the only signal victory at New Orleans too late to affect the terms of the peace. The terms too were inconclusive. The two countries fell back to the status quo of 1812.

All the bothersome questions that divided them were unsettled. Future negotiations would still have to locate the Canadian boundary and resolve disputes over the Newfoundland fisheries.

The war did leave American and English political leaders with the general conviction that, however fiery their oratory, in practice they had better settle their disputes peacefully. It took thirty years more to fix the details of the line between the United States and Canada in its full extent from Maine to Oregon; and fresh causes of irritation continued to appear. Yet though the popular slogans were often bellicose, the determination to keep the peace proved stronger than the temptation to take up the sword. Issues that could not be resolved or compromised were postponed.

The determination to find a basis for accommodation reflected subtle changes in attitude on both sides of the ocean. The Americans, gaining steadily in strength in the decades after 1815, were not as prone as formerly to interpret every difference of opinion as a threat to their territory or to their republicanism. Furthermore, the conquest of Canada had not been as easy as the War Hawks had imagined; no liberated populace had risen up to welcome the invaders. It was more prudent to hold off. Time was on their side and growth would add steadily to their strength.

The English position also changed. In the landed aristocracy, the army and the church, men of the old school, resolute defenders of the empire, still feared republicanism as a threat to all order and regarded the American variety as only slightly less dangerous than the French. But their influence diminished rapidly. A new type of politician appeared in the House of Commons to speak for the owners of the factories that had transformed the English economy in the half-century before Waterloo. They had no intention of diminishing the prerogatives of the Crown or of yielding to revolutionary tendencies at home. But they regarded the old empire as a source of corruption and inefficiency, a burden on all for the sake of the privileges of a few. The true sources of national strength were industry and commerce, with the natural course of which the government should interfere as little as possible. It was to England's best advantage neither to humble nor subjugate the United States, but to encourage the growth of the former colonies and make good customers of them. To that end it was desirable, as the economists since Adam Smith had demonstrated, that goods for trade, capital for investment, and men for settlement should all move freely to where they could most profitably be used. The diffusion of these assumptions supplied a firm basis for Anglo-American understanding after 1815.

The liberal viewpoint made fewer converts on the continent of Europe. The economic changes, already well advanced in Britain, were only just taking form across the Channel; and the dominant groups in the countries that had defeated Napoleon had no intention of tolerating any social changes whatever. In time, industrialization and the emergence of a new middle class would alter the politics of western and central Europe also; but for the moment, the old regime was practically intact.

England therefore divided from its former allies in the response to national revolution. George Canning, who had become foreign minister in 1822, regarded the uprisings in the Spanish colonies in America as blows not at legitimacy but at a corrupt empire that interfered with the free course of trade. He had no desire to collaborate with the plan of the great powers to aid Spain and feared that intervention might prove the cover for the extension of French interests in the New World. Calling upon the New World to redress the balance of the Old, he sought the support of the United States in 1823 to offset the influence of the Holy Alliance. Canning proposed a declaration by which the United States and Britain would both disavow all claims to possession of any portion of those territories and then go on to maintain that no other power had the right to interfere with the newly independent countries.

Secretary of State John Quincy Adams, however, wished to make an *American cause* of the matter. His interest in the collapse of the Spanish empire was not identical with the British. In 1819 the United States had persuaded Spain to hand Florida over by sale and had then recognized the independence of the rebellious colonies. But it had no intention of foreclosing the possibility of further expansion in the area. Nor did it wish to tie its hands for the future by a joint declaration. It preferred to make its position clear by a statement that would cope with the pretensions of the Holy Alliance in Latin America and also with Russian ambitions south of Alaska and yet that would leave it free to deal as it saw best with any future contingency.

The Monroe Doctrine asserted bluntly that Americans played a distinctive role in international affairs. They considered legitimate all *de facto* European governments and would refrain from interfering with their internal concerns. But any attempt to extend to this hemisphere *the political system of Europe, essentially different from that of America* was dangerous to the peace and safety of the United States. The Republic would tolerate existing colonies but not new ones; and the effort of any power to deny independence to its *Southern brethren* would be an unfriendly act.

The statement of hemispheric solidarity did not quite mean what it said. Americans could readily envisage a single political system — their own — reaching across the two continents. But they were by no means sure that they wished to join the founders of the new Latin American countries on equal terms. Invited by Bolívar, the liberator, to a congress of the independent states in 1825, the United States hesitated and then finally sent delegates too late to participate. Behind the procrastination were grave doubts whether the revolutions in the south would follow the American pattern or deteriorate as the French had. In time, of course, the common principles of republicanism would spread throughout the hemisphere, but whether in a single national state or many was not at all clear.

The Monroe Doctrine was a means of establishing the distinction between the Old World and the New, between the area still gripped by forces resistant to change and that immediately open to the forces of liberty. Here in America men could find room at once to be free; there in Europe, ancient restrictions for the time being still bound them. But the steady flow of people, capital and goods across the Atlantic would undermine the old order and bring the blessings of liberty to all. Of that Americans had no doubt.

After 1815, traffic between Boston, New York, Philadelphia, Baltimore and New Orleans in the west and Liverpool, Le Havre, Rotterdam and Bremen in the east grew heavier, more frequent, and more regular. The vessels engaged in it, which had scarcely changed in two centuries, now were larger, more spacious and safer. Craft of two hundred or three hundred tons no longer were adequate; nor was it necessary to carry armaments to ward off pirates or enemy raiders; and copper sheathing protected the bottoms. After 1840 steam powered great new boats of two thousand or three thousand tons in rivalry with the smaller, slower and less reliable, if cheaper, sailing ships. The increase was at first mainly for the purpose of accommodating the rising volume of cargo. But there was room also for the passengers about to debouch upon the New World.

The two forms of immigration which had earlier accommodated the largest numbers vanished, never to be restored. An act of 1808 forbade the further importation of slaves; and although some were still brought illegally from Africa and the West Indies the numbers were far fewer than in the eighteenth century.

The trade in redemptioners or indentured servants also disappeared. The Napoleonic wars and the dangers of travel at sea had blocked up the old channels of migration. They were not worth clearing because American institutions were hostile to servile obligations. Men felt free to work for whomever they pleased; neither the ties of apprenticeship nor indenture held them to unfavorable arrangements. Shipowners and prospective masters therefore anticipated no profit in revival of the older practice. The migrations after 1815 were to be primarily of free individuals or families, making their own plans and going their own way after their arrival.

The volume of new arrivals rose steadily. Only a few thousand entered each year in the 1820's. In the 1830's the level soared to about sixty thousand a year and in the 1840's, to about two hundred thousand. The flow reached a peak of well over four hundred thousand in the single year 1854. Thereafter the wave subsided to a low point of about a hundred thousand in 1859. In all, some six million newcomers landed in the United States in the forty years after 1820; they helped to lift the total population from the seven million of 1810 to the thirty-one million of 1860. About half the newcomers were natives of Great Britain and Ireland; two million more were Germans; about fifty thousand, Scandinavians; and the rest of Europe contributed smaller groups.

Several distinct components entered into the movement. Europe did not altogether settle down to the internal stability envisioned by Metternich. Periodic revolutions erupted against the established governments in almost every part of the Continent in 1820, in 1830, in

1848, and in 1852. Each produced a flow of disappointed emigrés who sought refuge in the United States.

Carl Schurz, for instance, had enlisted as a student in the effort to make Germany a liberal democracy. He fought in the Revolution of 1848, gained fame by arranging the romantic escape of his teacher from Spandau prison, and then decided that where liberty was there his country would be. He came to the United States to find a congenial setting for ideas that could not then be expressed in Europe and went on to a successful career as soldier, statesman and writer. Francis Lieber, John Mitchel and thousands of others, like the planters of the seventeenth century, were unattached people who formed part of no integrated movement, but came for entirely personal motives. Although their numbers were always small, they played an important role in the United States. Literate and educated, they assumed the leadership of larger groups of immigrants with whom they had little in common other than language.

Some Europeans also regarded America, as the Puritans and the Quakers had, as empty space that offered opportunities for experimentation. Dissatisfied where they were, they made the New World the scene for the realization of their utopias, religious or secular.

About 1817, for example, a poor tailor, a peasant woman and a carpenter revived an eighteenth-century German pietistic sect which had claimed to live by direct spiritual inspiration. Widespread popular suffering in the aftermath of war added to their membership. They abjured private property, shared goods and labor, objected to the formalism of the established churches, and refused to send their children to school or their young men to military service. They were constantly in trouble. In 1826 an inspiration came; God wished them to find new dwellings in the wilderness. They were to leave for America. Lacking the means, they set themselves to saving for the voyage. After sixteen years, the time came; eight hundred men and women moved to Ebenezer, a great tract in western New York. The Lord was with them. In 1854 the land had so risen in value that they sold out at a profit and moved farther west to Amana, Iowa.

Scores of such groups crossed the Atlantic from England, Norway, France, Switzerland, and Germany, bringing with them their own particular schemes of redemption. They settled at Zoar and New Harmony, Icaria and Bishop Hill, in picturesque colonies, not far different from those of the native Mormons or the Brook Farm socialists. There was space for all.

Much more important were the migrations which reflected the economic disturbances through which all Europe passed. In the century after 1750 the population of the Continent just about doubled; in England it tripled, in Ireland it rose fourfold. That unexpected growth put intolerable pressure on ancient systems of land-holding and craftsmanship already in process of change.

First in England, then spreading eastward everywhere on the Continent, new modes of production crowded out the old communal ones. Immense factories and great landed estates took the places of thousands of family workshops and of millions of peasant holdings. The new enterprises produced goods at a far lower cost and in far greater quantities than the old techniques. Yet the machines made the skills of the artisans and peasants quite valueless. Those people, some once prosperous and secure in their ancient communities, now faced a simple choice of alternatives: they could remain where they were and sink to the level of factory hands or farm laborers; or they could migrate. In the 1820's and 1830's, increasing numbers of them determined to salvage what resources they could and make the move across the ocean.

Another element, larger still and also displaced, at first had no resources to salvage and was immobilized by its poverty. In Ireland, Scotland, England, southwest Germany, and Scandinavia, numerous landless peasants, or cottiers, had lived off the inefficiencies of the old system. Although they lacked land, they had been part of the village community, and that entitled them to throw up a hut for shelter, to graze a cow in the common fields, and to hire themselves out to labor for others. Living always on the brink of destitution, they were virtually indistinguishable from paupers who had no fixed means of support. The disappearance of the old village forms and of the common fields left them with no livelihood at all.

Yet they could rarely move in the 1820's and 1830's. Their inherited poverty bound them where they were. Some worked as migratory laborers; others drifted to nearby cities where they sought employment in the factories; and still others gave up and settled for a subsistence on charity.

Disaster clarified their position in the 1840's. The potato rot of

1846 brought famine to Ireland, Scotland and Germany; and a cholera epidemic literally decimated the enfeebled populace. Those who survived faced a simple choice: they could seek to live by escaping or remain where they were to die. Lack of funds was no longer an insuperable obstacle. The fugitives walked to the seaports or begged for assistance or got subsidies from public authorities anxious to be rid of the expense of supporting or burying them. One way or another those who could do so, got away. Ireland in 1841 had held almost a half million one-room cottages. In 1861 there were only eighty-nine thousand. The cottiers had not improved their housing; they had either died or emigrated.

Those newcomers who arrived with any means at all were well aware of what they faced in the New World. Scores of guidebooks and hundreds of transatlantic letters made the opportunities known. The ambitious and hopeful were not to crowd in the cities or remain in the East. They were to join the movement of people already in westward motion. Unfamiliar with the wilderness, the Europeans generally preferred to take up cleared lands, buying out the earlier settlers. The capital brought across in immigrant chests thus accelerated the shift of population. By 1860 a vast domain had been peopled. The line of settlement that year was well west of the Mississippi, running through western Minnesota and Iowa, down through the corners of Nebraska and Kansas, to take in the eastern counties of Texas.

The process of migration followed lines more than a century of experience had made familiar. First came the trappers and traders, isolated men at home only in the wilderness and capable of dealing with the denizens of the forest — human and animal — on equal terms. Occasionally they collaborated with parties of exploration dispatched by the government to make known the face of the land.

With the trails defined — by Stuart, Long or Frémont — the pioneer families followed. Burly men hacked out clearings for their cabins and fought off the Indians while they subsisted by the gun and the fishing rod; hardened women managed the crude households by doing without; and children grew tough in the struggle to survive. In their wake moved the agents of civilization, land speculators, lawyers, officials and shopkeepers who established the links that drew the frontier close to the rest of the world. The court held sessions; the boats moved regularly down the river; a printer set type for the newspaper. This was the time of decision for the pioneer. The fish and game grew scarce and disappeared, the tax collector appeared and there was the wearisome business of establishing title at the land office. The first arrivals then had to choose between striking permanent roots and settling down to farming or taking to the move once more.

Escape was possible because a train of new families from Europe and the East was on the way to buy out old claims and to devote themselves to more permanent agriculture. Usually the pioneers preferred to keep in motion. Disqualified by temperament and character from adjusting to a routine, they pursued their dreams westward in the never-ending quest for space.

The farmers who intended to stay followed routes that kept them in contact with the homes they had left. They preferred to be near towns where they could trade their products for supplies, where a sheriff could maintain order and where they could find the support of neighbors like themselves. There was therefore some pattern to their migration. The foreign-born formed their own clusters of English, German or Norwegian settlement; and the natives also maintained lines of continuity with the places of their origin. The New Englanders who left the hill towns, depopulating the recently settled northern counties of Maine, Vermont and New Hampshire, moved in a steady stream across New York state, through the upper tier of counties in Ohio, Indiana, and Illinois, and on into Wisconsin and Iowa. When they arrived they built villages like those they had abandoned, formed Congregational or Presbyterian churches, and began to think of the provision of schools and colleges. The Southerners, by contrast, moved up through Kentucky as Lincoln's family did, then on across southern Ohio, Indiana and Illinois to Missouri or south through Tennessee into the Mississippi delta. They were generally self-sufficient, each household to itself, and less likely than the Yankees to feel the attractions of an organizing town center. The ministrations of the circuit-riding preachers and judges gave them all the service they needed; and they depended more upon the connections of kinship than upon places in a fixed community sustained by formal institutions.

At the edge of the great plains, the movement paused. Here began the *Great American Desert,* an environment totally unlike any the Americans had theretofore encountered. The absence of trees and the sparse rainfall frightened men accustomed to life in the heavily wooded East. What would here serve for fencing, fuel or shelter? What crops would grow in this heavily crusted sod? There was a widespread impression that the region would remain forever barren.

Only scattered handfuls had moved into or beyond it by 1848. Religious zeal had persuaded the Mormons, expelled from Illinois, to follow Brigham Young to a new Zion in Utah; and a few families had made the long, hard overland crossing to the Oregon country, where they formed the nucleus of a thriving settlement in the Willamette Valley. But not many, for the moment, wished to follow them.

Other Americans occasionally found reason to intrude into Mexican territory. The temptation of great land grants drew some impresarios into east Texas, where they revolted in 1836 to form their own republic; and the silver of Santa Fe attracted regular expeditions bent on trade. A group of merchants and ranchers was tolerated in California. Word of the riches of that province occasionally induced a party of settlers to make the hazardous crossing. But to get there took months of marching across the desert, then an exhausting climb up winding canyons, to altitudes always covered with snow. Sometimes near the summit it was necessary to lead the oxen, one at a time, through a narrow crevice and laboriously pull the wagons over. And not all who started got through.

The great desert was an imposing barrier to those who attempted to cross or live in it. But imagination lightly carried over it those who dreamed of the farther west and what lay beyond. The strange, infertile plains and the forbidding western mountains could not obscure the land of promise along the Pacific coast. Upper California alone would provide homes *for millions of future Americans,* Thomas Hart Benton told the Senate, as he gained support for topographical expeditions in the 1840's to map the way there.

And still farther west, in a closing of the great circle, was the Orient. American trade with China had risen steadily down to the 1830's; if it seemed to fall off in the next decade, energetic steps would revive and stimulate it. In the hope of doing so, Caleb Cushing, in 1844, negotiated a commercial treaty with the Celestial Empire.

Within the next decade Commodore Perry's ships would force similar concessions from the Japanese.

It took but the least calculation to realize how much more successful that trade would be, conducted from an American base on the Pacific. Asa Whitney, who had gone from New York to Canton a bankrupt, in a few years returned a man of wealth. In January 1845, he petitioned Congress for an immense land grant to finance a railroad westward from Lake Michigan that would enable the United States to *reach out one hand to all Asia, and the other to all Europe.*

California was the objective, but Texas was the means of acquiring it. After the butchery at the Alamo Stephen Austin and Sam Houston had led that province in a successful revolt against Mexico. The Texans were Americans and, having gained their independence, sought admission to the Union. After nine years of negotiation, a joint resolution of Congress in February, 1845, made that possible. Mexico had stubbornly refused to recognize the loss of the province, but had cautiously refrained from any forceful steps to regain it. Presented with the fact of annexation it protested vigorously but seemed disinclined to go beyond verbal objections. President Polk was not to be denied his chance at California, however. Having goaded the Mexicans into firing the first shot, he was able to ask for, and secure, a declaration of war by Congress in May, 1846. The contest was brief, one-sided, and eminently successful. From it the United States emerged with New Mexico and California.

Virtue had not long to await its reward. The American regime had hardly been installed when the Swiss trader Sutter found gold at his fort. The word flashed round the world and touched off a rush that transformed the Pacific Coast. Clerks left their ledgers and farmers their plows to claim their share of the riches. They came overland by covered wagon through the steep mountain passes; or they sailed to Panama where a railroad carried them across the Isthmus to the ships that brought them to California. The rush sucked in Europeans as well as Americans and also drew a substantial group of Chinese in a reverse eastward migration. San Francisco at once became a great city and little mining camps sprang up by the scores on every interior stream. Gold was the symbolic reward for having come as far west as the continent permitted.

The acquisition of California by no means satisfied the urge for expansion, however. Already some Americans complained that all Mexico should have been annexed; others foresaw an imminent union with Canada, which had only recently been embroiled in a conflict with Britain; still others had their eyes on Cuba and the Caribbean. No single stage of growth could complete the process which involved not merely individuals seeking their own success but the destiny of the nation.

These decades of rapid growth had endowed the concept of a distinctive American mission with renewed vitality. In a half-century, the United States had overleaped the Mississippi and more than doubled its size while its population had grown fourfold. There was not the least reason to believe that the Republic had spread to its full dimensions. Some day the hemisphere as a whole would join in one truly United States of America. Nor was Europe's day of redemption indefinitely to be postponed. The revolutions of 1848 for the moment had failed. But the despots would not long hold their thrones; and America would ultimately show its sister republics of the Old World how to build a new society of liberated men. Meanwhile, missionaries in Africa, Asia and the Pacific islands were laying the groundwork for the future emancipation of those benighted areas.

Soon would begin the *boundless era of American greatness. In its magnificent domain of space and time, the nation of many nations would manifest to mankind the excellence of divine principles.* From its base in the Western Hemisphere would develop *a Union of many Republics, comprising hundreds of happy millions, owning no man master, but governed by God's natural and moral law.*

The great nation of futurity, proclaimed the *Democratic Review,* would come into being without war or military conquest. Its secret weapons were of another sort. Its high example alone would *smite unto death the tyranny of kings, hierarchs, and oligarchs and carry the glad tidings of peace and good will where myriads now endure an existence scarcely more enviable than that of beasts of the field.* The people of the world would cast off their own yokes, stirred to emulation by the success of republicanism in America. The evidence that free men of every origin could govern themselves in harmonious co-operation was plain on every map that showed the expansion of the country and in every indication of its growing economic power.

The Mexicans humiliated at Guadalupe Hidalgo, the Nicaraguans invaded by filibusterers, might question the sincerity of such professions of peace and good will; and some native critics of American policy might also doubt the purity of expansive motives in these decades. In actuality, altruistic ideals and the hope of gain were meshed inextricably together in the drives that forced men on toward mastery of the continent. But the ideals had at least this influence, that neither in thought nor in action did it occur to Americans to make subjects of the people of the territories added to the Union. All were to be Americans, citizens of states absolutely equal in rights with those of 1776.

Beneath the high-flown rhetoric was a core of ideas which accurately described the antagonism of the New World to the Old in the half-century after the Congress of Vienna. Insofar as the Holy Alliance aimed to stabilize the old regime, America was inevitably its enemy. The power to expand demonstrated the viability of republican institutions, unsettled millions of Europeans, and helped create patterns of trade, investment and industry that were a constant threat to the status quo.

15

New Modes of Production

*N*ever take great hazards. The habit of mind which is induced is unfavorable and generally the result is bad. To keep what you have, should be the first rule; to get what you can fairly, the second. — Thus a collection of maxims and morals for merchants and men of business in 1857. Much had changed in the character of American enterprise since the days of Gray and Dexter.

The volume of overseas trade had certainly increased rapidly. Almost at once, with the restoration of peace in 1815, the ships had begun to come; the arrivals scarcely slackened thereafter. In the forty years after 1820, the value of goods exchanged jumped almost sevenfold. Yet the growth was not primarily in the forms of commerce upon which Americans had formerly ventured. The relaxation of imperial controls eliminated the advantageous position of neutrals; and the exotic exchanges with remote corners of the world languished after 1830. Instead, the direct transfer of merchandise between Europe and America supplied an ever larger share of the cargoes. In 1860, more than seventy per cent of the exports and more than sixty per cent of the imports moved in that manner. England was both the largest seller and the largest purchaser.

The merchants now had regularity with a vengeance. They rarely owned their own vessels, but received and made shipments on scheduled liners. They kept abreast of current developments through the pages of *Niles' Weekly* or *DeBow's Review* as well as through the local press. The goods they handled commanded fairly stable prices and were dispatched to known destinations. Prosaic articles of daily use moved westward across the ocean and into the interior — cottons, woolens, silks and linens; china and earthenware; iron and steel products; wine, coffee, tea, dried fruits, nuts and spices. In return went the raw materials — bales of cotton, fish, meat, wood and wheat.

In almost every year the United States imported more than it exported. Fees from the carrying business and gold from the California hillsides made up some of the deficit; the capital immigrants brought with them also helped. But most of the gap was filled by British investors who purchased American securities and supplied the short-term credit that financed overseas trade. English exporters commonly allowed transatlantic merchants a full fifteen months to make payment; the merchants, in turn, usually gave jobbers and shopkeepers a whole year. In the interim return cargoes earned the exchange to clear the accounts. English capital thus financed much of the United States' international trade. After 1830, the amount outstanding in sterling bills averaged about $100,000,000 a year and almost all the transactions went through the hands of a few large London mercantile banking houses, of which Baring Brothers was most prominent. By accepting these arrangements, the American merchants became, in a sense, agents of British exporters. The relative stability and order of these conditions were a welcome relief from the more venturesome overseas enterprises of an earlier generation.

However no merchant could altogether avoid great hazards. Business was subject to marked fluctuations, although the general trend was upward; and the alarming panics of 1819, 1837, and 1857 showed that risk had not been excluded from commerce. Bills could be met when due only if the purchasers of goods created commodities sufficient to command the means of payment. Prosperity depended upon the constant expansion of the number of customers for imports and of producers of exports. The rapidly mounting population was eager enough to consume the manufactures of Europe, but it also had to turn out the articles to be sent back in payment.

Cotton was the most valuable export to pass through the ports of New Orleans, Baltimore and New York. After 1815 conditions were ripe for its phenomenal spread. Hundreds of mills in England, France, Germany and Russia, as well as within the United States, clamored for supplies and thousands of planters, attracted by rising prices, hastened to meet the demand. At first the Carolina uplands, Georgia and Virginia were the chief centers of production. Then the callous removal of the five civilized Indian nations from Georgia opened the way into the incredibly fertile black belt of Alabama and Mississippi. Before long the cultivation of cotton reached up the Mississippi River to Arkansas and Tennessee and then around the Gulf of Mexico into Texas. By 1860 Mississippi, Alabama, Louisiana, Georgia, Texas, Arkansas and South Carolina supplied the largest portion of a crop of over four and a half million bales from which fully one half of all American exports were drawn. *Cotton was king,* Senator Hammond proclaimed; it could *bring the whole world to our feet.*

This spectacular development firmly fastened the Southern economy to the plantation and to slavery. Many small farmers raised cotton with a half-dozen hands or even fewer. But there was a consistent tendency toward larger holdings. Steadily rising demand and prices increased the speculative value of both land and Negroes. The larger units of production were desirable because they brought their owners substantial capital gains as well as profits and provided them with a hedge against soil exhaustion.

Most planters counted it advantageous to expand their possessions as far as their capital and credit allowed. Bennet Barrow of Louisiana considered the plantation *as a piece of machinery; to operate successfully all of its parts should be uniform and exact.* By careful management he accumulated five thousand acres, two hundred slaves and an estate valued at $150,000. Yet his account books reveal continual borrowings and lendings, purchases and sales. And it was through speculation that Joseph, Jefferson Davis's older brother, who came almost barehanded from Kentucky to Mississippi, gained his million dollar holdings.

Far from disappearing, as an earlier generation had hoped, slavery was more securely fixed in the life of the region than ever before The rising value of the black men's labor stabilized the plantation system among the sugar and rice growers of Louisiana. It also created a booming market for the surplus slaves of tobacco- and corn producing areas in Virginia, Maryland and Kentucky. An enormous internal slave trade stocked the new plantations. Heavily guarded coffles moved endlessly on foot or came down by boat to take place in fields that reflected the glare of the hot southern sun. Thoughts of gradual emancipation faded in the light of the brutal calculation of returns from breeding stocks of colored people. By 1860 fully four and a half million Negroes were bound to perpetual servitude.

In that year cotton dominated the life of the South and influenced a good part of the rest of the nation. Concentration upon that single staple absorbed the full attention of the men who were, or aspired to be, planters. The older practice of setting aside little plots on which the slave could raise corn or vegetables tended to yield to the in clination to give every acre over to the most profitable of crops, even if that meant importing from elsewhere the very food consumed on the plantation. Every penny of surplus capital went into land and Negroes; little remained for industry or internal improvements. Free labor would not compete with the bondsmen; therefore few im migrants chose to settle in the plantation districts and the status of the poor whites, who did not share the advantages of the system, sank inexorably unless they too gained possession of the black soil and black hands that made the white gold grow.

The overseas merchant found somewhat less pleasure in a survey of the accounts of free agricultural enterprise. The farmers were willing enough to buy tea, cloth and cutlery. But they could not supply return crops as readily as the planters. The output of wheat, corn and meat was also climbing; but these products were not as scarce as cotton and could not compete in Europe unless their price were low enough to offset the cost of transportation. For the time being, they found their major outlet in the internal American market, which grew rapidly as more people crowded into the cities, more slaves labored on plantations. Yet gratifying as such sales were they did not themselves produce the means of paying for the flow of imports.

These considerations scarcely troubled the immigrants who expected to till the soil in Illinois, Missouri or Wisconsin as they had in England, Germany or Norway. They bought as little as they could, diversified their crops, spared the land but not themselves and shunned debt like the devil. Theirs were the moderate gains of men whose ambition was to leave a proud freehold to their sons.

By contrast, speculative zeal was the birthright of native farmers on the move, whether of Yankee or Southern origin. Generations in pursuit of success had taught them the exploitative techniques of how quickest to mine from each plot whatever it could give. They kept their eyes fixed to the market, determined to bring to it the commodities that commanded the most favorable price. With land abundant and labor short, they bent every energy to production of the most remunerative staple.

The patterns of free agriculture were therefore in constant competitive flux. The center of wheat production moved steadily westward as new areas opened to settlement. Until 1820, the Mohawk and Hudson valleys were pre-eminent, then the Genesee country and Pennsylvania. After 1830 the nation's great wheatfields spread in a wide band across northern Ohio, Indiana, Illinois and Wisconsin, chiefly areas of New England settlements.

The farmer of Southern origin showed a greater affinity for corn, whether because of habit or because of the physiography of the districts to which he came. In the 1830's, Kentucky, Tennessee and Virginia were the leading producers of that crop; but by 1860 they had been outdistanced by southern Illinois, Ohio and Missouri. The mode of marketing also changed. Formerly corn had most conveniently been transported in its distilled form, whiskey. Now it was stuffed into the razorback hogs who were no longer allowed to root for themselves but were fattened to be driven to the nearby packing houses.

Cincinnati became the great *porkopolis* which shipped everything but the squeal to the tables of the whole country. Chicago in the 1850's became its rival, reflecting the shift westward of the source of supply. For those whose tastes ran to beef rather than to pork, great herds of cattle moved to the East, fattened in regular stages on the way as they approached the slaughterhouse. In 1860, Texas and Illinois were the great cattle states.

Enterprising farmers in the older areas soon learned they could not pit their rolling hills, quickly worn through misuse, against the fresh prairies of the West. If they did not themselves migrate, they had to find new products for the market. Agricultural societies diligently labored to improve techniques through fairs, contests and experiments. They counseled the importation of shorthorn cattle from England and of merino sheep from Spain; and for a while those patient beasts rescued the agriculture of Massachusetts and Vermont from stagnation. But in time the herds and flocks drifted West also, to leave dairying the last recourse of the East. The husbandmen who remained where they were faced an unremitting, and generally losing, struggle to hold on in the face of the outpouring of commodities from the newly settled areas. Often they were driven to a desperate quest for additional income in the handicrafts and later in manufacturing.

Intense competition made the farmer almost everywhere a speculator. Since he could never estimate the future condition of the market, he bent every effort to raise as much as he could. Meanwhile, hoping for a rise in values, he took title to as much land as his credit permitted. He still dabbled in trade and was willing to try any improvement that promised to save labor and lower costs; he bought the new cast iron or steel plows and the Hussey or McCormick reapers as they appeared, even if it meant going into debt to do so. He worried constantly about improvements in transportation, for the cost of carrying his products was the critical element that determined the size of his markets and the adequacy of his reward.

The overseas merchants joined the farmer in that concern. Cheaper means of conveyance would stimulate the increased volume of exports that all sought, and, properly directed, would channel the traffic through the particular city that each favored.

Hence began the determined quest for improvements that occupied four decades. The turnpike had proved its inadequacy, but the work of laying out public highways continued; and the federal government supported a national road across the mountains into the Ohio region. Sidewheel steamers learned to navigate the inland waterways, slipping from landing to landing along the coast and down the tortuous courses of scarcely navigable streams.

The greatest hopes, however, now rested not in making use of nature's channels but in surmounting its obstacles. Americans plunged hastily into the task of building elaborate canal systems to match those of Europe. The Erie Canal, which linked New York City with the Great Lakes in 1825, paid for itself almost at once in tolls and touched off rival projects in Pennsylvania and Maryland. Other ambitious ventures connected the lakes with the Ohio River and reached into the Southern back-country. These were no sooner a-building than a new form began to displace them. In 1830, the first railroad lines were laid out; and a veritable frenzy of construction seized the nation. In the next three decades, fully thirty thousand miles of track crisscrossed the interior of the country.

It took labor, capital and some skill to put them there. Of these, the last-named was least available and least valued. The United States as yet lacked the services of a body of qualified engineers; badly designed locks on the canals, flimsy wooden trestles and insecure rails would all shortly have to be replaced. But hands to wield the shovel and pickaxe were abundant. Hundreds of immigrants who disembarked without resources labored in the construction camps until they discovered how mean were the rewards for doing so. It did not matter if they left; there were plenty of more recent arrivals to replace them.

Capital was somewhat more difficult to come by, particularly since estimates of cost frequently fell far short of reality. The canals were generally state enterprises. The funds to construct them were raised, however, not through taxation but through bonds floated among venturesome investors. By the time the railroads were projected, the first enthusiasm had worn off; greater inducements were necessary to dislodge the savings of prospective participants. Therefore chartered corporations, often sustained by government guarantees, offered the promise of limitless profits and elicited the speculative dollars from merchants, farmers, municipalities and foreign investors. Sometimes English banking houses were ready to take these securities in payment for rails and equipment.

The South lagged far behind the North because it lacked all the necessary elements to effect the transportation revolution. Slave labor could not effectively be used in construction gangs; and foreign investors were dubious about ventures in the region after some states repudiated or devalued their debts in the panic of 1837. Above all, the Southern merchant was lured by ambitions different from those of his Northern counterpart; the attractions of the plantation soaked up his surplus capital. His image of success was fastened to the great homes not far from New Orleans or Charleston; and the projects he turned in his mind were those of transforming himself into the master of a gentlemanly estate rather than of improving his position as a trader. He missed the opportunity that others seized, to shape canal and railroad routes to his own advantage.

In a fluid economy past experience was no guide to the needs of trade. Instead, transportation patterns were defined by the expectations of merchants, each of whom envisaged his own city as the future metropolis of the continent. Cautious enough in their own transactions, they plunged boldly into enterprises which promised both personal and communal rewards. The result was speedy construction, but also waste and planlessness.

New York won out in the rivalry; by 1860 *some magnetic virtue in their compass needles* seemed to attract the whole world's ships to Manhattan. Smaller ports like Charleston, Newcastle, Providence and Portland quickly dropped from the race. But Boston, Baltimore, Philadelphia and New Orleans remained serious competitors through most of the century. In the struggle for position as entrepôt where the interior of the continent would exchange goods with Europe, New York had substantial advantages. The Hudson and Mohawk valleys and the lakes gave it a water-level route through the mountains. It was central to the most heavily populated region of the country and could efficiently distribute every type of commodity to internal as well as foreign markets. The success of the Erie Canal gave it a head start in the race and attracted outsiders who were encouraged to come by its tradition of cultural diversity. Shortly after 1825, for instance, shrewd Yankee merchants began to move the base of their operations from New England to New York.

These factors were cumulative. The growing volume of trade made available warehouses, banks and brokerage facilities that drew still more business. Ships that brought woolens from England or silks from France could take back cotton from the South and wheat from the West. It was often more convenient to ship these goods by way of New York than directly from New Orleans or Charleston.

Many-masted Manhattan was evidence that trade still brought great gains to some — and great losses to others. Success now depended not on chance stumblings on opportunity in remote parts but on the efficient arrangement of the links among the far-flung sectors of an expanding economy. John Murray Forbes understood that early. He had come back to the United States after his years in Canton with a fortune sufficient to give him a position of importance in commerce. He perceived that the railroad builder's opportunity lay in Michigan rather than in Massachusetts and shrewdly put his capital into lines radiating out of Chicago.

The merchant in Boston or New York who invested in, or dealt with, the West carefully followed the fluctuations of the currency. The movement of goods depended as much on money and credit as upon rails and canals.

All the speculative groups in society wished for inflation. Farmers and planters always anticipated higher prices and assumed debts on the gamble that the future would pay them. Investors in land or stocks or new enterprises of any sort also believed that additions to the store of currency and credit would spur on the economy and raise the value of their holdings. They pressed the states to charter new banks which would make available the paper they wanted.

But not everyone speculated; and those who did not, found inflation a cruel enemy that silently ate away the worth of their labor and their savings. Laborers suffered when wages, low as they were, came in notes of uncertain value and when the price of bread rose. But they were neither articulate nor powerful enough to make their voices heard. More important and more influential were the artisans. As handworkers, they were in no position to profit by expansion; they lacked the techniques to meet rising demands. Indeed speculation, by stimulating trade and improving transportation, weakened their control of their own markets and threatened their independence. The bootmaker at his last, the hatter at his form, and the cutler at his forge watched with trepidation as the ships and trains brought in, from distant places, shoes and hats and knives that the merchant would put on sale to deprive them of their livelihood.

The artisan could not deny the desirability of improvement. But he protested bitterly about the form it took. The magic of the soulless corporation conjured out of nowhere the money by which it created its monopoly. The craftsmen demanded that only specie serve as currency and that charters be limited to public agencies so that all men could compete as equals.

Between the two extremes were the overseas merchants. They had a stake in the expansion that made their trade possible; yet they had no desire to receive in payments from the interior bundles of bank-notes they could not use in their own transactions or exchange for remittances to Europe. In the larger cities, they tried uneasily to main-tain a balance between the twin hazards of contraction and overex-pansion.

For a time, the Bank of the United States, rechartered in 1816, promised an exit from that dilemma. In 1822, Nicholas Biddle be-came its president. He was then in his middle thirties, a scholarly Philadelphia gentleman who had already served as one of the govern-ment directors and before that had tried his hand at diplomacy, literature and editing. He hoped to create order and stability in the chaotic American economy. The country, he thought, had been *crippled and almost destroyed by banking in the interior.* It was time to *concenter its business in the large commercial cities.* The Bank was in a unique position to do so. Into its local branches merchants brought paper money from every part of the Union. It could send the notes back for redemption to the issuing banks, which would have to be prudent in their use of the printing press with that threat sus-pended over them. The effect would be to centralize decisions about fiscal policy instead of allowing them to remain dispersed in hundreds of local banks.

Biddle's policy antagonized both the artisans who thought it too soft and the speculators who thought it too hard. But he was in-vulnerable until he thrust the Bank into politics and made an enemy of Andrew Jackson. The President had no rigid ideas on the subject of the currency; there were both hard-money and soft-money men in his following. But he was suspicious of the moneyed Easterners whose corrupt bargains, he thought, had deprived him of victory in 1824; and he smelled a design for monopoly in Biddle's maneuverings at the Bank. He removed the Government's support, prevented an extension of the charter that expired in 1836 and ultimately destroyed the institution. No other agency of central control took its place. Each state created what banks it wished and those in turn set their own policies of credit and currency. There were no limits to expansion except those temporarily imposed by panic in 1837 and 1857. There was no way the merchants could fully protect themselves against those hazards.

Nor did they find much solace in national commercial policy. Many Americans had sought to raise the tariff since Hamilton's proposals had proved abortive. Apart from the simple desire for protection that moved Louisiana sugar planters, Pennsylvania iron manufacturers and Missouri hemp growers to seek safety in import duties, the residual hope survived that the tariff could be an instrument of national economic policy. Henry Clay thus dreamed of an American system which would protect domestic industry and yet yield sufficient revenue to finance internal improvements. Manufactures and agriculture would then sustain each other in a mutually profitable exchange. Such proposals met the relentless opposition of the cotton planters convinced that a tax on imports would simply siphon away some of the returns from the staple they exported.

Again the merchants took an intermediate position. They opposed barriers that might restrict their trade. But they believed that a moderate tariff increase would lower some of the perennial excess of imports over exports, reduce the drain of specie out of the country and establish the conditions of orderly growth. Again they were frustrated. Tariffs remained low through almost the whole of the period.

Indeed, the overseas merchants who linked the American to the European economies were practically alone in the desire for order. Almost everyone else plunged feverishly on in the speculative effort to hasten the gains of the future, and did so on borrowed capital. The merchants profited as intermediaries but they remained insecure while planters, farmers and promoters hurtled perilously along at the edge of disaster.

Some merchants, in the desire to generate a dependable body of exports, looked to the example of England and ventured off into an experiment as bold as that of any Westerner. Manufacturing had made Britain great. Why should it not do the same for America?

They had in mind not the small workshops of the interior where smiths fabricated wagons, hammers and shovels, protected by distance from competition; nor the rural household where craftsmen pointed nails or made shoes, shingles and pencils; nor yet the mill to which cloth was brought for fulling and dyeing. Merchants participated in such enterprises, putting out the iron bars, the wire and the yarn and distributing the finished products. But the more imaginative thought also of integrated factories after the English model where a single building housed all the steps of production which were performed by power-driven machines operated by wage laborers.

Cotton goods were the first to be worked up by the new methods. There was no domestic competition and the merchants knew the market from their experience as distributors of English wares. The hazard lay in going into production; the plants called for a substantial investment which might be lost without a reliable force of workers to tend them. But then, even if they earned no great return on their capital as stockholders, the merchants could at least gain a commission as selling agents. In 1813, Francis Lowell persuaded a group of Bostonians to invest in the first such venture at Waltham. Ten years later they built the city of Lowell on the Merrimack River particularly to house such enterprises; and thereafter the idea spread rapidly. The value of cotton goods turned out in the United States had climbed well above $100,000,000 in 1860. By then the factory had appeared in Utica, New York, in Paterson, New Jersey, and in scores of other villages through the North. The system had also extended to the production of woolens and paper.

The early factory was rural, pitched near the water supply which turned its wooden machines. Yet it was large, employing 150 laborers or more. It drew its labor from the only available source in the countryside. North of Boston, many a depressed farmer was willing to let his daughters work for a few years in the mills while they awaited their true careers in teaching or in marriage. Lucy Larcom, the ninth child in a poor family, welcomed the opportunity to become one of the ladies of the loom, to live docilely, safe from temptation in the carefully superintended boardinghouses where she spent her spare time writing for the *Operative's Magazine*.

That disciplined order of life did not take root in other parts of the country. The factories in southern New England and the middle states were smaller and more often individual rather than corporate enterprises. Richard Borden, for instance, had left the farm to work in a gristmill, then opened an iron works at Fall River in 1821. He plowed the profits back into cotton mills, banks and a steamship line, employing whole families — men, women and children — which could not get by on farm incomes. The bleak factory and the laborers' cottages straggling down the road became familiar sights of the rural countryside.

Industry lost its rustic aspect after 1840. Immigration then piled up an abundant labor supply in the coastal cities. Thousands of penniless Irish and German peasants came ashore in Boston, Philadelphia and New York with no resources and with a desperate eagerness to work at any wages. These people accepted what terms were offered; and if the labor of a man would not support his family, then the women and children could work too. Their strangeness and the recollections of the hunger they had escaped kept these people from protesting. Some drifted off to the mill towns where they began to replace the girls and the casual farm hands. Others laid the streets and raised the buildings of the expanding towns; or they took to tailoring or similar simple tasks for contractors in the cities where they landed.

Within a decade, the availability of cheap labor, unprecedented in America, sparked the appearance of many new industries and transformed those already in existence. Wooden machines gave way to bigger and more ingenious iron ones and water power yielded to steam; great brick factories replaced the earlier structures and the scale of enterprise grew steadily larger. By 1860 manufacturing had become an urban pursuit. Furniture, carriages, machines and numerous other objects poured out of newly designed workshops in which the former peasants toiled; and all these products entered into the flow of internal and foreign trade.

Some of the consequences of industrialization had begun to emerge by 1860. The use of steam and the great machines of the new plants created an expanding demand for coal and iron, on the basis of which heavy industry would later develop. The railroads and canals facilitated the movement of goods in and out of the manufacturing centers and in turn were sustained by the traffic thus generated. The ability to supply the domestic market, and even to export, articles once imported narrowed the deficit in the balance of trade. Those were encouraging aspects of national development.

There were also less palatable effects. As factory methods spread to more branches of production they completed the destruction of the traditional handicrafts; the hired laborer took the place of the independent artisan. Furthermore, the innocent paternalism of the Lowell boardinghouse and the family unit of Fall River employment both vanished. The entrepreneurs in the city hired an individual for as long as he was useful, by the hour or the day. Each worker appeared at the gate when he was needed and disappeared when he was not; whether he could live on what he earned was solely a matter of his own concern. The exchange of wage for service was a purely impersonal transaction. In the 1850's a steadily growing proletariat paid through its deprivations for the efficiency of the new factories.

A world relatively tolerant of the free movement of people, goods and capital permitted the Americans to expand their economy in new directions after 1810. Their response was the development of the plantation, the mechanized farm and the factory. The virtue of each of these modes of production was the capacity for generating a great outpouring of goods. Between 1820 and 1860, the national wealth of the country increased fivefold. A considerable portion of those riches accumulated as capital and began to relieve the old dependence on overseas sources. But a good deal of the increase in output moved directly into the hands of consumers and raised the standard of living. Cloth and bread and meat were more abundant than earlier, although not all men shared equally in them.

Yet the new modes of production also raised troublesome questions. The gains were frequently counted up. The costs were less often calculated. The slavery more deeply rooted in the South than ever, the restless movement along the frontier, the decay of the artisan crafts, the villages abandoned within a few decades of their settlement and the failures in the aftermath of panic, all were visible, but by now so familiar that none stopped to reckon the losses they entailed.

Less familiar and more shocking were the human costs of industrialization. Before the machines, *like so many mares haltered to the rack stood rows of girls, all steady workers — twelve hours to the day, day after day, through the three hundred and sixty-five days, ex-cepting Sundays, Thanksgiving and Fast-days.* This was the rag room of a paper mill in 1855, *a great white sepulchre* it seemed to the visitor who observed the living death of its inmates.

Their condition was more extreme than that of other Americans. But was it essentially different? *The mass of men lead lives of quiet desperation,* a rebel observed in 1849. *From the desperate city you go into the desperate country,* he warned, *and have to console yourself with the rodents' bravery.* It could not have been for this — for the endless striving of the speculator, for the painful calculations of the merchants, for the dreary toil of the laborer and the slave — that the American, this new man, had become free. Yet that was the price of the economic growth in which many took pride. There were no fewer hazards here, although of a different sort, than in the old whaling, trading days.

16

Intellectual Ferment

CHARLES DICKENS was thirty years old and flushed with his success, when he made his first visit to the United States in 1842. The novelist found little to admire in the New World. But an experience in Boston, only a few miles from the factories of Waltham and Lowell, in another institution built by merchants, touched his deepest emotions. He sat down in a room before *a girl, blind, deaf, and dumb; destitute of smell; and nearly so of taste; walled up in a marble cell, impervious to any ray of light or particle of sound, with her poor white hand peeping through a chink in the wall, beckoning for help.* He observed the miracle that had transformed her into a being radiant with intelligence and pleasure.

Laura Bridgman had been a sickly child from the time of her birth in New Hampshire. At the age of two she had lost all her senses but that of touch. Six years later, in 1837, her parents brought her to a benefactor, who determined to release her from darkness. Weeks of patient loving effort stretched into months as she was taught the arbitrary signs of language by feeling raised letters. The poor child learned mechanically as a knowing dog his tricks, imitating in mute amazement everything her teacher did. Then *the truth began to flash upon her: her intellect began to work: she perceived that here was a way by which she could herself make up a sign of anything that was in her own mind, and show it to another mind; and at once her countenance lighted up with a human expression: it was no longer a dog or a parrot: it was an immortal spirit, eagerly seizing upon a new link of union with other spirits!*

Samuel Gridley Howe, who for years devotedly led Laura by the hand, was then thirty-six years old, an able doctor, well connected and in a position to strike for any of the forms of success his countrymen valued. He chose to sit, hour after hour, with a little girl who could not see or hear or speak. He did so with the same courage and determination with which he had a few years earlier fought with the Poles and the Greeks for independence. He intended to prove that Laura's immortal spirit could not die nor be maimed nor mutilated, that even within this least accessible of beings was an irreducible human element that the will of man could improve.

He was one of that company of reformers which had undertaken to revise the whole social structure, the state, the school, religion, marriage, trade, and science. Their total pattern of belief had inflamed the people of his generation with enthusiasm; any sacrifice was justified to hasten the dawn of a nobler morning in history.

Those heady ideas emerged from the assimilation of new intellectual trends that transformed the life of Europe even while Metternich schemed to keep the Old World from changing. In France, Germany and England, philosophers, poets, scientists and historians reinterpreted man, the world he inhabited, his religious faith and the means by which he was to improve his condition. Their thoughts were attentively received in the New World. Americans no longer counted themselves the rivals of Europe; more confident and less defensive than formerly, they regarded the older culture across the Atlantic as a source from which they could draw inspiration, as a stimulus to their own thinking. Eagerly they went back to the universities at Göttingen, Berlin and Paris and to the ateliers of Florence and Rome. They became avid readers of the books and magazines that flowed in a steady stream across the ocean; and they patiently listened to the lectures and concerts by the famous foreigners who made them visits. Most important of all, native writers and thinkers absorbed and restated the European concepts in terms that accorded with the heritage and experience of the Americans themselves.

In this age, oratory was the most successful medium of communication. The persuasive effects of the spoken word established the influential politicians, preachers and philosophers who made themselves heard from the lecture platform before they were widely read in the book or magazine. The lecturer could not marshal his thoughts in private; he had to be aware of the audience with which he sought to share his meaning and he had to turn his phrases to hold the attention of the men and women who sat before him. The necessity of doing so significantly affected the ideas of such men as Ralph Waldo Emerson, who regularly mounted the rostrum.

Few Americans were more carefully listened to than he. For years he traveled a national circuit, working over the subjects he later published as essays. In the process, he gave the German idealism and the English romanticism that had stimulated him a distinctive American cast.

Emerson's vision perceived a mystical unity in the universe. Every object of nature had not only the particular form of its own being but was also a part of the transcendent oversoul called God. In this pantheistic communion, every man shared a spark of the divine. The natural impulses that animated each in his free actions were divine; and self-reliance was God-reliance. Man had only to turn to nature for reason and faith. *Standing on the bare ground, — my head bathed by the blithe air, and uplifted into infinite space, — all mean egotism vanishes. I become a transparent eyeball. I am nothing. I see all. The currents of the Universal Being circulate through me; I am part or particle of God.*

Many of these phrases remained obscure to the earnest men and women in the audience; few Americans in the 1830's considered themselves transparent eyeballs. Yet they nevertheless found a meaning in Emerson's message.

Theologically these transcendental ideas were remote from the forms of Christianity most Americans professed. Emerson indeed had thrown up his pulpit because he could not accept even the Unitarian doctrine, undemanding as that was. Yet the citizens of Cincinnati or St. Louis who begged him to lecture in their cities did not consider him an infidel. Sober churchgoers nodded in approval as they followed the convoluted clauses of his sentences.

The message they heard was not quite that which the orator intended to convey. He spoke of nature; his listeners summoned to mind the features of the earth as they had been before man's arrival, not capriciously thrown together but arrayed in a coherent order which reflected the rule of law that governed the universe. None, examining its convenient disposition, could deny that it was the handiwork of a benevolent Creator. But neither could any doubt that change was an integral element of that order; *nature slept no moment on an old past, but every hour repaired itself and improvement was its law.* Man, as one of its creatures, was an instrument in the process. His canal corrected the inadequacies in the course of the stream and his clearing rid the land of its superfluities of forest. Indeed, their own experience persuaded Americans that such advances were the rule: otherwise how account for the subdued wilderness, the never-ending expansion of settlement, and the steady growth of wealth?

Progress, in fact, was a law of history. Humanity had always advanced, thwarted sometimes by obstacles, deviating occasionally from the true line, but in time moving onward to perfectibility. Whatever was just, humane, good and true, according to an immutable ordinance of Providence, would in the sure light of the future prevail. It was inherent in man's nature that he should be able to improve himself, for he came into the world endowed with infinite capacities, inspired by infinite desires, and commanded to strive perpetually after excellence. Common to each and every one — even to Laura in her utter darkness — was that seed of spirit susceptible to improvement. The common man was every man, in his original state, waiting to be made perfect. Whatever impediments held him back were extraneous and removable; his own character was innately good. Evil was no gloomy mystery, binding the world in everlasting thrall, but an accident, destined to be surely subdued as the Human Family pressed on to the promised goal of happiness.

The reason and the will were the means of effecting that improvement, the former by permitting man to discern the laws by which the universe functioned, the latter by enabling him to manipulate the forces about him. To use either well he had to disencumber himself of the bonds of tradition, habit and authority and, looking squarely at the world about him, strive to recast it. The practice of self-reliance summoned forth the best qualities of each person and strengthened him to leave his mark upon the times. Self-improvement was therefore the cardinal virtue.

It remained only for society to create the conditions under which the individual could develop his capacities, by removing the unnatural obstructions in the way of correct understanding and righteous action. All shared the obligation of participating in those labors, for all were members of a single human family and held a common stake in the future progress of mankind. There was no reason to believe that the process would be long or difficult. But neither was there any excuse for delay; every obstacle leveled brought nearer the moment of redemption for all.

In arriving at this faith in man's ability to perfect himself, the Americans had come a long way from the time when they had conceived themselves helpless sinners in the hands of an angry God. They had recast, in terms of their own experience, the ideas derived from the Great Awakening and inherited from the enlightenment of the revolutionary period. The expansion and growth of a half-century were the manifestations of their own power and merit; the painful deficiency in what had thus far been achieved was the unfinished business of the future. The assurance of indefinite progress alike gratified the successful and consoled the failures.

It was not in the least difficult to reinterpret traditional Christian doctrine in the light of these basic assumptions; and the loose sectarianism of American religious life offered men ample latitude to do so. The broad band of New England settlement that stretched from Vermont through upper New York into Ohio was repeatedly burned over by fiery prophets who made converts by pointing out that progress was merely another term for the familiar millennial Second Coming of Christ. William Miller may have erred in the calculation of the precise date in 1844. His disappointed followers came home from the hilltops where they had waited in vain; but the zeal of their adventist faith did not abate in the least. Joseph Smith, having founded a church with the discovery of the Book of Mormon, gave the believers a cause by revealing that they were latter-day saints enduring a period of trial by preparing for the coming of the Kingdom.

Others were bolder in their theological speculations. John Humphrey Noyes formed Perfectionist colonies in Putney, Vermont, and Oneida, New York, where, like the Shakers earlier, he hoped to establish social institutions appropriate to the Millennium. Unlike his celibate forerunners, however, he preached the perfection of love in both a carnal and a spiritual sense and devised a pattern of complex marriage that earned his colonies a lurid reputation.

More significant than these picturesque offshoots was the subtle process by which the central body of American religious thought assimilated the concepts of progress and perfectibility. Unitarianism was already susceptible by virtue of its roots in the Enlightenment; it rejected any imputation of natural depravity in man and from the premise of his essential goodness conceived of a *Christian revolution* that would create a new social order based on recognition of the obligations of the moral law. The Quakers too were prepared to shift the emphasis of their concern to the improvement of the world about them. The preaching of Elias Hicks precipitated a schism among the the Friends, not because of divisions in basic points of view, but out of disagreement about the speed with which traditional doctrine could be abandoned.

Orthodox Trinitarians in various Methodist, Baptist and Presbyterian groups effected the same transition, although not without bitter doctrinal dispute. The essential element in the change was the surrender of the sharp distinction between the regenerate and the unregenerate and the insistence that all men were capable of perfection. Although the Disciples of Christ, formed by Alexander Campbell in Kentucky, acknowledged that only God's gift of grace truly freed the sinful, they nevertheless believed that the work of the church was not merely *to Christianize some, but to moralize more and, in some degree, to civilize all.*

The change was less overt in the Congregational churches, which were custodians of a contrary tradition that led directly back to the Puritans and to John Calvin, and which had been hardened by experience to resist the enthusiasms of unorthodox preachers. Yet the old doctrine was doomed. The learned ministers wrestled with the inherited body of theology that argued man's helplessness against the will of God. They could scarcely go directly to Perfectionism; but a circuitous route brought them to an accommodation with the spirit of the age. Nathaniel Taylor, a frail, thoughtful divine in New Haven, found the means of persuading many of his colleagues that freedom of choice was not an illusion and that anyone was therefore capable of being saved if he wished to be. His neighbor in Hartford, Horace Bushnell, concluded that there was no caprice in the divine selection of candidates for redemption; God fixed on those whose families reared them to recognize Him in their actions. Correct Christian nurture that trained people in good behavior would open a way to salvation that could comprehend all.

Even revivalism showed an unexpected affinity for Emerson's doctrines. The great meetings which continued through these decades were still enlivened by extreme manifestations of emotion; remorseful sinners rolled upon the ground, shrieked and were seized by the jerks before they found the peace of repentance. The preachers' extemporaneous inspirations and wild gesticulations were in marked contrast to the lecturers' careful reading of prepared manuscripts. Yet common content showed they spoke to the same audience. Charles Finney threatened his listeners with hellfire and damnation but also assured them that they could *get right with God* by laboring to create a New Eden in which people would voluntarily live in harmony with the moral law which governed the world. The Y.M.C.A. and the home missionary movement, each in its own sphere, preached the same gospel.

A reform movement among the growing Jewish congregations showed much the same tendencies. Indeed, faith in the essential goodness of man and in his capacity to progress toward perfectibility rested squarely upon American experience. The ideas borrowed from Europe supplied the concepts to make meaningful the energies expended in growth and in expansion across the continent.

The new faith demanded action. The test of virtue was the practice of goodness; and that required men actively to ameliorate the condition of humanity. The decade after 1815 defined the tactics and strategy for doing so; then, in one area after another, Americans launched efforts to recast their world.

Precisely because the sources of support were so widely diffused, these movements needed dedicated leaders willing to devote their full time to organizing societies, collecting dues and contributions, publishing journals, making speeches and traveling through the country on missions of persuasion. Naturally such people were exceptional; often by the standards of their countrymen, they seemed eccentric. Some, like William Lloyd Garrison or Elihu Burritt, were the sons of artisans and farmers who had not done well or were frustrated by personal, emotional, or economic difficulties. Others, like Wendell Phillips, sprang from well-to-do families and had the advantages of education and position; and occasionally established merchants like the Tappan brothers or Gerrit Smith took a prominent part.

Efforts at a total reconstruction of society were rare and were uniformly unsuccessful. A few enthusiasts, having read the works of the French socialist Fourier, set themselves to building utopian colonies in the suburbs of Boston and New York or in the wilds of Indiana. But Brook Farm and other such experiments were harmless diversions, with little general support or influence. The way to improvement was not through the destruction of property that the socialists proposed, but through its diffusion. And the impediments to progress would not be blasted out by a general assault but would yield one by one to the patient efforts by which the reformers removed all unnatural restraints that impeded man in the pursuit of perfection. If Dr. Howe could thus liberate Laura, surely there were no limits to what could be done in aid of the less afflicted.

Any bold spirit who could wield a pen or mount a rostrum could launch his own movement. The air was heavy with schemes for redemption, each with an irrefutable logic of its own. *What a fertility of projects for the salvation of the world!* The soldiery of dissent attacked evil on every flank. One thought that all men should go to farming and another that none should buy or sell; another, considering that the mischief lay in diet, made unleavened bread and fought fermentation to the death. The adepts of homeopathy, or hydropathy, of mesmerism and of phrenology, all claimed to work their miracles.

With this din of opinion and debate, there was nevertheless a keen scrutiny of institutions that produced lasting changes in American life. Education was the most powerful weapon in the struggle for self-improvement, for knowledge would free men from the shackles of ignorance. What schools existed were farcical, deficient in both organization and pedagogical methods. They were to be entirely reformed, borrowing from, and improving upon, the best European models. Horace Mann and Henry Barnard led a struggle for free, secular public schools open to all. They asked the state to supervise and support local boards, to maintain standards and to provide a supply of trained professional teachers. It would then be possible to end the philosophy of *Authority, Force, Fear, and Pain that indissolubly associated together the ideas of Childhood and Punishment.* Instead the school would humanize and refine, *show that there was something besides wrath and stripes and suffering in God's world* and by dignity, learning and benevolence encourage the child to develop his innate capacities for learning.

In 1860, the task was far from complete; but it was well under way. Teachers trained in normal schools took up their vocations seriously rather than as a temporary expedient. They taught in buildings erected for the purpose and used the Peter Parley and McGuffey texts written with the specific needs of students in mind. And scores of mechanics' institutes, libraries and lyceums, as well as the flourishing daily press and hundreds of magazines, carried education beyond the years of childhood. There was also hope of converting the college to some useful end. Although the older Eastern institutions remained encrusted and inert, their ancient curricula still at war with common sense, the new state universities were to serve the people by spreading practical learning.

Self-improvement also required liberation from any force that limited the individual's capacities. The stupefied drunkard was remote indeed from perfection; by 1830 a thousand temperance societies had exacted three hundred thousand pledges of abstinence. In the next two decades the movement achieved national organization and borrowed the tactics of the revivalists. J. B. Gough and his imitators wandered about the country, pointing to the example of their own conversion and describing in lurid detail the noxious effects of whiskey on man. They enlisted thousands of followers, but not enough. As long as the weak in will remained unpersuaded the work was not done.

In the 1850's, the reformers called upon the government for aid. Twelve states followed Maine's example in enacting prohibition laws. This was not a denial of liberty but an extension of it, for these statutes simply removed temptation from men incapable of freeing themselves from its corrupting effects. And no doubt the virtuous who painfully surrendered vice were reluctant to see it too easily enjoyed by the unredeemed.

All those rendered dependent by their situation were similarly to be encouraged to lift themselves. Laura's example showed the way. On a visit to the East Cambridge jail in 1841, Dorothea Dix saw the insane chained naked to the wall. She learned that there were only eight asylums in the country, not one of them adequately maintained. She then made it her life's work to travel from prison to poorhouse, from cellar to cave — wherever these unfortunates were incarcerated. Legislature after legislature yielded to her plea for help in rescuing the least of humans. Other reformers lavished their concern upon the victims of vice and poverty. The poor, the criminal, the orphaned and the ill were no longer to be counted subjects of an overpowering fate, useless and worthy only to be shut out of the way. They too were human beings, capable of being redeemed and of becoming useful members of the community. The dependent female half of mankind also needed liberation. In 1848, a feminist declaration of independence at Seneca Falls set the goals for the emancipation from the legal and social discrimination that kept women inferior in status.

The same reform impulse animated the efforts to guarantee every person one day of rest. The Sabbatarian movement enlisted not only the tradition-minded, but also humanitarians persuaded that human dignity required at least this relief from ceaseless labor. A somewhat similar motive lay behind the efforts to protect the workingmen. The artisans displaced by economic growth were torn between the desire to protect their existing position and that of finding an exit from it. On the one hand, they supported the demand for a ten-hour law for the employees of corporations and fought to abolish imprisonment for debt. On the other, they agitated for a homestead law that would give a free plot of land to every prospective settler.

The new point of view undermined the old justification for property qualifications for suffrage and officeholding. The artisans most directly affected were in the forefront of the movement to repeal these restrictions which disappeared in most parts of the Union in the 1820's and 1830's. But their appeals met a sympathetic response at every level of society. One could not deny political equality to the common men, if all were on the way to being perfected. For the same reason, Americans actively championed the revolutionary struggles of Poles, Greeks, Frenchmen and Germans for democracy.

But the brightest star in the whole galaxy of reform was abolition. The Negro was the most deprived, the least free of beings. Yet within him too the divine spark glowed, the common human element demanded liberation. Slavery was the greatest indignity of all, for it denied to millions the most elementary human qualities and, by its degrading effect upon both master and slave, stood in the way of the whole nation's progress. Abolition gained steadily in strength after 1830, drawing support from both revivalist religion and rationalistic humanitarianism.

That slavery was an evil — some would have said a sin — evoked little serious difference of opinion in the North, although only a few zealots saw their way clear to effecting immediate emancipation. Respect for property and law induced others to hope for the curative effects of time. For the time being, the institution would remain in the South, where constitutional guarantees protected it. But it was certainly not to expand, nor was federal power to sustain it. Yet there were serious questions: how long was the *time being* to endure and what means would finally root the evil out where it existed? Meanwhile there were grave problems at home, in elevating the free Negro and in according him his full rights as a man.

Questions of pace and method were often vexatious despite the widespread agreement upon ultimate objectives. The reform impulse expressed the general belief of Americans unsettled by expansion and economic growth that they could contribute to human progress by perfecting themselves and their society. At once, or gradually? And at what cost? Some counseled patience; others were willing to tear down every existing structure to speed the rebuilding. In 1842 a meeting of the Massachusetts Anti-Slavery Society voted against the following motion: *Resolved, that the sectarian organizations called churches are combinations of thieves, robbers, adulterers, pirates and murderers, and as such form the bulwarks of American slavery.* The extraordinary logic of that statement bespoke the unwillingness to wait of those who thought millennial perfection imminent. More moderate men expected some delay. Only a few refused to enlist at all in the armies of progress.

Reform created the greatest problems for those who somehow stood apart from most Americans, not sharing fully the same social situation or the same basic religious premises. Progress and perfectibility, for instance, had little meaning to the mass of immigrants of the 1840's and 1850's, who saw no prospect of immediate reward in the promises of the New World. Their faith was a consolatory one, which directed their vision toward the life eternal of the hereafter rather than toward the transient pleasures of this world. The German Lutherans and Irish Catholics wished their churches to be stabilizing elements of communities they hoped to rebuild rather than agents of change. In their view, the reformers all too often discounted the evil that was real in man and interfered with the simple gratification of his wants. The recently arrived remained entirely apart — often suspicious, sometimes overtly hostile.

The great merchants of the Eastern cities were also qualified in their enthusiasm for reform. The lack of respect for familiar landmarks distressed men who valued order and wished to minimize hazards. They were willing enough to support education and to aid the blind and insane but they grew uneasy when enthusiasts proved heedless of the rights of property and discounted the worth of wealth. Respectable men wished the safeguards of law to limit the disruptive effects of excessive social change. Some, Congregationalist or Presbyterian by birth, sought stability in the Anglican Church, attracted by its ritual and its air of permanence that was a welcome relief from the turbulence of the sects.

The direct path from reform to abolition alarmed Southerners. Long reliance upon the faith that the future would solve the unsolved problems of the present had permitted the planters to evade responsibility for the Negro's bondage while the plantation fastened slavery permanently into the life of the region. After 1830, they could no longer contemplate emancipation, even in the remote distance, not only because of the guilt and the fear of the social consequences that had troubled Jefferson's generation, but also because it would ruin the whole economy. The servitude which had enthroned cotton as king of the productive system could not be wholly bad; it had made progress possible. The laborious search for a defense of slavery phrased in terms that all Americans could accept increasingly occupied Southern thinking. There was little persuasive power in references to the bondage described in the Bible or in Greek and Roman antiquity; the religious and social standards of the New World were loftier than those of the past.

The most useful expedient was a counterattack to prove slave labor more progressive than wage slavery. William Grayson and John C. Calhoun argued that the hireling of the North was actually less well off than the bondsman of the South; and George Fitzhugh demonstrated that a great civilization could only rise on the patriarchal basis of slavery.

Yet there was an awkwardness to that line of thought: why confine to the Negro *the kind and affectionate relations that usually existed between master and slave and that could never be created between the capitalist and the laborer?* Alas, the great planters were a minority in the South and the poor whites had no desire to be part of the sill that kept their betters out of the mud. In 1858 Hinton Helper warned the *Non-Slaveholders of the South* that slavery threatened to degrade them and demanded its abolition.

There was as yet no way of accounting for the Negro's peculiar fitness for bondage that would reassure the whites. Fitzhugh believed that the blacks were innately inferior, but because he could not bring himself to deny their common humanity, he had to reject, root and branch, his contemporaries' ideals of equality and freedom. Only a few speculative doctors like Samuel Morton and Josiah Nott were willing to conceive of a multiple creation that would exclude the Negro from descent from Adam and make him a special species of man. Most Americans, North and South, clung to the literal accuracy of the Bible, to the Christian belief in the unity of creation and to the faith that a common divine spirit animated all men.

The Southern attitude therefore remained equivocal. For three decades the slaveholders were on edge. Year after year they made great issues of abolitionist petitions to Congress, of the inflammatory statements in obscure newspapers, of the rantings in distant meetings. Yet they had little reason to fear that Congress would act upon those petitions or that some stray copy of the *Liberator* would find its way to an illiterate slave. Why then did they care?

They cared because they had to justify and defend themselves to themselves. Like the merchants, they shared the premises of their countrymen, but feared the conclusions that followed from them.

Many Southerners remained quiet abolitionists, resenting their peculiar institution yet incapable of doing anything about it. Some reforms, like temperance, women's rights, and aid to the dependent found as much support in the South as in the North. But a growing anxiety about the implications for the Negro qualified the slaveholders' attitude toward progress and perfectibility; and a few, like Fitzhugh, were bold enough to renounce altogether the common intellectual heritage of their times.

The merchants and the planters often took refuge in the pretense that they were the products of stable paternalistic and patriarchal traditions. The Brahmin or the Knickerbocker pictured himself the offspring of several generations of gentlemen, untroubled by material concerns and dedicated to culture and to political leadership. If there was a country estate in the background, then he was the genial squire, respectfully greeted by a contented yeomanry. If not, then he was a captain of commerce whose ships brought wealth from distant shores.

In the South, the dreams were feudal. The plantation became a manor, the slaves humble serfs, and the planter a mounted knight, gallant in war, chivalrous, disdainful of materialistic considerations. His highest obligation was to his honor, affixed to the woman who was his own true love. Surrounded by the voluminous skirts that were the symbol of her ladyhood, she occupied the center of his household. Chaste and virtuous, affectionate but not sensuous, hospitable to her equals and kind but firm to her inferiors, a competent mistress but free of all manual tasks, she glided gracefully through the drawing rooms that were her — and his — domain, all as described in the novels of Sir Walter Scott.

The participants in these fantasies did not really deceive themselves. They had no such traditions. The merchant had as recently moved into his Beacon Hill home as the planter to his Mississippi plantation. They were only trying to shake off the uncomfortable weight of ideas they could not totally reject. The tension of that effort diminished their ability to work with other groups and itself demonstrated the disruptive consequences of the awareness that progress in America depended upon the perfectibility of every man.

17

The Tensions of an Expanding Society

O N THE LAST DAY of its 1855 session, the House of Representatives of the Great and General Court of the Commonwealth of Massachusetts unanimously adopted an act to incorporate the Gridiron Newspaper Company. Among the incorporators were the Governor and a group of distinguished Boston citizens. Only a few issues of the journal appeared, although for a time it enjoyed the patronage of the federal government. The editor, Daniel Pratt, was a well-known figure in the community. He traveled a good deal, was a popular lecturer, and at one point announced his candidacy for the Presidency. His platform: *I am for the Constitution and the Union. Christian Virtues. Faith, Hope, Charity, Benevolence, Hospitality.* Among those who encouraged him to write his autobiography and helped him publish it were Professor Joseph Henry of the Smithsonian Institution, General Winfield Scott, Daniel Webster, Jared Sparks, John Pierpont, Edward Everett, Rufus Choate, and Abbott Lawrence.

Pratt's speeches to various groups earned him numerous tokens of recognition. On one occasion, Longfellow composed an Ode expressly to celebrate his oratory — which lifted

Americans up in heart,
To play their great and exalted part;
And win a name that can never fade,
And leaving smaller ones in the shade
While he himself goes high in air,
And comes down plump on the President's chair.

Not among the bard's best efforts, of course! But few lecturers had the distinction thus to be honored.

Pratt was a lunatic. A poor boy who had never succeeded in any of the trades at which he tried his hand, he had shipped on a whaler and gone out too late to the California gold rush. He returned to Boston to spend the rest of his life drifting through New England, a figure of fun among his distinguished contemporaries.

Such a readiness for amusement the Americans displayed! Half-mad eccentrics turned up in many communities, to the huge enjoyment of the inhabitants. Richard Locke established the success of the New York *Sun* by a series of stories in 1835 describing the one-horned goats and strange flora on the moon, seen through a gigantic telescope. The ladies of Springfield, Massachusetts, having subscribed to a fund to send missionaries to the unconverted batlike lunar men, no doubt were carried away with genteel laughter when they learned it was all a hoax. Trickery of this sort was long to be P. T. Barnum's stock in trade.

What did Americans find so funny in the demented antics of an unbalanced lunatic?

They were laughing to keep from crying. Focusing on the one who was the travesty of themselves, they could quiet the emotions and satisfy the intelligence with ridicule. All those caricatures — Sam Slick, Hezekiah Bigelow and the buncombe oratory — transposed the solemn into a bearable form. Hidden in the black face, the slave became a minstrel who was not a Negro at all. Only thus could men relieve the unbearable tension under which they suffered, held back by their limited capacity for achievement, pushed on by their own limitless expectations and aspirations.

A general ache seized hold of Americans shortly after adolescence. The women complained constantly of debilitating headaches and the men worried themselves with unidentified pains. Not uncommonly on the frontier, the passing stranger pushed open the door of a windowless cabin to find father and mother down with the ague while the unheeded children fended for themselves. The private correspondence of this period kept an unending record of invalidism and of the fear of disease. This was entirely apart from the panic caused by more spectacular disasters, as when Asiatic cholera swept through the coastal ports in 1849 or when yellow fever descended upon cities in the South.

These people were no weaker than their forebears nor more disposed to debilitating illness. Their diet was far from meeting later standards of adequate nutrition; but it was no worse than earlier. By any objective criteria, the health of the Americans probably improved in the half-century after 1810; certainly the death rate of the native-born generally declined.

Yet the complaints and miseries were not simply imagined. They were, in part, the product of an altered view of disease. Physical disorders were products of natural causes and therefore were not to be passively accepted, but controlled, either by prevention or cure. The correct mode of life and the use of correct remedies were guarantees of health. It remained only to know what was right. Feverishly the quest went on for the proper nostrum. Every town worried about its provisions for public health; and individuals diligently endeavored to select among the rival medical sects that purported to know how to treat their ailments. Numerous Americans also sampled the patent remedies and pain-killers compounded by chemists or offered by medicine sellers of every degree of honesty. Daniel Pratt too had a secret cure in a bottle that could relieve any ill. Undoubtedly the liberal use of alcohol in these preparations served some purpose; and, in any case, whiskey was a recognized specific for weariness. The unremitting anxiety about feeling good created a morbid sensitivity to pain that heightened the eagerness with which people welcomed the oblivion of anesthesia.

It also explained the persistent hope of discovering a clue to the means by which an act of will could itself conquer disease. Some believed that Dr. Spurzheim's charts of phrenological bumps were the key; others accepted Dr. Mesmer's notion that animal magnetism was the answer. In Belfast, Maine, Phineas Quimby discovered that a subject he threw into hypnosis could diagnose and prescribe effectively.

Quimby gave up clockmaking and took to the road, then concluded that the curative power came not from the insight of the subject but from the faith of the patient. He settled down to a prosperous career of mental healing, comforting his clients with the assurance that the human mind, functioning properly, could control every physical reality.

With this preoccupation with bodily ills went a shuddery fascination with death. In 1832 a twenty-two-year-old Divinity School student at Harvard went in the middle of the night to the tomb of a cousin who had died a few months earlier. They had been in love when he had been sixteen. Laboriously he unscrewed the coffin to catch a glimpse of her undecayed features, hoping there to find some clue to the meaning of life. In fiction, too, the blonde girls went unfulfilled to the grave. The death scene in the novel or play could always bring emotion to a crescendo. The thoughts of this generation ran frequently to *the last bitter hour, the stern agony and shroud, and pall, and breathless darkness, and the narrow house. Surrendering up their individual beings,* they knew, *each would go to mix forever with the elements, to be a brother to the insensible rock and to the sluggish clod, which the rude swain turned with his share, and trod upon. All who walked the globe were but a handful to the tribes that slumbered in it.* But could they really console themselves with the thought that approaching the grave, they would *wrap the drapery of their couch about them and lie down to pleasant dreams?*

The burial place ceased to be an adjunct of the church and became, as at Mount Auburn, a site of sepulchral beauty designed to touch the emotions. Sensitive young people wandered through the lanes, holding communion with nature in its visible forms and pausing to contemplate the elaborate monuments to mortality. Here were Poe's materials. Figures of decay ran through much of the imaginative writing and painting of the period.

Broody wonderings about death touched off a curious strain of speculation about the afterlife. In 1844, Andrew Jackson Davis, a poor shoemaker boy sent off on a *psychic flight through space* by a hypnotist, concluded that the departed shades were not gone forever; communication with them could unlock the secrets of the universe and establish the brotherhood of man. A few years later, the Fox sisters in Rochester learned how to interpret the knockings of the spirits in order to carry on conversations beyond the grave.

The men and women who worried about their bodies in health, in illness, and in death, also anxiously sought to understand the mysterious sexual impulses linked to so many other of their tensions. At some point in that undefined area in which spirit and matter overlapped, the intercourse of love in a sacred act gave birth to life. Yet to yield incautiously to the obscure urgings that led to that point was to risk defilement; there was a fate worse than death, and its name was love. Man, innately good though he was, could blunder into unaccountable guilt and corruption. The various connotations of the word love muddled the whole problem: love of God, mother love, love of country — were these the same as the love of a man and a woman? There was no clear answer because the question could not be discussed openly; one could only guess by indirection from the characters of fiction.

The stories reveal a consistent pattern.

Men and women exert upon one another a physical attraction not unlike that of Dr. Mesmer's hypnotism; a current passes between them as between magnetic particles. So much is physical and susceptible to either good or evil ends. The seducer's wiles can have the same effect as the true lover's declaration of faith; and the victim may actually be deceived by the appearance of pleasure in the disaster. Yet the purely sensual union surely destroys the spirit and forever ruins its participants. There is a nobler way. The hero and heroine fall in love; they feel the same physical force; but they transcend it, by subordinating it at whatever sacrifice to a spiritual union that elevates them both. Thus the last chapter. The implication is that the sanctification of marriage will in due course lead to a consummation in the flesh, which will have no brute carnal purpose but rather will serve the future through the family.

Strains on family life, however, made the criteria of romantic love burdensome. The falling mortality rate created unexpected problems. Husbands and wives had to spend longer lives together and parents, spared the painful duty of burying some of their children, discovered the prolonged anxiety of trying to provide for all of them. It was no easy matter to supply a proper start on the plantation or the farm. To divert land, slaves, or capital to the use of a son was to curtail the father's chances of expansion. The elders counseled the postponement of marriage, the youth were anxious to strike out for themselves, and the hidden rivalry between the generations extended the pain of separation. Meanwhile, the young men who went West or delayed their entry upon family life abandoned increasing numbers of women to spinsterhood.

The choices were even harsher in the city. Between the merchants and the immigrant laborers, a vast middling population struggled for respectability, its hopes fastened to the chance of rising to wealth, its fears fixed on the danger of the descent to poverty. The artisans, shopkeepers, clerks and bookkeepers had the limited assets of their skills; but their chance of bettering themselves rested upon the ability to accumulate a modicum of capital and yet to maintain the decent style of life that commanded the confidence of those with whom they dealt. The bachelor living with his parents was in the best position to do so. When marriage proved irresistible, the prudent man established his wife in a boardinghouse until he could afford the expense of an appropriate household; and thereafter he constantly balanced the charges of family life against his need for capital. If he managed well, his every move would be upward. But if he miscalculated, rushed too early into wedlock, or begot children too soon or too frequently, then his opportunity for success vanished.

The excessive family damaged the offspring as well as the parents. It deprived the young both of the stake to set them on their way and of the orderly Christian nurture to aid them to perfection. The heedlessness of one generation thus endangered the welfare of the next.

Under these circumstances the size of the native white families shrank steadily in the nineteenth century. The effort was painful, for the American family had already ceased to orient itself by the norms of a stable community and its members had to make every decision for themselves, self-reliantly, by their own standards of individual fulfillment. Year after year, in the darkness, the men and women examined their desires in the effort to understand what they wanted.

They were unhappily ill-informed about the alternatives. The spectacular experiments of John Humphrey Noyes reflected the pervasive curiosity about birth control. The less overt manifestations were more significant. Licensed physicians worried about the number of abortions; and the columns of the press carried frequent advertisements of pills and potions of an undescribed effectiveness. Did the notice mean what it said? *Must not be used during pregnancy. Certain to produce miscarriage during that period!* Lectures, in many towns, *for men* [or *women*] *only* drew unabashed audiences of growing size, and the sales of popular books which spoke in private and in confidence, and told the honest truth, mounted to the hundreds of thousands.

The expressed attitudes of society were clear and unanimous. Any artificial form of birth control enfeebled the frame, produced a horrible train of disease, and was a crime against nature and God. Abstinence, repression and self-restraint were the only safe means of regulating family size. Only by careful exercise of his will and reason could man avoid the debilitating effects of carnality and enjoy a pure, spiritual love, consummated only when justified by the purpose of procreation.

Whether Americans fully succeeded in doing so or not, the strain was severe. Prostitution in the cities and concubinage on the plantations revealed the extent to which some men found restraint unbearable. No such release was available to respectable women, married or spinster, who suffered in addition from a constricted role that denied them passions, as their extravagant costumes denied them femininity. Resentment at their bondage to a romantic model — ethereal and fleshless — sparked their struggle for rights, much as it did the Bloomerite revolt against fashion.

Men and women alike displayed acute sensitivity to any image with the least sexual connotation. Drapes modestly covered the piano legs, or rather, limbs — the bolder word was not used in polite conversation; and the replica of Hiram Powers's Greek Slave was decently outfitted in a sober garment. Lurid reports of vice in the slums, among the poor, or in heathen lands made shocking but interesting reading, for indignation offset the thrill of peeps at the depravity of others. Often indeed, the successful, stiff in the unremitting postures of self-control, regarded with pity the poor, the Negroes and the foreigners whom they sought to reform. There, in the slave quarters or tenements, people gave themselves over to animal-like unrestraint; drinking and breeding without calculation, they bartered for momentary pleasures their birthright of perfectibility. Or did they?

The men and women striving to succeed could not afford to doubt it. Their own investment in goodness was too heavy. Some at least of those feminine headaches, of those all-pervasive masculine aches and pains were the products of the tensions their efforts generated.

The men expended much of their energy at work, an outlet open only to the women of the poor. The others, having completed the chores of households plentifully staffed, after 1840, with Irish and Negro servants, turned to the most available resource, reading. A flood of magazines, novels, giftbooks and annuals supplied them with romances in which they sought the meaning of their lives. In these tales, they could suffer vicariously the dangers their own experience excluded and take pleasure in the ultimate rewards of virtue. Sometimes, too, they led their husbands to the concerts, plays and exhibitions of traveling companies, where both could edify and improve themselves.

The need remained for activities that would give participants a more direct sense of belonging and thus endow them with a consciousness of identity they could not feel alone, detached in their own families. Compelled by their restless moving about always to share their lives with strangers, these people were eager for external means of orienting themselves as they made the vital decisions in illness or health, at birth, marriage and death. The burden of choice upon the unaided power of their reason was otherwise far too heavy.

Hence they urgently desired to form associations to take the place of the communities they had left or had never known. A multitude of societies appeared to serve every type of American, rich and poor, Eastern and Western, urban and rural, native and foreign. Whatever other function they performed, they relieved the loneliness and supplied the norms by which their members located themselves.

The churches were the most common, sometimes the only, form of group life. Having by now altogether separated themselves from the state and become purely voluntary bodies, they were entirely dependent upon local support. Those who joined existing sects or created new ones satisfied not only the need for worship but also that for belonging. Attached to the religious rites were pleasure of participation in common activities which the whole family shared — fairs and picnics or the simple exchange of talk with neighbors.

Other groupings turned about some important communal function. Militia and fire companies offered protection of a sort but also allowed their members to meet, elect officers, parade in uniform, and roister at their annual feasts in which a laudable purpose forgave the relaxation of the usual restraints. Those recognized purposes set the good citizens off from the Plug-Uglies, Knuckle-Dusters, and other gangs, in which less respectable types entrenched themselves in the unpoliced sections of the cities, such as The Five Points in Manhattan. Innumerable philanthropic, cultural and reform organizations offered somewhat more austere outlets for the urge to belong.

Americans became a nation of joiners, creating groups for purely fraternal objectives when nothing else drew them together. The Masons, after stirring up a flurry of political hostility in the 1820's, settled down in convivial lodges. A host of other societies assumed grandiloquent names, gave their officers exalted titles, and established their identity in ceremonies, rituals and uniforms. Some cloaked themselves in secrecy to unite the initiates by excluding the outsiders. Within the sanctum the individual changed; he could be what he was not in ordinary life, behave as he would not usually permit himself to. Staunch republicans threw off their somber garments as they passed through the portal, proudly bore monarchical titles, arrayed themselves in snatches of Oriental or medieval finery and became Knights and Potentates, for the moment absolved of the bonds that restrained other men. In the group the individual thus found relief from the stern obligation of self-reliance he accepted outside it.

Secrecy, however, evoked the fear and resentment of the excluded. The uninitiate could only guess at what went on behind the drawn curtains and their guesses traveled along all the illicit avenues they would not permit themselves to enter. The unidentified probably hid to do what they could not do in the open; lewd orgies, murders, conspiracies to subvert the state were the order of their meetings. No ordinary power could put them down; only the secrecy of counter-conspiracy was effective. The anti-Masons organized to do battle with the Masons, the anti-Mormons with the Mormons, and the Order of the Star Spangled Banner with the Roman Catholics.

Violence and the symbols of violence tinged all these activities. Every initiation rite included some gesture of brutality or some touch of blood as if this overleaping of usual restraints would best establish the unity of the group. The lodge members did not ordinarily resort to the illicit use of force, common on the frontier or in the slums. But they were fascinated by it and now and again yielded to temptations to violence in riots or vigilante action. When some laudable purpose justified it, they hanged thieves, burned down a nunnery to liberate its inmates, destroyed the presses of unpopular editors or the houses of prostitutes, and drove away Mormons or rival fire companies. In the initiation ceremony, the participants joined in the taste of the forbidden, both to seal the secret and to throw off temporarily the restraint by which they ordinarily bound themselves.

Many, but not all, associations fell within ethnic lines. Common language, religion, culture, and habits spontaneously drew men together when they had a choice. The process of migration emphasized these elements; distance from the homeland added value to its heritage. The Vermonter and Bostonian were more likely to acknowledge their likeness as Yankees in San Francisco than in the East. For the foreign-born and their children, who had come a greater way, such ties were more binding still.

There was more scope for association in the city than in the country. The visible needs for common action were greater and the density of residence provided opportunities for more frequent and more varied contacts. But the urge toward affiliation was a common characteristic of the whole country. *Americans associate as freely as they breathe,* wrote a visitor from Scandinavia. They had to if they were not to stifle in their loneliness.

The one association to which all Americans belonged was the Republic; the one activity in which all participated was politics.

In a calendar meager with ceremonial moments, election day was one of the year's few memorable occasions. Now every man became a king, for he was the maker of his rulers. Crowds stayed close to the polling places in town to observe the course of the contest; and farmers came in early to the courthouse to cast their votes and to observe the outcome. Whiskey flowed freely and the excitement mounted as the leaders mobilized their forces; and now and then heated tempers spilled over into an exchange of blows. This was the culmination of a campaign designed, by an exchange of slogans and charges, to involve the greatest numbers possible.

The electoral process organized the fragmented population into two parties. In ordinary life, people were merchants, laborers, farmers or clerks, Congregationalists, Methodists or Baptists, Yankees, Yorkers or Irishmen. But to win they had to be on one side or another, just as there could only be two armies in the field or two teams in the play. *All voting was a sort of gaming;* and the contestants, striving for victory, had to draw the maximum number of voters to their side.

The issues involved in government action were of some consequences in establishing party affiliations. The artisan was likely to enlist behind a candidate who favored the ten-hour law and opposed monopoly, while the frontier squatter took the side of one who came out for free land. But these were far from the determining elements. Men entered a party for the same reasons that they entered other associations, to identify themselves with a group that gave them a sense of participation in a significant social process; and economic and social position, ethnic heritage and personal outlook on life shaped their choices, in this case as in others. Partisanship, like other forms of belonging, descended in the family. The candidates were more likely to tailor their stand on issues to estimates of the preference of their following than the latter were to alter voting habits under the persuasive effect of an abstract argument. The campaign aimed not to convert the opposition but to mobilize those already loyal and to swing over the unaffiliated.

Since its object was to win a majority in a population composed of diverse elements, the party was an alliance rather than a homogeneous body. It operated primarily in the state legislature, which made the decisions that most directly affected the lives of the voters who elected it regularly. Here the local leaders organized, shaped the legislative program, and distributed the patronage and other rewards of politics. Compromise was the essential element of their tactics; no individual or group could altogether have its way without risking the alienation of some part of its support. The governor was a consequential figure, but he knew that the representatives in the state house or capital not only controlled the destiny of any measures he proposed, but in the last analysis, also had the local power that determined whether he would be re-elected or not.

An analogous process slowly extended to federal politics. The government in Washington was remote and was elected indirectly and at infrequent intervals. Although the President was not only a ceremonial figure who symbolized the unity of the nation but also the custodian of considerable power, his selection until 1828 involved little popular participation. He served for two terms and was succeeded by the Secretary of State, the official with the widest experience in administration. A Congressional caucus confirmed the succession, its members going back to their states to mobilize the necessary support. All other federal officers were either appointed or elected through the machinery of state politics. Parties therefore did not exist on this level; everyone called himself a National Republican.

The system began to collapse in 1824. Andrew Jackson, a military hero of great popularity, who had moved on to a career in speculation and Tennessee politics, presented himself as a rival to John Quincy Adams, the heir presumptive. To some extent Jackson entered the contest to avenge the personal slight of a censure he ascribed to Adams. But the candidacy also reflected the discontent of Westerners who thought they had been unjustly excluded from a share of federal power. Jackson lost in 1824, but four years later had drawn together a national alliance that made him President. His charges that the old system was corrupt and his claim that the President should be the tribune of the people put the election of the chief executive on a new, more popular basis.

Jackson's activities in office between 1828 and 1836 precipitated the gradual coalescence of state organizations into two national parties. Controversies over the Bank, the tariff and internal improvements aligned his supporters and opponents on opposite sides. By the election of 1840, the Whig and the Democratic parties were clearly defined along lines that held through the election of 1852.

The two national parties were heterogeneous alliances cemented by common interests. Their conventions selected candidates and framed platforms; they enjoyed the support of loyal newspapers; and they rewarded faithful followers with office. The westward movement of population supplied a basis for co-operation; the migrants carried their political affiliations with them and established links between the parties in the states to which they came and those which they had left. Whig support followed the line of New England settlement from Massachusetts to Iowa, Democratic, that of Southerners from Virginia to Missouri. Questions of policy also evoked broad national groupings. Massachusetts merchants, Pennsylvania ironmakers and Louisiana sugar growers favored a protective tariff and tended to become Whigs. Artisans in New York City, planters in Virginia and farmers in Ohio fought the national bank and tended to be Democrats. The political leaders sought to join these elements into a working majority, at the expense of what compromises were necessary.

The Senate was the chief scene of these operations. Here representatives of the state organizations who held office for extended periods came to know one another well and learned to collaborate. Here was the forum in which Webster, Clay, Calhoun, Benton and their colleagues made clear their positions and exercised their ability to maneuver. With the exception of Jackson, and to some degree Polk, the Presidents had considerably less power and influence; even their use of patronage was conditioned upon senatorial acquiescence.

The process was effective. On both the state and federal levels it permitted an orderly use of governmental power that was responsive to the will of a majority of the people. Popular influence was exerted not through referenda on specific questions but through the mediating efforts of elected representatives who carried the mandate of the governed to arrange tolerable accommodations.

In 1855, when the Massachusetts legislature chartered Pratt's newspaper, the system had collapsed. The perfectionist demands of the reform movement had already strained its capacity for compromise. The slavery question brought it tumbling down.

The issues raised by reform in the 1830's and 1840's were not readily voted up or down both because they were novel and because they hinged on moral questions that admitted no qualified response. Many state parties held together through those decades only with the greatest difficulty. But the problem of the extension of slavery after 1850 reached a point at which no further adjustment was possible. The compromises of 1820 and 1850 had used up all the space there was. The long-postponed future had arrived. Anything more would circumscribe the scope of free settlement.

Patience had run out. The majority of Northern people had gone as far as they could in extending the area open to bondage and in protecting the South's peculiar institution. Yet the planters and their poor white neighbors were no more content than before. They too wanted no boundaries to their opportunity to expand — as they were doing, with their families, slaves and plantations. They saw their influence shrink as they became a minority in the nation and feared that any further concession would open the way to an abolitionist assault upon their social system. Southern hotheads seriously demanded guarantees not only that slavery persist where it was but also that it grow indefinitely in the future. Where was now the goal of progress?

Few men in either section as yet perceived the consequences of the division. The machinery for effecting an adjustment quietly fell apart, as the leaders stood helplessly by. The long struggle over the Compromise of 1850 had sapped the strength of Whigs and Democrats alike. The antislavery men deserted to form various new political organizations and left the old national parties in disarray in the election of 1852. Two years later, the Kansas-Nebraska Act compounded the confusion, by opening to slavery territory Northerners had theretofore considered safe for freedom. That year, in protest, many men throughout the Union joined and voted for the Know-Nothings, a strange society, half secret lodge, half political party that stood inchoately for native Americanism. Its meteoric rise was a sign of the collapse of the other parties and with them of the apparatus for compromise.

In 1855 an old man, who perceived connections obscure to the totally sane, left Ohio to join his sons in Kansas. At his arrival John Brown learned of the illness of his wife, who had stayed behind. He could *discover no reason why this country should continue sickly, but it has proven exceedingly so this fall. I feel more and more confident that slavery will soon die out.*

Remorselessly the crisis unfolded. Kansas bled in civil war; the Supreme Court held that Congress had no right to exclude slavery from any territory; political loyalists froze in a sectional mold; the Republican party, entirely Northern in composition, prepared to elect a President the South would not accept; and the attack on Harpers Ferry brought to the gallows *that new saint than whom none purer or more brave was ever led by love of men into conflict and death* — Emerson's words for John Brown.

They had need to laugh, those about to learn that love of men led to conflict and death. With what great faith and confidence they had embarked upon the conquest of a continent, certain that their formula for freedom would make them perfect. Their exalted role in human history justified every sacrifice.

O days of the future I believe in you — I isolate myself for your sake,
O America because you build for mankind I build for you.

They had succeeded. No external force could halt or harm them. Yet in the 1850's some inner inadequacy pushed the government — on which they most prided themselves — to the brink of failure. That would be the greatest hoax of all, to have borne the ills and suffered the deprivations, to have held themselves in and suppressed alike the urge to love and the fear to die, and then to have the dream of perfection dissolve into a spectral nightmare. The thought was intolerable except as a joke.

VI

The Trials of Industrialization
1860–1900

18

The Failure of War

WEARY OF decades of postponement, the Americans drifted into war in 1861. Almost with relief, they slipped finally into a conflict that none expected would materialize. After a decade of wrestling with slavery's expansion they were glad once and for all to cut through the knot with a stroke of the sword. Some welcomed the opportunity to break away from the restraints that confined them in daily life. To shed routine cares, march in uniform, have an identity in a company, join with others in the disciplined ritual of dedication gave them that sense of belonging they avidly sought. Glory, for the moment, displaced success as the object of the young men's striving. North and South, the militia went jubilantly off to a training-day holiday.

Many more put their faith in power. They had been accustomed to think that their government was not like others. Free and uncorrupt, it could achieve whatever the reason and the will of its people directed it to. The law was the law and what was right was right; and force should command obedience. Confederates and Federals alike were blind to the possibility that there might be problems which even the power embedded in a free republic could not solve.

The war was not a single event, with a single set of causes and results. No chain of inevitable causality linked the succession of incidents that led one to another — from Lincoln's election to secession
to the kind of conflict that was fought, from the war to the peace
that was its outcome. A particular configuration of forces at each
point of decision shaped these developments. Furthermore, the
participants could not in advance envision the relation of their own
specific actions to the whole drama. The war crept up upon its victims
in steps of limited consequence which, only in their as yet unknown
totality, added up to a cataclysm.

The election of a Republican still left Southerners effective control of Congress and of the Supreme Court. Lincoln could not conceivably have touched slavery within the states; again and again he
explicitly assured his countrymen that he would not do so. Ironically,
every outstanding question about the future of bondage in the territories was, for the moment, settled. There was no immediate crisis
that men themselves did not create. Nevertheless, South Carolina,
in December, 1860, dissolved the union and *assumed her position
among the nations of the world, as a separate and independent state.*
Six states in the deep South followed her lead and in February, 1861,
the seven republics formed a Confederacy curiously like the Union
they had just left.

The politicians who made those fateful moves had no glimmer of
the results. They could not imagine that secession would redress their
grievances; less than ever before would they be able to share the space
of the West or secure the return of their fugitive slaves. They were
swayed not by any such reasonable estimates of the situation but by
fury at the humiliation of having lost. To have accepted the election
as a national judgment would have acknowledged the correctness
of the direction in which the North moved and, implicitly, the wrong-
ness and guilt of their own social system. Secession, said the future
Vice President of the Confederacy, *was the height of madness, folly
and wickedness*; yet even he did not understand the depth of the
current that would soon sweep him too along.

In their hearts, many believed that secession might not be permanent, but might lead to concessions and a graceful return; and if
separation were irrevocable, an amicable adjustment would arrange
the terms. Therefore the efforts at compromise continued. Experience

deceived many into the belief that a peaceful outcome was inevitable. The seceders pursued the time-honored maneuver of the excessive demand and Northerners resisted the familiar Southern bluff. But each side expected an ultimate settlement. War was unthinkable.

It was all a waste; the mechanism and the will to compromise had disappeared. The delusions dissolved when the earnest bargainers who met in a peace convention in February learned that the North could not accept the only Southern alternative to secession — slavery fixed in the Constitution, forever unchangeable, and assured of the opportunity to expand.

So then, secession was a fact; and the border states could no longer remain aloof. They had no sympathy for the hotheads who had precipitated the crisis. *Believe me,* wrote Mrs. Robert E. Lee of Virginia in February, 1861, *my feelings are all linked with the South, but those who have been foremost in this revolution will deserve the reprobation of the world for having destroyed the most glorious confederacy that ever existed.* Yet they had to decide whether to be isolated islands of slavery among the free states or throw in their lot with those which had withdrawn. Virginia, Tennessee and Arkansas chose the latter commitment and North Carolina, which had earlier refused to do so, reversed itself to join them. Maryland, Kentucky, Missouri and Delaware remained, although somewhat uneasily, in the Union.

The slowly unfolding perspective of what was to come also shaped the decisions of Northern men. When it became apparent that compromise was no longer feasible, that secession would be permanent and that the border states would divide on the subject, war still did not seem the inevitable result. Let *the wayward sisters depart in peace;* in time they would come penitently back to the fold. It was not by choice that the Northerners took up the sword. Nor did any absolute calculus of alternatives inform them that they would suffer more by the dissolution of the Union than by the conflict necessary to preserve it.

Lincoln had shown no more foresight than others in dealing with the efforts at compromise; and he was no better prepared for war than any of his contemporaries. His career had been that of a politician and lawyer who lived by mediation, by the arrangement of settlements within the rules of the game. As the months went by after his elec. tion, he continued to hope that some agreement would take form; the Americans could not separate. They could not *remove their respective sections from each other nor build an impassable wall between them.* They would remain face to face, and intercourse, either amicable or hostile, would continue; it would certainly not be more advantageous or more satisfactory after separation than before.

In the crisis, as he considered the issues before him and the nation, Lincoln fastened on one guide to conduct, which he described as preservation of the Union. The phrase, as he used it, connoted not simply the antithesis of secession, but the totality of procedures of orderly government which alone made the Republic viable.

Lincoln remained a stickler on one point — the inviolability of the rules. He was willing to concede much on the future of the slave in the South; he was willing to negotiate the question of the territories, on which he might have taken a less rigid stand than did the Republican party platform. But he simply could not yield to Southern demands without jeopardizing the future of republican government. The *central idea of secession was the essence of anarchy.* If determined resistance by a minority could permanently frustrate the clearly and constitutionally expressed will of the majority, then there would be no rules and no game, but only an endless succession of stalemates as rival groups checked one another.

Yet Lincoln saw no clear way, within the rules he respected, of coercing the recalcitrant states. His inaugural address in March shunned the idea of bloodshed or violence unless forced upon the national authority. He assured the South that there would be *no invasion, no use of force against or among the people anywhere.* Where hostility to the United States was so great and so universal as to prevent competent resident citizens from holding the federal office, there would be no attempt to force *obnoxious strangers among the people for that object.* The attempt would be so irritating and so nearly impracticable that it would be better for the time being to forego the exercise of power in the South. But the President could not recognize secession by surrendering federal property anywhere.

Other Northerners followed Lincoln's course. The failure of the compromise efforts convinced them that they could not now give way before the pressures of the South and still preserve the processes of orderly government. Yet they did not know the war would come until it was upon them. Desperately they and the President hoped for some exit from the impasse.

The shots that rang across Charleston harbor in the early morning of April 12 set the federal fort afire. The flames would not subside for four years. Some of the Carolina officers had gone to their posts from the *merriest, maddest dinner* they had yet enjoyed; they had no apprehension of what a blaze they kindled. The reproachful flag, once theirs and now foreign, had floated too long in their air; and a supply vessel threatened to keep it there indefinitely. They only wished to bring it down.

Violence took them across the line of the forbidden. This was war. Lincoln had been patient, had held strictly to the line of legality, not only to win the loyalty of the border states and of waverers in the North, but also because he understood better than most the cost of destroying the fragile order that kept men from becoming beasts. Aggression ended his indecision. There seemed no alternative but to fight back and end the rebellion. The hesitant fell into place; the pacifists, the men of Southern sympathies, the political opposition discerned no other choice.

There was still no comprehension of the full meaning of the war. The Confederate aides had dashed gaily about in red sashes as the shells fell on Fort Sumter. Lincoln issued a call for three-month volunteers; and the Zouaves hastened down in their gaudy uniforms. On both sides loyalty and the habit of obedience to constituted government drew people into the ranks. The beat of drums, the blast of bugles, *burst into the solemn church, into the school, scattered the congregation, drove out the scholar, left not the bridegroom quiet nor the peaceful farmer peace.* All put on their new identity, suspended the old rules, and went off confident of an early return.

It was to be far different from what they expected. Many months would pass before they came back and there would be empty spaces in the ranks. The fighting dragged indecisively on, for the accepted tactics of the day gave the defense an immense advantage. The masses of men dug in along lines that took advantage of the topography and, supported by the artillery, mowed down the charges of the oncoming enemy. The attackers attempted to concentrate power at one point heavy enough to break through and stave off a counter-attack. Each side therefore accumulated ever larger forces in the lines that faced each other day after day. Accident and skill turned the tide in particular battles; but in the end each realized that it could win only by wearing down the other.

The Union strategy at first was simple. A naval blockade would starve the Confederacy and a frontal attack upon the capital at Richmond would destroy it. That failed, first at Bull Run and then in discouraging repetitions of disaster. The strategy then shifted. Superior resources permitted the federal armies to begin a long en-circling movement that cut the deep South off from the West and made possible a war of attrition that exhausted the enemy's resources and gradually drew narrowing rings around the remaining centers of resistance.

Confederate hopes rested upon the ability to stave off these attacks, to establish the permanence of independence, and to achieve the support of the European powers. They had, however, been slow to gain diplomatic recognition, despite the persuasive power of their cotton. The Continental monarchs had been willing enough to aid a movement which demonstrated the failure of republicanism. Napoleon III, indeed, was almost indecently eager to do so; the French economy would profit and destruction of the Union would secure the shaky Mexican empire he had given his puppet Maximilian. But the other countries were not free to act without the assurance that the British navy would be friendly.

In England, a substantial body of conservative opinion, pleased with the collapse of American democracy, favored the South. A majority in the Parliament awaited a favorable moment for ex-pressing that sentiment. In October, 1862, William Gladstone, then an influential member of the Cabinet, openly announced that Jeffer-son Davis had made a nation; and at the end of May, 1863, Southern sympathizers in the House of Commons gave notice that they would move to recognize the Confederacy. Support would then snowball in the capitals of Europe and the North would realize that recon-quest was hopeless. Such were the calculations in Richmond. Vice President Alexander H. Stephens of the Confederacy, an old friend of Lincoln's, prepared to negotiate the terms of such a peace. It was only necessary through some dramatic demonstration to show that the South could not be conquered. The task of doing so fell to General Robert E. Lee.

Lee was a gentleman and a professional soldier. He had gained distinction in the war with Mexico and had risen rapidly in rank. In 1861, he could have commanded the federal armies. Instead, though he had strong national feelings, abhorred slavery, and deplored secession, he resigned and took service with the Confederacy. Loyalty to his neighbors outweighed the obligation to the Union. He could not envisage the Virginia landscape other than as it was, its harsh features — slavery and the plantation — softened in the romantic glow of his affection for home and family.

Then, for two years he had seen the South torn apart by invading armies, while he held back in a purely defensive posture. He could recall the swift marches and bold stabs of the costless Mexican adventure and now determined by one daring thrust to earn a satisfying peace.

On June 3, he led the Army of Virginia northward to disaster. By the end of the month he had come to within ten miles of Harrisburg, the Pennsylvania capital and the prize which would prove that the South could not be crushed. Then a chance encounter at Gettysburg precipitated a four-day battle in which 160,000 men tore at each other in suicidal fury; one-third were casualties. On July 4, Lee knew he had lost. Somberly, in a torrential rain, his army retreated south to the Potomac.

There remained two years of brutal fighting. After Gettysburg, the flow of aid to the South, from across the ocean, dried up as the blockade gained in effectiveness. Hostile armies chopped the land to pieces. Devastation spread. War became hell. But not until April 9, 1865, did the Confederacy recognize the inevitable and surrender.

The wounds were slow to heal. The embittered soldiers fought with a ruthlessness that left destructive scars for years. The unrecognized passions that had brought them to the conflict emerged into the open; the men who passed through fields littered with the dead felt the blinding need to obliterate the enemy who was none other than the brother-betrayer. Millions of Americans learned how to kill one another and learned also to hate.

This was not at all what they had known in novels or in Mexico. This was the first of the great modern wars in which battles were fought in deadly seriousness. No longer, as in the eighteenth century, did an exchange of desultory fire for a half-hour precede a wait of another six months before the next encounter. Here the soldiers confronted each other in trenches for days on end; and they shot to kill. The toll was monstrous — 360,000 dead on the Union side, 258,000 dead on the Confederate side, a stupendous mound of corpses, all American.

Civilians were also helplessly involved in the many-threaded drama with *its sudden strange surprises, its confounding of prophecies, its moments of despair, its interminable campaigns, its mighty and cumbersome green armies engaged in bloody battles — with over the whole land an unending universal mourning wail of women, parents, orphans.* Their men left, not all to return. They lived under military control, were taxed heavily, and suffered from many shortages. Pockets of disaffection appeared on both sides; desertion was a constant problem. A deep uneasiness spread through the land as people demanded to know why they were fighting.

In both the North and the South, the leaders reached back to a common heritage to supply the explanations. In the Confederacy, liberty became the key to the struggle. They fought to protect their freedom from an aggressor who wished to destroy their social system. They suffered thus, to preserve the sanctity of their homes; and at the thought, their minds ran off to the black figures, moving quietly through the hallways, awaiting the invader. *They make no sign. Are they stolidly stupid? or wiser than we are; silent and strong, biding their time?* The recollections survived the last battle to embitter the peace.

In the North the explanation was more complex; it had to satisfy the men in the ranks and their relatives behind the lines, the party in opposition, and the rebellious part of the country ultimately to be reunited. On the battlefield at Gettysburg, Lincoln responded. The war was a test of whether a nation *conceived in liberty and dedicated to the proposition that all men are created equal* could *long endure.* The sacrificial dead had fallen to give the nation *a new birth of freedom,* so that government *of the people, by the people, for the people, shall not perish from the earth.* The words rang with the familiar tones of the revivalists and reformers of the 1850's. The call to conversion could not mean a return to an earlier unregenerate condition. The unsought war was an opportunity. The power mobilized to conduct it might serve some good universal end that would justify its costs. Its pain and misery might wash away the problems of the past.

Slavery! That had been the original sin; its marks were still evident through the war and after. In the areas controlled by Union armies, Negroes fled from their masters. Should they be handed back as private property or treated as contraband? Why should they not fight and relieve the drain upon Northern manpower? The Union would enlist more support in Europe if its struggle was for men's liberty rather than for the subjugation of rebellious provinces. Thus argued the congressmen and editors who wished to give a broad meaning to *a new birth of freedom.*

The President was hesitant. He had always known that slavery would someday disappear. A house divided against itself could not stand; the Union could not endure half slave, half free. But he worried about the loyalty of the border states, about closing the door to a possible softening of Southern attitudes, and about dissension among his followers. Moreover, he had the lawyer's concern with legality. He hoped at first for compensated emancipation, preferably joined with some scheme for colonization to remove the blacks from the South. By 1862, he understood that was no solution. He drafted a proclamation that used his war powers to emancipate the slaves of rebellious citizens. Shrewdly he insisted, at the same time, that reunion was the only aim of the war and waited until after the victory at Antietam to make the decision public.

The problem did not disappear; it assumed another form. The Negro, cast loose without resources, was helpless. He needed a stake and aid to adjust to the conditions of freedom. Furthermore, he would finally be secure only if Southern society were entirely purged of the evil that had formerly debased it. All the millennial dreams of the abolitionists and reformers now shifted to the unredeemed states which were to emerge reconstructed from their suffering, free of vice, the happy home of thriving yeomen and industrious workingmen. Canny Republican politicians, anxious lest their party become a minority after the peace, fell in happily with schemes which promised to recruit them loyal voters in a region barren of their supporters.

Reconstruction therefore started with high hopes. An army of missionaries descended upon the ravaged South, some on behalf of the Freedmen's Bureau created by Congress in 1865, some on behalf of private philanthropies. They fed the hungry, opened schools and hospitals and tried to bind up the wounds of war. New men appeared in some of the state legislatures anxious to further the work of reform. Meanwhile the Thirteenth Amendment completed the process of emancipation; the Fourteenth forbade the states to infringe upon the liberties of any of their citizens; and the Fifteenth assured the ballot to all men.

The great design failed. Too many Southerners came home embittered by war and determined to restore rather than reconstruct their way of life. To counteract their influence called for a sustained use of federal power; and the poor white Tennessean who became President after Lincoln's assassination lacked the skill and the will to govern effectively. Imbued with prejudice against the Negro, flattered by the attention of the planters once so far above him, confused by ambition, he precipitated a division between those who favored a radical approach to reconstruction and the more conservative elements unwilling to experiment with forms that might upset existing property rights. By the time Andrew Johnson left office in 1869, enthusiasm had waned; a growing number of Northerners were tired of the issue, were anxious to concentrate upon their own affairs, and were willing to allow the Southern states to govern themselves as they wished.

The reconstruction legislatures were no less effective than their counterparts elsewhere but they were unable, without aid, to break the local patterns of control. The old masters came back to their ruined plantations, gallant losers but unrepentant and resolved to step back into the roles they had filled before 1861. They quickly regained power, sometimes in an alliance with men of new wealth. Amnesties and pardons gave them access to politics, sharecropping proved a substitute for the plantation, and terror repressed opposition. The Ku Klux Klan, the Black Codes, and segregation deprived the Negro of the ballot, held him in a state close to peonage and established his social inferiority as firmly as slavery had. Northerners remained sympathetic but satisfied: the Negro was free; let him improve himself.

And with time, the black men acquiesced. Jubilee had come — but not for them. They had proved their manhood in the ranks and died like the whites for liberty. But they were not yet to live like the whites. Freedom and equality faded into a distant future which the Negroes could only approach through years of humble apprenticeship. In 1876, the centennial year of Independence, the last vestiges of Reconstruction disappeared. By then, the desire to forget the costs and failures of the war had spread to the whole nation. The hope that some good would come of it was an illusion.

A PARABLE. The tricky transmigration of a soul took to King Arthur's court a Connecticut Yankee, practical, ingenious and full of fight. He became *The Boss*, proclaimed a republic, abolished the privileged class and the established church and declared all men exactly equal. The priests, the nobles and the gentry, however, shriveled up the commoners and led them like sheep in the battle for reaction. Having the advantage of modern armaments, the Boss and his soldiers, *champions of human liberty and equality*, won. But *in that explosion all our noble civilization-factories went up in the air and disappeared from the earth. Ye were conquerors*, concluded the magician, *ye are conquered! These others are perishing — you also. Ye shall all die in this place — every one.*

There remained, North and South, a great pain among those whose homes had vanished and whose husbands, brothers and sons had returned with crippling souvenirs of the battlefield or had not returned at all. Those who lived on could give themselves no true account of the war, for it had not settled the important problems that had divided the nation in 1860, neither the future of the Negro nor the kind of society the United States would become. A generation nurtured in the spirit of Emersonian optimism and in the belief that human beings could re-create the world in an ideal image could not face that actuality. Instead it made the conflict a symbol of that which had alone been saved, national unity. Decoration Day drew the North and South together in the shared commemoration of their dead and the war became an experience that had united rather than divided Americans. Every base element vanished in the memories of the conflict; only nobility remained, as if those who survived could thus banish the guilt of having failed those who died. There were no villains, only heroes in a splendid pageant which could be recalled without embarrassing reflections on what it had been for.

The failure of the war subtly discredited the notion that the state could be an agency for reconstructing society. The capacity to shape visions of reform was by no means dead; but that the normal operations of government offered a means of making them real was no longer credible. Politics settled down into a contest for power between the two parties, now stable, national, and well organized. On Election Day, as distinguished from Decoration Day, the war hardened ethnic, sectional and economic affiliations, as the Grand Old Party waved the bloody shirt in the claim of credit for the glory, while the Democrats nursed the wounded sensibilities of the losers. No great issues of policy consistently divided the two parties. The excitement of campaigning remained; but the battles were primarily for victory.

Few expected any longer that government could take any positive action to ameliorate society. Its function was simply to preserve order. An elaborate body of law administered by technically trained professional lawyers enabled it to do justice abstractly without reference to goals of its own and without disruptive changes in existing social relations. The Supreme Court, at the apex of the structure, kept strict watch on what was constitutional and permissible.

Yet paradoxically, political victory was also expected to bring a share of the spoils. As so often in war, when there were no common goals, it was each for himself. The veterans, having come back, would not admit that the world made by their fighting was imperfect. Their organizations were dedicated to inertia, except when it came to pensions for their members. And a host of avid men, liberal in the use of bribes, circled the agencies of government in the hope of carrying off unrecognized booty in the form of favorable laws and grants of franchises and contracts.

This was a great barbecue. The boss surveyed with complacency the machine through which he controlled the city. His gracious favors satisfied the voters while the greedy interests courted his support. Local political leaders retained their influence in the state legislatures, while the governor became the party chieftain controlling the elaborate administrative machinery and dispensing patronage.

The focus of federal authority remained in the Senate. The Presidents, with the exception of Grover Cleveland, were weak and indecisive; and the House was unmanageably large and stifled by anachronistic rules of procedure. Senators, on the other hand, enjoyed continuity in office and powerful connections with the legislatures that elected them. In this body lawyers joined men of great wealth, attracted by its club-like features. Access to patronage and the ability to influence, indeed frequently to dominate, the process of selecting Presidential nominees buttressed their dignity and prestige.

The disconcerting frequency of corruption and the absence of great new ideas or new causes shocked sensitive observers. The war seemed not only to have deflated all hopes of constructive action but also to have released men from all salutary restraints. The result was often cynical disillusion. *In politics we cannot keep our hands clean,* says the protagonist in Henry Adams's novel *Democracy. To act with entire honesty and self-respect, one should always live in a pure atmosphere, and the atmosphere of politics is impure.*

Efforts at reform were singularly ineffective. Generally, the leaders were respectable men, fed up with the degradation about them and anxious to oust the rascals. In 1872, they momentarily captured the feeble Democratic party, installing as their Presidential candidate Horace Greeley, the veteran hero of many old reform battles. But their program was weak and indecisive; and they went down to defeat. In the 1880's, small groups of Mugwumps, with similar futility, objected to the dominant powers of the Republican party; and pure-minded citizens occasionally purged a graft-ridden city.

But the questions the reformers raised had little relevance either to genuine problems or popular interests. They fought corruption and sought civil service reform; they objected to high tariffs and asked the government to refrain from interfering with the lives of its citizens. Only a handful of Americans in the 1870's and 1880's cared about these issues, which could not offset the loyalties and organization that gave the entrenched parties power. As a result a declining percentage of the eligible population took the trouble to participate.

The spreading apathy reflected the conviction that common action was vain; individuals did better to occupy themselves with their own concerns. The prosperous pursued their interests while the aggrieved and underprivileged saw no prospect for improvement through government. The problems of farmers and laborers had grown no easier with the end of the war, with industrialization and with the expansion of settlement into the great plains. But their efforts to secure ameliorative legislation in the 1870's and 1880's were not well rewarded and they usually looked to nonpolitical measures for aid. The existing machinery of politics seemed invulnerable to change.

The mounting frustrations of these decades generated a wave of discontent. Leaders of organized labor, farmers burdened with debt, visionary reformers, temperance men and good citizens dismayed by corruption concluded that the old parties were beyond redemption; a new People's Party would save the Republic and uplift mankind. In 1892 the Populists put a Presidential candidate in the field. Their platform protested against the callous indifference to the welfare of the population and asked for positive action to expand *the power of government — in other words, of the people — to the end that oppression, injustice, and poverty shall eventually cease in the land.* They attracted more than a million votes and sent a dozen spokesmen to Congress.

But the spirit of the times trapped the Populists too. Alone, the road to office seemed long and tortuous; an alliance with one of the old parties might bring them there quickly. In 1896, they set aside their more radical demands and threw in their lot with the Democratic candidate. His defeat not only deprived them of the prize of power but destroyed their capacity for future independent action. When the century ended there seemed little prospect, and even little desire, for far-reaching changes in government.

Ironically, Americans were never more prosperous. While they had passed uneasily through a tragic war and an uneasy peace, other impulses out of their past had generated new sources of power, created a new culture, and diffused new ideas that diverted their attention from the effort to use force to create a good society.

19

An Industrial Economy

SOME MEN refused to let the war touch them at all. Other concerns turned their minds from the fighting. They were not tempted to volunteer; and if their names came up in the draft, they could, as was the custom, send substitutes to take their place.

In Cleveland, a determined youth meticulously kept his accounts. He had been trained by his father to get on, to drive a sharp bargain, to save, and judiciously to nurture his interests. When the firing broke out in Charleston harbor he was twenty-two, and a partner in a firm of commission merchants; and the rising prices of pork and beef added to his capital. In 1863, he invested in an oil refinery, understanding that the recently discovered Pennsylvania wells would soon give light to the homes of the continent. Just before peace came, John D. Rockefeller bought out his partners and launched upon a career of expansion. In the same years, Andrew Carnegie, who had begun as a poor Scottish immigrant, shrewdly appraised the need for steel as he went about his duties on the Pennsylvania Railroad.

Entrepreneurs were not the only ones to keep the experiences of war vicarious. The farmers' drive to bring fresh acres under cultivation did not slacken; and thousands of newcomers, landing from the ships that shuttled across the ocean, entered the New World's workshops. Through the war, the task of developing the economy went on, largely within channels already defined in 1860.

Upon the foundations earlier laid, the Americans constructed an elaborate system of national communications. The 30,000 miles of track of 1860 grew to 193,000 in 1900. Five transcontinental routes connected the two oceans and a network of trunk lines carried freight and passengers among the great cities. In addition, substantial cargoes moved along the inland waterways; and new pipelines brought oil from fields to markets. Meanwhile the telegraph and the recently invented telephone established direct contact among businessmen in various parts of the nation.

The speed and ease of movement permitted the development of elaborate sales organizations to distribute goods to every part of the country. A hierarchy of brokers and wholesalers supplied the credit and the facilities for exchange that brought shoes, soap and beans from the manufacturer to the shopkeeper and thence to the consumer anywhere in the country. Each night, in the dreary small-town hotel, the drummer repacked his samples and checked off the orders, fanning the hope of a promotion to the inside salesman's job. In many places the bargains of the first chain stores and mail order houses opened other channels for the transfer of commodities, while the one-price, no-haggling system and the low overhead of the department stores, in the larger cities, attracted crowds of buyers by ads in the press. Enterprising manufacturers also took to advertising, hoping thus to create a national market for their wares. The result was an increase in the volume of sales that encouraged large-scale production.

With this stimulus every branch of industry expanded swiftly in the four decades after 1860. Light manufacturing grew rapidly. The New South followed the course the North had earlier pursued; but demand was so heavy that growth there did not affect adversely older enterprises in New England. Cotton factories, which had the longest history, still quadrupled their capacity; and shoes, soap, sewing machines, hats, silks, processed foods and cigars poured forth in mounting volume. Workers continued to make ready-made clothing in their homes, but used mechanized techniques under the control of large-scale contractors.

Railroads and pipelines, bridges and new buildings, factories and machines, all generated a demand for steel. Great new plants supplied it. By the end of the century the United States produced ten million tons a year and led the world. Meanwhile a complex of other heavy industries made tinplate, locomotives, machines and carriages. Enormous mineral stores were dug out of the earth to keep the plants going. The output of coal went up from 14,000,000 to 257,000,000 tons; and the performance in copper, lead, zinc, iron, and petroleum was no less impressive. Meanwhile the forests of Maine, Wisconsin and the Pacific Northwest were stripped for the timber and pulp the economy required.

Industrialization stimulated agriculture by expanding the number of consumers enormously. Every additional laborer in the factory or the mine was a customer for the bread and meat of the farm. At the same time, the spread of manufacturing in Europe opened up vast foreign markets for American grain, cotton and oil. Every ship that carried immigrants to the New World took back cargoes from the fields of the West and the South. New improved reapers, harvesters and combines — some powered by steam — raised the level of productivity, and easy transportation carried commodities swiftly to the elevators, warehouses and docks.

These results were evident in the increased volume of production. In the forty years after 1860 the output of corn and wheat both rose almost fourfold, while that of cotton tripled. The acreage under cultivation more than doubled between 1870 and 1900, as did the number of farms. Great herds of cattle moved through the open range and when fencing ended the long drives, grazed on ranches that kept the stockyards of Kansas City, Omaha and Chicago busy. The $271,000,000 farmers had invested in agricultural implements in 1870 had more than tripled by the end of the century. In the same years the value of farms went up by a full one hundred per cent. On the surface, agriculture enjoyed a bonanza almost as striking as that of industry.

The expansion of American industry called for unprecedented supplies of both labor and capital. Both were available. Into the cities rushed an army of young men and women, the sons and daughters of farmers or small-town businessmen. They came in pursuit of the opportunities for advancement hidden there. They found jobs at the counters and ledgers, cherishing the dream that a few made real, of a rise to independent proprietorship or to a place in the professions.

A movement of another sort filled the positions at the machines. A new tide of European migration had begun before the end of the Civil War. It mounted steadily to a peak of seven hundred thousand in the single year 1882, then stabilized at about four hundred thousand annually. In all, some thirteen million newcomers entered the United States in the four decades after 1860. They helped raise the total population from thirty-one million to more than seventy-five million in 1900.

The old sources continued to supply substantial numbers. Britain and Ireland sent some three million and Germany almost as many, while the movement of Scandinavians was much heavier than before the war. But the economic revolutions which had begun in those countries also spread eastward. By the end of the century about one hundred thousand immigrants left Italy each year for the United States and contingents of equal size were on their way from Austria and Russia. Smaller but more exotic groups also arrived from Portugal, Greece and Turkey; and northern New England learned to welcome thousands of French Canadians from Quebec.

The volume rose as the crossing grew easier. Railroads brought the peasants quickly to the port of embarkation in Europe, and distributed them to their destinations in the New World. The ocean voyage in the steerage of great steamships was swift and cheap, if not comfortable.

The newcomers fell into an established pattern of employment. Those with the means to equip themselves suitably found places in agriculture easily. The railroads, anxious to develop traffic and to sell land grants with which the government had subsidized construction, encouraged them to come West. Immigrants were not eligible to stake out claims under the Homestead Law, but they could purchase the holdings of natives who did. There was no shortage of space for those who could get to it.

To buy a farm and support the family until the first harvest took more capital, however, than the majority of new arrivals possessed.

Most postponed the dream of an independent yeoman's life and sought a livelihood in construction gangs, in the factories and mines of the mill town, or in the shops of the great manufacturing cities. The basic conditions were the same — no unskilled breadwinner by himself earned enough to support a family; only the labor of his women and children made ends meet. An abundant supply of hands was therefore available to industry at the lowest possible charge. Concern about this item never troubled the entrepreneur eager to expand.

Immigrants supplied the bulk of the migratory labor force in agriculture, in lumber camps and in construction. They laid endless miles of railroads and streets and dug gas and water lines. In the country they moved with the crops at harvest time; and in the city they lifted and carried as the buildings rose. Unfamiliar with the language and law of the new country, helpless in the absence of alternatives, exploited by avaricious contractors, they mingled their labor with the stone and earth that built the industrial economy.

Some laborers settled down at the head of the pit where the coal or iron or copper was. Or they found employment in Braddock, Pennsylvania, or Pullman, Illinois, typical mill towns where heavy industry now often located its plants. Such places were close enough to a city for access to capital, management and marketing facilities, yet detached enough to permit effective control of the workers. Generally a single enterprise dominated the community. Its employees, once settled, were immobilized. Their jobs, the houses they rented, even the churches in which they worshiped belonged to the company, and they were held to a rigid discipline established by an impersonal, remote organization. The only form of protest left to them — such violence as the Molly McGuires spread in the Pennsylvania anthracite fields in the 1870's — did not long challenge the corporation's ability to control its labor force as it wished.

Immigration also supplied the demand for hands in the metropolitan cities. In 1900 thirty-eight municipalities had populations of more than one hundred thousand and six had gone beyond the half-million mark. New York alone counted more than three million inhabitants. Yet the laborers were never lacking to raise their buildings, to supply them with every service, and to tend their machines. Here, as elsewhere in the economy, the newcomers were indispensable.

The unrestrained flow of people across the Atlantic, rising with demand during prosperity, subsiding in depression, relieved every American entrepreneur of concern about this element in the productive system. Docility compensated for the immigrants' lack of skill. They did what they were told and, lacking fixed work habits, adjusted to mechanization and technological changes without the arguments that experienced mechanics put up. Above all, the cost was low. Satisfied with a meager level of consumption, they left their employers a substantial surplus of profits that could flow back into economic expansion.

Capital moved as freely as men. Thousands of investors were ready to buy the stocks of the corporations which organized the great enterprises and a loose, flexible financial system encouraged the venturers to do so.

No central agency aimed to direct the process. Land grants and other subsidies by the state, local and federal governments helped accumulate the necessary resources but did not interfere with the control of the entrepreneurs. A national banking act of 1863 taxed the notes of state institutions out of existence. The currency was therefore no longer an instrument of expansion; if anything, it tended to contract during these years, at least relative to the size of the population and the growth of the economy. Credit, however, suffered from no external restraints. The number of banks and trust companies rose from 1500 to 10,300 and their total resources and their loans outstanding each multiplied tenfold. The suspension of almost a thousand of these firms between 1893 and 1897 revealed how much of the boom was speculative.

The banks did not simply create credit; they were the media through which it was disbursed. The deposits that permitted them to honor drafts came from accumulations in the hands of potential investors of various sorts.

Families with old wealth often had the means to strike out in new ventures. The rewards of the fur trade had earlier permitted the Astors to buy New York City real estate that zoomed in value and that in turn enabled them to put a surplus into railroads and industry. Quincy A. Shaw, H. S. Russell and Henry Lee Higginson sent their Boston funds into Michigan copper; and his heirs were free to invest elsewhere the gains from old Cornelius Vanderbilt's speculations.

Some promoters generated their own capital. Rockefeller and Carnegie saved and plowed the profits of their enterprises back to new productive uses. They were intermediaries — not at first the owners of oil wells or iron mines, but processors and fabricators; the one refined oil, the other built bridges. They were therefore sensitive to the market and to the needs of consumers. When costs were low, shrewd management of their funds permitted them to expand in the direction they anticipated demand would take. When prices rose, they raked in the margin cheap labor charges assured them and prepared for other opportunities to spread out. They were careful not to waste their substance and bore the tiny taxes they paid with no pain. Successful entrepreneurs usually followed this course.

Thousands of Americans emulated them. Speculation was every man's heritage; and the war which made it a patriotic duty to buy bonds stimulated the habit. The clerk whose expenses did not quite consume his income, the farmer in a good year, the neighborhood doctor and the country storekeeper, each had a chance to buy a share of fortune. Often it seemed only sensible to go into debt to get in on a sure thing. An elaborate network of brokerage services permitted the residents of Omaha or Atlanta to deal with the stock exchange as readily as any New Yorker. In 1900, investors throughout the country traded almost 140,000,000 shares there; and the little sums they contributed had mounted up to the gigantic capitalization of the great corporations. Panic in 1873 and 1893 wiped out many a paper gain and ruined those who had borrowed to plunge. But hope was resilient and was fulfilled often enough to sustain continued optimism.

Foreigners also were still attracted by investment in the United States; and a thriving international trade provided them with the means of getting their funds across. Englishmen, Germans and Frenchmen were eager to send their surpluses overseas and American securities offered as good returns as those anywhere in the world. The holdings of Europeans in the New World more than doubled between 1860 and 1900.

Management of these great sums converted the most successful merchants of a former day into investment bankers. Jay Cooke had begun as a storekeeper in an Ohio country town and by 1860 had raised himself to a banker's desk in Philadelphia. During the Civil War he became the prime distributor of Union bonds and later drew upon that experience in mass selling techniques to float industrial and railroad securities until the panic of 1873 wiped him out.

The more successful investment bankers, however, had ties with both domestic and foreign investors. August Belmont came as an agent of the Rothschilds, while Kuhn Loeb and Company worked with German houses and J. P. Morgan with the English. Hence their insistence upon the necessity for preserving the international gold standard which seemed to them essential to the free flow of capital. Their services as middlemen brought them stupendous fortunes.

The investment bankers found their opportunity in an economy fragmented by local control. No general plan had established the routes of the railroads or determined the location of mills or refineries; hundreds of individual decisions left each unit unco-ordinated except through the trial and error of competition. Yet expanding markets and technological innovation revealed the efficiency of large-scale production. To the calculating banker, industrial combinations were essential to extend the benefits of big business to all the states of the Union and into foreign countries as well. Mergers or other forms of association, arranged through stock transactions, were his solution. Of course, he personally gained a substantial commission for his services and usually also took a neat insider's profit on the rise in the stock values. The only cost was *water*. It was an old drover's practice to force the beast to drink its limit before sale; the same principle added a ten-million-dollar firm to a twenty-million-dollar firm to get a fifty-million dollar corporation.

The financiers were not alone in perceiving the possibility. It was clear to railroad men like Vanderbilt and Hill that the trunk line had an advantage over the local road, just as an oil man like Rockefeller or a steel man like Carnegie understood the utility of integrated enterprises that united wells, pipelines, refineries and marketing organization or mines, furnaces and fabricating plants. The strategic assets of combination were also apparent to the manufacturers of sugar, glass, whiskey, and meat products. Scores of great entrepreneurs moved to compete with the bankers in the effort to control the process.

Hunting on the fringes of the pack were the speculators, pure and simple. They had no interest whatever in factories or rolling stock, only in securities, which they traded with unscrupulous shrewdness. Jay Gould, for instance, was twenty-four when he came to New York City to enter the leather business in the year of Lincoln's election. The son of a poor upstate farmer, he had ruthlessly scraped together the means of making his start. By the time the war was over, he was buying railroad shares and was on his way. Manipulation of Erie stock alone brought him at least ten million dollars by 1872; and he probably gained as much more from his flyer in gold a few years later. He and his peers prowled the exchanges, on the lookout for the consolidations which were important means of adding to their wealth.

By the end of the century, oil, steel, electrical equipment, rubber, starch, and sugar were among the industries organized into trusts, the popular term for the various legal arrangements that made these empires possible. These mammoth organizations certainly added strength to the economy, although many Americans wondered whether the result was always to maximize efficiency. But that the development permitted some to gain great fortunes was beyond a doubt.

What were they after, these men who could not pause in the quest for more, who took in by the minute what others could not earn in a year's labor, whose stores of wealth already exceeded their capacity to spend, or their children's, or that of their children's children? They gave their goal various names — order, efficiency, duty — and they described it as God's plan or economic law. But power was what they sought and business was the form in which their society recognized power. They took pleasure when the press referred to them as captains of industry, barons, kings and czars; and Morgan appropriately called the yacht he loved *Corsair*. Zeal for battle led them on, in fascinated absorption with the luck that would test their pluck. They were self-made, not in the sense that they had all risen from nothing, but in the sense that their achievements demonstrated their merit. Therefore they demanded that they be let alone and angrily fended off any hint of interference.

They succeeded because thousands shared their lust and bid up the prices of securities as fast as water was pumped into them. To Morgan and the respectable bankers, Gould, Dan'l Drew, Jim Fisk, Bet-a-Million Gates and the rest of them were an unsavory lot. But in the speculative arena all were equals. The security market remained vulnerable to raids because the investment process, in which all who were able wished to share, was free of any external control.

The alternative, integration under government supervision, was unthinkable, given the state of politics. The businessman turned to government when it was to his interest to do so; he sought tariff protection for his product, favorable rates from regulatory commissions, and franchises or subsidies where possible. But he did so without reference to general goals, seeking only his own advantage. Better protection for him meant higher costs for others. With the state he negotiated as with a rival power, and he had no illusion that the men with whom he dealt were animated by any larger interest than his own.

A few public servants, such as Charles Francis Adams or Elizur Wright, aspired to regulate railroads or insurance to protect the users and investors. But any entrepreneur, naïve enough to believe that such administrators were representative, was quickly disabused by the scandals that regularly rocked municipal, state and federal governments. If he conducted a national enterprise, he could cut through the complex obstructions of overlapping jurisdictions, anachronistic laws, and avaricious officials only by bribery or evasion. Brazenly the bagmen disbursed the boodle from their satchels and contributed lavishly to campaign funds. Skillfully the lawyers worked out the means of stepping around the inconveniences of the statute book. Business was a battle; as in war, the usual rules were suspended.

There were protests. The socialists and anarchists, for all their furor, attracted little support. But millions of Americans read Henry George's demonstration that *progress, marked by a prodigious increase in wealth-producing power* had only given *poverty a darker aspect* by widening the gulf between *those who got an infinitely better and easier living and those who found it hard to get a living at all.* Edward Bellamy vividly pictured the economy as a great coach on which a few rode in luxury, pulled on by the painful toil of the mass of men. Each author outlined his own remedy; and dozens of other schemes for salvation competed for attention. The readers recognized the validity of the diagnosis but would not buy the nostrums offered as a cure. They preferred, each group for reasons of its own, to acquiesce in the situation as it was.

The unskilled laborers, mostly immigrants and their children, had no desire to overturn the social system. Their thoughts focused on the immediate problems of creating a decent, orderly way of life in the face of crushing hardships of existence in the slums of the city or mill town. Full-time pay for a sixty-hour week might rise to nine dollars, but few enjoyed that much security and most got along by scrimping on consumption or by depending upon the labor of their women and children. Such men valued the small gains that made for stability and, eager to conserve the family and the church shaken in migration, shunned rather than sought change.

However slight the rewards, the laborers were still mobile and free, so that an occasional one among them could rise either in petty trade or in the hierarchy of industry. It was not for ease but for work that they had come to the New World; and poor though their lot was, so long as the avenues upward were not closed, it was better than what they had left. They made no exact calculation of the chances or of how many succeeded; if not they, then their sons could share the promises of the expanding economy.

Skilled laborers had a taste of the rewards and were therefore less content. The wages of railroad engineers and carpenters, of machinists and loom-fixers rose steadily; and so did their expectations. Generally native-born or immigrants with experience in English or German industry, they knew their rights and were ready to strike for them if necessary. They were ready also to meet violence with violence when employers were intransigent. Organized in craft brotherhoods, most of which affiliated with the American Federation of Labor, they shook off any involvement with social theory or political action, turned their backs upon the unskilled and the underprivileged and pursued the pure and simple objectives of the larger wage check and the shorter working week.

All the other elements of urban society were acquiescent. The shopkeeper often groaned under the competition of the chain or department store; the trust pressed the small manufacturer to lower prices; the army of clerks, salesmen and managers labored to preserve their respectability and yet to get ahead; and professionals squirmed to adjust their own values to the exigencies of the new society. From these groups there arose occasional cries of outrage at the revelation of some particular instance of iniquity and they sometimes mobilized the strength to purge the local Tweed. But no sooner had they done so than they reverted to their party loyalties and resumed their own quest for individual success.

From the rural population, still a majority in the nation, rose an endless lament. The rising domestic output and competition from Canada, Australia, Argentina, Egypt and Russia drove prices down: corn, which had averaged about sixty cents a bushel in the 1860's, was down to about twenty-eight cents between 1896 and 1900; wheat declined from more than one dollar to about sixty cents, cotton from sixteen cents to eight cents. In poor years the rewards were even lower. Yet costs remained inflexibly high. Charges for machines, transportation, processing and credit drained away the returns and led to foreclosure. In 1900, one-third of the farmers were tenants.

Local causes exacerbated the discontent. It took a long time before the South repaired the damage of war and adjusted to the crop-sharing system that replaced slavery. On the Great Plains, isolated families fought a harsh, unfamiliar climate that subjected them to parching drought and freezing blizzards. These two regions were the loudest in complaint.

But the problems of agriculture were general and emanated from the old dilemma of the market farmers. They were not satisfied to live by the sustenance of the soil as the immigrant did. Like other Americans, they sought success through speculative expansion; in 1900, nearly a third of them paid interest of seven per cent or more on mortgages. They were businessmen. Yet the farmers were not able to adjust their production to the needs of the market as others could; they could not close down the plant or lay off a few hands, because their enterprises were not simply economic ventures, but also homes. Instead, their routine drove them to maximize production, whatever the demand. Industrialization heightened their difficulties, by widening opportunities and deepening temptations. They too wished their share at the great barbecue. The ideal of the happy yeoman contentedly tilling his soil still supplied the stock figure of their rhetoric, but in actuality they raced on in avid pursuit of the same success that was the common goal of Americans.

Any man could do it. The starting point did not matter. There were *Acres of Diamonds* in every backyard. It was *a duty to get rich*, for *money was power;* and success, through pluck and luck, was a demonstration of individual merit. The failures — the tramps who wandered workless and familyless, and the outcasts who sank to the level of immigrant laborers — *were made poor by their own short-comings. It was all wrong to be poor, anyhow.*

The farmers, like the salesmen or doctors or mechanics, waxed indignant at the banker's nefarious trust. He was grabbing too much for himself! In the extremity of depression between 1892 and 1896, a good many Americans voted Populist to combat the conspiracy of the international monopolists. But prosperity restored party loyalty and a hint of admiration, all along, tempered the indignation. Morgan and Gould were many a man's villain, but involved in a villainy not a few secretly wished to emulate. Everyone wanted to strike it rich; and much of the currency agitation of these years fed on the desire to diffuse the magic of money that bankers seemed to monopolize.

Across the country, the stands of wheat ripened in fields where once only buffalo had grazed; the blast furnaces brightened skies that just yesterday had looked down on the wilderness camp of a major from Virginia; and the locomotive pulled long lines of freight through the pass Meriwether Lewis had painfully crossed. The United States was the world's greatest industrial power; in forty years, its wealth had increased fivefold.

The free movement of men and capital in an unrestrained market had created an enormous capacity for production which an enfeebled political system could not govern. *The lack of any common control and the consequent impossibility of orderly development* was wasteful and left the weak prey to the strong. It was consoling to believe that the fittest would survive. Yet now and again, the individual businessman or farmer, involved in an unequal contest over rates with the railroad or pushed to the wall by the unfair tactics of a great competitor, wished there were some authority to mediate. But even were the government able to act, by what standard could it judge what was right and what was fair? There was no answer to that question in a world where each sought his own advantage.

As the nineteenth century moved to a close, Americans were uneasily aware that, while all shared the promises, few shared the rewards. The divergence in experience, between those who gained great fortunes and those who did not, profoundly influenced the order industrialism imposed on society.

20

Cultural Transitions

THE POET looked curiously at the crowd of men and women *attired in their usual costumes* on the ferry. He could not know *the hundreds and hundreds* who crossed in daily intimacy, total strangers to one another. Work drew them together in the morning; in the evening they scattered, each to his home.

The millions who lived in New York or the hundreds of thousands in Cleveland or San Francisco could not know one another. Nor could they meet their needs for mutual aid, co-operative action, companionship and culture by becoming part of any social organization that encompassed them all. To begin with, they were divided by religion, color and national origin. The impact of industrialization further separated them by increasing the distance between the extremes of wealth and poverty.

Each man could push his own way ahead — devil take the hindmost. But he could not always be self-made and self-contained. Illness, bad luck and, if nothing else, death made all dependent on others. The joys of the birth or marriage of a child or of good fortune in business were the richer for being shared. None could stand altogether alone, not even the most successful, who wished at least admiration and respect for their power and achievements. Everyone had to belong somewhere, if there was to be order in the world.

The problem was simplest for the laborers. Poverty compelled them to live where housing was cheap; and within the range of available accommodations, they chose places where they could associate with people like themselves in language, habits and religion. They moved spontaneously into the ghettos that increasingly pockmarked the face of the great city. No one forced the Germans to settle in Yorkville or *Over the Rhine,* or the Jews in the East Side or West End, or the Italians in Greenwich Village. The newest arrivals knew the addresses before they stepped off the boat and gravitated thankfully to the islands of familiarity in an environment in which all else was strange.

They quickly sought equivalents for the tightly knit communities they had left. They worshiped in churches and synagogues like those of the old home, erecting the tabernacle booths in the back yards of the tenements, and parading through the crowded streets in honor of the saint. They formed fraternal and benevolent societies to assist them against the hazards of the New World. Their own newspapers in their own languages gave them word of one another; plays, choruses and dances were their amusements; bars, coffee houses, and beer halls supplied them with convivial meeting-places; and the group here preserved the folk wisdom that had proved efficacious in the past.

The immigrants, therefore, did not find it difficult to identify each other. Back in the Old World they had not usually thought of themselves as Italians or Poles or Germans; their own districts limited their horizons. In the United States participation in common activities and organizations brought to light the heritages they shared and shaped the ethnic groupings within which the foreign-born led their lives.

The newcomers of native birth also sought equivalents of the homes they had left for the city. The model in their case was the country town that every American boy and girl thought he remembered — its neat green dominated by the church spire and courthouse tower, its orderly streets lined with sturdy houses, each set off by its plot of lawn. No matter what the actual experience of the young men and women who returned each evening from the pursuit of fortune to dreary lodging-house rooms, their aspirations for stability turned to that image of orderly personal relationships.

Some never succeeded. Inadequate incomes kept them from settling down. When they married, they could do no better than move into flats in the rows of identical houses, in Philadelphia, Baltimore or New York, that struggled for respectability against the encroaching slum. They moved frequently but got nowhere in the exchange of one apartment for another. They belonged to nothing; rootless and anonymous, the city was for them a wilderness in which they foraged alone.

Those who succeeded escaped. Only New York in these years saw the appearance of commodious apartment houses in which some of the well-off chose to live. Most people there — and elsewhere, all — sought the rewards of a rise in status in the spreading suburbs. In the 1860's the streetcar had already begun to reach out toward Brooklyn and Harlem, Roxbury and Dorchester, the South Side and the West Side. In the 1880's electric traction supplanted the horse and further extended the commuting radius. Meanwhile the balloon frame and stucco had cheapened costs of construction so that a family in moderate circumstances could have its own single house on its own plot of land — a proper home. In the privacy afforded by rooms of special function — parlor, bedrooms, dining room, kitchen — the decent family could arrange its life away from the dangers of the city.

Virtue was the price it paid. Caution, abstinence and planning stretched income to cover expenditures, savings and provision for the children. The birth rate among these Americans fell by about thirty per cent between 1860 and 1900; that helped, although at the cost of painful restraints. But then it was always necessary to pinch where it did not show in order to keep the little house intact.

Therefore men clustered with their own kind in the suburb also, to be able to sustain one another by common attitudes, habit and knowledge. They came to districts with churches and lodges familiar from their youth, and resumed the diversions and activities interrupted by migrations. Here neighborliness prevailed and the opinion of the community disciplined disorderly elements or excluded outsiders. Here, in the unrecognized ghetto of the well-off, was a refuge from the strangeness and loneliness of the city. Such interior communities within the great community spread across the metropolitan areas to balance the meaner districts in the center.

It was good to settle down. Yet it was also good to move upwards. Social mobility destroyed the stability of the ghettos whether in the slums or in the suburbs. The extreme case was that of the men of exceptional wealth, whose fortunes made them as much strangers as foreign birth made the immigrant. Few had the inner resources that kept Carnegie or Rockefeller largely self-sufficient. Most required a new style of life, a new mode of thought and new groupings with which to identify.

The Boston Brahmins, the Knickerbockers of New York, and the Philadelphia Main Line families developed a group life as separate from that of their contemporaries as any other ghetto. Lacking the usual appurtenances — association with a royal house, a hereditary nobility and political power — they themselves contrived the visible symbols of a distinctive style of life. Their model was the European, and particularly the English, aristocracy. The Americans built lavish town and country homes, equipped themselves with carriages, liveried servants, and crests, and took to sports and to frequent trips abroad.

Alas, these tokens of distinction were available to anyone who commanded the price; and, displayed by any buyer, the Fifth Avenue address lost its symbolic value. Yet the group could not define itself as in Europe by legal privilege or by birth. Eagerly the girls sought titled husbands. But the exceptional heiress who captured a duke disappeared into a foreign society and scarcely advanced her own family's status.

The truth was that only riches distinguished the would-be aristocrats in America; and dollars were still democratically available to men of many backgrounds. Those who wished to draw off in a circle of their own could do so only by the arbitrary exclusion of outsiders.

By 1900 an elaborate apparatus for doing so had been created. In some places, the process was conscious and deliberate. Up from Georgia came Ward McAllister to be the autocrat of New York's drawing rooms. He had filled out by marriage a not-quite-adequate fortune of his own and had spent an apprenticeship in Europe fawning upon the genuine nobility. From a base in Newport he moved in on Manhattan, then divided between the sober old-time *nobs* and the lavish-spending *swells*. Capturing the ladies by his precious airs, from which there was nevertheless no hint of danger, he argued persuasively that *Society* — those in — would appear when it became known who was out. There were by definition to be four hundred families in the city; and he presided over the selection. No others existed.

Elsewhere, less formal means achieved the same end. Private clubs and associations conferred the accolade of membership. The invitation lists to balls and dinners were carefully scanned for clues of affiliation; and the proper churches had to limit the access of new families eager to join. A place in Newport or its rival summer resorts and attendance at correct preparatory, dancing and finishing schools, and colleges, were also signs of acceptance. Here the friendships were made and marriages arranged that extended the group lines into the next generation. Ultimately, published Social Registers made known who belonged and who did not.

In all cities, exclusion demanded an object. Which object was of secondary importance, although recency of wealth was the most general criterion. Jews, the most mobile immigrants of the period, were usually denied admittance to *Society*, but the Coreys of Boston were equally reluctant to receive Silas Lapham of Vermont and Mrs. Astor had to be persuaded to accept Mrs. Vanderbilt.

The aristocracy scrupulously refrained from taking note of its members' behavior or associations in the business world. But leisure activities were subject to a fixed code, English in antecedents. Politics, except for the individuals sent to the Senate by compliant legislatures, involved too many contacts with the populace. But sports, avocations and hobbies showed a man's freedom from the humdrum concerns of the masses; and culture and philanthropy afforded him an opportunity for the display of distinction and leadership.

Society developed after its own fashion in each of the great cities. Boston and Philadelphia were the most rigid. Firm family ties, strengthened by education and religion and by trusts that controlled the transmission of wealth from one generation to another, gave their elite groups powers of discipline no other enjoyed. Old New Yorkers, by contrast, could not cling to their pre-eminence, and strangers with enough wealth found an entrée relatively easy.

Chicago, St. Louis, Baltimore and San Francisco were more recent and therefore more fluid. The possessors of great fortunes there attempted to organize *Society* in emulation of the Easterners. Mrs. Potter Palmer reigned as Queen of Chicago in a great limestone castle, but everyone knew that her husband, a few years back, had stood behind the counter of a dry goods store. Society in these places remained loose and provincial, frequently weakened by the desertion of its members to the East.

Society in smaller cities like Cleveland and Pittsburgh had all the same deficiencies of recency and fluidity. In addition, the select groups were too small to sustain themselves. The families, occupied with culture and propriety, were too few to hold on. When their children grew old enough to think of alliances by marriage, they often shifted their operations eastward.

New York denuded most of the country of its plutocrats. Gotham was more receptive than either Boston or Philadelphia and had greater social resources than the national capital, which remained a Southern town visited by transient diplomats and politicians. The newcomers brought their wealth to Manhattan and added to the capital resources disposed through that financial center. By the end of the century, New York *Society* also considered itself *American* society.

The would-be aristocracy demonstrated its leadership through good works and culture. It dominated the boards of hospitals, orphanages, colleges and other philanthropic and educational institutions. And it established itself as patron of American art, music and literature.

The art, music and literature it patronized, however, was not that which Americans — or any group of them — saw, heard or read for pleasure. A few, like Morgan and Higginson, understood and loved painting or the symphony orchestra. But generally, *culture* as *Society* defined it served another function, that of establishing the status of its patrons.

Necessarily, that *culture* was imitative and eclectic. The railroad king could model his new house on nothing in his own past or in American experience. He constructed a French château or a Tudor mansion — or some extravagant combination of the two. Great country homes were transplanted from Europe — if not physically, then on the drawing boards. Churches, libraries and other public buildings displayed the same pathetic dependence. Only the stores, factories and office buildings escaped as they rose in skyscrapers freely into the air.

Interiors showed the same unhappy taste. Professional decorators searched Europe for the appropriate pieces to fill the proper period rooms. By making one chamber Japanese and another Louis Quinze they expanded the scope of their borrowings and gratified their clients with the assurance of having the best of all worlds. Whatever space the persuasive purveyors left uncluttered with objects of art, the family itself filled with bric-a-brac brought home as trophies from its tours. Painting became a somewhat exotic branch of interior decoration. The content of the picture was less important than its source which certified that its possessor was a man of taste and wealth.

The opera, the symphony concert and the theater became important social occasions. The music or the play were the least of the attractions. The stiffly costumed holders of the boxes sat the hours through in bored discomfort in order to be identified; they played a role as demanding as that of the performers on the other side of the proscenium. Books were not to read but to own. The collectors began to assemble great libraries they never expected to use, incunabula, first editions, fine printings, extravagant bindings and presentation copies. Rarity and price were the sole criteria. To the extent that these people read at all, it was in the genteel magazines and in the books there guaranteed to be important.

Culture was thus an inert thing to be possessed rather than a medium through which the individual expressed himself. It was *good* because it helped establish the status of its owner. The opera was no more expected to evoke emotion in its audience than the Gainsborough. Both were signs of refinement.

These Americans differed therein from those of earlier generations. The contemporaries of Jefferson and Emerson had also borrowed from the Greeks, Romans and English, but they had done so themselves, attaching a specific meaning to the classical pediment or the Gothic arch. *Society* had no standards of its own and sought no meaning in the objects it possessed. It depended instead on the services of intermediaries who established the canon of what was good and what was not, of what was polite and what was vulgar. The promoter or impresario informed the purchaser's taste and set the price. One went to Duveen for pictures, to Damrosch for music, and to Carrère & Hastings for buildings, just as one went to Morgan for bonds, because one could there get a certification of worth. Respected institutions buttressed the judgments of the experts and maintained stability of values. Museums and libraries removed any excess from the market, and with the opera and orchestra made a public display of what belonged and to whom.

The consequences of the alliance between *Society* and *culture* were far-reaching, both for the producers and the consumers of art. The creative work became an abstraction with no relevance to the function it served. The battlements that surrounded the country estate were not designed to shield archers any more than the fine edition was to be read. People learned to look at a church and see architecture, to look at a Crucifixion and see a painting, to listen to a mass and hear music, as if the content of those works had no relationship at all to their form.

Americans who wished to compose or paint or design buildings had to conform to the same values. They served a clientele which had ceased to look or listen, ceased to feel, and which searched only for the arbitrary signs of worth. An exceptional architect like H. H. Richardson managed an accommodation by struggling to express his own talent while pleasing his patrons. Louis Sullivan gave up in disgust after the success of his early efforts and spent his life on petty commissions. Many more simply acquiesced and surrendered to the innocuous manufacture of sounds, words and color for the demands of the market. Only toward the very end of the century would Howells, Crane and Norris begin to break away from the confining conventions in literature.

The results were even more depressing for those deceived into the belief that the canvas and the stone they bought were culture. They had ransacked Europe and carried away what was authoritatively best. What good did it do them? In the process they had lost the capacity for being directly and personally touched by the work of art. They had ceased to expect creations of the spirit of man to add meaning to life. The master wandered through the marble halls bedecked with Flemish tapestries; he sat in chairs made for princes; and he lifted his eyes to the portrait of someone else's distinguished ancestor. He was heir of all that money could buy. But his possessions informed him not in the least who he was or what was the purpose of his power. The culture of his ghetto served him less well than did that of the immigrant in the slum or of the salesman in the suburb.

That sector of *culture* which was science was immune to some but not all of the pressures of society. An awesome technology commanded respect and was evidence of the power of knowledge. The collection of right information and the mastery of proper techniques had drawn steel from the blast furnace and oil from the refinery; the same methods could solve other problems as well.

To arrive at truth, the scientist accumulated and classified into meaningful categories a great fund of information, from which he drew generalizations. He tested those principles by reducing them to operational terms and applying them to practice. In doing so, he assembled new data to modify the generalizations in an endlessly circular process. In medicine, for instance, the physician observed cases, developed theories, prescribed remedies and examined the results, which gave him new data. An individual could labor in his own surgery or laboratory. But an organization like a clinic was infinitely more effective. The same procedures applied to every area of knowledge, to social, physical, and natural science alike.

On the continent of Europe, Americans observed, the university was the seat of science. But the United States in the 1880's possessed no comparable agency. The old colleges — venerable Eastern schools and the hundreds of recently established sectarian seminaries — aimed as in the past to turn wild boys into Christian gentlemen. Their curricula, student bodies, and faculties were utterly alien to the needs of science. Nor were the state universities appropriate seats of the new learning; they were buffeted on the one hand by the demand of parsimonious legislatures that they confine themselves to practical subjects and on the other by the desire of faculties and alumni to turn them into imitations of Harvard or Yale. The new task called for the conversion of the old institutions or the creation of altogether new ones.

Americans followed both lines. Johns Hopkins, Clark and Chicago started afresh with staffs oriented toward research and in close association with hospitals and other scientific institutions. Harvard, Yale and Columbia joined the same functions to their existing structures and emerged, schizophrenic, to serve an incongruous combination of purposes; barbarous undergraduates droned through courses in return for indulgence in the fun of the playing field and club while serious scholars pursued learning in the libraries and laboratories. Michigan and Wisconsin found the means of adding similar branches to their expanding holding-company operations.

These developments cost money and called for choices; and the ability to provide the one brought control over the other. As in industry, the resources for expansion came primarily from private investors, and mostly from the possessors of great fortunes, who took an interest in the university both as a center of culture and as an instrument for making gentlemen of their sons. Hence the advantage of the older Eastern schools. Johns Hopkins and Chicago had the support of individuals of great wealth, but Yale and Harvard could draw upon the resources of large and growing bodies of alumni.

In education as elsewhere, the patron-investor depended upon the counsel of influential experts. Science had the answers, but the layman could not decide alone which physician or physicist, which economist or biologist had the right results. Validation, as in the case of *culture*, came from impresarios who defined what was good and what was not. One consulted President Charles W. Eliot of Harvard on educational problems, or William H. Welch on medicine, or H. B. Adams on history. Through their influence *Society* accepted an officially defined *science* as it did a defined *culture*. The university by 1900 was the ultimate medium for the certification of both.

The process was somewhat less damaging in scholarship than in art because the professor, in most fields, had some autonomy. He could write what he liked within fairly broad limits. But unless he was one of the exceptional men who always commanded a respectful hearing, his conclusions would pass unread, without the approval of the arbiters of knowledge; and heresy in economics or religion invited retribution. Boldness of thought was rarely counted a virtue in the university which conceived of its task as that of establishing correct standards for the guidance of *Society*.

Most Americans thought of their clubs and newspapers as means of organizing their own lives; it did not matter to them that others followed different ways. The Irish Catholic laborer who was a member of the Hibernians took it for granted that the Yankee clerk would be a Methodist and a Mason. But the would-be aristocrats could not accept that tolerant parity. Their *Society* had to be *the* society, their *culture*, *the* culture, to bring them the status they sought. They did not want the whole population crowding into the opera or applying for admission to Groton, Harvard and the Racquet Club; but they wanted possession of a box and membership recognized as signs of their own leadership. And they hoped that respect for correct knowledge would keep the population from being misled by disruptive fads.

A concerted effort to diffuse the appreciation of *culture*, including science, to the whole society utilized both governmental sanctions and the educational system. The long effort of the professions to achieve a monopoly of practice now approached fulfillment. Licensing laws in many states admitted to medicine and the bar only those qualified by a prescribed course of training. Preparation for these careers generally followed a defined route through college and professional schools, access to which depended upon graduation from high school. Secondary education was more available than before, but it was uniformly tailored to standards prescribed from the college. A tightly articulated system thus took form to diffuse *culture* to the whole country.

The pressure was disruptive. The other urban communities, and the farmers as well, respected wealth and read the accounts of gala dinners with interest. But they hesitated to accept the dominance of a self-constituted elite. They had their own cultures, their own societies and their own leaders. Indeed, exclusionary policies sometimes drove rising men of new wealth back into the ethnic group and strengthened its cohesiveness. The banker of humble or foreign birth, repulsed by *Society*, threw his energies into the affairs of the community of his origin. By developing independent institutions of their own the ghettos thus evaded the pretensions of *Society*.

They were not, however, able to hold their children. By the 1880's, many sons — of immigrants in the slums, of natives in the suburbs, and of farmers — were breaking away from parental communities and culture. They hoped to rise by education; and education demanded acceptance of the defined *culture*. The boy who learned what he was taught did well in the high school and went on to college and the professions or to a desirable job in industry. *Culture* was the price he paid for position, status and power. It ceased therefore to provide authentic satisfaction or to answer his most troubling questions. He learned to identify good music and great art, but without expecting any personal response to them. The result often was an inner conflict between the success all Americans esteemed as a goal and the break it entailed in the continuity of their experience.

The need to conform was particularly irksome because other modes of thought and expression outside the canon of propriety and good taste cut across all group lines and did move people, cultivated and vulgar alike.

Side by side with the official *science* there existed a science which was popular in the sense that it thrived, without institutional support, solely by its service to a clientele drawn from every sector of the population. Its means of validation were simple and untheoretical. The only significant test was practice. If the little liver pills ended the pain, explanations were superfluous. One could speak through a wire, have light without fire, and be drawn in a wagon without horses. Wonderful. One might equally well fly through the air or ride beneath the sea, as the Sunday supplement said.

The men who learned to use the telephone, to put on the electric lights, and to ride daily on the trolley car had no understanding of physics or even of the operations of the mechanism. They treated these devices as a kind of magic in which a given cause produced a predictable result: one turned the crank, a voice was heard; one threw the switch, the light went on; one pulled the lever, the car moved. In the same way, one swallowed the bitter liquid to take the pain away and one printed paper or coined silver to raise prices. It was unnecessary to wonder why; the scientist was as credible a figure as the magician on the stage.

The heroes of popular science were not at home in the university but in the workshop, not Willard Gibbs or William Graham Sumner, but Thomas Edison and Coin Harvey. The media that made their achievements known were not the publications of learned societies but the Sunday supplement, the magazine and fiction. The same pages also described the lost continent of Atlantis, illness that had no physical cause, and machines that flew through space to other planets or burrowed down among the strange creatures within the hollow shell of the earth. It was not a question of whether Lydia Pinkham was as good a doctor as a graduate of Johns Hopkins; the remedies of one were as likely to be effective as those of the other. But popular science had this advantage, that its practitioners, unfettered and undisciplined, were attentive to experience and more imaginative about its potential.

Popular culture, like popular science, was related to the life of its participants rather than to their status. The official literature and theater commanded only a tiny audience. Most Americans read the *yellow* penny press and dime novels and went eagerly to the circus or to vaudeville performances. The Bowery theater and the troupe that brought *Uncle Tom's Cabin* or *Rip Van Winkle* to town lacked the polish and dignity of Richard Mansfield in Clyde Fitch's *Beau Brummel*. But they, like the press and the popular novel, implicated the audience by involving it in real problems. The happy ending permitted a brutal realism in the treatment of some subjects. Others touched the senses of awe and wonder; and burlesque mocked the pretensions of society. In much of the comedy, the audience recognized itself. The ethnic stereotypes — drunken Irishman, avaricious Jew, grasping Yankee, blustering Southern colonel — were sometimes cruel exaggerations, but they touched on actual types and situations and they permitted the audience to apprehend, through laughter, the world about them. These spectacles were not simply to be observed across the footlights but to be participated in.

American humor, said the *Nation* in 1883, *had the same relationship with literature that the Negro minstrels or Harrigan and Hart had to drama.* The difference between the uptown and the downtown theater and literature was that of its authenticity. It was the same with popular music, which was not to be *appreciated* but to be sung or danced to. The art of the comics was to laugh with. And, unlike the sport of *Society*, the organized athletics of the baseball field or prize-ring involved a bitter struggle for success in which the victor beat down the loser with no pretense of good feeling.

Popular culture had its own promoters and impresarios, but it lacked patrons, prestige, or institutional props. It thrived only by being popular, that is, by attracting customers, and therefore it was responsive to the mood and attitude of those it served. It borrowed freely from the classics, from the defined *culture*, and from the folk traditions of the groups it hoped to draw within its orbit. But it assimilated those borrowings by a sharp awareness of the men and women it addressed.

In 1900, American culture was no more orderly than American society. The effort to organize stable aristocratic, suburban and immigrant communities was momentarily successful. But they could not exist in isolation; and while *Society* had the power to give its own *culture* status, it could not satisfy the needs of others, or for that matter, its own. The ladies too used patent medicine, but surreptitiously, without telling the doctor. As the century drew to a close, the growing attractiveness of popular culture reflected the inability of these communities to hold the support of their own members and of the next generation.

Rural America remained apart from all these developments and hostile to them. Increasingly the city became alien, and increasingly its influence reached out to the farms and to the stagnant small towns left behind by industrialization. The Chautauqua lecturer, in the tradition of the lyceum, brought to the hinterland the congenial wisdom, humor and tastes of the wider world, but could not offset the urban pressures. The great metropolitan centers had changed the face of the country; and the men who could not cope with the new situation were bitter as they contemplated the results. The bankers and the immigrants had created not only an economy that bore harshly upon the farmer, the courthouse lawyer, and the owner of the general store, but also a culture strange in values. And the agents of both intruded everywhere; the lighthearted slicker in the circus and the hardhearted freight manager of the railroad alike sought to deprive the *rubes* of the fruits of honest toil.

Yet they could not stay away, either from the market or from the show. The prospect of gain and of pleasure were standing temptations. More ominous, their sons and daughters panted to plunge into danger. Nostalgically the old-timers thought back to the good old days before the railroad broke in upon the serene countryside, when, they imagined, life had been good and pure. Was the promised land no longer in their future but in the past, behind rather than before them?

The same uneasiness penetrated the less successful sectors of the suburbs inhabited by the children of the country folk. There came a time when some drummers realized they never would gain the promotion and would travel the same monotonous round to the end of their days. There came a moment when the bank closed and swept away

the savings of a lifetime or when an enterprise failed and left its proprietor too old to start over again. Then the weary men, reckoning up
the meager rewards of their striving and deprivation, eagerly longed
for what they now lacked, for what they fancied had once existed — a
whole community with satisfying values of which to be a part.

Some revolted and fastened their resentment to a cause. Prohibition and Populism were alike in their hostility to the city — *Babylon
the great, the mother of the harlots and of the abominations of the
earth,* where *the animal man, drunken with the blood of the saints,
fed off the multitudes.* Prohibition was more than a crusade against
liquor, Populism was more than a demand for political and economic
reform. Among those who listened to the bloodcurdling accounts of
the vice that emanated from the saloon and the bank were many who
responded, out of the depths of their own frustration, with hatred
toward both the foreign-born poor and the rich.

Those emotions subsided with the renewal of hopes for success, but
they did not disappear. Festering beneath the surface, they generated
a gnawing anxiety about the meaning of Americanism. The Civil
War had shaken the polity and industrialization had transformed the
economy. Could the image of the American — that new man — survive the painful personal and social adjustments of these decades?

21

Americanism

In 1890, the editor of *Youth's Companion* was shocked to observe some boys throwing snowballs at girls. It was not alone the offense to chivalry that led him to take up his pen for a stinging editorial, but the fact that the heinous deed had occurred within sight of the flag. *The American flag means fair play, equal chance, protection to the weak and honor to women.* In hoisting it, pupils at school *make a profession of the American religion, a leading principle of which is respect and consideration* for women. The meaning of faith had changed profoundly since 1860, if raising the flag could conventionally be taken as an act of worship.

The intervening three decades had shaken accepted maxims and forced many churches to reconsider their role in man's life. Americans were particularly vulnerable to these unsettling tendencies, for they had taken nothing on authority but relied on the unaided reason and on experience. The intellectual turmoil of those years left them in confusion, anxious to believe, but uncertain in what. Groping for an answer, some attempted to cut loose from the nation's heritage, but could not altogether shake off the cords to the past. Veneration of the flag was an aspect of their determined search for faith.

They had tried to preserve an orderly community life so that fixed norms could guide them in a changing society. They had not succeeded. One could not be sure after 1860 that success was the reward of proper behavior; too often the ability to get ahead ran counter to traditional ethical precepts. Earlier, each man had hoped to better himself because all were perfectible and because it was the manifest destiny of the individual as well as of the nation to expand. Now the fortunes of a few rested on the poverty of the many; and the proper standards of behavior fluttered in the winds of convenience.

Furthermore, man's stature had shrunk disconcertingly. Without Emerson's divine spark, self-reliance became but a term for selfish callousness to the needs of others. Yet the transcendental eyeball, that particle of God, ceased to be credible in the light of the war and of science. Americans suddenly discovered that they knew little of man and of his place in the universe.

Since early in the nineteenth century the geologists had gone tapping about over the face of the earth. They had the soundest credentials — academic status and the ability to turn their information toward useful ends. They demonstrated that the planet was far older than traditional accounts allowed it to be. The Bible was therefore not literally accurate. It was a metaphorical, poetic document — one of divine inspiration, if one wished, but not a precise record of events. At the same time, the astronomers' telescopes began to show the immensity of the universe; the solar system receded to a corner of space, the dimensions of which none could guess. Man then was but a speck on one of several planets that revolved around one of many stars.

While reeling from these discoveries, Americans also had to absorb the impact of Darwinian theories of evolution. Science showed that man, like every other living object, was in constant process of development. His features and character were not formed at a single moment in the beginning, to remain forever the same, but rather were evolved slowly in time — and they would continue to do so. He was not now what he had been nor would he remain what he was. Change, furthermore, came through natural selection; random occurrences, the products of blind chance, made some organisms fitter to survive than others.

At once the familiar conception of human history as a drama with a known beginning and a predictable end collapsed. Man's development was a process devoid of purpose, proceeding from an obscure origin to a shadowy future. He was not a unique being created in the divine image of God but one of nature's creatures, not unlike the monkey from whom he may have descended, and he could only guess what shape his own remote offspring would take.

In bewilderment, thousands of men and women came to hear the great orator Robert Ingersoll demand that they surrender *the hope of ascertaining the first or final causes, of comprehending the supernatural.* They were to proclaim themselves agnostics. They did not know. They could not know. And the church which made a pretense of certainty only deceived the credulous. *With sword and flame, it destroyed the brave and thoughtful men who told the truth* about its fictions. This impressive figure planted boldly on the platform was no wild-eyed radical, but the son of a minister, a war veteran, a wealthy lawyer and a power in the Republican party. Speculators plunged heavily in tickets for his lectures, so avid was the demand. And his words were moderate by comparison with those of the outright free-thinkers, atheists and anarchists.

It was titillating to listen to the bad boy — an older Huck Finn — dare God to strike him dead where he stood. The boldness of the irreverence gave thousands of listeners a vicarious release from restraints they had not imagined could be lifted from them. It was as if all the naughty words they knew but feared to utter came suddenly tumbling out in one uproarious joke.

Respect for the clergy ebbed. That Henry Ward Beecher, a figure of national prominence, became enmeshed in a trial for adultery was symptomatic. The preachers were misfits, good for nothing better. *Only the shrimp in a family was sent to the theological seminary,* wrote Peck of the respectable Milwaukee *Sun.* The *human dried prune* grew up with *never a generous impulse or a natural dose of perspiration on his brow, called from one place to another, investigated for conduct prejudicial to good square religion, whitewashed by committees and delivering tracts on the evils of smoking and drinking.* Read in the new perspective, the Bible lost its awesome quality. *Adam and Eve may have been all right in their day,* but they were far behind the times. Adam was *a regular sucker. Going into that apple speculation* proved *what kind of man he would be to run a farm at this age of the world.* As for Eve, she was just *a woman who could not say no.* That much was reasonable and in accord with experience.

Yet it was not easy to surrender faith. A lingering worry persisted: where would they be without that ultimate restraint? The church embraced too many personal recollections and satisfied too many emotional wants to be abandoned. It may no longer have offered a credible explanation of the universe or held forth a reliable guide to daily conduct. But it was here that neighbors met, and it was here that ritual imparted order to life's mysteries. The sacred acts sustained the family, kept marriage from being merely a transient relationship, and marked the birth of the oncoming generation. Above all, it buried the dead, and death was more than ever in the consciousness of Americans.

Often in the parlor, they stood about the piano to sing. The music, derived from old hymns, raised waves of feeling in the group and the words reminded them why: *The Shiloh drummer boy lay dying, a prayer on his lips; John Brown's body lies a-moldering in the grave.* In almost every family there was *One Vacant Chair.* It could not have been all in vain; the glorious dead could not have been reduced to nothingness. Ingersoll preferred to think that those he had loved and lost had *returned to earth, to become a part of the elemental wealth of the world, unconscious dust, gurgling in the streams, floating in the clouds.* His audience did not follow him. It had come to hear him *give Hell hell,* not to see heaven demolished; and it could not put away the faith that John Brown's *soul* went *marching on.*

The will to believe conquered reason and experience. At the extreme, spiritualism, in a variety of guises, attracted a growing number of adherents. From Russia by way of India came Helena Blavatsky. In 1875, with Henry S. Olcott, she formed the Theosophical Society in New York, teaching that death was only an incident in the cycle of migrations of the individual spirit. Julius Dresser and other earnest devotees of the New Thought movement formed a variety of churches. And Mary Baker Eddy, inspired by Phineas Quimby, joined the old and the new, in Christian Science. Man was not material but spiritual; and neither illness nor death existed except in his own mind.

The older churches gradually accommodated their creeds to the new situation of their communicants, making a place for the new knowledge, yet retaining the familiar ritual and emphasizing the comforting assurance that there was room in heaven for all the departed dead. John Fiske, the popularizer of Darwin, achieved his greatest success with the scientific demonstration of the immortality of the soul. Beecher, despite his personal debacle, convinced many that evolution and faith were compatible in the heart of man. Ideas that did God's work were worthy of belief. All others could be disregarded; *whether they were true or not, they were not true to me.* By the end of the century, modernist clergymen in all the Protestant denominations had achieved a similar adjustment; and the same tendency was evident in Reform Judaism and in the liberal wing of American Catholicism. The Deity became conveniently the first cause or the force behind evolution, another designation for the nature described in Norris's *Octopus.* Lost in the process was the relationship to a personal God who cared.

Atonement for the guilt of the loss came in the periodic revivals staged in the great cities. These occasions, quite unlike the camp meetings of the past, were carefully managed, supported by prosperous businessmen and attended by audiences from the middle classes. In these dramas, the preacher, the leading actor, pitched his themes to the tastes of the participants. Dwight L. Moody, the most popular performer, neither addressed the men and women before him as sinners nor threatened them with hell. Instead he vividly described concrete scenes of suffering on earth, the martyrdom of Stephen or the whippings of Paul or, in painful detail, Christ's last hours — the scourging, the crown of thorns, the mockery, the nailing to the cross, the death cry. On this platform, the events no longer credible as history became as real as the fiction of *Ben Hur* or *Quo Vadis.* In the mounting horror, the audience perceived that Christ had been their *burden-bearer;* a sentimental identification would *make room for Him in the heart* and purge sin.

Or, alternatively, the preacher, like Sam Jones, was a rustic comedian whose homely wit expressed the plain truth of common sense. Conversion was *a business contract binding on both parties.* God saved those who *enlisted in His army* in the crusade against alcohol, theaters and dancing.

But in either case, action, not belief, counted. Christianity, said Moody, *was not a dogma, not a creed, not a doctrine. Theology,* said Jones, *was a good thing — a good thing to stuff with sawdust, like a fish, and put in a museum as a relic of antiquity.* It was therefore not altogether incongruous that people who clamored to hear Ingersoll should on other evenings come to the revival which, without critical demands upon faith, gave them a momentary connection with a personal God absent in their usual religious life.

Resolution of the dilemma between the will to believe and the evidence of the world comforted men not pressed too hard by either horn. The undemanding creeds satisfied the social needs of those whose lives were orderly and free of want. The wealthy parishioner of the Episcopal Church took comfort in its institutional stability, its respect for authority, and its English antecedents. In the suburb, the Presbyterian or Baptist Church established pleasant links with their members' rural past. But the working people, the marginal clerks and salesmen, and the depressed farmers would not be put off without an explanation of their condition. Their existence was an endless crisis. They had to know why; and they wanted a God who listened attentively to their prayers.

Some flatly rejected the evidence. It was not their science! Refusing to mediate with the universities and books, with the theories and logic of a society strange to them, they clung to fundamentals — the literal accuracy of the Bible, a heaven to reward them and a hell to punish their oppressors. Evil emanated from sin and dominated the world. But they would be saved by turning to God. To restore *the religion of Jesus Christ,* it was necessary to *destroy all existing institutions, aristocracies, governments, churches, colleges, penal institutions, and business generally.* And it was worth it.

The cataclysmic tone which, in the West, animated both Populism and fundamentalism was unnecessary in groups with institutions deeply rooted in tradition. The inherited churches and faiths of the immigrants, Negroes and Southern poor whites were agencies of stability that needed no rational defense. As long as these people stood apart in their own communities they could disregard the questions that troubled Americans higher in the social scale and hold firmly to the God of their fathers.

Compromise or intransigence settled or evaded the issues of personal faith raised by science. But Darwinism also cast doubt upon the traditional understanding of the nature of man. Adam was out of date. All humans were not his children, common offspring of a single

family. In an indefinitely enlarged time-span, they might well have
evolved into altogether different species; or, natural selection might
have led various breeds along quite divergent lines of development.
Good Christians no longer had to consider mankind as a unity; after
1860 they could think in terms of distinct races, each with its own
inherent biological traits, separate and unequal. The new understanding helped account for anomalies in the American social situation; it
was in accord with the findings of science; and it offered many people
an escape from emotional tension.

For Southerners, race explained the whole Negro problem — the
propriety of slavery in the past, the failure of Reconstruction in the
present and the need for segregation to control the blacks in the future. All whites, poor and rich, North and South, had reason to unite
to eliminate *social contacts contrary to natural law* and to confine the
freedmen to the inferiority to which heritage condemned them. These
arguments won over Northerners who wished to justify the failure to
intervene in the South and the inability to improve the lot of the
colored men at home. Successive judicial decisions accepted the premises of the racist position and nullified the guarantees of the Fourteenth Amendment.

The indelible mark of color also justified hostility to other groups.
The Indians, after being so long pushed from place to place, now had
nowhere else to go. They were skulking savages, their base nature
made plain in dime novels and in the lithographed ambush of General Custer. The Chinese in California were the scapegoats of the
Workingmen's party and of the organized labor movement. Low
character, lack of moral sense and criminal instincts made their exclusion necessary.

In the last decade of the century, perception had become acute
enough to distinguish racial differences even among the whites. The
New Englanders who then formed the Immigration Restriction League
had witnessed the change in their section with distress. Industrialization had despoiled the countryside and slums the cities. Politics were
corrupt and culture was debased; and it was all the fault of immigrants who were no longer the sturdy settlers of the past but *beaten
men of beaten races*. Some Populists, concerned with the money
power of the Jews, and some labor leaders, concerned with the competition of Italians and Slavs, echoed the phrases.

The prestige of science in Europe and America sustained the racist argument. The writings of Count Gobineau had shown the importance of physical, cultural and spiritual differences among the species of men and had revealed that all civilization was the product of the efforts of Aryans. Anthropologists measured thousands of skulls to arrive at a precise index of race; and geneticists showed statistically that no degenerate or feeble stock could ever be made healthy by education or favorable environment. A mixture of strains was dangerous, for the poorer quality inevitably caused the deterioration of the better. Superior and inferior races *could not live together on any other terms than as masters and slaves.*

The danger to the purity of the blood was immediate and personal as well as social. Contact with the lower breeds threatened every man and woman who struggled painfully for abstinence and restraint in the interest of a sound family life. In the South the blacks threatened to drag the whites down to their own brutal level; on the Pacific Coast, the Orientals beguiled little girls to their laundries to commit crimes *too horrible to imagine*; and everywhere the Latins, Jews and Slavs were implicated in vice, as in liquor and crime. All were threats precisely because they were inferior. Sensuous rather than spiritual, they exercised no self-restraint, as their large families showed. Soon they would outnumber the superior stock. Then a relative handful of the able, thrifty, and hard-working would be left to support a great mass of degenerates. Thus civilizations declined.

Hence the prolonged concern with the future, which Darwinism had also unsettled. The familiar millennium disappeared; and the years stretched endlessly ahead in an unknown direction. Americans could no longer be confident that time would solve the problems of the present. They reread with interest the warning, of George Perkins Marsh in 1864, that the earth had been given them *for usufruct alone, not for consumption, still less for profligate waste.* Question: what would happen when the wells ran dry, the last trees crashed down, the cars rose from the pit empty of ore and the abused soil refused to yield? Participants in the conservation movement, in growing numbers, cast fearful glances ahead as they reckoned up how little was left. In 1892, Frederick Jackson Turner explained that the free land of the frontier — now gone — had shaped the political, social and economic institutions of the United States. A turn in a new direction was imminent.

A flood of utopian novels in the last two decades of the century speculated about the shape of things to come. The happy endings that made them tolerable did not conceal the fear of the cataclysm upon which many of the plots turned. In Ignatius Donnelly's *Caesar's Column*, an oligarchy of wealth led by Prince Cabano (born Jacob Isaacs) dominates the country and pushes the world toward destruction. In desperation, the people revolt. But their uprising degenerates into anarchy, base elements seize control and all civilization is consumed in a holocaust. The images are real to those who recall the Paris Commune, the labor riots of the 1880's and the activities of anarchists at home and abroad, and who jumble in with these events what they have read of lost continents, decayed civilization, alien races and other worlds.

These were the reflections of men worried about the future because they could not control the present as they thought they should. The failure of the war and the massive changes wrought by the factory city freshened the ancient anxieties of the Americans, forced again and again to abandon that which they cherished. As often as they had cut themselves loose from home and the past to seek opportunity, so often had they been overtaken by an overwhelming longing for what had been left behind. Yet the past could not be recaptured nor the future held firm; and the posterity for which they sacrificed would desert them as they themselves had deserted their parents.

Neither the family nor the immediate community seemed to offer men secure moorings. Filed away in the numbered flats of numbered houses on numbered streets, people who wished to be more than anonymous integers ardently desired to know who they were — what father's son, what group's member, what God's creature. They could find the answer only by seeking out their brothers. And in their confusion they attempted to locate one another by excluding the outsider who was not one of them. Hence they were drawn to the fancied unity of race.

But however imagination might people the past with Aryans or Nordics or Teutons, daily life was more complex. The white might set himself off from the Negro, the Christian from the Jew, and the Anglo-Saxon from the Italian; prolonged indefinitely, the subdivision brought him back to himself — alone. Their history deprived Americans of the refuge of common descent.

They came back therefore to what they did share, their Americanism. But in doing so they transformed the concept to accommodate their longing for a group with which they could feel one and to which they could attach their loyalty. They were *one people*, united, descended from a race of patriots, custodians of liberty and virtue and thereby set apart from lesser men. It was only necessary to hold together to share common beliefs and repress divisive impulses, to be secure in the present and in the future.

Precise definition was not important. Vaguely, Uncle Sam, like Brother Jonathan, had rural Yankee features. But that did not bar Southerners from identifying with him — or, for that matter, the children of immigrants. The Irish-Americans, the German-Americans, and the Jewish-Americans proudly displayed the records of their achievements that entitled them to share the same identity. Indeed, even the Afro-Americans could participate, although rarely on an equal plane.

What was important was the opportunity for ceremony and ritual. In the national holidays, the parades, and the veneration of the flag, the American shed the burdens of being a person alone and dissolved, at least temporarily, into the national entity that made him secure.

Although a separate and superior race, Americans still had duties toward the rest of the world. In *Our Country*, Josiah Strong, a popular Congregationalist preacher, explained the obligation of extending the blessings of rule by the United States over inferior breeds. In *The Problems of Civilization Solved*, the Populist Mary Ellen Lease foresaw a global conflict with the black and yellow races of Asia and America. The Americans would emerge victorious and go on altruistically to govern the colored people of the world for the benefit of all. Brooks Adams, in *America's Economic Supremacy*, explained that economic growth compelled the United States to acquire colonies. Captain Alfred T. Mahan showed that national strength depended upon sea power which, in turn, was contingent upon the naval bases of a far-flung empire. Meanwhile restless young men like Theodore Roosevelt who had only read about war lusted for glory and vociferously urged that a fight would be *a good thing* to tone up Americanism.

These arguments for imperialism differed from the doctrines of manifest destiny in one vital respect. Citizenship was not to follow the flag. The *dull and stupid* peoples about to be conquered could not govern themselves. Nor could they become citizens equal in rights with the Americans. They were to be subjects governed for their own good by their superiors in the United States. In that respect the colonies for which the imperialists longed would also be unlike Alaska and Hawaii, territories acquired with the assumption that they could advance to statehood.

In 1898, a *splendid little war* with Spain created the opportunity for implementing these ideas. President McKinley had fumbled his way into the conflict, pressed on by the popular clamor from men genuinely concerned with the liberty of the Cubans and from those with an economic stake in the island, along with racists, imperialists, the yellow press and jingoists of every sort. At the peace, the United States stripped Spain of its Caribbean and Asian colonies, and, to retain the Philippines, ruthlessly suppressed an insurrection by other men who wished to be free. The conquerors in Manila had certainly come a long way from Valley Forge. The senator from Indiana gloated that the islands were *ours forever*; and just beyond were *China's illimitable markets. We will not renounce our part in the mission of our race, trustee, under God, of the civilization of the world. God has not been preparing the English-speaking and Teutonic people for a thousand years for nothing. He has made us the master organizers of the world to administer government among savage and senile people.*

Other Americans watched with despair the subversion of the ideals of the Republic in the name of Americanism. Some joke! *The red-letter days of the calendar are April 1 which reminds us that we are fools and October 12, Columbus Day. It would have been wonderful to find America, but it would have been more wonderful to miss it.*

The crowds cheered as the boys came home. This time there had been no pain, only glory.

Once the first fever subsided, however, the traumatic shock of the imperialist outcome called for a reconsideration. At many points the new Americanism did not fit what Americans actually were. In the special Columbus Day song, 1892, every school child in the country repeated:

> *Humanity's home! thy sheltering breast*
> *Gives welcome and room to strangers oppress'd.*
> *Pale children of Hunger and Hatred and Wrong*
> *Find Life in thy freedom and joy in thy song.*

No reference here to the inferiority or superiority of the children of want promised life in freedom! The teachers who led the singing were patriotic and had no desire to make rebels of their pupils. But the history of the country and the experience of all who sat in the classroom ran counter to the assumptions of the imperialists.

Men and women who actually worked with the immigrants, the Negroes, and the native white poor in the settlement houses of the urban slums or in missions to the rural countryside, could not believe that all domestic problems had been solved or that the United States had adequately demonstrated its capacity for self-government. From the pulpit, Washington Gladden and George D. Herron insisted that the church had a duty toward the world in which it existed. Setting aside for the moment questions of the afterlife and of theology proper, they focused upon the implications of the ethical imperatives of Christianity for economic, social and political behavior. In the universities, Richard T. Ely, John B. Clark and Charles H. Cooley used their learning to criticize their society. They deplored the widening gulf between the rich and the poor and sought a basis for restoring the sense of human solidarity infused with religious values. In their conceptions of the social gospel they outlined another version of Americanism.

For the moment they were a minority. But their appeal touched responsive chords of conscience in many people. It could not make sense to serve a dinner on horseback on Sherry's second floor with the steeds prancing about the magnificent dining room, *each bearing, besides its rider, a miniature table.* Perhaps it was true that men had descended from monkeys; but surely they were not still in the jungle. *He that hath plenty of peanuts and giveth his neighbor none, he can't have none of my peanuts when his peanuts are gone.* Any man — or monkey — could understand that.

A handful of other scholars, by 1900, had begun to re-examine their culture. William James and John Dewey dealt at first with limited technical problems — the ways of knowing or the place of the child in the school. But in doing so, they exposed the empty formalism of the defined *culture* divorced from experience; and they encouraged a reversion to the pragmatic approach of earlier generations.

Sporadic actions showed the explosive consequences of these ideas. Andrew Carnegie, unshaken in his immigrant's faith in opportunity, decided that *the man who dies rich dies disgraced* and set about disposing of his fortune to further human progress. In Toledo, Samuel M. *Golden Rule* Jones read Herron and concluded that if God were indeed *our Father*, then all men were brothers and deserved to be treated as members of a single family. In 1895, he raised wages, lowered hours and let his employees share in the profits of his machine factory. Elected mayor, he reformed the city and held office despite the combined opposition of the major parties, the churches and the business interests.

Charles M. Sheldon's novel *In His Steps* was the most popular of a genre, in the 1890's, that revolved around *golden rule* experiences. It showed what would happen if Americans, at each decision in life, would ask themselves as Jones had: *What would Jesus do?* The question worried millions of readers.

As the century turned, many Americans were taking stock. They were a world power. They had built an economy of tremendous capacity and had created impressive social and cultural institutions. But they were unsure of the uses for the factories and farms, the schools and churches, and the abundant energy of a growing population.

A tragic Civil War had cast the shadow of doubt across the older dreams of perfectibility, of mankind liberated by free government, of a Kingdom of God in the empty space of the New Jerusalem. Overwhelmed by industrialization and urbanization, unable to form a stable community or a satisfying culture, some were tempted to turn to newer goals and strange gods. But few were willing to surrender altogether these last best hopes of man. The shock of becoming conquerors forced them to think once more of the means of shaping a good society. They had still in mind the words of the poet:

Democracy was not perfect, but it was the only means by which the future could enter upon a decent course. The true New World of orbic science, morals, literatures was yet undefined, unform'd, advancing, absorbing the present, transcending the past. But they could feel in its ominous greatness, evil as well as good.

VII

The Dilemmas of Maturity, 1900–1939

22

Isolating America

THE VERY FIRST year showed that Americans had been right to await the twentieth century with both hope and trepidation. In East Texas, Spindletop blew in, throwing up oil in a gusher of wealth, 160 feet high and six inches in diameter. That was the promise. In Buffalo, a demented anarchist shot down President McKinley, revealing the dangers of daily life in the great cities. That was the threat. The potential was unlimited, both for riches and destructive madness.

The assassination brought to office the first of the powerful twentieth-century chief executives. Theodore Roosevelt in 1901 was just a little more than forty. Offspring of a good New York family and educated at Harvard, he was convinced of his personal ability to govern and determined to lead the nation to a more strenuous life. A confirmed imperialist, a friend of Mahan and Brooks Adams, he had gained his reputation as a hero in Cuba; and he was anxious to increase the country's military strength and to acquire the colonies appropriate to a world power.

Teddy waved a big stick and often spoke belligerently as well. Yet neither he nor his successors developed an American empire. Instead, they prepared to disembarrass the nation of the acquisitions it had already made. Imperialism proved a temporary aberration of American policy.

It was not through want of opportunity that the United States refrained from acquiring new colonial possessions. Certainly the Europeans had been there first and had gobbled up the choicest morsels in Africa and Asia. But there was plenty of space left, and other newcomers to the game, like Japan and Germany, did not hesitate to claim what they could. Americans held themselves to a smaller overseas domain than Portugal, Holland or Belgium because imperialism in practice proved incompatible with the institutions of a free republic.

The Philippines were a striking case. Even in 1898, a resolution assuring the islands independence had gained a tie vote in the Senate and was defeated only through the intercession of the Vice President. No sooner was Aguinaldo's rebellion suppressed than the work of pacification began. The United States reorganized the civil administration, provided medical and educational aid, and gradually extended individual liberties to the residents. By 1917 Filipinos held many appointive posts in the territorial government and were represented in its legislature. The independence they would ultimately attain was postponed largely because of fear of Japanese aggression and because of the economic advantages to the islands of maintaining their connection with the American market. This was a far cry from the subjugation Beveridge had envisioned.

Nor did the nation expand elsewhere in the Orient, although an occasional statesman was tempted by the thought of coaling stations or concessions. Consistently the United States supported the territorial integrity of China and argued for the equal rights to trade of all foreigners there. If this *open door* policy served American interests, it also served those of the tottering Manchu empire. The United States returned a large part of the indemnity received for damages during the Boxer rebellion, to be used for scholarships; and it withdrew from a brief participation in a condominium of international banks which managed Chinese finances because that smacked too much of foreign control. Ironically, in view of his professions of belligerency, Roosevelt's signal achievement in this area won him the

Nobel Peace Prize for his efforts in negotiating the treaty that ended the Russo-Japanese War.

Involvements in the Caribbean were deeper. The United States was eager to ease communications between its two coasts by an isthmian canal; and it wished to keep out the European powers that threatened to intervene in the region from time to time. But American moves toward those objectives, with one notable exception, were largely negative and defensive. President Roosevelt's impatience made him the accomplice — if not the initiator — of a Panamanian revolution against Colombia in 1903, by which he secured favorable terms for the canal. But an apologetic indemnity to Colombia later repudiated that personal act of aggression.

The feeble republics in Nicaragua, Haiti and Santo Domingo were in perennial disorder. The corrupt dictators who ruled them borrowed freely abroad, failed to make the payments and then uncomfortably looked out at the harbor for sight of the foreign warships come to collect. A debt was a debt. Yet Americans were uneasy at the thought of Europeans re-established in an area from which Spain had just been excluded. President Roosevelt in 1905 added a corollary to the Monroe Doctrine: to forestall the intervention of others, the United States would temporarily take control of such countries. For the same reason it retained the power to step in in Cuba, although military occupation ended in 1902. On the other hand, Americans were patient in the face of provocations after the Mexican revolution of 1910 and refrained from interfering there; and in 1917 Puerto Ricans became citizens. These were far from imperialist measures and far from the common practices of the great powers at the time.

Little circles of army and navy officers, businessmen, and intellectuals continued to urge a more expansive overseas policy. But popular sentiment was overwhelmingly negative and made further adventures politically hazardous. There had been a margin of only two votes in the Senate when the treaty with Spain had been ratified; and the peace influence grew steadily in the first decade of the new century. Most voters agreed with Mr. Dooley that, *if they were chinamen, they'd tuck their shirts into their pants, put their braids up in a net, an' go out an' take a fall out of the invader if it cost them their lives.* It was a good thing *they ain't Christians an' haven't learned properly to sight a gun.*

In any case, inhibitions restrained Americans in the use of power. The little brown and yellow men were no doubt inferior and probably never would stand on their own feet or be able to run an honest election. But the weight of a tradition, laden with the rhetoric of freedom and human dignity, prevented Americans from acting upon that assumption. A concern for legitimate procedures and for the welfare of the native population impeded the efficient exploitation of the new possessions and diminished their value. It was best to leave those races to their own devices as soon as possible.

The failure of policy was one of omission rather than of commission. The occupation of Haiti or Nicaragua was less important than the fact that, once installed, the Americans made no attempt to create democratic institutions. They were content to restore order even though that left a dictator in control, because they had lost faith that other peoples could govern themselves.

Those who wished to involve themselves with the backward people of the world could do so without the force of government. Missionary enterprises expanded rapidly, carrying with them not only the gospel but also modern medicine, education and agricultural techniques. Meanwhile the entrepreneur cast appraising glances at the unsatisfied wants of the uncivilized areas. Here were millions of new customers for kerosene and clocks; here were thousands of laborers willing to carry out the bananas and rubber to send in return. These were the ways to deal with the outer world. Even so, trade with Latin America, Asia and Africa played a minor part in the whole economy and despite occasional confusion of the dollar with diplomacy, such commercial penetration as occurred was peaceful.

Racist thinking subtly affected attitudes to the civilized countries also. Gone was the thought of the coming unity of mankind. The social set, intellectuals and recent immigrants still valued connections with the Old World. But most Americans had become dubious not only of colonialism but of every type of foreign contact. The Republic was uniquely theirs; its ways could not be exported; and association with any strangers would enfeeble it. Some sections began to suspect that even overseas trade lacked value. Contraction of the export market for grains and meats, as the European countries adopted protectionist policies, nurtured the idea in the West that the United States ought to become entirely self-sufficient. Better to stand alone.

Preoccupied with their own domestic affairs, Americans were indifferent to foreign policy, which they were content to leave to those
with the inclination to play at being diplomats. President Wilson,
soon after his election in 1912, was willing to let his friend Colonel
Edward M. House travel through the chancelleries of Europe on
his behalf without bothering to clarify the purpose, or to compose
precise instructions, or to consult the State Department.

Turning inward, Americans found cause for satisfaction in their
record of economic growth after 1900. The familiar indices were
reassuring and the depression of 1907 halted the upward trend only
momentarily. National wealth, income and the output of manufacturing more than doubled in the first twelve years of the century. A
steady flow of immigrants supplied all the manpower required and
raised the population from seventy-five million in 1900 to well above
one hundred million in 1917. In six of the ten years after 1905 more
than a million newcomers entered the United States annually. In all,
about twelve million arrived by the time war broke out.

Everything boomed, gold in Alaska, oil in Texas, fruit in California. The wages of unskilled labor rose, as old industries thrived
and new ones appeared. Railroad mileage went up by thirty per cent
in the two decades after 1900. Meanwhile, the automobile manufacturers, coming from nowhere, converted the little carriage shops
into great integrated plants, using armies of hands at the advanced
technique of the assembly line. By 1917, the value of their product
had risen to above a billion dollars. Capital was abundant, still
speculative and still available for expansion. For the farmer, too, this
was a period of relative prosperity; the rising purchasing power of
the urban population more than compensated for the loss of some
foreign markets. There seemed no reason, therefore, for concern with
events outside the United States.

The effort to remain aloof nevertheless failed; there were more
ties to Europe than Americans realized.

In August, 1914, the great powers of the Old World went to war.
Ancient sores, disputed boundaries and imperial contests had aligned
them in two rival blocs, suspicious, hostile, and weighted down with
expensive armaments that fear would not let them lay aside. Two
decades of diplomatic maneuvering had only made the divisions

more rigid. When the crisis came, none would yield and the Continent plunged toward disaster. At the outbreak of fighting, President Wilson had asked his countrymen to remain neutral in thought as well as in deeds. Therein he expressed the fervent wish of his countrymen for peace. A poet imagined Abraham Lincoln come back: *when the sick world cries, how can he sleep? Too many homesteads in black terror weep.* But the pain sprang from the *sins of all the warlords and the folly of kings who must murder still.* The New World fortunately was free of those corruptions.

Yet the dream of Lincoln's spirit and Wilson's request for neutrality were alike to be futile. Too many connections — ethnic, social and economic — ran across the ocean to permit men disinterestedly to watch Europe destroy itself.

German-Americans, for instance, hoped for the victory of their fatherland while the Irish joined them out of hatred for the English oppressor. These groups quickly realized that they could aim only to keep the United States from aiding their enemies. They therefore joined the Scandinavians and the pacifists in working for neutrality. On the other hand, the Czechs and other subjects of the Austrian Empire and the Italians wished for an Allied victory.

The most pervasive influence, however, was that of the friends of England and France. British immigrants were important, particularly since they were often unrecognized as foreigners. Even more powerful were the native-born Americans accustomed to thinking of England as a model and of English culture as linked to their own. The President himself was a great admirer of parliamentary government and of the traditions and manners of the land of his ancestors. Much as he wished to at first, he himself was not long able to maintain the neutrality in thought he considered desirable.

Since 1896, American diplomats had learned to co-operate with the British, who assiduously cultivated their friendship. The war added an economic interest to the existing social and political ties. Anglo-American trade and financial connections had always been important; the fighting made them more so. In the crisis, England turned to the United States for the goods it could not produce itself and, to facilitate the shipments, asked Morgan and Company for credits. The bankers requested the approval of the government.

Secretary of State William Jennings Bryan was reluctant to agree;

money was the worst of all contrabands because it commanded every-thing else. But the President refused to interfere and the loans were made. In the next year the American economy grew more dependent upon exports to the Allies; further loans were then necessary to prevent *the restriction of outputs, industrial depression, idle capital and idle labor, numerous failures, financial demoralization and general unrest and suffering among the laboring classes.* Insensibly the United States had acquired an economic stake in Allied victory. After 1915 it could ill afford to have Germany win.

Such considerations operated in the background of the President's consciousness, but he was unwilling to let them influence him directly. His own thinking concentrated on the moral issues of the war. An effective wave of British propaganda had portrayed the Germans as Huns sweeping across civilized Europe; and the Kaiser's disregard for form made plausible all that was exaggerated and false in these reports. His reference to the Belgian treaty as a scrap of paper came back frequently to haunt him; and he continued to rely on naked power whenever it pleased him to, as in the declaration of unrestricted submarine warfare. Americans, still attached to the doctrine of freedom of the seas, resented violations of their neutrality by both sides. But the callous indifference of the Germans to inter-national law made them seem the more culpable.

The crisis came in May, 1915, with the sinking of the Cunard liner *Lusitania;* one hundred Americans were among the passengers who lost their lives. The outraged President presented the Germans with an ultimatum so strong that his Secretary of State Bryan resigned out of fear it would lead to hostilities. After months of negotiations, however, the Kaiser's government suspended submarine warfare. In good conscience, Wilson could go to the polls in 1916 proud that he had kept the country out of war.

There was only a flimsy basis to his hope for neutrality, however. Ideally, he preferred a negotiated peace with the moral weight of the United States thrown in favor of an amicable adjustment. But in actuality, neither side would settle for less than victory; and the only victory the United States could accept was that of the Allies. When the Germans announced the resumption of unrestricted submarine warfare after the failure of their winter campaign of 1916, Wilson felt he had no alternative but to take up arms against them.

The President made that step with trepidation in April, 1917. On the evening before he delivered his message to Congress, he spoke his heart out to a friend. The war, he said, *would overthrow the world he had known. A majority of the people would quit thinking and devote their energies to destruction. They would forget there ever was such a thing as tolerance and the spirit of ruthless brutality would enter into the very fiber of national life.* But to the Congress and the public Wilson spoke with confidence and assurance. The war would end war and make the world safe for democracy. Only a handful of Congressmen voted against the great crusade.

To most Americans the war came as a great surprise but, for a time, as a relatively painless one. The Spanish outing had been their only direct experience with battle and had given them no glimmer of what modern technology did to fighting men. The factories and farms of the United States stepped up their output to meet the immediate need of the Allies for supplies. Prosperity spread, wages and profits rose, and the excitement of remote adventure gave a lift to life.

Teddy Roosevelt impatiently awaited a summons to unsheath his sword once more and a few ardent young men who had already prepared for action began to move across the ocean. But at the end of 1917 only two hundred thousand troops had reached Europe and few had seen action. The war was *Over There.* Over here, the country enjoyed a year of relatively easy involvement. This was the time for hunting out slackers, pacifists and German spies, for turning sauerkraut into *liberty cabbage,* for preventing the teaching of the German language or the playing of German music. Liberty loans rallied the patriotic, and gay parades sent the boys off.

Then the fun stopped. Two million doughboys went overseas; they helped halt the German spring offensive of 1918 and went on to win the grueling Meuse-Argonne Battle that ended the war. The cost: almost twenty-two billion dollars, 115,000 dead and 260,000 ill or wounded. By the summer of 1918, many a parent, dreading the coming of a telegram from the War Department, had forgotten the gaiety of the year before.

In November, it was over. The titles of the Emperor, Sultan and Czar disappeared; it was only necessary by a just peace to complete the task of making the world safe for democracy.

The President had already outlined the conditions: freedom of the seas, self-determination for all peoples, no revenge, open diplomacy and a great league of nations to settle amicably any future conflicts. The President knew of course that the Allied powers, by secret treaties, had already agreed to divide the spoils in quite a different spirit from that expressed in his Fourteen Points. But he went to Paris confident that he could persuade them to mend their ways. The exhausted people of Europe eagerly awaited his arrival. Never had the prestige of the United States been higher among the common men of the world whom Wilson hoped to enlist in his support. He had forgotten his own earlier insight into the effects of war and would be overwhelmed by the demands for retribution, by the hatreds that would not die.

Wilson could not afford to fail. He had staked much on the faith that this would not be like other wars; its outcome would justify the costs. Yet his determination to succeed doomed him to failure. He could no longer afford to be intransigent, he had to return with an agreement; and he had to give way to the unyielding stubbornness of others or confess that the decision to fight had been a mistake. At point after point he conceded to the Allies who united against him. Versailles in its final form was poles apart from his Fourteen Points. Of all the high hopes he had brought to the conference table, he rescued just one. The Allies had cynically given in to his demand for a league for peace, expecting that it would help the victors retain their spoils. This sole concession, Wilson desperately wished, would make up for the loss of the rest; it would provide the means for rectifying the injustices he could not keep out of the settlement.

When he returned to the United States to present his handiwork to the Senate, Wilson had thus exhausted his capacity for compromise. He had salvaged so little there was nothing left for bargaining. He insisted that the treaty be ratified as it stood. The Senate refused.

The country, weary of a war that had improved nothing, was disillusioned with the peace. The defects were evident not only to German sympathizers but to all who had sincerely hoped with the President for a peace without victory. Punitive clauses ascribed total guilt to the central powers and exacted steep reparations; and self-determination was far from the decisive element in redrawing the boundaries. In addition, Irish-Americans feared that the league covenant might some day force the United States to help Britain suppress an Irish rebellion. More generally, there was a will to be done with the complicated politics of Europe. People who had silently doubted the wisdom of fighting felt justified, while those who had been too vociferous in their belligerence reacted in guilt against the mistake. In the course of a vain effort to win the nation over to his views, Woodrow Wilson collapsed in Pueblo, Colorado, in September, 1919. He served the rest of his term as a semi-invalid.

For the next two decades, the memory of the war and of the peace remained a standing reproof of those who wished to draw the nation into conflicts that were not its proper affair. The victorious Allies in the 1920's selfishly pursued their own interests, and convinced Americans that the best defense of virtue was aloofness. Europe had not improved in the least. The collapse of kings had brought worse regimes to power. The Americans had, at first, welcomed the change of regime in Russia. But they quickly perceived in Communist disrespect for legality a fearful force with which they could not mediate. The specter of revolution everywhere stalked the Continent. The new states of eastern Europe, except for Czechoslovakia, proved no more worthy of support than the empires they had replaced. A dictator who expounded a new fascist doctrine seized power in Italy while the German Republic seemed incapable of solving its economic and social problems.

Under these circumstances, it was best to allow the professional diplomats who controlled the State Department after 1920 to arrange the terms of peaceful coexistence by settling war debts and by negotiating disarmament agreements. But Americans were through, for the moment, with the effort to reform Europe.

They did not realize that in turning their backs on the Old World they abandoned it to the grim alternatives of Communism or Fascism.

Men who sought the refuge of isolation found satisfaction in total — one hundred per cent — Americanism. Whatever did not conform was to be excluded.

The immigrants were an obvious target. During the war an Americanization movement had aimed to obliterate their recollections of the places of their birth; and a literacy test, enacted over President Wilson's veto, aimed to limit the number of new arrivals. When, to the astonishment of the proponents of restriction, the newcomers proved capable of learning to read and write, a restrictive quota system under the laws of 1920 and 1924 effectively reduced the totals to be admitted and also discriminated between the desirable racial types of Northern Europe and the undesirable ones of Southern and Eastern Europe. People of Asian descent were altogether barred. Immigration thereafter fell off sharply. That long chapter in American history closed.

The country was also to be purified of the foreign elements already in it. The *Reds* — dissident radicals of every sort — were assumed to be aliens; deportation was the fate of many who actually were, while criminal syndicalist laws hounded into jails those who proved, surprisingly, to be citizens. Voluntary associations like the American Protective League, the American Legion, and the Daughters of the American Revolution hunted down disloyal elements; and Mayor *Big Bill* Thompson made known his readiness to repulse any effort of King George to invade Chicago. The vigilance against un-American activities continued on into the 1930's, although in less frenzied forms.

Nationalism was also economic. Other nations furthered their own interests; Americans would do the same — export as much as possible and dump their agricultural surpluses where they could while rising tariff walls protected them from the need to buy from foreigners. Since the United States had become an international creditor during the war, its customers lacked the dollars with which to pay. No matter; a steady flow abroad of loans and investment capital made up the deficiency.

In the 1920's foreign trade seemed of little consequence. A productive miracle took care of everything. The manufacture of automobiles, refrigerators and radios expanded by supplying a growing domestic market; and if demand slackened, improved sales techniques, better advertising and planned obsolescence restored it. Meanwhile, chemicals and aluminum added to the strength of heavy industry and speculative finance raised security values. The farmer did not share the prevailing prosperity; but he seemed only to be paying in the usual fashion for his orgy of wartime overexpansion.

Few worried about the effects of the end of immigration or about the fact that the rate of population growth was declining. The free movement of capital and goods into the United States that had sustained its growth for more than a century was over. But at the time, it seemed enough that Negroes coming up from the South filled the empty places at the machines.

The complacency vanished in the great Depression. The stock market crash in the fall of 1929 wiped out inflated security values and discredited the banking and investment system. The slump in agriculture deepened; industrial production declined; and unemployment became a standing weakness of the social order. For the whole decade that followed, at least ten million men — one-fourth of the total labor force — lacked jobs. Nothing helped. The wheels of industry did not resume their motion of themselves, nor did government action induce recovery. Speculative expansion may have touched off the initial panic; but the long decline after 1929 showed that something more was wrong.

The shock of discovering the vulnerability of their economy did not, however, alter the determination of Americans to concentrate on their own affairs and let the Old World take care of itself. There was no inclination to restore the prewar conditions of growth. Suggestions for international co-operation fell on deaf ears. With the abandonment of the gold standard in 1933 the United States, like other countries, managed its fiscal policy with an eye only toward domestic considerations; and planning proceeded entirely on the assumption that the productive system of the nation was to be largely detached from the rest of the world.

There was a further withdrawal from foreign political entanglements. The last embers of hope that the United States might join the World Court or the League of Nations died early in the 1930's; and the disarmament treaties expired at about the same time with no effort at renewal. The plight of Europe's refugees in that decade led to not the least relaxation of restrictive immigration legislation.

The surviving legacies of imperialism were also liquidated. Puerto Rico, offered its independence, chose an intermediate commonwealth status. The Philippines, on the other hand, were set on the way to total separation. The remaining protectorates in Latin America also terminated and, while a collaborative *good neighbor* policy replaced the Monroe Doctrine, the sense of involvement in the affairs of the hemisphere faded. In an ultimate expression of the wish for isolation, a succession of neutrality laws controlled loans and the sale of munitions to belligerents in an attempt to forestall a repetition of the mistakes of 1917.

Americans were fully aware that the threats to peace grew graver by the year. In Japan, a clique of army officers already had considerable freedom of action and moved to gain power over the whole state apparatus. They invaded Manchuria in 1931, installed a puppet regime, and six years later opened a long undeclared war with China. By then Mussolini, the Italian dictator, after years of bluster, had attacked Ethiopia; and, in Germany, Hitler's Nazis had begun their career of open aggression by tearing up the remnants of the Versailles Treaty.

The crisis came in Spain, where fascist army officers revolted in 1936 against their democratically elected government. The republic, which had only recently replaced a corrupt and decadent monarchy, sustained itself with difficulty in the face of betrayal by its armed forces. Yet the United States denied Spain's request for the right to purchase supplies. The neutrality laws had not been designed to apply to civil conflicts and, indeed, President Franklin Roosevelt found reasons for continuing to send oil and scrap iron to Japan for use in China well into 1941. But in the case of Spain he was content to follow the vacillating policy of England and France and, above all, was anxious to avoid involvement. Hitler and Mussolini had no such scruples about aiding their ally, Franco, who marched victoriously into Madrid in 1939.

Spain taught the fascists that they had nothing to fear from further adventures. The Germans moved into Austria; the settlement at Munich gave them parts of Czechoslovakia; and they shortly took the rest of that unhappy country themselves. They were then ready to move on to Poland in their quest for an eastern empire.

There was no doubt where American sympathies lay. If occasional individuals earlier had a kind word for Mussolini's reform of the Italian railroads, they were alienated by the attack on Ethiopia in 1935. The Nazis and the Japanese warlords had no support in the United States except from a few right-wing fanatics. Roosevelt had the approval of the whole country in 1937 when he explained that there was *no escape from international anarchy through mere isolation or neutrality.* The contagion of war would spread in the absence of *positive endeavors to preserve peace.*

The sentiments were unexceptionable. *America hated war. America hoped for peace.* But when it came to the positive endeavors there was only the vague wish that the English and French would, in time, be strong enough to put down the fascists. In 1938, the Americans disapproved of appeasement and wished that Chamberlain and Daladier would take a stronger stand in defense of the Czechs. Yet it occurred to few that the United States also had an interest in the preservation of international law or that the same reluctance to be involved in other nations' quarrels that made the Americans isolationists, made the English and French appeasers.

When finally, the Western powers, incapable of making further concessions, determined to resist Germany's designs on Poland, Americans welcomed the decision. It was time that the democracies showed their strength — the other democracies. They themselves would give their moral support and *cash and carry* aid. That they might some day be called upon to fight in Asia, Europe and Africa was unthinkable; their oceans cut them off from unregenerate strangers. The Americans devoted most of their energies to the improvement of their own society.

In clutching that illusion, which the First World War had only strengthened, they forgot that the sea in their past had always been a mode of access rather than a moat. Japanese aircraft carriers in the Pacific would shortly remind them of that.

The quest for isolation was, in part, a reaction against the manner of American involvement with the outer world earlier in the century. The United States withdrew into its continental fastness in the effort to liquidate the undesired results of imperialism. But isolation was also the result of the desire of Americans, after 1900, to devote most of their energies to the solution of their personal and social problems. Domestic issues in those decades generally overshadowed all others.

23

Searchers for Stability

THE AMERICANS who sought vainly to break off contact with Europe attempted at the same time to reorder the contacts among themselves. The closed communities established before 1900 had not remained stable. The effort to compensate through racism or through the patriotism that masqueraded as Americanism was evidence that the ghettos and their culture had failed to pass from generation to generation. Nationalism was the reaction of dissatisfied men who groped for a deeper emotional commitment than the old forms supplied. After 1900, those not lulled by pleasures available to all continued to search for security.

There were early stirrings of revolt within the confines of high *Society*. The young people who had inherited wealth and position attached to neither one nor the other the values their parents had. Nor, having escaped the need to struggle, did they feel the desire for success. Business rarely had a place for them; they had been trained to despise money-grubbing, and the fathers whose names they bore overshadowed them. Only a few like John D. Rockefeller, Jr., took satisfaction in philanthropic, communal or political leadership. Most of them had nothing to do.

Henry James, returning to the United States in 1906, saw *a great circle of brilliant and dowered débutantes and impatient youths waiting for the first bars of some wonderful imminent dance music.* They longed for the thrill of involvement and they were not likely to find it in the cotillion or in the box at the opera. Already before the turn of the century Mrs. Stuyvesant Fish had become known as the *enfant terrible* of New York Society; she dispensed with elaborate formal dinners and, at her suppers, replaced the usual staid orchestra with a lively band. It was more *fun* that way.

Anyway, the real fun was downtown. There gaiety was unrestrained. There music set the body in motion and the leggy chorus lines stirred the blood. Boys came in from college for a weekend and learned to make the round of the amusing places. Gradually, downtown moved uptown, vaudeville became the variety show and the musical comedy; and the half-world of café society provided a meeting place for the offspring of the quondam aristocracy and the ladies and gentlemen of the theatrical, sporting and gambling domains. The angry fathers frowned; the worried mothers sighed; the anxious debutantes waited. There were no means of enforcing discipline.

After the First World War the barriers were completely down. *Society* receded to the back pages while life moved into the country club and the speakeasy. The deb joined her brother; and the parents hastened on in their own pursuit of pleasure. The world of Ward McAllister collapsed.

Mobility continued to pull other men out of the groups into which they had been born, but with more disruptive effects than before. Industrial growth generated a tremendous demand for managerial talent and for technical and clerical services, for which generally only natives were trained. As the base of the occupational pyramid broadened, the space at the top became ample. The expansion of the unskilled army of the foreign-born on the assembly lines increased the number of vice-presidents, engineers, foremen and salespeople. In addition, laborers needed the services of lawyers, doctors, and shop-keepers. These opportunities drew young men from the farms to the cities and persuaded parents to support their children through high school. Yet every ascent of the ladder took the boy of ambition farther away from the home and from the habits of his father.

Furthermore, Americans continued to shift about long after Turner announced the close of the westward movement. In no year between 1900 and 1939 did more than two-thirds of them live in the state of their birth. Preponderantly those who changed their places of residence went to the cities, which spread to hitherto undreamed-of dimensions — New York, 7,500,000; Chicago, 3,400,000; Philadelphia, Detroit and Los Angeles, all over 1,500,000; and Cleveland, Baltimore, St. Louis and Boston not far behind. To lead an orderly life or preserve any continuity with the past in this environment was more difficult than before.

Mobility in space and in status had begun to breach the ghetto walls before 1900; it tumbled them down after the turn of the century. New arrivals from the countryside and from Europe continued to form their own communities, but the public school and the office encouraged the association of people of diverse backgrounds and pulled the children away from their parents' beliefs and organizations. The short stories of O. Henry and the paintings of John Sloan from various perspectives caught glimpses of the detached individuals who moved about the metropolis without a place to which they really belonged.

The break was particularly sharp for the children of immigrants in the first two decades of the twentieth century. The continuing flow of newcomers from Europe then replenished the population of the East Side or Little Italy as rapidly as the fortunate old-timers left. On his way to the desk the neatly dressed young man turned away from the shabby laborers; he could smell the Hester Street Jewishness, the Mulberry Street Italianness of them and wanted no part of an association that could only drag him down. Whether he changed his name or not, he cut the visible connection with the foreigners he wished to escape. Nor did his discomfort ease after 1920, when immigration slackened and the old communities weakened for want of replacements.

The sons and daughters of immigrant parents only felt more intensely the deprivation that troubled many other Americans in the twentieth century. The Old Gentleman wished to rear *an Institution national in character, such as the Magna Carta or jam for breakfast in England*. He wanted a son who could come after he was gone, to stand strong and proud and say, *In memory of my father*. Flitting from furnished room to furnished room, singing "Home Sweet Home" in ragtime, all remained forever *transients in heart and mind*. The shopgirl and the drayman, the steno and the medical student reached out for marriage and success, but needed also a place in which to locate the rose-covered cottage and appropriate activities to fill it with meaning.

Detachment was an advantage only for the exceptional persons who rejected the rose-covered cottage. Sensitive young men who felt stifled in the old communities moved because they needed space in which to express themselves. T. S. Eliot and John Dos Passos were sons of proper families who had learned too well the lessons of college; applying the standards of the classics, they saw through the shabby pretenses, the empty formality of the established writers of their own time. Edgar Lee Masters and Theodore Dreiser, who left the small towns of their birth, discovered that the formulae of the genteel tradition did not match their experience. Jack London and Carl Sandburg were children of the poor or of immigrants — marginal, half one thing and half another, able to compare and to question. They came to the cities seeking freedom from the old milieu and access to the media through which to speak out. In 1900 they were already a formidable company; and disillusionment after the war increased their numbers through the 1920's.

Rejecting the society and culture of their origins, they emigrated, literally or figuratively. Like Hemingway and Eliot they went off to Paris or London; or like Sherwood Anderson and Tom Wolfe they drew together in a domestic *Bohemia* in the immigrant quarters of the metropolitan centers. Greenwich Village in New York, Beacon Hill in Boston, the South Side of Chicago gave refuge to the exiles. Here life was real; the immigrants, idealized, dealt with the serious problems of bread, love and death. The observers wished their literature and painting also to be real and sought, in the contact with a more vital world, to break through the sterile formulae they had inherited.

These people considered themselves an advance guard in the revolt against official culture. They plunged into experiment, eagerly welcoming stimuli from their counterparts in Europe and struggling to develop new forms of poetry, painting, architecture and music. Their posture as rebels and the necessity for battling the established guardians of taste persuaded them that the only valid standards were those the artist developed for himself. They learned to discount the marketplace and the best-seller list and they no more expected the patronage of the banker than the comprehension of the corner grocer. They directed their *little* magazines and their *little* shows at self-contained audiences and felt no sense of involvement with the societies about them.

The separation cost the culture that served most of the population the loss of some of the best talent of the time. But many creative personalities also suffered. When they were not entirely preoccupied with their own sensations, they dealt with the outer world as reporters, as detached observers regarding an alien scene. To achieve any more intimate relationship with other Americans called for entanglements with popular culture that few cared to assume. If they flirted with Communism or with Southern agrarianism in the 1920's it was less out of any positive identification with those causes than as a further form of rebellion against a restrictive environment.

Outside Bohemia popular culture flourished as it developed facile means of communicating with an expanding audience. The mass of men cut loose from habit and traditional modes of expression lacked inner resources and needed dependable associations. They formed a great body of consumers for entertainment. New technological developments supplied their wants. The high-speed press, the phonograph, the cheap printed picture, the moving picture, and later the radio made the performer or writer accessible in every part of the country.

All the media grew bigger, livelier, less restrained. The yellow press now came into its own, less crude than before, more competently edited and visually more appealing through the use of photographs. Pulitzer's *World* subsided and began to strive for the respectability that would kill it, but William Randolph Hearst's empire was firmly planted in every major city, briskly fighting off local emulators. Its policies sometimes gratified the caprice and the political interests of its proprietor; but it held its readers by sensation, that is by an accurate depiction of the brutal world in which they lived. After the war the tabloid, a form imported from England, further defined the techniques of popular journalism. Its size was manageable in a crowded subway or trolley car; its front-page picture drew the purchaser more forcefully than the most suggestive headline; sports, comics and human interest stories crammed its pages. The *Daily News* in New York and its counterparts elsewhere gained steadily in strength.

A new rhythm crept into the people's music. In the concerts at the park and in the beerhall, people still listened to the marches and the old sentimental songs. But a more singable, danceable beat drew them to their feet, relaxed the vocal chords. They came to hear, they came to cheer, the gay mournful ragtime bands. The drummer grinned, the fiddler swayed, and the tune swirled in the mind. It stayed for days, it went to work, and it made the hours pass.

Jazz welled up from deep ethnic sources. Its expositors were Negro, Jewish, Irish, and Italian; they had listened to minstrels and folk singers and to the popular ballads of the 1890's; and they were above all improvisers skilled at catching the mood of the audience to which they catered. By 1920, jazz had captured the dance floor, the stage and the market for phonograph records and sheet music. It had become the dominant idiom of the country's song.

It had readily found a place in the thriving vaudeville circuits, although by that time it had to share interest with the newer medium of the moving picture. The film had passed through a brief period of preparation when novelty was its chief attraction. Then the nickelodeon spread rapidly through the country and existing theaters quickly installed screens across which the flickering images could pass. In 1920, the movie industry was securely anchored in its Hollywood base and growing lustily. The next decade would mark its recognition in the extravagant oriental palaces that reached from Broadway to Main Street.

The motion picture in its early years was not far removed from its origins in vaudeville and the popular stage. The comic turns of the familiar clowns and the melodramatic confrontation of virtue and vice were simply recorded on film and extended to a wider audience than formerly. Improvisation was the rule, more often than not, and the tramp, the fat man, the passionate Latin, the vamp, the strong simple Western hero and the villainous mortgage-holder were all recognizable stock types.

Immense growth thrust a massive organization upon all expressions of popular culture. The movies became an industry, with a potential for great profit and with the need for substantial capital; it required the controls and the planned production that other corporate enterprises did. Furthermore, the audience was increasingly heterogeneous, drawn from every part of the country and from every social group; the successful film had to attract the children of the rich as well as those of the immigrant laborers. To set themes and characters at the common denominator of the whole population was an imposing problem requiring careful co-ordination and discipline. Radio's task was more imposing still, for by the 1930's it had a larger audience and was, in addition, subject to government regulation.

All the media yielded to the same pressures. Rigid organization made the relationship of the artist to his listeners or viewers impersonal. He rarely knew for whom he was acting or singing, only guessed at the reaction, and therefore developed a routine that pitched his performance to the taste of the mythical sixteen-year-old girl in Des Moines. Everything else was done out of sight and could be faked or covered over. As a result the outpouring of printed, filmed, and recorded matter was often limited to the sterile repetition of innocuous formulae. Each year's song or picture had to be *new* because only thus — not in content — could it be distinguished from last year's.

The loss to the performer was irremediable, but the *star* compensated for the loss to the audience. Hoot Gibson, Tom Mix, Rudolph Valentino, Charlie Chaplin, Paul Whiteman, and Rudy Vallee became as familiar in the magazine or newspaper as on the screen, their personal and their projected lives confused in a common identity, shadowy in outlines, yet capable of entering the reveries of millions of Americans.

Sport also became an organized sector of popular culture, but one not subject to the same degree of control as the others. The radio or movie producer could make or break a star and shape plots to his will. But in baseball and boxing, talent was absolute, chance unavoidable and the audience still present in the flesh. The performer knew the sound of genuine cheers and hisses and the viewers knew the thrill of participation in a genuine drama. When Babe Herman dropped the fly ball the scene could not be reshot; there was no predicting the precise odds of Dempsey's return to the ring when Firpo knocked him through the ropes; and nothing Colonel Ruppert did gave Babe Ruth the ability to clear the fences. The crowds in the stadiums grew rapidly in size and millions more followed the score at a distance. That gamblers should have attempted to fix the World Series of 1919 was almost unbelievable.

Athletics, like the other media of popular culture, supplied the material for daydreams. The hours of immediate involvement in the dark of the palace or in the ball park were only the start; memories of the turn of fate that saved the day, of the adventure and the passion, made the weeks of labor bearable. But since the events on the screen were totally separate from the reality outside, more often than not the men and women emerged hugging illusions with no meaning for the problems of their own lives.

The spread of popular culture and the decay of polite society struck at the roots of the official *culture* defined at the opening of the century. In the fastness of their entrenched institutions, the old guard for a while attempted to rally the forces of aristocracy and tradition. But Europe betrayed them, the war set them reeling and the Depression brought them down to defeat. In 1913, the Armory Show brought the new art of Cézanne, Gauguin, Van Gogh and the cubists to America and revealed that there was more to painting than the Old Master and his imitators. After 1918 Old World titles were cheap; it was ludicrous to ape Continental nobility when Russian dukes drove taxis in Paris. Under the impact of the stock market crash, most of the opera houses withered away and even New York's Metropolitan barely survived. Few of the genteel magazines and newspapers lived through the 1930's. Nor would the government, as patron, sustain the old order. When the New Deal stepped in, through the WPA, it dotted the country with Georgian post offices and permissively encouraged every kind of mural painter and writer.

The collapse of defined standards opened the way to an exciting intrusion into established institutions of elements from both the popular and avant-garde cultures. The Broadway theater now found a place not only for the comics and chorus, derived from vaudeville, in the Ziegfeld Follies, but also for the plays of Eugene O'Neill, who had served his apprenticeship in the *little* Provincetown Playhouse. The new magazines — *Smart Set, American Mercury* and *New Yorker* — were similarly inclusive; and the immensely successful *Saturday Evening Post,* in the effort to provide something for everyone, made room for the stories of F. Scott Fitzgerald and William Faulkner. There was no telling who would turn up on the best-seller list.

The temptation to pander was great. The critic called upon the writers to *meet the needs of the trade; by failing to do this, novelists of the Chaotic school have worked considerable harm to the industry at large.* But there were enough artists with inner standards strengthened by their refuge in *Bohemia,* to steel themselves against the lure of the industry. The quarter-century after 1914 saw more substantial contributions to literature, painting and music than any other in American history.

Most Americans were reasonably content to work for a raise on the job and enjoy a movie at night, to bet on the game or the market, and to follow the comics or the serial in the paper — at least until the Depression plunged them into economic insecurity. Liberated by the removal of restraints, they were able to have their cake and eat it too. Relaxed codes of behavior permitted them to pursue success and yet have fun at leisure.

But considerable groups felt left out and viewed the changes about them with dismay. In the suburbs the clerk and the foreman, in the small town the druggist and the lawyer, in the country the farmer and the minister witnessed with despair the disintegration of the orderly way of life for which they had labored. Though they themselves sometimes tasted the forbidden fruit, the successes and failures alike perceived that the twentieth century threatened values they cherished. The old fear that by seeking to rise they would lose stability was the more oppressive now that all society was *without form and void.* Their children still went off, still to be corrupted by the corrosive outer world. What was more, city habits reached out to engulf the whole nation. The motor cars raced through the resentful countryside; the phonograph and radio brought profane chants into the home; in every county seat the dark interior of the movie theater beckoned the unwary. Babylon had indeed conquered.

Some would not yield, but fought back against all that was alien to the style of life they wished to preserve. Discrimination now served many Americans as it had earlier served the Southern poor white against the Negro. It established a racial difference that defined the group, protected it against outsiders and gave it pride in its own superiority. The targets, however, were no longer the black men alone, but also the Catholics and Jews, the Italians, Japanese and Poles, who were to be excluded, held down, as a sign of the worth of the one hundred per cent Americans.

Discrimination had a twofold attractiveness. It freed those worried by the foreigner from competition and enhanced the chances of their children. At the same time, it prevented alien tastes and habits from gaining ascendancy. The prohibition movement became the rallying point of those who wished to save the Republic from the corrupting effects of alcohol, the saloon, machine politics, jazz and the movies, from all the sins which robbed the nation of its purity. Commander Richmond Hobson, hero of the Spanish-American War and Congressman from Alabama, warned that it was only a question of time. *We are making the last stand of the great white race.* If the destroyer, liquor, could not be conquered, the world would be undone, the yellow men would take over and *the human race would go from degeneracy to degeneracy till the Almighty in wrath wiped the accursed thing out.* Somberly, Madison Grant and Lothrop Stoddard added the prestige of scientists and historians to the judgment that a great race was falling to the assault of undermen.

Frustration pushed the angry ones to violence against the Japanese in California, the Greeks in South Omaha, the Jews in Georgia, and during the war, against Reds and slackers everywhere. Many joined the Ku Klux Klan, swelling its membership to four million. In the Midwest and on the Pacific Coast, as well as in the South, the hooded figures solemnly burned fiery crosses to exorcise the stranger. In 1924 they fought desperately to prevent the nomination of a Roman Catholic for the Presidency; and in 1928 when Al Smith was designated, their hate-filled propaganda contributed to his defeat.

The Eighteenth Amendment, which embodied the fondest hopes of the prohibitionists, did not conquer the destroyer. The speakeasy and bootlegger did their work as blatantly as the saloon and the brewer; and this effort at control, by lowering respect for the law, further weakened the moral fiber of the nation.

The Depression finally shattered the spirit of those who had resisted change. The repeal of the Eighteenth Amendment was disheartening but other causes for gloom overshadowed that debacle. The dream of self-sufficiency and success died. The accumulated savings of life-times of restraint quickly disappeared and men always proud of their ability to make good sought relief in the same lines as the despised industrial workers. Propertied farmers sullenly broke the law to prevent foreclosures and did not scruple to demand government aid.

New millennial schemes tempted some to vote for Upton Sinclair's Epic Party, persuaded others that Dr. Townsend's plan would give pensions to all, and induced still others to join the Silver Shirts or similar fascist groups spawned in the unrest. Many more, who resisted such movements and yet could not altogether surrender to apathy, put their last hopes in the New Deal.

The people under attack — Negroes, Jews, Irish Catholics — could not become racists. Their underprivileged position deprived them of that refuge. Yet there was a significant parallel between their response to social and cultural change and that of the native whites. The majority were content with the pleasures of popular culture. But clusters of aggrieved men judged the new conditions inadequate and sought more meaningful forms of identification and expression. They could not simply revert to the organizations and traditions of their parents for those bore the stigma of poverty and foreignness displeasing to people who wished to rise. When prejudice and discrimination reminded those who reached for higher occupational positions that they were not fully equal, they claimed their rights as native Americans. At the same time, fearful of rebuff, they also sought the security of renewed identification with the groups of their origin.

The problem was extreme for the Negroes. W. E. B. Du Bois, for instance, was a Harvard graduate who had earned a German doctorate. A brilliant and sometimes original thinker, and a lucid writer, he nevertheless realized that he could never hold the chair in a university to which any plodder could advance with the passport

of whiteness. He devoted years of his life to protest. Yet pride and
the fear of rejection induced him also to look inward, to describe *the
Soul of Black Folk* and the unique qualities of their own culture.

A growing number of mobile Negroes, particularly in the new
urban centers, shared Du Bois's dilemma. They rejected Booker T.
Washington's formula for appeasement and helped to establish the
National Association for the Advancement of Colored People and the
Urban League to fight discrimination and gain equality. Yet also
needing a cultural identity of their own, they took pride in Harlem's
black renaissance and sympathized with Marcus Garvey's *Back to
Africa* movement in the 1920's, knowing it a hopeless delusion, but
warming to it as a defiance of the white world.

After 1900 the Jews faced an anti-Semitism more virulent than the
unfavorable stereotypes and the restrictions of clubs and resorts in an
earlier period. Concerted efforts excluded them from some branches
of employment, limited their access to the universities and the professions and barred them from desirable residences. In some places
they were the victims of violence and the Klan sought to deprive them
of political rights. The United States then might not, after all, be
different; perhaps expectations of assimilation were a delusion and
their long history of separateness and persecution would continue.
They could not complacently look across the ocean and be sure that
what happened in Czarist or Hitlerite pogroms would not happen
here.

Some Jews decided that they were indeed a separate nationality
and required a homeland of their own. The Zionist movement attracted only a tiny minority in the 1920's, and when it grew in the
next decade it was sustained more by the hope of making a place for
European refugees than by the expectation that Americans might
actually leave for Palestine. It too reflected a desire for national
identification, a wish to be proud of the group to which one belonged.

The great majority of Jews, however, clung to their commitment to
the United States. They were a part of this society and no other; and
their congresses, committees and leagues struggled successfully for
equality. They too welcomed the promise of the New Deal.

Other minorities occupied less extreme, but comparable situations.
The Irish Catholics suffered from the recurrence of nativism and felt
the shocking weight of the Klan's hatred in the 1920's. The national-

ism that had absorbed their attention earlier in the century had subsided with the establishment of the Irish Free State; only a few die-
hards fought on against the partition of Ulster. A majority of these
people were in their third generation in the United States and their
reaction to discrimination was an attempt to prove that Catholicism was Americanism. They became prominent among the followers
of Father Charles Coughlin, the radio priest, who mobilized a
crusade *to keep America safe for Americans and not the hunting
ground of international plutocrats.* A minority of extremists were
members of the fascist Christian Front who joined hands with former
Klansmen and other isolationists on the platform of *America First.*
Like the other minorities, however, most Irish considered the fight for
equality primary and looked to the New Deal for support.

Nationality had become important for all Americans because they
expected it to compensate for the loss of the stable groups and traditional cultures of their parents. Their expectations would not be
satisfied. The concept of American nationality had changed radically
since the nineteenth century, when it had made room for men of
every background, demanding only that they involve themselves in
building the country. It had narrowed by 1900 to require also that all
be reduced to a common type in a melting pot that dissolved the distinctive features of their origins, class or section. Popular culture had
begun the process. Those who would not yield had to seek alternative
loyalties. But neither the inclusive nor the particular versions of nationalism was in accord with realities. The Americans were neither
fragmented into multiple national entities, nor one hundred per cent
homogeneous.

By the 1930's, two other channels of accommodation had gradually
been defined.

The labor movement had maintained the pure and simple character its leaders of 1900 had anticipated only in a few sheltered
branches — in the railroads and printing trades, for instance. Down
to the World War, other unions, pressed by employers who refused
to recognize them and by radicals who wished to make them instruments of revolution, held their members by giving a deeper meaning
to the affiliation. The Irish teamsters, the Jewish garment workers and
other unions with a distinct ethnic cast were social organizations in

which balls, picnics, and educational and insurance services were as important as collective bargaining.

Such unions moved into the 1930's in a relatively strong position. In that decade, depression and the legal recognition of their status gave them security and expanded their ranks. In addition the Congress of Industrial Organizations enlisted the unskilled in the heavy industries so that the number of unionized laborers rose from three and a half million in 1929 to almost nine million a decade later.

The new members sought more than an agency to increase the weekly paycheck; they wanted a cause. The union was to stand between the worker and the world and be a medium for political, cultural, and social as well as economic action. The Depression, which stifled hopes for continued social mobility, built up the expectation that most men would remain fixed in their trades and organize their lives around associations centered on the job.

A smaller group of intellectuals perceived an enduring value to ethnic group life. Observers like Hutchins Hapgood had remarked the cultural vitality of the immigrant ghettos in the first decade of the twentieth century. To abandon that richness of experience for mechanical sameness was a loss to American life. Randolph Bourne and Horace Kallen thought, instead, of society as an orchestra with each ethnic group *a natural instrument*; the harmony of all *made the symphony of civilization*.

The conception of cultural pluralism attracted support in the 1920's, and in the next decade, embraced the hopes of many Americans for a democratic group life. The decline of racism and the New Deal's emphasis on equality and experimentation sustained the faith that the unique elements of the American experience would teach men to live together while retaining their differences, to find unity in diversity. Basic to these hopes, as to almost all those raised in the search for stability, was the expectation that men could also learn to imbue their political relationships with social justice.

24

The Meanings of Social Justice

IN THE PRESIDENTIAL election of 1912, no candidate called himself a conservative. The unusual campaign that year found four contenders in the race. All were progressives, although of different sorts.

At the beginning of the century the crisis precipitated by the Spanish-American War had compelled people to rethink their attitudes toward their society and toward the world. Whether they were imperialists or anti-imperialists they became aware of the deficiencies in the existing order. The result was a radical change in attitudes and a growing conviction that the state needed reconstruction to be able effectively to advance the welfare of its citizens. Justice called for more than neutrality on the part of government; it required positive action to meet the challenge of rapidly changing conditions which the isolated individual could not control. The continuing evolution of society demanded corresponding progress in political forms.

Progressivism was not the platform of a single political party. Nor was it an articulated creed. It was a mood that embraced divergent, and sometimes contradictory, ideas. Its common element was the conviction that new times called for new measures and that the Republic bore the responsibility for helping men master the forces set loose by industrialization.

The roots of progressivism reached back into the last two decades of the nineteenth century. After 1900, the pioneer expounders of the social gospel found a wider and more attentive audience. Sales of Charles M. Sheldon's *In His Steps* mounted into the millions in response to the growing interest in the subject.

Clergymen of many denominations appealed for action to implement the religious idea of human brotherhood and sought out the poor to learn their problems at first hand. Charles Stelzle described slum conditions as he had actually lived them and Walter Rauschenbusch, who had worked in the depressed areas of New York, went on to examine the *social crisis of Christianity*. The existing economic system presented a serious threat to faith. *Competitive commerce made Ishmaels out of the best men* by exalting selfishness and mercilessness, the qualities most dangerous to the salvation of their souls. In a more moderate tone, the Reverend Endicott Peabody was teaching his students at Groton — among them Franklin Roosevelt — that wealth brought responsibilities for service. In response to these diverse impulses, the Federal Council of the Churches of Christ in America in 1905 began its labors to unite the Protestants of the country in support of the social gospel.

The Jews of the United States, in the same spirit, reinterpreted *the Messianic hope for the establishment of the Kingdom of truth, justice and peace among all men* as a mandate to solve the problems created by *the contrasts and evils of the present organization of society*. Rabbis like Stephen S. Wise, Emil G. Hirsch and David Philipson became teachers of morals and commentators on the affairs of the day from a progressive point of view. Meanwhile Father John A. Ryan's demonstration of labor's right to a *living wage* called attention to the social injunctions of the papal encyclical *Rerum novarum*, a document that had received little attention in the United States when it was issued in 1891. The same priest was active in the promulgation of the Bishop's Program for Social Reconstruction in 1919.

The churches thus responded to a common challenge. Altogether apart from the specifics of theology, they had been horrified by the conception of man that had taken form toward the end of the nineteenth century. Frank Cowperwood, hero of *The Financier,* had learned from watching a lobster devour a squid how life was organized. *Things lived on each other — that was it. Men lived on men* just as the lobster lived on the squid. The Americans who could not accept that conception of themselves found a religious imperative for altering it.

The task of reform was not confined to the church. Laymen shared the same spirit and performed the same labor in a secular context. The corps of professional social workers had direct contact with the effects of poverty on children, on living conditions and on morals, and began to wonder whether driblets of aid could be effective while the environment remained corrosive. The growing formality and the scientific organization of their endeavors did not obscure the underlying faith that their charges were worthy not only of compassion but of reform.

Still wider circles responded to the call for action. Altogether apart from the depressed laborers or the poor farmers who sought to better their own conditions, substantial numbers of Americans felt an impulse to benevolence, religious in nature though not necessarily in creed. Well-to-do daughters and wives, not themselves involved in business and endowed with ample leisure, were distressed by the effects of the competitive struggle upon their fathers and husbands; and they felt tinges of remorse as they compared their own comfort with the pervasive poverty about them. Girls from the country or from small towns, seeking careers, discovered with dismay the disorder of the city. Julia Lathrop, Anne Morgan, Mrs. Oliver Belmont, Jane Addams, Dr. Alice Hamilton, and Ida Cannon were among those who wished to do something about it. A few enlisted actively in philanthropy; many more supported such organizations as the National Consumers League which attempted to force employers to improve labor conditions.

The universities were also a seedbed of progressivism. Most professors stolidly carried on their work as teachers. But the role of the university as a seat of learning encouraged the more imaginative among them to look critically at the external world. They noted its features, in the first instance, as data that would serve in the formulation of scientific laws; but their own procedures demanded that they test their conclusions in practice; and increased autonomy permitted them to descend from the ivory tower to do so. While the university still depended upon contributions from men of wealth, the sizable grants were now usually made through professional intermediaries and foundations, sympathetic to the aims of scholarship. Meanwhile the state institutions, rising in importance, regarded themselves as servants of the community obliged to deal with its practical problems.

All the sciences gained by their greater independence. But the chief beneficiaries were the social sciences encouraged thereby to examine human relations and to prescribe the mode of their improvement. History, economics, government and sociology, defined as disciplines, addressed themselves to the task.

The prevailing assumptions of the social scientists were pragmatic; they favored *the impartial assemblage and mutual confrontation of all sorts of ideas*, to be supported by facts and verified by experience. Therein they had the support not only of the philosophy of William James and John Dewey but also of basic habits of American thought with roots far back in the eighteenth century. Truth was not an abstract proposition to be derived from authority or deduced from general principles but rather a tentative formulation of existing data that could be applied to practice.

There was, therefore, no generally defined body of conclusions upon which historians like Charles A. Beard and Carl Becker or economists like John R. Commons and Thorstein Veblen or sociologists like Edward A. Ross and Albion W. Small all agreed. But they wrestled with intellectual problems within a common framework of ideas that shaped their impact upon the public.

They had long since assimilated Darwinism. Evolution was the common language in which they thought. Nothing existed as given; every phenomenon developed and was therefore to be understood in terms of its origins and of the context that immediately influenced it. This essential characteristic was as true of institutions as of organisms. The church, the town meeting and family had not received a permanent form at a particular moment in the past and had no inherent qualities; extended evolutionary processes had made them what they were.

It followed that all the social scientists were inclined to emphasize the environment as the dominant influence upon development. Crime was a product of the vicious conditions of the slum; democracy, of the free land of the West; corruption, of the unrestrained pursuit of wealth. Changes in the environment altered the forces that molded men: good housing made good citizens and exposure to wholesome camp life suppressed delinquency in children. The insistence of the eugenicists that some traits were transmitted through the germ plasm was troublesome, as was the argument of the racists that some peoples were inferior. But the environmental hypothesis could incorporate even these data; long subjection to poor conditions had caused the degeneracy of the Jukes family and the Sicilians. The effort to save them might not be worth while, but their deterioration was explicable in environmental terms.

The evolutionary assumption also accounted for the impact of environment upon institutions. The Supreme Court, for instance, was not a detached body passing abstract judgment upon issues in which it was not itself involved. It was an agency of forces that emanated from the society around it. The law, Oliver Wendell Holmes pointed out, took form in response to *the felt necessities of the time*; and many scholars interpreted the judges' action in vitiating the Sherman Antitrust Act or in striking down state child labor laws as subservience to entrenched economic interests. The Constitution itself was similarly comprehensible. Charles A. Beard's analysis of the convention that composed it and of the ratification process thus attempted to expose the influence of certain property-holders on its adoption.

Environment played upon the society through economic impulses, for the primary connections among men were those established by participation in the productive system. None of the academic scholars was a Marxist, but socialist ideas, though not in a precise class formulation, markedly affected their thinking. For example, Beard and J. Allen Smith, whom he followed, were both indebted to Algie M. Simon's radical description of the *Social Forces in American History*.

More generally, the accumulation of criticism of wealth to which socialists, Populists and the followers of Henry George had contributed since the 1880's supplied the progressives with data and stimulated them in the search for the economic causes of social deficiency of their day. Conversely, the questioning process encouraged a mounting volume of muckraking literature which made sensational reading for the general public in the exposure of the dubious methods which had piled up the great American fortunes. These writings grew increasingly acid in the first decade of the century and gave weight to the more sober and more restrained judgments of the scholars.

An understanding of the basic forces that molded American civilization did not, however, diminish faith in progress. By isolating the causes that impeded development the scholar could aid in their removal; his explanation of the ill effects of unrestrained wealth would help the citizens control it through their government. Modern man did not have to allow the blind chances of nature to determine the course of evolution; the use of his intelligence could shape its direction.

For this reassuring idea the progressives were indebted to the sociologist Lester Ward, who wrote just before the turn of the century. Americans, he argued, found themselves *in the coils of plutocracy* from which democracy could not extricate them. It was necessary to replace *the puerile gaming spirit* of politics with a *sociocracy. The individual had reigned long enough.* Society could take its affairs into its own hands and be guided not by particular interests but by the *social intellect, armed with all the knowledge* it could command. The governors were to be experts who possessed the scientific information to plan and direct the future development of the whole system without regard to the specific wishes of its component parts.

The planning idea answered the need of the conservation movement. Wildlife enthusiasts had by now joined the people worried about the depletion of *natural resources* in the demand for a halt to the heedless exploitation of the continent. The use of water as a source of electrical power increased the insistence upon the utility of controls. The movement gained strength to prevent the defacement of nature and to assure the best use of the nation's wealth; and what was true for cattle, timber and oil, held also for men. The eugenicist sought the power to sterilize defectives *as a first very moderate step toward the development of the stamina of the human race.* The conservationists anticipated that a declining birth rate and the end of immigration would shortly give them a stable population to manage and improve. Planning was the means through which to attain all these objectives.

The test and the reward of successful planning was *efficiency*. No word was more frequently or more vaguely used by progressive thinkers. Sometimes it meant simply the ability to produce the greatest volume of goods at the lowest cost or the reduced tax rate in a municipality. But on the other hand, cut-throat competition or the depletion of the forests, though they reduced prices, were sometimes considered inefficient because they threatened more general goals of social welfare. Still, the very lack of clarity in the use of the term increased the attractiveness of the concept; people could agree that the machinery should work well, whatever the ultimate objectives for which it worked.

The conceptions of planning and efficiency were especially attractive to the growing numbers of engineers in charge of construction, maintenance, and operation of the vast economic plant. As technicians, they were trained to block out considerations beyond the task at hand; their job was to build factories and machines, not to worry about who would buy or sell the shoes. Yet their own experience taught them the importance of proper controls; and the humans — workers, salespeople and consumers — were the least dependable elements in the productive system. If only men too could be kept in step with the machines, the whole order would be neat, predictable and arranged in accordance with the sound principles of cost accounting. Frederick Taylor had already worked out the elements of a system of *scientific management* which Thorstein Veblen was about to generalize into a model of society.

The idea of efficiency also linked the academicians to the businessmen. Every factory owner or merchant understood the utility of planning, expertise, and low costs in his own affairs, and approved of the same methods in public life. Government, philanthropy, religion and education ought also to be businesslike. Planning therefore made sense to the entrepreneur. Fair rates from the railroads and public utilities and uniform or minimum standards of production and marketing would put all enterprises on the same plane and award success to the most efficient.

There were differences in the application to detail. At one extreme, the Morgan partner George W. Perkins thought of the corporation as itself a public body and he approved of consolidation into great trusts which could impart order to all industry under general government oversight. At the other extreme, bankers in the interior and small merchants and manufacturers considered dissolution of the trusts the first objective of regulation so as to ensure competition among small units. Both groups looked to the scholars for support.

Progressive social science therefore significantly influenced the emphasis of reform in the forty years after 1900. The weaknesses in this movement were serious. In its focus upon economic considerations it treated all men as integers in the productive system. It disregarded the problems of race and of the immigrant, assuming that the general improvement in the standard of living would eliminate all the difficulties emanating from those sources. Progressive social science was also blind to all non-rational elements in human behavior; the individual was a calculating machine moved entirely by estimates of his own self-interest. And it simplified social relationships into a clearcut conflict of contending social forces: Jeffersonians against Hamiltonians, farmers against merchants, East against West. Despite its professions of objectivity, moreover, it often endowed those battles with melodramatic moral overtones — good guys against bad guys.

Nevertheless the social scientists supplied progressivism with the idiom in which a new conception of social justice was to be formulated. Their ideas guided the millions of Americans attracted to change by the ethical impulses of their faith.

The general assumptions that arose from the convergence of social science and social gospel did not endow the progressives with a common platform, a coherent philosophy, or a unified program. The four candidates of 1912 represented the variety of tendencies implicit in the movement.

The Republican President, William Howard Taft, was running for the second term which had become the expected reward for service in office. A genial, kindly man, he had been a devoted follower of Theodore Roosevelt and had served with distinction as Secretary of War. He had had no intention of deviating from his predecessor's line and, indeed, in some respects was more consistent. But he was cautious and moderate by temperament and had the lawyer's respect for proper procedure. The progressive attacks upon the judiciary seemed to him insensitive to vested rights. His frightened efforts at compromise attracted the support of the Old Guard, resistant to any change, which had nowhere else to go and upon whose support he grew increasingly dependent.

The entry of Theodore Roosevelt supplied the contest with drama. His was the tragic dilemma of the young man who had reached the top too soon and had no further heights to conquer. He was only fifty when he left office in 1909, vigorous and still zestful for achievement. Politics seemed closed to him; he wrote, edited, traveled and shot big game, but remained restless. As an observer it was easy to find fault with his successor. Impatiently Roosevelt became convinced that he would have done better. When a boss-ridden Republican convention denied him the nomination he broke away and accepted designation by a new Progressive Party.

T.R.'s position in 1912 was clearer than it had been during his presidency. He had gradually been thinking problems through and, reading Herbert Croly's *Promise of American Life*, realized that he had moved away from his earlier position which the plodding Taft still followed. Croly had traced two forces that had struggled for mastery of the country in the past — the Jeffersonian concern for the welfare of the masses and the Hamiltonian insistence upon a strong government by the elite. His book had proposed that the United States now fuse the two by seeking Jeffersonian ends through Hamiltonian means. Roosevelt also believed that a strong government should control the economy, regulate rather than bust the trusts and direct all the productive energies of a *New Nationalism* to improvement of the conditions of the people. On that platform, *standing at Armageddon and battling for the Lord*, he attracted the support of intellectuals, social workers and independents as well as of those still held largely by his exciting personality.

The Democratic standard-bearer, Woodrow Wilson, was a political scientist, formerly president of Princeton University and, at the moment, governor of New Jersey. His nomination was a token of the respect now accorded academic men. A Presbyterian upbringing and a Southern background colored his view of reform. In the first instance, it meant decency and honesty in politics; although he had used the assistance of local bosses to gain office, he enhanced his reputation by turning against them once he was in power. Efficiency in government reduced taxes and strict regulation lowered utility rates, both policies which pleased the commuters of his state. Beyond that he believed in free competition, an open market and a low tariff.

Louis D. Brandeis, a Boston lawyer and veteran of many a battle against corporate interests, supplied him with the philosophy of his campaign for the *New Freedom*. Bigness was not an asset but a curse. It created massive, wasteful organizations and stifled the capacity for experiment and innovation that small units enjoyed. The trusts had acquired their power not through greater efficiency but through privilege, unfair tactics, and the use of other people's money. By destroying them the *New Freedom* would remove a drag from American development and unleash the forces of further growth.

The fourth candidate, Eugene V. Debs, was to earn the largest vote ever cast for a Socialist. His party attempted to unite the natives and the foreign-born, the skilled and the unskilled, intellectuals and middle-class reformers. Hopelessly given to splintering, since it had no patronage or machine, it was attacked by the radical followers of Daniel De Leon and by the Industrial Workers of the World, who distrusted political action and preached violent class war. Debs spoke for some sectors of the labor movement and called for government ownership of basic utilities. But his greatest support came from cities like Milwaukee in which Socialist municipal administrations had given the citizens honest and efficient government. In those places he was generally regarded as only a more radical progressive.

Wilson's victory was not the result of a considered choice by the electorate among the various programs offered it. The vote was distributed much as it had been for a quarter-century before; and the Democrats won because of the division within Republican ranks. The campaign was significant, rather, for the opportunity to reconsider the direction of national development and to educate the voters in the implications of the problems the candidates discussed. The election was a mandate to whichever party won, to carry forward the progressive reforms already initiated in the previous twelve years.

The impact of progressivism altered the structure of government and its relationship to society. On both the state and the federal levels, the machinery of decision and administration became more responsive to popular pressures. The chief executive — President or governor — grew steadily in power not only through command of the patronage but also because he alone *was expected to look out for the general interest of the country*. Access to public opinion, the ability to be heard, gave him a potent instrument with which to recruit support for his policies.

The courts remained largely unregenerate, and control of the legislatures and of Congress by local interests and bosses was only gradually loosened. The initiative and referendum, devices which some hoped would permit the people to intervene in the lawmaking process, had little effect. But redistricting in several states, the primary, the reform of the House of Representatives which reduced the power of the Speaker, and the direct election of senators after the adoption of the Seventeenth Amendment eliminated some abuses and coincided with a growing insistence upon honesty among public servants.

Strong executives and more responsive legislatures, between 1900 and 1917, developed an extensive program of action. There was no radical overturn of existing institutions nor any subversion of the rights of property. Rather, frequent compromises carefully and gradually extended the power of government to adjust society to the conditions of industrialism. The states embarked upon efforts to further conservation, education and public health. They inspected tenements and factories, provided for workingmen's compensation, regulated the labor of women and children and aided farmers through demonstrations and research. The federal government shared the same concerns, sometimes encouraging the states through conferences and grants-in-aid. In addition, it began to mediate in strikes, set the conditions of labor for seamen and railway workers, and attempted to assure the purity of foods and drugs.

Compromise resolved the most important controversies over control of the productive system. The trusts were not busted, but some types of holding companies were outlawed and the Federal Trade Commission was authorized to prevent unfair competition. The railroads remained privately owned, but the Interstate Commerce Commission's power to set rates was strengthened. The federal reserve system met the desire for more orderly and yet more flexible patterns of currency and credit; and it was to be operated neither by bankers nor by the government but by a combination of both, while a separate institution dealt with the farmers' special financial requirements. The income tax provided a new source of revenue, but the rates (one per cent over $4000) were so low that taxpayers were hardly inconvenienced. The administrators put in charge of these bodies were generally respectable if unimaginative men, drawn from business or the civil service, who tried to execute their functions with as little disruptive effect as possible.

The World War temporarily extended the scope of government controls. Patriotism justified a new economic nationalism. Mobilization on an immense scale gave unprecedented powers to the War Industries Board and put labor and transportation under the direction of federal agencies. There were no complaints; and the officials in charge had ample latitude for experiments in planning. Although most of the emergency bodies were dissolved after the peace, the precedents they established had far-reaching consequences in 1933.

In the 1920's the states were the chief arenas of progressive action. Many entirely reorganized their administrative apparatus and local governments; most launched ambitious programs for conservation, the development of water power, parks, urban planning, education and welfare. By contrast the federal scene was quiet when it was not comic. Warren G. Harding was a pathetic throwback to an earlier order; Calvin Coolidge was a competent executive but lacked the inclination to take the initiative in anything; and Herbert Hoover was overwhelmed by the Depression before his first year in office was over. The enduring achievements of these years were administrative, the results of such efforts as those of Joseph Eastman in the Interstate Commerce Commission and of Charles G. Dawes in the Bureau of the Budget.

The decade did witness a new and significant concern with civil liberty. The growth of bureaucratic power since 1900 had begun ominously to encroach upon the freedom of the individual. The first victims were pacifists, aliens and radicals; the fanatical zeal for enforcing the prohibition laws against the resistance of a large part of the population widened the possibility for the abuse of power. The excesses of the wartime sedition acts, of the Red scare and of the dry agents evoked a determined counterattack which reached its head in the agitation over the Sacco-Vanzetti case. Altogether apart from the guilt or innocence of the two Italian anarchists, that incident revealed that the poor, the foreign-born, and the unpopular could not get a fair trial in the Commonwealth of Massachusetts and evoked a widespread call for redress.

Relief began to come through the judges — not generally favorites of the progressives. The dissenting opinions of Justices Holmes and Brandeis had already laid the groundwork for greater solicitude for individual rights. That concern became more acute in the 1920's. The key was the provision of the Fourteenth Amendment which forbade the states to *deprive any person of life, liberty or property without due process of law.* In 1923 and 1925 the Supreme Court held that those words prevented the states from infringing upon the freedom of religion and of speech of their residents and thereby significantly expanded the guarantees of the federal Bill of Rights. The implications of that new interpretation were to be thoughtfully explored in the decades that followed.

The prolonged crisis of the Depression was also a crisis of progressivism. The Old Guard, encouraged to regroup during *normalcy,* was totally routed in the panic of 1929. By 1932 the country knew that prosperity was not just around the corner. Depositors who lost their savings in bank closings, unemployed laborers, foreclosed farmers, and members of the underprivileged minorities supplied the votes that swept Franklin D. Roosevelt into office. They were eager for action and preferred boldness of decision to a leisurely contemplation of alternatives. The President gave them what they wanted.

F.D.R. was the progressive incarnate, experimental and pragmatic, committed to no general theories or coherent policy, but animated by the impulse to service inspired by Rector Peabody at Groton and by his education as governor of New York. Roosevelt's experience in the World War, as Under-Secretary of the Navy, had taught him that the government could act, and he was determined to try whatever promised a hope of recovery. His entourage included trust-builders and trust-busters, proponents of national planning and of free competition, monetary quacks and sober corporation lawyers. And it was precisely that flexibility and the faith it reflected that something could be done which made the New Deal popular.

The efforts to induce full recovery were not successful. Federal provisions for relief reduced the likelihood that Americans might starve. But unemployment scarcely subsided and the farm problem came no closer to resolution than earlier. The NRA adventure in planning was already collapsing under its own weight when the Supreme Court held it unconstitutional. Tinkering with the currency had little effect; and pump-priming through public expenditures was not applied consistently enough to yield results.

But the New Deal could take credit for substantial permanent achievements, the further reform of banking and the regulation of the security exchanges; the imaginative Tennessee Valley Authority scheme for regional development; the Wagner Act's guarantee to labor of the right to collective bargaining; the minimum wage law; and the social security system. An effort to raise the levels of productivity in the South responded not only to the pressures of a powerful bloc of senators but also to the genuine needs of the least advanced section of the country. The increase in income and inheritance taxes to finance these measures began a redistribution of wealth which reduced the most glaring inequalities of the late nineteenth century.

The New Deal was the culmination of four decades of progressive development. It did not aim to overturn the old order according to any utopian design or abstract theory. Its major impulse was toward a reconstruction that would permit government to take positive steps toward the creation of a just society. Its strengths and weaknesses therefore were those of progressivism in general — pragmatism and moderation, the disregard for non-rational factors, the emphasis on economics and the preoccupation with security. But those deficiencies were more readily perceived after the crisis of depression had passed than while jobless men still lacked the means of subsistence.

The New Deal provided Americans with an escape from collectivism. The Socialist Party declined steadily in strength in the 1930's and the organized labor movement successfully resisted pulls to the left. Even the most vociferous radicals gained a hearing only by the claim that *Communism was Twentieth-Century Americanism*. The demand for a surrender of liberty in exchange for security was unattractive in a society that still promised people justice and individuality.

The reaffirmation that free men did not have to feed off each other like beasts, accounted for the popularity of the New Deal. The outpouring of votes that re-elected Roosevelt in 1936 was a response not to the handouts and relief checks but to the glimmer of hope that the state might now furnish citizens with the security and stability that they no longer found in particular communities and that they needed as individuals in the massive society America had become.

25

Individualism, 1900–1939

THE HAT AND CANE are symbols of borrowed elegance. The mustache may be real. But the battered shoes and shapeless coat give the show away. The nonchalance of the walk, walk, walk fools no one. From around the corner come the cops and the little fellow is off, game of the chase that is always a part of it.

Only the ladies do not run. If they move at all, it is to glide in their ankle-length skirts. But the ladies are not real. Their perpetual innocence and outrage, their inaccessibility to emotion, show they are not of this world. The society dame plastered with paint, mud, pie, remains as placid as the fair young maiden rescued in the nick of time.

Everyone else runs — the paunchy boss in his avarice, the brutal fellow-worker in his greed, and the law brandishing its nightstick cruelly. And the little fellow runs too because they are all against him.

They are against him because he is the outsider, alone, and belongs to no one. Often he has no name, but always he has an identity and, indomitably he fights back, using their own rules to defeat them. So what? At the end, the prize is usually not worth having and as he walk-walk-walks jauntily off, he shows it was not a reward he was striving for, but his own individuality.

Everyone was running — going away; there were not trains enough to take them. They were off for somewhere else because it was better for them there. Until quotas kept them out after 1924, the immigrants still arrived from Europe; and after that some newcomers still crossed over from Mexico and Canada. But native-born Americans were the most restless. The ambitious moved to improve themselves, from country to city, from East to West, from North to South, and South to North. Those with no hope wished at least to get going; they could not face the prospect of working, starving or dying where they were. Fired, closed out, foreclosed, they cranked up the old touring car or rode freights — away. Retired, finished, withdrawn, they sold out their farms and businesses to sit in the California or Florida sun. In a manner of speaking, all were tramps, like Chaplin on the screen, unwilling to be tied down, to be limited by the here and the now.

The frontier had disappeared, but movement continued, less coherent, less directed, less purposeful than formerly. Pulled by an unexpected tide toward the new Detroit factories, drawn in a swift current to the Pacific coast, subsiding neither in prosperity nor in depression, the flow carried along men who wished to be not members of families, not citizens of towns, not rooted where they were, but individuals free to go where they liked.

The automobile set them rolling ever more freely. In 1939, well over thirty million motor vehicles were registered in the United States, sixty times as many as in 1910, almost one for every four persons — men, women and children. They all loved to take the wheel of a brand-new Oldsmobile and be off for a long fast ride, away to the other side. Of what? No matter. Liberated from the fixed route of the trolley car or train, the driver moved off by himself in the privacy of his own chariot. Though it took him each day the same way to work and back, he was his own master, his the power at a touch of the accelerator. Nothing could be finer on the day of rest than to escape from home to the jammed highways out of the congested cities.

The automobile was a universal object of desire. Advancing technology lowered the cost and a rising standard of living enabled millions to make the down payment or at least to buy a used jalopy. But those were not the only reasons for the diffusion of ownership. The American wanted a car because it freed him from restraints, let him get away. It was the great symbol of his independence as an individual. The wheels that let him roll kept bringing him home yet assured him he was master of motion. Just so, he wished the community and family to be — at his service, available for stability, yet making no irksome claims to tie him down.

After 1900, *Society* tended to become valueless and glamourless. Wealth, it seemed, debased man; the pursuit and possession of it robbed him of emotional satisfaction. The rich were inhuman not only in the lack of sympathy for others, but also in their own inability to feel.

A STORY. *I want you to marry me,* said Maxwell as he snatched a moment from the telephone. *Won't you, Miss Leslie?* The stenographer acted very queerly. Overcome with amazement, the tears flowed from her wondering eyes. *It's this old business,* she said softly, *that has driven everything else out of your head. Don't you remember, Harvey? We were married last evening at the Little Church Around the Corner.*

Theodore Dreiser's novels spelled out the problems of the *Financier* and of his women in greater detail; money corrupted passion as it did every other personal relationship. The rich were as much to be pitied as envied. The song put it more simply. The society girl was *a beautiful sight to see. But happy and free though she seemed to be, 'twas sad that she'd wasted her life. For her beauty was sold for an old man's gold; she was a bird in a gilded cage.* The yellow press still gave space to the affairs of the swell families; but the tone was of amusement rather than of respect. All rich men were fair game, socialites or not. It was a field day when the *Daily Mirror* and the *Daily Graphic* got to work on the love affairs of Kip Rhinelander and his Alice or of Daddy Browning and his Peaches.

The Depression completed the debacle by revealing the ineptitude of the nabobs at their own business of business. The great families in their fine houses were clownish dolts; it took *My Man Godfrey,* from out of the hoboes' camp, to show them how to live and love. In 1903, Edward Steichen had photographed the elder J. P. Morgan; the corsair glared fiercely from the print and a trick of the light transformed the arm of the chair, on which his hand rested, into a dagger pointed at the viewer. Thirty years later, the newspapers carried a picture of his son, who bore the same name, smiling in genial bewilderment at a midget placed on his lap by a circus press agent. The poor old man about to testify at a Senate hearing had no idea of what was happening to him. So much for those pretensions to pre-eminence and leadership!

The disrepute of *Society* extended to all the communities in process of dissolution. None of the second generations wished to accept the handiwork of their parents. Even in the saccharined stories of Booth Tarkington, Penrod and Sam mischievously subverted the good behavior of the dancing school. More acute writers revealed how *Spoon River* and *Main Street* stifled the personality, crushed rebellion and turned their victims into religious and social hypocrites. The same hostile view of organized community life showed through the observations by young Jews, Italians, Negroes and Irish Catholics of the groups into which they had been born and which they sought to flee.

A phenomenally popular play pointed the moral. The individual could liberate himself by casting off inherited ties. Abie got his Irish Rose when the boy and girl decided to disregard the ancestral differences that kept them from blissfulness. At the happy ending, the priest and the rabbi grinned on in approval.

The old ways were not only wrong but ridiculous. The *booboisie* read Mencken with glee and laughed at their own former credulity. The muckrakers and debunkers shifted their attention from contemporary culprits of wealth to the national and religious heroes of the past. E. Haldeman-Julius sold by mail millions of *Little Blue Books* that gave Americans the inside story; and respectable books demonstrated that the *Real George Washington* had feet of clay, and that the Biblical King — David, the *Giant-Killer* — was a double-dealing opportunist who *could always get someone else to kill his giants for him*. Abstract standards of good and evil were delusions, explained *Helen of Troy* in a best-seller; and *society was only a name for a group of human beings*. The happiness of the individual was the important thing.

The individual did his best to pull away from the group and to follow his own inner inclinations because he could not trust communal standards or communal information. Everyone was trying to put something over. The news column was no more to be credited than the advertisement beside it; and the reader alternated between fits of wary skepticism and periods of utter naïveté. He often let himself be persuaded. But deep down, even as he paid the price, he was ready to laugh at his own gullibility. It was all ballyhoo, a fraud, bunk — history, society, everything outside himself.

Was nothing sacred any more?

Mammy! (The sun shines east, the sun shines west; but you're the one that I love best.) Ma-a-mmy.

No one would question motherhood. Every man wanted a girl just like the girl that married dear old Dad. But sung out by Sophie Tucker, the *red-hot mama*, the connotation became ambiguous, just as Al Jolson's blackface *mammy* did, as if the relationship were not altogether as clear as convention made it. A sardonic note sounded through the popular vaudeville ditty:

> *Don't swat yer mother, boys, just 'cause she's old*
> *Don't mop the floor with her face.*
> *Think how her love is a treasure of gold,*
> *Shining thro' shame and disgrace.*
> *Don't put the rocking-chair next to her eye*
> *Don't bounce the lamp off her bean!*
> *Angels are watching you up in the sky,*
> *Don't swat yer mother, it's mean!*

The serious play and movie did not trouble to hide the bitterness. *Yes, Mother* said Robert (*engulfed forever*), hopelessly tied by the *Silver Cord. Mother love suffereth long and is kind; beareth all things; believeth all things; hopeth all things; endureth all things.* Stifleth all things?

It was safer, on every account, to reduce the emotion to the formal, commercial terms of Mother's Day.

The whole family, in fact, was a threat to personality. Its arbitrary requirements dragged down the men and women who yielded to its constraints. Clyde Griffiths refused to allow the claims of his parents to impede his struggle for success; but his softness in dealing with Roberta's demand for marriage led to *An American Tragedy.* Happiness in fiction as in life often depended on the ability to divorce oneself from burdensome relationships, to be free to seek fulfillment wherever the opportunity presented itself.

Relaxed laws made separations easier and a tolerant code of sexual conduct recognized extramarital affairs almost as a matter of course. It no longer took restraint to achieve birth control; the means were available in the corner drugstore. Marriage was a convenience rather than a permanent union of souls; Judge Ben Lindsey recognized the logic of the situation and recommended a period of *companionate* trial before young people permanently committed themselves. The dating practices of the 1920's went a long way toward meeting his suggestion.

The unwillingness to accept external restraints also influenced significantly the institutions under more direct social control. The child-centered school pushed to an extreme John Dewey's protest against the formalism of nineteenth-century education. The progressive movement gained rapidly in strength after the World War and by the 1930's was altering the practices of the public schools. In the same years, the teachings of Freud modified the assumptions of social work and, more generally, encouraged the individual to seek adjustment in self-expression and in the resolution of inner conflicts through the satisfaction of irrepressible personal drives.

The churches had a more difficult time of it. Only the completely tradition-oriented could turn without strain against the spirit of the times and they did so at the risk of losing their children. Orthodox Roman Catholics and Jews held to their own ways with the support of the surviving immigrant communicants. The rural fundamentalists also stubbornly resisted efforts at accommodation. At Dayton, Tennessee, the prosecution of a teacher who brought evolution into the classroom mobilized the last line of defense: the monkey was not man's ancestor; the Bible was literally accurate; science was a falsehood. But these dogmatic assertions could not persuade the uncommitted; and the fiasco of Prohibition, with which the fundamentalists were popularly identified, made a mockery of their ideals. Billy Sunday's revival antics entertained many, but converted few even at the height of his popularity, before 1918. Thereafter he had trouble assembling an audience.

Only those churches waxed in membership which took the offensive in an uncompromising crusade against modernity among the marginal elements in American society. Jehovah's Witnesses, the followers of Father Divine, and scores of other millennialist sects attracted people who sought immediate divine direction in a confusing world alien to their inherited standards. The poor whites and Negroes who supplied most of the membership of these groups had learned by experience how slight were their chances of standing alone as individuals.

The growth of such new denominations was evidence that the churches in the mainstream of American life could not guard against the currents of change. Indeed, to the extent that they had dedicated themselves to the social gospel they had also committed themselves to being progressive; and they could not readily draw the line between progressive and permissive. In some denominations there was an inclination to assume a psychiatric function; the Emmanuel Movement among the Episcopalians, for instance, found a therapeutic value in religion. But that too centered faith upon the adjustment of the individual.

In the healing cults the identification of health with worship was complete. Out in California, Katherine Tingley, the Purple Mother, led one branch of Theosophy in the quest for *physical beauty, intelligence and spiritual wealth.* In her community former bankers and industrialists listened to lectures in an atmosphere *like poppy-scented champagne* while her own constant companion, the dog Spot, was the reincarnation of the favorite among her three former husbands. She and her rivals were outlandish but accepted as a matter of course. An American Legion post in Chicago which heard Annie Besant's Hindu World Master in 1926 ended its meeting with the whole assembly singing "For He's a Jolly Good Fellow." In a less exotic context, Sister Aimee Semple McPherson used popular music, chorus girls and the appurtenances of the stage to preach that Christ saved — and cured. Physical *culture* reflected in reverse the same identification of body and spirit. For Bernarr MacFadden and his followers the *Torso Beautiful* was the means to health and to salvation.

At whatever level of respectability and decorum these movements operated, they displayed the tendency, that also influenced the churches, to focus concern upon the personal problems of the participant rather than upon established rite or prescribed creed. Only thus could they hold the individual impatient with restraint and eager to cast off all external ties. They felt the same disruptive pressure of dismemberment that played also upon the family and the community.

Now man had struggled loose; he was free and alone. At this

hitherto unprecedented altitude he could regard himself in an unfamiliar perspective.

> *Luuu-*
> *cky Lindy*
> *He is the One.*
>
> *Luuu-*
> *cky Lindy*
> *He is the* ONE.

The greatest hero in the history of the human race. Fifty-five thousand telegrams agreed with the *World*. Even President Coolidge — Silent Cal — was moved to eloquence.

Thirty-five hours in the air, alone in space, above the endless ocean, between the two worlds. Master of the Machine. Lone Eagle who by will and daring soared.

His was the culminating experience of American adventure, not because of the nature of the feat — others had flown the Atlantic before Lindbergh did in 1927 — but because its solitude made him the absolute individual his countrymen wished to be. He came of a long line of men able to do things because they were unencumbered: cowboys — Owen Wister's Virginian, offspring of Natty Bumppo and sire of Tom Mix; the detective — Old Sleuth, now Nick Carter, about to be the Private Eye; the athlete — Merriwell, Dempsey, Ruth; the reporter — scoop. Nothing held them down, or him; self-propelled, they moved in response to inner impulses; they obeyed codes of their own making; and they came through because they wanted to. They were the models of every American's aspiring.

Women were American too, and having no models to emulate, they went farther in throwing off restraint than the men. Daisy and Lady Brett passed far beyond the goals defined years before at Seneca Falls; education, the ballot, public office and jobs, the cigarette, the highball and the golf course were accessible to them as to men. The double standard was gone and the resentful subjection to frequent childbirth. Easy marriage and easy divorce, small families and plenty of time became the rule. With their hair cut short and their legs unswathed, they were free and equal — and separate. The Gibson girl, at the beginning of the century, dreamily eyed the prospect; the postwar flapper greedily seized it. They were *nobody's babies now*, but persons with their own identities and their own desires to satisfy. The All-American girl moved through life, self-contained, giving when she received, taking what she needed, an individual like the dancing partner with whom she shared moments of intimacy in the solitude of the crowded ballroom.

Rebellion was the form the desire for an individual identity took. The city and town, the factory and office crowded people in, made them cogs, all alike, mass-produced, numbered and not named. The past, and the family which linked them to it, tied them down when they wished to fly. They could not yield without spreading their wings, without having their fling. Otherwise they would waste something within them.

No doubt the restrictions were somewhat more onerous than they had been in the nineteenth century, in Huck Finn's family or Maggie's city or Ed Howe's town. But in addition the twentieth-century individual revolted because he also wanted something more than his predecessors had, something which he feared restraint would crush.

It's a mouse and it's tough. Every day he lets fly at the cat with a brick. Pow! Then the cop is after him (the cop is a dog) and sometimes the mouse lands in jail. But this is the joke; the cat is on his side and both of them hate the cop (dog). *Krazy Kat!*

Why does the cop (dog) care? Because he is the law and has to keep people from doing what they want to do.

Why does the mouse throw the brick? Because he is tough and won't let the law push him around.

Then why does the cat bring cake to the mouse in jail, knowing that tomorrow he will again throw the brick? Because she loves him.

With all his faults I love him still. As she gave out the words, Fanny Brice thought of Nicky Arnstein, her swindler husband. She, a poor girl from Brooklyn, had earned fame and the appreciation of the great people of the world, while he, in the finery for which she paid, drifted from one disreputable affair to another. He wasn't true; he beat her too. What could she do? The great sums she handed over disappeared dismayingly. All his grand enterprises ended in nothing or brought him to the bar of justice and to jail. He was no good, her friends told her; and he dragged her down. But though it cost her a lot, there was one thing that she'd got. He was *my man*; and *whatever my man is, I am his forever more!*

This is how we understand the world. We love not by virtue of the merit of the object of our affections — *How come you treat me like you do?* — but because we need to love. We have been so long escaping from the stability we seek that we come to rest only in the arms of that solitary stranger who, knowing nothing of our connections, perceives our true identity. Thus, *it happens one night*, on the bus, when the reporter protects the waif, unaware that she is the heiress in flight from home. Love is the way we express ourselves and are happy, as we all must be.

Keep smiling, is Sister Aimee's constant refrain. *Glad, glad, I'm so glad*, says the little orphan in the best-seller. So Happy! We are all so happy.

The cop (dog) always interferes because he is the guardian of the encrusted rules by which parents, church, friends and state prevent us from being ourselves. We know that we must fight him because we can see that people without families or position have no inhibitions; neither are they bound by the law. Therefore they are happy, glad, smiling — white teeth gleaming in the dark face. They can tell the nicest man they ever knew — oo, oo, *I'd leave ma happy home for you* — oo, oo. That's natural. There are no blackface girls in the gilded cage.

> *Take me to your heart again and call me honey;*
> *All I want is lovin', I don't want your money.*
> *I'll put up a washin' sign outside the door,*
> *Alexander, take me back once more.*

The rest of us cannot do the same unless, like the Negro or the common man in the proletarian novels, we are stripped of all external possessions and, in our nakedness, learn our own nature.

Therefore we must fight whatever impedes our ability to express ourselves. We have, by now, gotten to read Melville and have given our own meaning to the pursuit of the white whale, which we take to be that self-designated goal within ourselves. However little faith we have, we must trust in the worthiness of that pursuit which will bring us out. We do not go forth because we believe in the whale; we believe in the whale because it justifies our wish to go forth.

STRANGE INTERLUDE. *I want to believe in any God at any price,* cries Nina, *a heap of stones, a mud image, a drawing on a wall, a bird, a fish, a snake, a baboon — or even a good man preaching the simple platitudes of truth. I want to believe in something! I want to believe so I can feel.* Anything is all right if it makes you love and keeps you from being *lonely and not pregnant with anything at all.* God Himself has thus become an instrument for the exercise of the sovereign human personality.

REPRISE. The little tramp, who has all along been indomitably defending his individuality, passes by the *city lights* and reaches *modern times.* The old antagonists have only slightly changed their forms but he still needs no props, nor any outer stimulus. Self-starting, he now walk-walk-walks into the finale hand in hand with the girl he loves.

For the mass of men and women the freedom of individuality was beyond reach. They lacked the inner resources to strike out without guide or companion. Many dreamed of flight; not many could take off.

Mostly they were content with second-hand experiences. The young girls studied the mirrors, seeking, in the lipstick line or in the drape of a gown, the distinctive reflection of unique personalities. They turned away — identical copies of the slick advertisement, garbed in the dresses the factory sewed up by the thousand. As they leafed through the pages of *True Confessions* — every one a boast — or teased at the drugstore soda fountain, or watched in the dark at the movie, they caught the feeling of bliss from the thought of the kiss that made the moment divine. But it was no fun to be alone. Every girl needed her *love nest.* They met the boys still absorbed in conflict — sport or getting ahead — and later tried to capture in marriage an equivalent of the romance the dream factories purveyed. Whether they found it or not, they were confirmed in the dependence upon the shadowy life of the screen or the printed page. Or, like Ring Lardner's Celia Gregg, who was *alone, all alone,* they helped themselves to sips of bourbon.

Through the first four decades of the twentieth century, these women and their husbands formed the rank and file of the searchers for stability. They were the voters for progressivism, which assured them that the nation — the great group of which all were a part — really cared for them. Yet political reform had not restored order to their lives. Exposed by the weakness of community and family, they needed love to protect their individuality; in search of it they established connections that submerged the very individuality they wished to protect.

Sensitive outsiders, detached yet close enough to understand, were horrified at the deception. They saw the aimless mob swirl about *Mr. Kahn's Pleasure Dome*, frustrated, cruel, eager for love but ready for violence, pressed so close together they could move only *in a great united front of screwballs and screwboxes* toward the flames that would consume them all. In the red light of death they would at last joyously dance.

Nathanael West reported only part of the spectacle. Fed up with the endless whining letters, with his countrymen's whimpering complaints of their lovelessness, he could no longer perceive the individuals in the mob. He read correctly the emptiness of the lives of those who gaped at Valentino's bier, the aimlessness of the flocks who watched the stars at *Grauman's Chinese* premieres, the violence that burst out in the San Jose lynchings, the cowardice of the gangsters, the avarice of the landlords. It was all true.

But his judgment was too harsh. They were not dirt but human beings and they were there because they were looking for something, dissatisfied with a purposeless routine. They wanted meaning to life and refused to be taken for granted or filed away in an impersonal account. The fault lay not in their striving but in their lack of the means of achieving or even articulating their desires. The inability of society to help them compounded the tragedy.

The gap between desire and reality also dismayed the most acute postwar writers. Their disillusion was a reaction not only to the war and the peace but also to the shortcomings of the nation; and it expressed not the abandonment of ideals but the depth of commitment to them. They were a lost generation because they would not make do with second-hand dreams. Whatever was worth doing, they knew, was worth doing well. O.K. then, what they could not do well, they would not do at all. Fitzgerald believed in the New World that had once flowered for Dutch sailors' eyes and *had once pandered in whispers to the last and greatest of all human dreams* — space in which to be completely free. Now in the great city that had betrayed Gatsby he still had faith in *the green light, the orgiastic future that receded before him.* It eluded him now. No matter, tomorrow he would *run faster, stretch out his arms farther.*

The young man from Montana (Minnesota) fought on in the hopeless battle and at the end there was only the dying at which he was no good at all. But as long as Robert Jordan (Hemingway) knew what it was he had to do he could wait. Let them come! He could fulfill himself.

This, wrote Sherwood Anderson, was the glory of earth-born men and women, never to yield, but standing, to take defeat implacable and defiant.

> *In this hard star-adventure, knowing not*
> *What the fires mean to right and left, nor whether*
> *A meaning was intended or presumed,*
> *Man can stand up, and look out blind, and say:*
> *In all these turning lights I find no clue,*
> *Only a masterless night, and in my blood*
> *No certain answer, yet is my mind my own*
> *Yet is my heart a cry toward something dim*
> *In distance, which is higher than I am*
> *And makes me emperor of the endless dark*
> *even in seeking!*

That affirmation, in its echoes of the Emersonian divine spirit, in the 1930's deeply moved Americans. With less certainty than their ancestors, but with fully as much determination, they wished only to be left alone to explore its meaning and discover themselves.

VIII

The Threat of Totalitarianism, 1939–1962

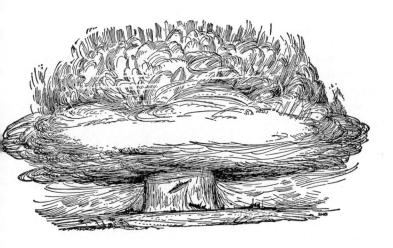

26

Holocaust

In October, 1938, Sylvia Holmes, a Negro housewife in Newark, grew more and more excited as she listened to the radio. When he heard *Get the gas masks*, that was the part that convinced her. She dashed out to tell the people: *Don't you know New Jersey is destroyed by the Germans?* She remembered that Hitler had not appreciated President Roosevelt's telegram a few weeks before. The Germans were smart and came down in something like a balloon — that's when there was the explosion. The world was coming to an end.

She went home, her knees shaking so that she could hardly walk up the stairs. She looked in the icebox and saw some chicken left from Sunday dinner that she had been saving for Monday night and said, *We may as well eat this chicken — we won't be here in the morning.*

The newspapers the next day announced that Mrs. Holmes, like millions of other Americans, had made a mistake. They had heard no news broadcast but a radio play, *The War of the Worlds*. And the invaders who were said to have landed in the Jersey meadows were Martians, not Germans.

But, after all, Mrs. Holmes was right. The danger did come from the Germans and her world was coming to an end.

The housewife in Newark knew it. But the statesmen in Washington did not — not even a year later when a pact with Stalin encouraged Hitler to invade Poland. For almost nine months after the outbreak of war in Europe a total miscalculation shaped American foreign policy.

The Nazi aggressors had swept easily through Poland and were massing their forces in the West, but the trump cards seemed to be in Allied hands. The Maginot line was impenetrable, the French army was the best in the world, and the British navy could easily cut the enemy off from the rubber, oil and cotton without which his *ersatz* economy would collapse of its own weight. In the winter of 1939, the democracies seriously contemplated the possibility of coming to the relief of the beleaguered Finns and thus taking on the Russians as well as the Germans.

American sympathies were clear. Only a few extreme fascist and anti-Semitic groups spoke out in favor of Hitler; even most German-Americans had nothing good to say of his regime. His defeat was certainly desirable and existing European forces were considered adequate for that purpose. The only question was the extent to which the United States should be involved. The isolationists, strongest in the Midwest, argued that the conflict was European and could never spread across the ocean. The interventionists spoke of a moral obligation to win the war *by aiding the Allies*. Neither side faced the issue events would shortly define. What if only American troops could halt the spread of Nazi conquests?

A spring of disaster followed the *winter of illusion*. In April, 1940, Denmark and Norway fell; in May, the Low Countries; on June 15, Paris. There was only *one more battle* to win. In September the *Luftwaffe* bombs rained down on England.

There was panic in Washington and indecision in the country. The President, dismayed at the miscalculations of the past year, declared in June that he would help *the opponents of force* and would prepare the nation for any emergency. He drew Republicans into his cabinet, gave the British fifty destroyers in return for some naval bases in the West Indies, and extended American protection to the Allied colonies in the New World. At the same time he decided that he could trust no one else in office and would seek an unprecedented third term for himself. But he repeatedly assured the people that these measures would go *short of war;* and in Boston, he solemnly announced: *I have said this before, but I shall say it again and again and again: Your boys are not going to be sent into any foreign wars.* The aid that flowed across the Atlantic would end the fear that they would die *in another Flanders.* Nor did the election clarify the matter; Willkie and Roosevelt held identical positions on foreign affairs; and neither spoke out candidly.

The Americans therefore moved confusedly into the decisive year that culminated at Pearl Harbor. Each month brought them closer to the involvement they were told would not come. By the fall their ships were actively shooting it out with Nazi U-boats. But they were unable to appraise the consequences; and the gap between people and leadership impeded the development of a consistent foreign policy.

Military unpreparedness made matters worse. Both services had been busy arming themselves — with the wrong weapons. Both underestimated the enemy; and neither had adequate awareness of the air power that was to prove decisive after 1941. Furthermore, the navy, still bemused by Mahan's theories, cherished the battle cruisers that were its admirals' delight and neglected antiaircraft defense, destroyers and carriers, no mean oversight in view of the war that was actually fought. Its plan of action called for massing the fleet at Hawaii, then a three-month cruise to the Philippines, picking off Japanese outposts along the way, and then a final confrontation with the enemy.

The Japanese were not waiting, however. In July, 1941, they had declared a protectorate over French Indochina; and the United States had responded with an embargo on the oil, rubber and credit essential to the Mikado's long-drawn-out effort to conquer China. The warlords at that point concluded that a conflict with the Americans was inevitable; and to succeed they had to strike the first blow. Through the months that followed, their emissaries in Washington made a polite pretense of negotiation while their armada in the Pacific set sail.

American intelligence, at the end of November, knew from intercepted messages that a striking force was in motion. But the responsible officers reading through the files of information could not believe that the objective was the invulnerable naval base in Hawaii. When a submarine was sunk in the harbor at 6:45 A.M. on December 7, 1941, and radar picked up unidentified planes at the same moment, it still seemed incredible that the little yellow men in their big eyeglasses would thus dare. At 7:55 A.M., the bombs fell on Pearl Harbor, destroying a hundred and fifty planes, six battleships and all hope of an easy victory. Nine hours later an attack on Manila wiped out the air force, sitting there — despite the warning — neatly before its hangars.

Within the next three days the United States was formally at war with Japan, Germany and Italy. There was no irresolution or division of opinion; the act of aggression resolved all doubts. But it did not clarify the purposes of the war. Americans knew they were fighting in self-defense but they would be a long time learning what they were fighting for.

The enemy was no wiser than they. The mistakes of the Axis leaders gave the United States time to gather its strength and make a fresh start that would ultimately turn the tide and yield victory. The greatest of the errors had already been committed by that master strategist Adolf Hitler. Stalin, frightened and insecure, was perfectly content to sit by and watch capitalists and fascists massacre one another. But early success went to Hitler's head; in June, 1940, he plunged toward the east and his great war machine blundered into a morass from which it would never extricate itself.

The Japanese errors also sprang from an excess of pride. Having won so easily at Pearl Harbor, they resolved to push their conquests further and fortify a ribbon of islands from the Aleutians through Midway to Papua, that would hold off counterattacks and permit them leisurely to complete the conquest and digestion of China. The effort overtaxed their strength while they still held strategic superiority and seriously weakened them for the future. At the battles of Coral Sea and Midway in the summer of 1942, the smaller American navy staved off the Nipponese battle fleet and gained the time for a renewal of its own power.

By contrast, the American commanders learned the lesson of their first disaster and displayed the consistent competence that came from an excess of caution. Careful preparation, limited risks and the massive accumulation of power were the marks of their successive campaigns.

A tremendous productive effort put the weapons in their hands. In the five years after the fall of France, the factories of the United

States turned out almost three hundred thousand aircraft, more than eight million tons of naval and fifty-five million tons of merchant shipping, almost three million machine guns and more than eighty-five thousand tanks. They did so while fully fifteen million men and women stepped into rank in the armed services. With these resources the commanders could take the time to be ready and could profit from the mistakes of the foe.

The European theater received major emphasis until the collapse of the Nazi regime. For almost a year, the movement of supplies to Russia, Britain, and the growing American expeditionary force was the chief problem. The Germans invested heavily and successfully in a submarine campaign which for a time sank ships faster than the United States could build them. In May and June, 1942, alone, more than seven hundred and fifty thousand tons went down. Not until then did the navy have a convoy system in operation; and not until the end of the year was the U-boat threat under control.

American strategy favored a frontal attack across the English Channel to throw the full weight of Allied power directly at the heart of the German empire. But the British preferred to use superior air and sea forces in a flanking movement from the south, while high-altitude bombing softened up the enemy's industry, transport and civilian population. The desire for quick action induced the Joint Chiefs of Staff to accept the latter alternative, which required less preparation. A vast flanking operation began with landings in Casablanca, Oran and Algiers in November, 1942; it had extended through Tunisia by May, 1943; and it led to the invasion of Sicily and Italy in July and September. The whole action went more slowly than anticipated, however, and came to a stop above Naples in October, 1943. Installed along the Volturno line across the narrow boot of Italy, the Germans and Italians halted further progress through the winter. The Americans were not to reach Rome until June, 1944.

Nor had bombing behind the lines brought the Axis down. Thousands of aircraft regularly spread fire and death through central Europe, but organized fascist power kept the battered population under control and at work. The destruction of hundreds of factories lowered productive capacity and created shortages; it did not, however, end German ability to continue the war. In February, 1944, a concerted attack by almost four thousand planes on twelve centers of Nazi industry crippled the *Luftwaffe* but it was still able to fly. Only a direct assault would bring Hitler's empire down.

The decision to launch such an invasion had been taken early in 1943. A year of preparation had accumulated almost three million men and well over two million tons of supplies in England. On June 6, 1944, a hundred and seventy-six thousand soldiers, carried by almost five thousand vessels, stormed the Normandy coast. Six days of brutal fighting established a beachhead five miles deep and seventy miles wide. Into this pocket the Allies poured three hundred and twenty-five thousand men, fifty thousand vehicles and one hundred thousand tons of supplies. In the last week of July they broke out of the Normandy peninsula and were on their way to the Rhine. Four columns, one Canadian, one British, and two American, moved swiftly across France. By the end of August they had reached Paris and Brussels.

In the fall of 1944 the Allied drive ground to a halt along a line that ran through Belgium and northern France. It had consumed supplies at a prodigious rate and needed time for regrouping. But the winter was far from leisurely for the troops. They threw back a German counterattack in December and a series of detached battles straightened the line. Meanwhile, the Russians had begun an offensive that carried them through the Ukraine, Poland, Hungary and Czechoslovakia toward Vienna and Berlin.

The final stage of the German war began early in March, 1945, with the seizure of the Remagen Bridge, which permitted a swift crossing of the Rhine. A series of deft encircling movements captured the Ruhr, the cornerstone of Nazi heavy industry, and ended the last serious hopes of German victory. In April, Hitler died by suicide and partisans took Mussolini's life. On May 7, General Eisenhower received the unconditional surrender of the remaining fascist forces.

The end of the war in Europe permitted the Allies, who had all along been fighting on two fronts, to devote full attention to their Asian enemy. After Midway, the Japanese had made one further effort to develop the shield of islands in the south that would protect their conquests. A new base on Guadalcanal in the Solomons was to ward off the danger of a counterattack from Australia. An exhausting battle for that island began in August, 1942, and lasted for six months, consuming staggering numbers of men, planes and ships. The Japanese withdrawal marked the failure of the last effort to keep the fighting remote from their home islands. The Americans were in a position to come back.

The way was long and hard. The United States gained steadily in air and sea power. But between its Australian and Hawaiian outposts and Japan were more than three thousand miles of dangerous waters, studded with archipelagos on many of which the enemy was strongly entrenched. Each could be reduced only by a painful, costly process. Yet without doing so, China and the industrial heartland of the Nipponese empire were out of reach.

Leapfrogging became the American strategy for the year after July, 1943. Powerful amphibious forces moved around the Japanese strong points to the weaker spots. A growing armada of aircraft carriers provided cover for these operations, while sizable submarine and destroyer fleets decimated the enemy's merchant shipping and crippled his efforts to bring relief to the scattered outposts. The Gilbert, Marshall and Mariana islands were thus enveloped and New Guinea cleared. On June 19, 1944, the battle of the Philippine Sea broke the back of the Japanese navy and gave the Americans freedom of action thereafter. In October, landings in the Philippines, protected by a great air and sea battle in Leyte Gulf, led to the reconquest of those islands. The seizure of Iwo Jima and Okinawa in the next six months permitted intensified bombardment of the great industrial cities of Japan. When Germany surrendered, plans were ready for an invasion; it was estimated that another year of fighting would force the Mikado's government to yield.

But the war was not to be won by these costly efforts, gallant as they were. Science, grown more magical and more powerful by the year in the twentieth century, put into the fighting men's hands a weapon of undreamed-of destructiveness. Albert Einstein, Enrico Fermi, Arthur Compton, Karl T. Compton, Leo Szilard, Isidore I. Rabi, J. Robert Oppenheimer, James B. Conant, James Franck — some of these names were familiar to Americans. But few people had an inkling of the enterprise that bound these scientists together. The refugees from fascist persecution had joined a band of physicists and engineers engaged in an adventure as exciting as any in the Pacific or in Normandy. Their secret Manhattan Project probed the microcosm to unleash the energy of the atom. On August 6, 1945, an explosion over Hiroshima leveled every structure in a four-mile radius and killed more than seventy thousand people. Three days later another blast over Nagasaki finally persuaded the Imperial Japanese Government, on August 14, 1945, to accept the terms of peace.

Bill Mauldin's G.I. Joes moved through the long campaigns in stoic silence. More than three hundred thousand of them lost their lives; more than a million were casualties. Stubble-faced, they crouched in the mud and asked few questions. Rosie the Riveter and the millions who waited and worked at home were similarly mute. There was a job to do.

Morale, on the whole, was good. There were fewer problems of discipline at the front or behind the lines than in earlier conflicts. The zoot-suit riots in Los Angeles exposed the uneasiness of some elements of the population; but protests against the war itself were inconsequential. Americans knew why they were fighting; they had been attacked. Life or death; them or us. *We are over here*, wrote Pfc. Donald Harkness from New Caledonia, *to prevent our homes from ever feeling a first-class bombing raid.*

All agreed on that. But the men in the foxholes and factories were hard put to say what else they were fighting for. *Just carry the messages we give you*, the cartoon sergeant tells the dove, *never mind the peace propaganda.* In the heat of crisis, men refused to think beyond the next moment, and grew tough, belligerent. A private who suggested, *When the Japs run out unarmed we should make an effort to take them alive*, drew a torrent of abuse. *Please notify the FBI, G-2, anything — but have that guy locked up.* A worried soldier, dismayed by events, wrote in the battlefield newspaper:

> *Across the world, the retrogressive waves*
> *Force back on Man his ancient love of caves.*

They knew that a disaster was on its way, but not why.

Their leaders had not been enlightening before 1941; and after Pearl Harbor offered only stammering explanations of the world's agony. On this vital point there was little communication between people and policy-makers. The failure hampered them all.

Franklin Roosevelt's was the greatest burden. He had some comprehension that the enemy was not Germany or Japan but totalitarianism — the massive deployment of power that reduced the human personality to absolute service to the state and that found its supreme outlet in aggressive war. After 1937 an awareness of that danger had grown in his consciousness. In January, 1941, he proclaimed his faith in the Four Freedoms; and that summer he and Churchill in the Atlantic Charter disclaimed any desire for territorial aggrandizement, called for freedom of the seas and of trade, and promised to labor for disarmament, peace and the rights of all people to self-determination. The President believed that those remained his goals until the day of his death in April, 1945.

Yet through 1940, he had not been able publicly to announce the consequences of these premises. To have acted more boldly would have called for a divisive political contest, with a strong risk of losing. He preferred to believe, as long as he could, that Britain and France could take care of the threat without direct American intervention; and he continued to assure those who trusted him that aid for the Allies would not involve the United States in foreign war. Hence the surprise and the blank incomprehension with which men and women greeted Pearl Harbor.

In 1941, the situation changed. The United States, attacked by aggressors, had to resist. The objective was to survive and to prevent a recurrence of disaster. All who fought the same evil — including the Russians — were united in pursuit of the same good. To pretend that the war aims of the Soviet Union were identical with his own, Roosevelt had to push to the back of his mind the troublesome freedoms in which he believed and Stalin did not. To have acknowledged those differences might have caused a breach in the alliance. Yet by concealing them, the President hopelessly complicated the problems of making peace.

In 1942, repeated disasters occupied his countrymen's minds. But the North African landings gave Churchill and Roosevelt the opportunity to review war aims at Casablanca in January 1943. The two leaders planned the next fighting steps and, in secret, agreed to develop and use the atom bomb. But their most important pronouncement was public: the war would end only with the unconditional surrender of the enemy.

The slogan aimed to reassure the Russians, disappointed by the failure to launch a cross-Channel invasion, and at the same time to bolster the morale of the English and American people. But it committed the President and the Prime Minister to a rigid policy before they had seriously considered the question they were reluctant to face: what would the world be like after the peace? They thereby reduced their freedom of maneuver when, later that year, they began to discover that the Soviet Union had quite clear ideas on the shape of things to come, ideas which were by no means in accord with their own.

Joseph Stalin was interested in neither the Four Freedoms nor in self-determination. He had two precise objectives when his blunders and Hitler's dragged him into war. A decade of terror in the 1930's had given him power; he wished nothing to diminish his control of the Soviet state. At the same time, his Communist faith informed him that war was the death struggle of capitalism and that it was his duty to prepare for the international revolution that would surely follow. He gladly took the aid laboriously delivered across the Atlantic but he refused in the least to accede to any proposal that might limit his future freedom of action.

In the succession of conferences that occupied the next two years, Roosevelt caught glimmers of these intentions. But he could not confront their implications and pretended they did not exist. He induced himself to believe that the Communists were really friends and would respond to kind treatment. As a token of his own good wishes, in May, 1942, he pardoned Earl Browder, leader of the Communist party in the United States, who had been convicted of an old passport violation shortly after the Russo-German pact.

To have done otherwise, to have faced up to the danger from Stalinism, might have entailed a break in the alliance and certainly would have called for a re-examination of past policies. Above all, to deal with the ruthless antagonist who sat beside him at Teheran and Yalta, the President would have had to consider questions he had trained himself not to ask. What would governments of their own choice mean in Poland and China after the war? Would those countries be worse off under German and Japanese domination than under Russian? Did Americans have an interest in those remote parts of the world, other than peace? Moving from emergency to emergency, straining every energy to the utmost, making decisions that involved the lives of millions of men, he tried to *minimize the general Soviet problem as much as possible* in the hope that compromise would straighten it out.

His countrymen were as confused as he. Herbert Hoover was certainly aware of the aggressiveness of militant Communism in the past; but his analysis of war aims in 1943 contemplated no serious future difficulty from that source. Others went even further. Vice-President Wallace hailed the approaching *century of the common man* and asserted that Russia was as committed to freedom as the United States. Two million copies of Wendell Willkie's *One World* pointed out that the great danger to peace in the future was Western imperialism, but anticipated no serious problems from the Soviet Union, which, Stalin had assured him, sought only *the right of every nation to arrange its affairs as it wished* and the *restoration of democratic liberties. We do not need to fear Russia*, Willkie concluded. *We need to work with her.* How could the President, after two years of war, admit to himself and others that mistakes along the way would blight the fruits of victory? The necessities of survival made collaboration with the Communists necessary; the necessities of rhetoric fostered the tragic illusion of their democratic intentions.

Stalin would not compromise. At Teheran (November 28–December 1, 1943) he agreed to declare war on Japan once the fighting in Europe was over — a painless undertaking that brought him a share of the spoils with none of the risks. He would also join in the punishment of war crimes, the occupation of Germany, and in a commission to work on the details of peace. Finally, he would take a place in an international organization that would replace the League and unite the whole *family of democratic nations.*

The last phrase, which replaced the *peace-loving nations* referred to in the Atlantic Charter, was the key to the difficulty. The Soviet Union was not a democratic state; during the war it nurtured a conspiracy to subvert all the countries with which it dealt. It was an ally insofar as it fought the Germans, but it was also a rival insofar as it sponsored regimes hostile to the governments-in-exile of Poland and Yugoslavia recognized in Washington and London. In occupied Europe the Communist party apparatus never ceased to function — even in the concentration camps.

Roosevelt and Churchill came closer to reality in February, 1945, at a meeting of the heads of state in Yalta. They gained Stalin's consent to the formation of the United Nations, to plans for the occupation of Germany, and to the recognition of France as the fourth great power. They paid a heavy price for these concessions. Persuaded by their military advisers that Russian aid was critical in the Far East and assuaged by the promise of future free elections in every liberated territory, they were induced to admit to the Polish and Yugoslavian governments the very forces that would soon turn those countries into Russian puppets. Hoping against hope that the Communists would yet be won over to reasonableness, Roosevelt secretly agreed to a voting formula for the United Nations, to repatriation of fugitives from the Soviet Union, and to the concessions Stalin demanded in Mongolia, Manchuria and the Kurile Islands which ran directly counter to promises given China. The President even then could not afford to let himself or the public know that his Russian ally was not a democracy and was a potential enemy.

His successor, Harry S. Truman, was quickly disabused. At Potsdam in July, 1945, he learned that Russia intended to dominate eastern and central Europe and had no intention of conducting free elections. Yet neither he nor his countrymen were ready to act upon the implications of that discovery; certain that they had earned total victory, they proceeded rapidly to demobilize their armed forces and thus weakened their hands in future dealings with Stalin. The Soviet Union, by contrast, did not intend to follow the example of the United States in disarming. Nor in the months that followed would it make a serious effort to control nuclear power. It did not yet have the bomb; but it was unwilling to expose its own internal disorders to foreign inspection. The surrender of Hitler and Tojo had brought not peace but a cold war against another dictator.

The United Nations was ineffective in this situation. It had rested on the premise that unity of opinion among the great powers would prevent any infraction of international law. But it could not act while the Soviet Union liberally exercised the veto in the Security Council. Furthermore, neutralist sentiment divided the free world. The prominence of the Communists in some resistance movements during the war and the socialist sympathies of many Europeans generated anti-

Americanism. *Yankee go home.* That sentiment nurtured the impression that Europe could be a third force mediating between the United States and the Soviet Union, both equally culpable of breaches of the peace.

In 1947, satellite regimes were solidly entrenched in most of eastern Europe, strong Communist parties contested the control of France and Italy, and a revolution threatened to sweep through Greece to the Mediterranean. Two bold measures in May and June of that year saved western Europe. By the Truman Doctrine, the United States undertook *to support free peoples who resisted attempted subjugation by armed minorities or by outside countries.* And the Marshall Plan offered Europe almost twenty billion dollars over five years to reconstruct its economy, in the expectation that a rising level of production and improved standards of living would form an effective barrier to Communism. Two years later the North Atlantic Treaty Organization created an alliance that reached from Norway to Turkey in the effort to further the process of containment.

The Soviet Union would not participate in the Marshall Plan and refused to allow Czechoslovakia to do so. Although secrecy kept the world ignorant, behind the Iron Curtain the people were paying in terror and deprivation for the mistakes and the dogmatic ideology of their leaders. An aggressive foreign policy kept them mobilized in the effort to bring closer the day of total revolution and redemption. The Soviet Union did not want war, but its probes short of war located weak spots which it exploited by subversion. The United States, on which fell the chief burden of the free world's protection, could only respond with defensive measures in the hope of gaining time.

Berlin, left as a four-power enclave in the midst of the Russian occupation, was one such weak spot; China, weakened by decades of war and inefficiently ruled, was another. An airlift in June, 1948, saved Berlin but led to the permanent division of East and West Germany. China fell to the Communists in 1949; and the next year satellite forces crossed the line that divided North from South Korea. Russian efforts to paralyze the United Nations by absence from the Security Council enabled the United States to enlist the support of the world body in resistance to the aggression. On the other hand, the Chinese moved massive forces down from the north in support of their Red allies and the costly three-year war ended in stalemate.

Stalemate was to be the whole story of the 1950's. The Russians had exploded their own atom bombs in 1949 and thereafter moved to build an arsenal of nuclear weapons and the rockets with which to deliver them. By the end of the decade the U.S.S.R., like the United States, had the power to wreak frightful disaster upon its enemy. The balance of terror injected an ominous factor into the maneuverings for position.

The United States gained the advantage in Europe where men could compare its social system with that of the Soviet Union. The reconstruction of the economy of the Continent ended the threat of subversion and reduced the force of neutralism. Meanwhile, the failures of the Soviet productive system led to discontent in the satellites, revolution in Hungary, and disquiet everywhere behind the Iron Curtain.

Outside Europe, the situation was different. Peoples who had suffered under colonialism directed their grievances mainly against their former rulers — England, France, Holland, Belgium and Portugal, all American allies. To aspiring nationalists Communism offered a vision of liberation and, in addition, a model for rapid economic development. Though the meager achievements and aggressions of Red China somewhat tarnished that image, there was no increase in friendship for the United States, which was identified with the past racial crimes of the white man in the colored world.

The result was a steady contraction of Western influence. The Chinese, having been repulsed in Korea, directed their attention southward. Turned back in Malaya, they moved into Indochina, where they ousted the French and entrenched themselves in North Viet Nam. Meanwhile, Indonesia, Laos, Burma, India and Ceylon acquired independence; and, although they stood off the Communists, they adopted a neutralist posture that made them unwilling to take any steps to halt aggression or to develop an order of law that might stabilize international relations.

Western influence in the Near East also began to crumble. Revolutions in Egypt and Iraq brought to power young army officers imbued with nationalist ideas. Within the next few years the ouster of the French from North Africa put similar regimes in control of Tunisia,

Morocco and Algeria. All regarded the United States with suspicion and ascribed to it Israeli independence, which they bitterly resented. Not even the peace-making role of the Americans in the Suez crisis of 1956 mitigated that distrust. The neutralist double standard emerged with painful clarity in the course of that incident. England and France were condemned for their attack upon Egypt but the uncommitted countries winked at the Russian assault upon the legally constituted Hungarian government. Yet by 1962 the new nations of Africa south of the Sahara had added weight to neutralism in the United Nations; and Cuba had become a center of Communist influence in the New World.

The American response was primarily defensive. Collective security agreements in the Near and Far East and in Latin America offered some chance of resisting open aggression, but were ineffective against the more insidious processes of internal subversion. Containment, in the sense it had been conceived in 1947, could not prevent hungry peasants from following demagogues, adventurers and dupes into the enemy camp. Only bread and hope could give men a stake in order, endow them with the will to resist Communism, and establish the basis for a peaceful future. The miracles of reconstruction in western Europe and in Japan encouraged the expectation that economic development might rescue other parts of the world as well.

President Truman's Point Four Program began a prodigious outpouring of assistance that reached every part of the world outside the Soviet Union and its more abject satellites. By 1962, expenditures, apart from those in western Europe, had mounted to some forty billion dollars, far outdistancing Russian efforts. Not all these sums were well spent; a good deal was diverted into wasteful armaments or into the pockets of corrupt local politicians. But this was the only available means of creating swiftly an attractive alternative to Communism.

Even so, there was the possibility that there might not be time enough, that impatience or error might trigger the disaster all dreaded. There was no assurance that aid in any amount would itself overcome the impoverishing effects of rising populations, rigid traditionalism, lack of skills and tribal divisions that held back the underdeveloped countries. Nor was there any assurance that the Soviet Union would gracefully accept defeat in peaceful competition, that it might not be tempted to take by force what it could not get by coexistence. But that was a situation within which Americans learned to live early in the 1960's.

Before 1939, they had been aware of the disorders that afflicted nations beyond the oceans; but most Americans had hoped that the United States would somehow remain immune. When war came at Pearl Harbor, they made the sacrifices required. But they did not realize until after the peace that their own future safety required them to take part in the active redemption of the whole world. And few looked back for a model to a period in their own history, a century earlier, when the New World had been charged with faith in its mission to bring freedom to mankind.

The dawning apprehension of the danger suspended about them, if it did not drive them to the extreme of denying reality altogether, persuaded Americans that it was at least time to take stock. The efforts in 1960 and 1961 of various governmental and private groups to define national goals or national purpose revealed a widespread concern with the future of the Republic. What did the people wish their country to be? That question, which once hardly needed asking, now had no clear answer. And the Presidents of the 1950's and 1960's still did not speak frankly, but alternated between the belligerent rhetoric of election campaigns and bland assurances that all was well.

27

New Conditions of Group Life, 1939–1962

AT HOME, the war made the impossible possible. The immediate job at hand was so pressing, no distractions could divert men from it. The targets were set — so many planes, ships and tanks — they had to be built, and they were. The productive system, lethargic for more than a decade, moved with new vigor and acquired a momentum that carried it along well after the peace. Its tremendous expansion in the 1940's and 1950's profoundly influenced the conditions of American life.

The economists no longer spoke of national wealth or income, but used a more precise measure, Gross National Product, the total output of goods and services. That index rose consistently between 1939 and 1962 — from about 200 to well over 500 billion dollars (of constant value) despite occasional setbacks in intervals of recession. All the other indicators of growth — numbers of jobs, personal income, and the sheer volume of commodities produced — showed the same general upward trend.

The forced draft of war did not in itself account for the economic revival. The emergency touched off a dramatic reorganization of industry, the effects of which persisted through the next decade. The needs of the armed forces made questions of cost secondary and required careful, orderly planning. The navy could not shop around for carriers or bombers; it had to collaborate with manufacturers on mutually acceptable terms. There was not enough steel or rubber to go around; only the allocation of priorities prevented the services from competing with one another and with civilian users. Price, wage and manpower controls during the war tightened up the processes of production and established precedents for future intervention by government in the national interest. This experience, while businessmen held the chief administrative posts, revealed that intelligent direction was compatible with competitive free enterprise and indeed improved the effectiveness of its performance.

The war also stimulated technological change. The auto makers, for instance, helped the aircraft manufacturers convert to a mass-production basis. Persistent shortages of manpower and the mounting backlog of orders encouraged entrepreneurs to expand and modernize their plants. After 1945, automation further modernized existing facilities. As a result, the output per man-hour almost doubled, and agricultural and industrial capacity both expanded enormously.

Growth in the decades after 1939 was free of some of the earlier extreme speculative disorders. The New Deal banking and security reforms showed their worth; the government, through changes in tax and interest rates, moderated the swings between inflation and deflation, prosperity and depression. In any case investment patterns were more balanced than in the past. Large philanthropic institutions and mutual funds held great blocks of stock which they generally managed so as to avoid sharp fluctuations. The increase in the total number of shareholders was also a stabilizing influence. Speculators still roamed the exchanges and gamblers still gained or lost, but their activities were less likely than formerly to damage the whole economy.

There was no shortage of capital. Directly or indirectly, the government underwrote a good deal of expansion. During the war, its orders and its financial assistance sustained the increases in capacity. They continued to do so thereafter. Military needs did not end with peace in 1945; Korea, nuclear development, and space kept federal agencies in the market as purchasers. Meanwhile, aid to housing and road-building programs strengthened important industries. Through the whole period a gradual inflation, never so steep as to undermine confidence, was perceptible enough to encourage risk-taking by the anticipation of rising prices.

Growth made room for new branches of manufacturing in new areas. Petrochemicals and electronics spread phenomenally around the Gulf of Mexico, in the upper South and on the Pacific coast. The former made available a multitude of new synthetic materials, the latter sparked a revolution in communications, data processing and automation.

An effective and flexible, if costly, distributing system carried the products of the fields and the factories to all parts of the country. Plane, auto and truck traffic rose rapidly, stimulated by extensive airport and highway development supported by government. The new forms of transportation had an inestimable advantage in the ability to shift part of their charges from the users to the taxpayers. Their competition seriously damaged the railroads, which were also weakened by unimaginative management, an unco-operative labor force, and a heavy burden of debt.

The increased speed of communications encouraged the appearance of a complex of sub-plants. All the processes of manufacturing did not have to be carried on under the same roof or in the same town. They could be dispersed in numerous fabricating and assembly plants. While mergers and combinations continued at the top in the interest of capital management and planning controls, production itself was often more dispersed than formerly.

The distributive system also carried goods more swiftly to consumers. Self-service food supermarkets had appeared just before the war; they expanded rapidly in the 1940's and 1950's. Discount houses extended the same techniques to other commodities. Mass distribution lowered the margin between costs and sales prices, permitted retailers to operate with smaller inventories, and reduced charges for overhead and credit. Installment buying was expensive, but the cost to the consumer was not greater than when the corner grocer or country storekeeper sold by the book and made his own reckoning of accounts. On the whole, Americans got more for their money than ever before.

They also had more money to spend.

All wages rose steadily, though not spectacularly, during the war; after 1946, with the end of controls, they bounded upward. As significant as the general average was the steady decline in the number of unskilled employees through the effects of automation, technological improvement, and the diffusion of education. Their percentage in the manufacturing labor force fell by almost one-half in the two decades. By contrast, the size of the white-collar and technician contingent increased rapidly. In addition, many families enjoyed the income of more than one wage-earner.

The result was unprecedented material well-being. The farmers, a dwindling proportion of the population, faced essentially the same problem as in the past — the tendency of production to outrun demand and the lack of controls to maintain a balance. But the political power of the rural states and the sentimental assumption that there was some unique value to agricultural life induced the government to support even the marginal farmers. The rest of the economy was rich enough to afford the continued subsidies.

Pockets of poverty survived in the rural South and in the great cities where men were either unwilling or unable to keep pace with change. Some poor whites, fiercely conservative in habits, fundamentalist in religion, and resentful of strangers, would neither emigrate nor improve themselves by education and remained in a mire until outsiders brought in the factory. In the cities, discrimination and poverty often prevented Negroes, Puerto Ricans and Mexicans from acquiring the training to take the new jobs; and these minorities remained mostly in the unskilled labor force. Often unemployed, they formed a pool of migratory agricultural hands or sought odd jobs in the urban slums. Their condition was by no means as desperate as that of immigrants in the 1890's. The government at least bore the responsibility for relief. But there remained a somber contrast between their destitution and the affluence of others.

Resentment toward wealth declined as many more Americans shared it and as the owners of great fortunes learned their responsibilities. The millionaires could spend lavishly, but so could the salesman on an expense account. The disappearance of the pretensions of *Society*; the graduated tax on high incomes; and the increasing involvement of the rich in philanthropic, political, cultural and social activities brought the day of the muckraker to a close. Indeed, Americans tended to assume that they were closer to economic equality than they actually were.

They had by no means solved all the problems of an industrial economy. The involvement with government created opportunities for influence-peddlers who knew their way through the intricacies of the bureaucracy and whose freezers, rugs and genial entertainment brought access to favors. The small entrepreneur had a hazardous time of it, squeezed as he was by great competitors. It was not clear in 1962 whether the research and development programs of the mammoth corporations offset the possible loss in innovation his restricted role entailed. There were questions, also, of whether the rate of growth was rapid enough while many plants used only part of their capacities, or of whether productive energies were best deployed as they were or could be deflected to socially more useful ends. Grave as these considerations were, they did not offset the achievements of this period. The economy had shown a renewed ability to expand despite the disappearance of the frontier and of the transatlantic movement of people and capital which had sparked development before 1929.

Underlying the rapid expansion of the economy was a surprising reversal in population trends. No proposition had been more firmly fixed in the thinking of social scientists in the 1930's than that the birth rate would decline, that population would soon level off and would perhaps even fall within the forseeable future. The number of residents in the United States grew by only seven per cent in that decade, the lowest in history, and confirmed the demographers' prediction.

The forecast was totally incorrect. The census of 1950 counted 151,000,000 persons, an increase of fourteen per cent in ten years, that of 1960 showed 179,000,000, an increase of eighteen per cent. And the rise showed every sign of continuing; projections anticipated a total of 210,000,000 in 1970.

Immigration contributed only slightly to the new tendency. Sympathy with the plight of the European refugees opened a thin crack in the country's closed gates after the war. There was also some movement from Mexico and Canada; and 200,000 Cuban exiles fled from the Castro regime after 1958. But the total of new entries in the two decades after 1940 was not much more than 3,000,000. Migration was primarily within the national boundaries.

The chief cause of growth was a change in the native birth rate.

After declining steadily for decades, it suddenly began to move upward during the war and continued to do so until 1960. Despite the ease, accessibility and efficiency of birth control methods, the number of children in each household mounted steadily. Young people married at an earlier age than before 1940 and they planned to bear offspring sooner and more frequently. The altered attitude increased the consumers of shoes, toys and baby clothes; it also profoundly affected important features of American social organization.

During the war, Pfc. John Behm, stationed in England, had tried his hand at poetry in *Yank*, the soldiers' newspaper:

> *We are bewildered and weary,*
> *Lonely to the point of madness,*
> *And if we shout and curse*
> *Through our quiet dreams,*
> *Forgive us.*
> *We are merely looking for a way to go home.*

He expressed a mood which had quietly spread among his contemporaries. They were all looking for a way to go home.

Raised by parents committed to individualism, they had passed through adolescence during the Depression, torn between the need for security and the desire to be free personalities. They had pitifully few roots, external props or even illusions. The war, they knew, would bring not only separation but obliteration. Everything would be finished, including their own precious individuality. And this time there was neither rebellion nor innocent enthusiasm — blue-eyed blondes kissing the volunteers — but rather the quiet acceptance of an obligation by men who had seen *All Quiet on the Western Front* and knew they were off for no big parade.

They did not wish the best years of their lives — for some the last years — to slip away while they reached for the elusive butterfly of romantic love. Before they went away, and after they came back, they wanted to be sure that some part of them would remain alive, seed immortal, kicking in the belly, running in the sun, surrogate triumphant in the father's empty space.

And after the war came Korea and the permanent draft and in every morning's newspaper some reminder of the world's dreadful vulnerability that increased the longing for an anchor in posterity. At the very same time, prosperity put security within the reach of all. The youngsters who pushed into parenthood did not think they were surrendering their individuality, but guaranteeing it.

The early marriage became usual. Boys and girls *went steady* in high school and many slipped into domesticity soon after. Continued education was no obstacle. The returning veterans brought the baby carriage to college; indulgently supported student couples kept it there. Later there would be jobs of a sort for all. Those who never finished high school or did not go beyond it were as ready for unskilled jobs and for the responsibility of a family as they ever would be.

There were mistakes. Hastily arranged unions frequently ended in separations and led to a rising divorce rate. Adolescents encouraged to *express themselves* did not automatically assume adulthood with the bestowal of the ring. But the norm was durably fixed.

Personal fulfillment remained the heart's desire of this generation. But the focus of its attention shifted from the striving for individual achievement to concern for the child. There had been enough of loneliness, of the sacrifice of all extraneous considerations to the demands of the *One*. Security was the value postwar youth cherished; the needs of their personalities were best satisfied in *Togetherness*. The intimacy of shared relationships compensated for the inability to manage the great affairs of society and gave assurance of continuity in an otherwise uncertain world. The young couple, wheeling the cart through the shopping center while the future toddled along, turned away from the insoluble questions and concentrated on those Dr. Spock could answer.

Employment bound these families to the metropolis. The farm and the small town continued to lose ground; the jobs worth having, and the opportunities for professional practice and entrepreneurship, were in the offices and plants that clustered around the city. But the great brick buildings and the paved streets were not an appropriate setting for life. The low level of construction in the 1930's had left a shortage of space, and rents were high despite controls. Limited budgets drove the young marrieds into marginal areas, close to the slums and the dangers of contact with Negroes, Mexicans and Puerto Ricans. Latent prejudices against these strangers and the fear of violence and dirt made the city undesirable; a stable household could not thrive in the disorder of the three-room apartment, the walk-up building and the crowded street.

The concern became urgent when the babies grew up. Where would they play, and with whom? At what school would they acquire the manners and skills to move on to a good college and a good job? Not in the promiscuous urban neighborhood where one was lost among thousands and outsiders could not know who was whose child.

They fled to the suburb. The automobile and the new highway systems made the move possible and government policy encouraged it. Loans were available to veterans for the purchase of little houses, but the low-rental projects in the city were only for the relief of the poor. Roads that led away from the center enjoyed lavish support, while public transportation, dependent upon inadequate fares, decayed. There was a clear advantage to getting out of town. Of the nation's great cities, only Los Angeles and Houston grew between 1950 and 1960, and they mostly in the outlying districts.

The postwar suburbs differed significantly from their predecessors. The sprawl of little communities across the countryside was on a much vaster scale than ever before and it involved a different type of person. The commuter of the 1880's or the 1920's had been born on a farm or in a small town and had brought to the city memories of rural life which he wished to recapture. The new residents of Levittown or Crestview had no such model from their own experience. The urban influences they sought to escape were the only ones they knew. They could draw on no fitting recollections of their own when they came to choose a dwelling or fill it with activity. Their only models were the tinsel images of the mass media. They had to learn from TV and the slick magazines how a proper home should look and how its occupants should behave. They also had to give content to social forms. A host of co-operative organizations and societies increasingly occupied their time; the PTA, the Red Cross, the March of Dimes, the Community Fund and the League of Women Voters were opportunities to participate in communal life.

The pressure of complying with these demands often left men and women *tied in knots and very depressed. Today's housewife does not know what is expected of her,* wrote one of them. *She sees the perfect mother portrayed on television. This only adds to her frustrations. The strange part of this is, I have had many people wonder how I ac-*

complish so much. They say how clever I am, yet many of these things I did not want to do. I did them because I thought that was what a perfect wife and mother did.

The task of integrating one man's family into a larger unity also remained difficult even in the suburb, because these people were still mobile; they moved from job to job and traded in their houses almost as frequently as their cars.

Therefore, they desired enough uniformity of background with their neighbors to provide them and their children with continuity in the jumps from the suburbs of Baltimore and New York to those of Dallas and Seattle. Tokens of ethnic and religious identity that a previous generation had often discarded now acquired unexpected value. Diligently, behind the picture windows, they labored to give authenticity to recovered rituals and earnestly tried to persuade themselves and their offspring that all would be as they wished it had always been.

They were only partially successful. The docile youngsters did their homework, tried to rank high in class and only rarely let themselves wonder why they were striving. Others, refusing to be simply the means of fulfilling their parents' needs, rebelled. Juvenile delinquency was a problem in Greenwich, Connecticut, as in Greenwich Village, New York, although in a different form. At night the cars raced along the highways or lined up at the drive-in, while the boys and girls sought each other out. The adults themselves often turned away from the television still hungry for the peace of mind all desired.

In the cities, poverty made the lack more visible. Around the periphery, the older people lingered in the gray area they were too tired to abandon. They stayed by the old parish and the old neighborhood, to which their sons and daughters returned for occasional visits. But houses and services deteriorated, awaiting in resignation inundation from the onspreading slums.

The central districts long were unredeemed wildernesses where the poorest and strangest found a home. Like their immigrant predecessors, their problems were primarily those of inadequate income and space. But the residents of Maxwell Street in 1960 lacked stable communities or families and in addition usually suffered from the disabilities of color. Crime, violence, delinquency and vice had never been absent from these places; the spreading use of narcotics and the images of brutality conveyed by the tabloid and TV now made the impact more intense. Great public housing projects supplied some of these people with improved amenities but neither added to the total available space nor furthered the reconstruction of communal life. The effect of more comprehensive schemes for urban renewal was still not clear in 1962.

The affluence of the economy affected the suburbanite and the slum-dweller differently. Prosperity enabled one to get away; poverty compelled the other to remain. But they shared the inability to see themselves in any meaningful relationship to the whole society. Each thought primarily of the security of his own household. The one desperately protected his ranch-type stronghold; the other bitterly resented exclusion. Those conditions set the terms of the encounters among the variety of Americans who met one another in the postwar world.

The war dissolved some of the hatreds that had formerly divided group from group in the United States. In 1960 a Roman Catholic became President and a majority of his countrymen in public opinion polls said they would accept a Jew in the highest office in the land. People who bore Italian or Polish names were no longer counted inferior; and even the Japanese emerged from the internment to which a stupid blunder had consigned them in 1942 without difficulty or resentment. There was no revival of the xenophobia or prejudice of the years after 1918. Instead, discriminatory barriers in education, housing, employment and social accommodations rapidly collapsed.

Racism as a consistent philosophy with respectable scientific support disappeared. The work of the social scientists in the 1930's and 1940's showed that the cultural or genetic differences among various groups of humans did not divide mankind into distinct and separate species. The war hastened the acceptance of these ideas. Americans of all sorts learned in fighting together that they shared the same strengths and weaknesses, the same fears and emotions; and they recoiled as one from the revelations in the Nazi extermination camps of the logical corollary of the doctrine of Aryan supremacy.

Since 1928, moreover, the minorities had taken an increasingly prominent role in politics. Al Smith's campaign and the New Deal had taught them to expect the government to intervene on their behalf; and, after twenty years, they had power enough to demand and secure aid in their quest for equality. Twenty states and many municipalities by law forbade discrimination in employment, housing, and education. The mere enactment of a statute was not enough to secure compliance, of course, but even without stringent measures of enforcement it established a standard of proper action which people learned to accept. It was easier to do so while prosperity and secure family life eased the strain of competition. But more important, the growing understanding of their own national character induced Americans to value the plurality of their society.

The Negroes shared some of these advances; fair employment practices acts helped them too and they too gained by the general growth of tolerance. But color made them more visible than religion made the Jews, or national origins, the Irish; and blackness was still a sign of the shame of slavery. Furthermore, the Negro had farther to go than other minorities; decades of degradation had left him ill prepared to cope with the problems of twentieth-century life. The lowest place in the economy did not yield the income with which to live decently or educate children or assert the right to vote; and the lack of political influence, training or capital prevented the rise to a better job. As a result he sometimes diverted his energies to inessentials, failed to exploit opportunities as they developed, and suffered from poor leadership. Nevertheless he too was to struggle for his rights and with some, although not complete, success.

The black corporal who could not be served in the railroad station while German prisoners of war lolled at their ease in the dining room emerged from the war determined to claim his heritage as an American. *Why are we pushed around like cattle? If we are fighting for the same thing, if we are to die for our country, then why does the government allow such things to go on?* He would be as full a man in civilian clothes as in battle.

The independence of the new African nations in the 1950's imbued the Negro with pride. Nigerians sat as equals with whites; colored Americans could do the same. The mounting consciousness of Africa also reminded many Americans of Wendell Willkie's warning in *One World* that peace depended upon extending the idea of freedom to cover all men of whatever color. The United States had to distinguish itself from the Boers, and cast out the residues of prejudice and *apartheid* or suffer irreparable damage in an important part of the world. The diplomats denied service on Route 40 in Maryland or barred from hotels in Knoxville and Salt Lake City were likely to carry away resentments that outweighed the millions in aid granted their countries.

Above all, the Negro appealed to a creed to which almost all Americans adhered — the faith, imbedded in their past, in equality of opportunity, individual dignity and personal rights. In response to the obligations of that faith, millions of white men and women learned to conquer inherited prejudices, to break through old customs and habits and to make room for the disadvantaged among them. Only a minority of Southerners, as in Oxford, Mississippi, or Little Rock, Arkansas, bitterly resisted because they were themselves unprepared for the life of their times. The tragedy was that inadequacies in the social and political system of some states gave control to those who could display their own superiority only through the oppression of others.

The first steps toward equality met little opposition. There was no protest when an executive order desegregated the armed forces; and black men and white served together in Korea with no difficulty. The President's Commission on Civil Rights in 1947 drew up an agenda for resumption of the task of liberation suspended eighty years earlier; and the inability of the Dixiecrats to exert the slightest influence upon the Presidential election the next year offered hope that progress might come peacefully. The National Association for the Advancement of Colored People and other agencies embarked on a campaign of political and legal action to break through the vicious circle of discrimination that held the Negro down.

The crucial bastion of segregation was the doctrine of *separate but equal* set forth in the case of *Plessy* v. *Ferguson* (1890). Under cover of that decision, the Southern states had been able to set the Negro apart as an inferior, not fit to share a seat on the train, a table in the restaurant or a desk in the school with the white.

Since the 1920's, however, the Supreme Court had been exploring the implications of the Fourteenth Amendment's guarantees of liberty; and it had already modified some features of segregation when it reviewed the whole issue in 1954. By a unanimous ruling it held that the Jim Crow system did in fact produce inequality and deprived Negroes of their legal rights. It directed the offending states, with all deliberate speed, to integrate their schools. There were no immediate indications of more than token resistance to orderly compliance.

A few large cities in the border states at once gave way and admitted colored and white children to the same schools. Elsewhere the progress was slow. Year by year the issue arose at the start of each term and slowly the number of desegregated places increased.

Lethargy and the unwillingness of the nation's leaders to take a firm stand unnecessarily prolonged the process. Once the judges had spoken, most whites were content to let matters take their course until some spectacular outbreak attracted attention to the latest trouble spot. And the politicians, courting Southern votes, closed their eyes to the problem until it crept up on them in an inescapable crisis. In the campaign of 1956 both Presidential candidates studiously evaded the issue; and after the election President Eisenhower refrained from any expression of opinion beyond the wish that the law be observed. Only after repeated turnings of his cheek, in the face of Governor Orval Faubus's obstinate disobedience, did the Chief Executive act to sustain the courts; and it was several years more before the schools of Arkansas were on the way to desegregation.

The delay offered demagogues an opportunity to make themselves heard. John Kasper thus descended upon Clinton, Tennessee, in search of trouble and White Citizens Councils sprang up in some parts of the South to organize defiance. However loud the sound and fury from these sources, determined local authorities could, if they wished, control the disturbances.

Increasingly, Negroes wondered whether the will was there. Others cried patience, patience; but time was running short for moderation. Set against the hope that the intransigent racist minority would some day see the light was the immediate reality; while others moved ahead rapidly, the colored man fell behind by standing still. Without education, without access to opportunity, he sank hopelessly into that pool of excess unskilled labor the economy no longer required. Each recession in the 1950's left larger numbers unemployed in Detroit, Cleveland, New York and Los Angeles and narrowed the hopes of escape from Georgia, Alabama and Mississippi. To wait indefinitely was to forfeit a share in American life.

A small, but significant, number of colored men gave up. They turned against the deceptions of Christianity and rejected the false god of whiteness. They read nothing but cruelty and betrayal in the record of Africa's contact with Europe and America and wished to have no more of associations that they thought brought them only hardship and degradation. They looked to Islam for an alternative and, taking up Marcus Garvey's old standard, asked for separateness rather than integration. Every defeat in the struggle for equality added to the Black Muslim membership.

Most Negroes clung to the old expectations, however. They too no longer worshiped at the shrine of whiteness. They were *glad to be black* and took pride in an identity they had no wish to conceal. They also knew that they were Americans, not Africans, and that they would serve themselves best within the whole society rather than cut apart from it. But they wanted prompt action to remove the restraints that kept them inferior.

The comic colloquy between President Eisenhower and Governor Faubus injected new militancy into the movement for civil rights by persuading many Americans that good will was not enough. Action was needed. Young Negro leaders emerged, some of them ministers like Martin Luther King, others dentists, lawyers, students. Imbued with faith in their country and convinced of the righteousness of their cause, they would settle for nothing less than their due — absolute equality of rights and opportunities, North and South. Their campaign attracted widespread sympathy.

The chosen weapon was non-violent protest. Ordinances enacted by local governments in violation of the Constitution did not deserve to be obeyed. Recourse to the federal courts led, by a long, costly road, to years of litigation and to further evasion by officials who had no respect for the judicial process. The militants therefore made a direct appeal to the conscience of the country. The method had its first extended trial in a boycott of segregated buses in Montgomery, Alabama; the Committee on Racial Equality adopted it as an instrument; and lunch-counter sit-ins, pray-ins, and freedom rides applied it widely. It called for the courage not to strike back and the willingness to suffer the brutality of depraved jailers. But by 1962, non-violence and the simultaneous pursuit of remedies at law had begun to work.

In the North, there was no dispute over principles but rather an uneasy exploration of the implications of full integration. Desegregation worked no miracles; schools in the colored neighborhoods of New York and Chicago remained colored even without the intercession of the law. Indeed it required positive action on the part of the government to compensate for the inequalities that retarded the Negroes. Often immediate results were disappointing, and the suburbanite, looking out of the window as his train pulled past the chaos of 125th Street on the way to Westchester, took comfort in his own distance from the source of contagion. Yet the situation improved steadily if not spectacularly; and above all there was hope.

The border states and the larger Southern cities grudgingly acquiesced in a start toward desegregation. Enough responsible men were aware of the costs of the old order to wish to alter it. Industrialization and a rising standard of living, which were the region's only mode of progress, could not proceed with part of the population permanently depressed and with the society forever divided against itself. Conditions in 1962 were far from equal anywhere below Washington, D.C., but the principle was established and a start made in the process, that threatened still to be painful, of discarding the habits and prejudices of slavery for those of freedom.

There remained the surly resentment of the rural deep South. In Louisiana, a hysterical woman brandished the Bible at the Archbishop responsible for her excommunication; in Georgia night riders burned down the church where Negroes had been urged to vote; in Alabama the Freedom Riders' bus went up in flames; and in Ole Miss a tight-lipped governor said No, No to every hint of change in God's own plan of segregation. For decades these areas had stood lowest in the Union in income, wealth, education and literacy. Theirs were the smallest proportions of eligible persons to vote. Theirs was a political system that subjected the growing cities to a decaying countryside. And there, the stubborn men rejected the progress that would uncover their guilty sin and, though they destroyed themselves and their world in doing so, resisted to the end what was bound to come. The only question was, how much damage the rest of the country would let them do.

The forces they hated were beyond their control. There was no room for slaves in the American economy that emerged from the Second World War. The abundance it was capable of yielding could not be withheld from some to satisfy the prejudice of a few. The Negro too had a claim to split-level security without which he would remain forever alien, a constant source of irritation from which no suburb could isolate itself.

28

Men in Space

AGAIN AND AGAIN, in the 1950's the government was slow to move; and when at last it acted, did so hesitantly and with qualifications. Its immense power remained potential, largely unused.

The questions were pressing. When was a tax cut or budget deficit necessary? Was it desirable to subsidize highways and air transportation at the expense of the railroads? By what standards should regulatory commissions fix rates or award franchises? What were the criteria for fair wages or prices? The economist pointed out the consequences of one choice or another. But he could not supply the answers; that was the task of those who made political decisions. Yet in these matters, as in implementation of the Supreme Court's ruling on desegregation, the machinery operated ineffectively.

The states and municipalities were no more adept in the use of power through established processes than the nation. Conflicting interests often produced a deadlock and made it necessary to entrust long-range planning or large projects outside the ordinary routine to extra-political individuals or agencies; things got done only in bypassing the usual procedures. Authorities and public corporations to build bridges or turnpikes antedated the war; but their spread was evidence of a growing lack of faith in politics.

The contrast with the earlier period was striking. The New Deal, the culmination of progressivism, had raised to a peak the confidence in the ability of government to apply intelligence to human affairs. After 1939, the best leaders often seemed incapable of arriving at decisions and the most exciting elections settled nothing. What was the use?

The Presidents and governors lost the capacity to establish policies that commanded assent. Often the executives were competent men with patronage and popular influence at their disposal. But they had their way only at the cost of laborious compromises. Congress and the legislatures, stiffened by routine and by rigid institutional forms, became strongholds of local interests capable of resisting any broad pressures. Some states had not redistricted for half a century, and their lawmakers did not represent the population as it actually was. In the Senate and the House, seniority, the cumbersome committee system and the right to filibuster gave strategic minorities permanent power of obstruction. The stubbornness of a single gentleman from Alabama or Arizona could delay indefinitely measures that seemed vital to a great majority. Lacking the votes to defeat proposals of which they disapproved, such men could maneuver a measure to death or stifle it by crippling compromise.

An informal alliance of rural elements dominated the Congress. The entente had already shown its power against Roosevelt in 1937; it emerged into the open in an effort to cut Truman down to size and in 1962 still held sway. Northern Republicans, for the most part hostile to any further *welfare* legislation, and Southern Democrats fearful of civil rights joined in a mutual assistance pact that kept the Presidents on the defensive. Since most of these legislators spoke for constituencies that did not change, they enjoyed uninterrupted tenure and retained control of the decisive committees, whichever party was in power. Elections, therefore, ceased to be means of resolving disputes. No choice the voters made could loosen the grip of the alliance on the legislative machinery. Only redistricting offered a hope of doing so.

The President was more representative, since the electoral college more accurately reflected the whole population than did the Congress.

But after 1936, his election also ceased to test issues or policies. Everyone knew that Roosevelt, Truman, Stevenson and Kennedy were Democrats, that Willkie, Dewey, Eisenhower and Nixon were Republicans. But the minor variations in their platforms and campaign rhetoric did not convince many Americans that the choice of one candidate rather than another would fundamentally change foreign or domestic policy. On the genuine issues of isolation, foreign aid, intervention in Cuba, deficit spending, civil rights, or aid to education, the voter almost never faced a decision between opposing points of view.

The crucial battles occurred in the nominating conventions in which the electorate were only observers. The dynamic force in those gatherings was the desire to blur rather than to define differences. Candidates — from Taft to Goldwater, from Wallace to Russell, Harriman and Humphrey — who were identified with a distinctive position were dangerous. They were certain to lose some votes. The party managers preferred a moderate nominee who could attract support from every sector of the population. Sensitivity to public opinion polls and the mechanics of the convention tended to soften differences that would, however, re-emerge after the campaign. Against the forces entrenched on Capitol Hill, therefore, the President enjoyed neither a positive mandate from his own election, nor a strong party organization committed to the line he established as leader.

The progressive movement which had vitalized politics after 1900 was in no position to do so once more. Roosevelt's personal strength and his long tenure of office had overshadowed every other potential leader of the forces that supported him. There was no apparent successor at his death. The old New Dealers seriously underrated Harry S. Truman, vainly searched for an alternative in 1948, and then halfheartedly accepted him. Meanwhile Henry A. Wallace borrowed the Progressive label in his race as an independent that year; and his fervent protestations of friendship for the Soviet Union confused matters further.

The issue of Communism was unsettling because progressives became scapegoats for a wartime collaboration in which the whole country had participated. The Party members or fellow travelers had never played a significant role in the Roosevelt administrations, but the former New Dealers were slow to define their attitude toward Red conspiracy. The old assumption that there were always two positions in politics had nurtured the impression that Communists were only more extreme liberals. Everyone who was against Hitler and Franco and for social security and the Scottsboro boys seemed on the same side. Furthermore, many well-intentioned believers in civil liberties leaped instinctively to the defense of Alger Hiss when he was accused of handing secret information to the Russians; and the unfolding of that case against the background of the Wallace campaign nurtured a misleading popular suspicion of progressivism.

In time, the domestic Red issue faded. But in the 1950's efforts to frame a renewed progressive program failed. The New Deal battles had mostly been won; much of the population was content with its material well-being; and intellectuals raised in the belief that economic considerations were primary could not readily envision attractive new goals. Local reform problems created pockets of strength in various parts of the country where liberals won occasional skirmishes, but they could not mobilize a national campaign or assert themselves effectively in Congress.

Labor and ethnic minorities still attached their loyalties to progressivism, but not as firmly as earlier. The sons and daughters of those who had gained in security and equality under the New Deal retained sentimental memories of F.D.R.; and when nothing else intervened the auto workers, sharecroppers, Jews, Poles and Negroes and their children voted for the Democratic party. But other considerations did intervene. Such people had themselves risen in status; they lived in suburbs or aspired to do so; and reform seemed safely locked away in the past. Middle-income concerns were primary for many — taxes were too high and there was too much inflation; their children deserved better schools; and Communism should be rolled back, although without war and without too much expense. The slogans and the militancy of the New Deal were not particularly relevant to these matters. The Negroes' grievances more sharply defined their demands. But in 1962 neither they nor the others had formulated a political program to replace that of the 1930's.

To a somewhat lesser extent the same deficiency reduced the political effectiveness of the organized labor movement. The leaders gave serious thought to the effects of automation, to the future work week, and to the necessity of cleansing their own houses of corruption, of gangsterism and of Jim Crow practices. But they could not mold a consistent set of policies that attracted widespread support or controlled the votes of their members. The CIO learned the limits of its strength when it failed to defeat Senator Robert A. Taft's bid for re-election in Ohio in 1950. Meanwhile increasing prosperity and the decline in the number of unskilled gave union members the tastes and interests of other middle-income people and further limited the political effectiveness of the unions.

The millions in their voting booths lacked dependable guides by which to orient themselves. A growing number referred to themselves as *independent*; no party or program claimed their allegiance. The machines lost steadily in influence in the face of the willingness to split tickets and of the inclination of many Americans to make their own patterns on the ballot. The citizens listened to various reasons for one choice or another; but the alternatives were never clear-cut and everyone knew how little faith to put in campaign promises.

The man alone before the long list, if he did not simply make his X or pull his lever out of habit, anxiously sought a name known to him. At some point in the campaign he had decided this was a personality he could trust. He acted not as the disciplined member of a group, nor on the basis of a confrontation of issues, but in response to the familiar appeal of the candidate as a man. He knew the Presidents and the governors and the military heroes from TV and the newspaper, where they put on a show for him. Or he had actually seen the nominees, or shaken a hand. He made his choice almost instinctively, almost unpredictably, in response to gestures that evoked his personal confidence. In the absence of any more direct sense of involvement, political apathy spread. The total vote rose, although not in proportion to the rise in the numbers eligible. People cast their ballots as a token of good citizenship rather than as an instrument by which they seriously expected to alter their own lives.

The extent of disillusion was accurately revealed in the reception of *Advise and Consent*, Allen Drury's best-selling novel, later adapted into a play and a movie. Earlier fictional treatments of the Washington scene — *Of Thee I Sing* or *Mr. Smith Goes to Washington* or Henry Adams's *Democracy* — had joked about the foibles of statesmen, or had expressed faith in or doubts about the effectiveness of popular government. But they had taken politics seriously. *Advise and Consent* made politics the background for personal melodrama; in it the most critical national decision — the relations of the United States with the Soviet Union — turned on the accusation of homosexuality directed against a senator. That millions of Americans found this picture of what determined their destiny credible revealed their uncertainty about the character of their political order.

The political vacuum permitted a freebooter like Senator Joseph R. McCarthy of Wisconsin to crowd into the limelight. People reluctantly engaged in the Korean War uneasily wished to know why the fruits of victory of 1945 had slipped out of their hands, and were ready to ascribe their predicament to internal subversion. But they believed McCarthy's assertion that card-carrying Communists infested the State Department, because the responsible political leaders were not willing to stand up against the wild charges. The damage to the morale of the Foreign Service and of the federal administrative system that resulted would not be repaired for years. But once challenged, after an attack upon the army and the Presidency, the McCarthyite menace collapsed. Nor could the John Birch Society a few years later stand exposure to public criticism.

Efforts on a more serious level to locate a conservative tradition ran up against the blank wall of the American past, which offered men no heritage but that of change. The ideas of the founding fathers were no consolation to Barry Goldwater or William Buckley in the quest for authority. The absence of any firm intellectual base imparted a querulous tone to conservative comments that made discourse with these writers and politicians difficult. Most Americans had no desire for extreme measures of either the right or the left. They preferred to tend to their own suburban gardens.

Widespread questioning of intelligence and reason as guides to life encouraged them to do so. In *The Caine Mutiny*, another popular best seller, play and movie, the villain was not the mad Captain Queeg, who almost brought his vessel to disaster, but the introspective intellectual Lieutenant Keefer who found a loophole in the regulations in order to save the ship. *The idea is, once you get an incompetent ass as a skipper there's nothing to do but serve him as though he were the wisest and the best, cover his mistakes, keep the ship going, and bear up.* Only discipline and obedience to authority could bring men through trying times.

As at earlier moments when Americans desired the security of reliable rules of conduct that would absolve them of the need for individual decision, they felt most keenly the lack of continuity with the past. If only they had not moved so much, then they would know what authority to obey. As it was, having left the homes of their fathers, they were always exposed to the burden of making up their own minds. And when the pressure was too great they embarked upon an earnest, frenzied search for antecedents to supply the props that freed them from the necessity for uncomfortable choices.

The descendants of the immigrants, now in their third generation, endowed the ethnic group with sanctity, wholeness, and security. Edwin O'Connor described the political boss as a benevolent rascal expressing the warm good humor of Irish-American life. Paddy Chayefsky, Philip Roth and Herman Wouk regarded Italians and Jews through the same nostalgic lenses. *Marjorie Morningstar* found nothing but anguish in the pursuit, through intellect, of her own personality; she was safe only in the warmth of a communal nest. Poor Marjorie was silly to have tried! The suburban housewife put the book down, content for the moment with the security of her own little house and her own little group.

A revival of religious interests sustained her and her family in that withdrawal. The postwar years witnessed a reversal of the indifference of earlier decades and a return to all the churches. Membership rose rapidly; new buildings appeared; and a multitude of related social, educational and cultural activities occupied young and old. Yet the question remained — what were they returning to? And, were they actually coming back to what they had left or seeking a refuge they had never enjoyed?

For those who had all along been guided by tradition there was no conflict. The Pentecostalist sects, the Hasidic Jews, the Negroes in the store-front chapel and the devout Roman Catholics simply continued practices they had never interrupted. That they were now in the main current was no more significant to them than that they had formerly been out of it.

The return was much more difficult for those who had grown up before the war in another environment and who were literally coming back to a faith which had once lapsed. Such people could accept the church as a social institution particularly appropriate to suburbia; they could recognize the utility of firm belief as a device for protecting their children against the trials of a disordered world and as a means of creating continuity across the generations. That was enough for the man who was *a sort of pale Christian* who had seen too much *to go on ignoring God* and who guessed that *a Christian is a Christian* — no matter of what sort. But the Americans who returned to the church wanted also authoritative answers to problems too great for the individual, and they were not readily satisfied in that quest.

The growth in affiliation coincided with an outburst of interest in theology, a subject subordinated to ethics for almost a century in the United States. In the 1930's it had not been taken seriously except for the mild involvement of intellectual Roman Catholics in Thomism. After the war the situation changed for Protestants and Jews as well as for Roman Catholics. John Courtney Murray, Reinhold Niebuhr, Paul Tillich and Abraham Heschel expressed a deep concern with the nature of man, with his relationship with God and with the presence of good and evil in the universe. European crisis theology, stemming from Kierkegaard by way of Karl Barth and Martin Buber, and existentialist philosophy after 1945 acquired fresh meaning for men perplexed by the postwar confrontation with the moral crisis of the use of violence to resist violence. The anguished apprehension that the world might destroy itself drew many of these thinkers in fear and trembling to a demanding faith that accepted and thus accounted for the paradoxicality or the absurdity of the universe.

It was not to these expositors, however, that the mass of new church members turned. The popular guides were Joshua Loth Liebman, Norman Vincent Peale and Fulton J. Sheen. The popular texts were *Peace of Mind, Peace of Soul, A Guide to Confident Living,* and *Faith Is the Answer.* Religion, these works assured their readers, was not a source of, but a cure for anxiety. For Rabbi Liebman faith was a superior form of psychoanalysis; *thou shalt transcend inner anxiety, recognizing thy true competence and courage.* For Dr. Peale prayer was a method of gaining energy and success; *you will become more popular, esteemed and well-liked, enjoy a delightful new sense of well-being and experience a new and keen pleasure in living.* For Monsignor Sheen conversion was a means of achieving certitude; *the mind is through with a search for a place to live and can settle down to the making of a home.* Belief soothed; it relieved personal anguish; and it made unnecessary the self-examination that many feared.

In the end, however, the worshiper could only say: *I believe.* He could not say: *I know.* Nor could he account for the difference between his faith and that of others, except on the grounds of habit and ethnic affiliation. *Go to the church of your choice,* said the advertisement; all were equal and what counted was that each man should belong to something, not to what. *Life's* account portrayed all the great religions sympathetically. Judaism was for the Jews, Catholicism for Catholics, Methodism for Methodists and Buddhism for Buddhists; each in his own pigeonhole. The question of *truth* was evaded. It became conventional to speak of the *Judaeo-Christian tradition* as the common element that made particularities of creed irrelevant.

Yet the question could not wholly be crowded out of mind: did men really believe who believed because belief was good for them? The furor in 1962 when the Supreme Court declared unconstitutional a state-prescribed school prayer showed that some Americans considered government intervention necessary to foster a piety the family could not, just as they demanded censorship to maintain moral codes the home could not.

The questions that really concerned men remained unasked. The black rain that had fallen from the mushrooming cloud over Hiroshima never washed away. The rent in the heavens as Sputnik passed through never closed. Men preferred to avert their eyes from these matters about which there could be no certitude. In the 1950's conformity to everyone's ways was only the easiest method of doing so.

Those who wished to understand the serious problems of their times had to grope through a thicket dense with irrelevancies. The media of communication had become so ponderous that the speaker often could not tell who was listening, nor the hearer whence the words emanated. Television — the union of the motion picture and radio — all but absorbed popular attention. Every other form swelled to the same gigantic scale. The book clubs, paperbacks and records distributed literature and music to the multitudes while the circulation of the surviving magazines soared into the millions. In the vast outpouring of sights, sounds and words there was no control, nor any consistent standard of selection. The philharmonic followed the western with only a station break between; and Mickey Spillane appeared in the same series as William Faulkner. There was room for the good, the bad and the indifferent; but there was no room for calibration or judgment and the confusion enfeebled all the signals. Each man had to be able to sort out the extraneous matter before he could find what he sought in the bombardment of information directed at him.

Even the dissenters were unsure of themselves. The rebels of this generation lacked the positive standards of their predecessors in Bohemia forty years earlier. Norman Mailer, the beats, the hipsters and the *sick* comedians knew what they were against; the world around them was a sham. But they were unable to say what they were for.

The uncertainty was particularly troubling for the young people growing up. The wind nipped at the bare legs of the drum majorette as she twirled her baton and her bottom. Behind her marched the Holy Family Reveries in leather boots, short skirts, brass-buttoned tunics and shakos. They were on their way, they hoped, to the Legion's national competition in Las Vegas. But they would never be able to square the pious verities they learned at home with the rows upon rows of slot machines and the steepled offices of Nevada where marriage or divorce was equally easy to come by.

Togetherness absolved none of the youth from the obligation to create a life of their own. No more than their parents could they forget that they were individuals with decisions to make in a distressed world. But they had little aid in learning to do so, despite the solicitude of the fathers and mothers. From the mass media came a vast array of images — confused, distorted, disordered. Violence showed frequently beneath the sentimental platitudes; they believed none of it or all of it, with equal coolness. Somehow they had to make their own way.

The effort varied according to the social situation and heritage of each person. They went marching along or carried the ball; they raced the cars, unthrottled the motorcycles, roved in gangs, or tried the needle; and, as platter followed platter in the juke box, they threw each other around — big apple, rock and roll, twist. Others read Salinger and *Lord of the Flies* — it was all futile — or found the same answer in *Mad* that mocked the inanities of their elders.

Youth gave over a large part of its life to formal education. In 1962, more than fifty million Americans were in school, almost the whole of the eligible age group. Attendance was the normal experience of their generation. Elementary school, high school, college and career followed each other in automatic sequence. Even marginal students went through the motions because the labor market had no use for them. This was the expected routine.

Yet however much the learning experience helped some become doctors, engineers, lawyers or businessmen, it threw little light on their own problems as persons. Overwhelmed by numbers and by the competition for places, education had become a filtering device, testing as much as teaching. Changes in the traditional curriculum had generally been beneficial, but many of the new subjects, like the old, were unresponsive to the serious questions of the students; often, alas, study only stifled the impulse to question. Hence the eagerness with which the young leaped at any possibility for immediate constructive action — sit-ins, SANE or the Peace Corps.

The quite different world of science existed on an island, never more important for Americans, yet, paradoxically, never more detached from the other aspects of their common life. Science enjoyed the prestige of great achievements. A dialed box operated great machines; from the burbling test tube came miracle drugs that lengthened life; and mysterious rays and lenses brought the infinitely remote and the infinitely small within sight. In return, private foundations and the government were generous in their support.

Yet science remained utterly alien to the people, who paid tribute to a powerful magician but could not understand his occult capacity for aiding or injuring them. His ultimate concern was the truth while theirs, they thought, was certitude. They brought their illnesses to the doctor not for an explanation but for a cure. Americans wanted the help of science, not the endless questions it raised. Therefore, they gladly spent billions on research, but preferred not to consider its import. They carried about the vague foreboding that this force might destroy their world. But they instinctively desired only to remember that the same force was equally capable of redeeming them.

The scientists felt the same mixture of fear and anticipation more sharply because they were better informed. On the plane, returning from that first fateful mission, with Hiroshima only a few miles behind him, one of them wrote to his four-year-old son: *The days of large bombing raids are finished. That means that nations will have to get along together in a friendly fashion. This terrible weapon we have created may bring the countries of the world together and prevent further wars.* The letter-writer then paused: *Alfred Nobel thought that his invention of high explosives would have this effect, by making wars too terrible, but unfortunately it had just the opposite reaction.* Reluctantly the physicists and engineers understood that the shadow of the mighty power they had created would hang over them indefinitely. They consoled themselves, as other Americans did, with the reflection that the same power could take them to the moon and beyond.

Why they should wish to go to the newer worlds was as difficult to explain as it had been for Columbus 470 years earlier. Competition (now with the Russians, then with the Venetians), the desire to prove that it could be done, discontent with the older worlds, and the inability to make more immediate use of available energy, all were elements that sent off the caravels and the rockets. The Americans had come full circle — back where they had started from when the Atlantic had limited the known universe.

They were already adrift in 1939 when the war broke into their lives. The old communities had dissolved; and confidence in the capacity to transform the world had left men proud of their individuality, unprepared for the shocking disorder before them. In the trauma that followed, the plenty and self-sufficiency of the suburb tempted them to retreat. But there seemed scant likelihood in 1962 that they would be more successful in this most recent endeavor to withdraw in little closed groups than they had been in the past. Now, as at the beginning, they were men in space, headed for great achievement or great disaster, as they had been through their whole history.

Out there is Venus, Betelgeuse. Space in unimaginable distances. A universe so large, no conventional terms can express it — and constantly expanding. In one of its numerous reaches, is a nebula, among the hundreds of stars of which the sun warms one of its planets, earth. Speck.

Man, a recent tenant. A billion years (two?) before he appeared, the continents took shape and strange beings roamed the emerging land. And before the AmeriMAN arrived thousands of years more went by. An instant in time on a speck in space was his experience.

In here, at the typing machine, a man wonders: meaning? How fond his predecessors were of geometric analogies — progress, a straight line up; decay, a straight line down; a spiral upward; a wavy, wavy cycle. How fond they were of purpose — the hand of God, the Oversoul, the evolutionary first cause, the dialectic of the class struggle. Perhaps.

It is not his task to subject the complex drama the words tap out to any such enfolding figures. If he can explain *how*, let others believe each their own *why*. There is meaning enough in the story itself.

In 1962, there are 180,000,000 Americans. A number? Also a multitude of individuals in their wonderful variety — no two the same, and each a product of forces that reach back into the nation's past.

She flies out once each year from the Eskimo village in which she teaches, also keeps the heating system going and registers births, marriages and deaths; Alaska is her frontier. He follows the ripening fruit up the California valleys; the soil still supplies his sustenance. They stand on the line or transcribe the tapes that issue from the computer to keep the wheels of trade and industry in motion. Such people have much in common with earlier pioneers, farmers, laborers and merchants.

Down the street, in the great celebration, come the Shriners. One of the potentates wipes his right hand across his baggy oriental trousers; the perspiration keeps loosening his grip on the scimitar he fiercely waves. Now and then an embarrassed grin shows through the pasted-on beard as he glances toward the crowd on the sidewalk. Does he know why he marches, why his neighbors, the druggist and the clerk, have crowded into bright yellow kiddie cars or have uneasily mounted unfamiliar steeds to be part of the parade? It is an anniversary of something. Yes, and they still need anniversaries to be part of something.

Often the Americans of the 1960's seem to be fighting the same battle as those of the 1660's, for the abundance to satisfy material want, for the stability to end their rootlessness, for the community to protect but not crush their individuality, for the unity that would acknowledge their diversity and for the faith to explain their unique situation in the universe. In the past the outcome of each successive stage in the struggle had only been the discovery of a new front on which to continue it.

But there are times also when the men and women of the 1960's seem totally different from their predecessors.

At the double drive-in, they adjust the rear-view mirror to catch a glimpse of the second movie while the first flickers through the windshield; they are interested in neither. In Las Vegas they pull away from the gambling tables at the Starlight to watch the bare-bosomed beauties descend from the ceiling. In St. Pete, they look at television in the dimness of the Senior Citizens Club while the noonday sun beats down on the pier outside. These aspects of New World life are unfamiliar in their aimlessness, lack of purpose and wasted energy. Question: is there an analogy here to the government, economy, science and culture that also are uncertain of the end to which to use the tremendous power they enjoy?

And much more is changing than is either quite the same or quite different. It is six hours across the Atlantic by commercial airline, less by bomber or rocket. The unfamiliar faces are closer than before and more demanding; no suburb is an adequate refuge. The machine's capacity for work grows greater by the day; and science does not pause in discovery. How will the products be used?

In their brief interval on one corner of the earth, the Americans tried a wonderful experiment. They had come to a wilderness which did not permit them to remain Europeans, but forced them to break age-old custom and depart from behind familiar tradition. Emptiness gave them room to spread out, to develop their own character without the oversight of home. Becoming aware of their own identity as a people, they dissolved the ties that bound them to the Old World and justified their independence by the laws of nature that made men free. They could then use the resources of the continent to reform society and perfect the personalities of all who came to the New World.

But the political failure of Civil War bewildered them just when science and industry made fresh demands upon their power to understand themselves. Laboriously in the twentieth century they resumed the effort to develop their individuality and to improve the society in the light of reason. Only by now, the space was gone; the brutal world closed in; the bomb dangled; and the question that had all along troubled them could not be evaded. Could man risk the freedom of faith in his own impulses or did he require the security, discipline and confinement of the group?

Now the writer, one of them, who shared their anxiety, reviewing the span of 355 years of American experience, could make out neither sure grounds for confidence nor unavoidable reasons for doubt. Their history had not been an unqualified success story. But it had created the best environment for freedom men had yet enjoyed. Here the earthbound humans had soared in moments of grandeur, when the frontiersman's wife came through the gap to see the whole valley planted with homes about to be, when the immigrant or Negro, escaped from oppression, cast his first ballot as a citizen, when husband, wife and child understood that beyond — apart from — the respect of convention, they could love each other as persons.

The radio audience that had listened in 1938 to *The War of the Worlds* had been right to flee in terror from the perils of outer space. The danger was genuine. But space and the freedom to move in it were the heritage Americans could not escape. Their alternatives were simple: they could either seize its opportunities or be helplessly lost. In 1962 the outcome was still open.

Index

Index